AIRCRAFT IDENTIFICATION GUIDE

HISTORY OF AVIATION

AIRCRAFT IDENTIFICATION GUIDE

Edited by John W R Taylor FRHistS AFRAeS FSLAET
and Kenneth Munson

HAWKER SIDDELEY 125

Powered by: Two 3,360 lb (1,525 kg) st Rolls-Royce Bristol Viper 522 turbojet engines
Wing span: 47 ft 0 in (14.33 m)
Length: 47 ft 5 in (14.45 m)
Wing area: 353 sq ft (32.8 m²)
Gross weight: 23,300 lb (10,568 kg)
Max cruising speed: 510 mph (821 km/h) at 31,000 ft (9,450 m)
Typical range: 1,762 miles (2,835 km)
Accommodation: Crew of 2/3 and up to 12 passengers
First flight: 13 August 1962

One of the two most successful jet executive aircraft produced in Europe, the HS 125 has been in production since 1964 and more than 200 have been sold. These include small batches of the Series 1, 1A, 1B and 3; and 20 Srs 2s equipped as Dominie navigation trainers for the Royal Air Force. The data apply to the current Series 400, which since 1970 has been marketed in the United States as the Beechcraft Hawker BH 125.

Published by The New English Library Limited,
Made and printed in Great Britain by C. Tinling & Co. Ltd
London and Prescot

SBN 4 50013 863

INTRODUCTION

WHAT WERE the Wright biplane and the world's first jet aeroplane really like? Only one photograph was taken during the first brief flight by Orville Wright in December 1903; there are no good, unretouched photographs of the Heinkel He 178 jet-plane of August 1939.

The best way of depicting the true shapes of such aircraft is, therefore, by means of three-view general arrangement drawings, or silhouettes of the kind used by the world's military services for accurate and quick identification of aircraft seen in combat.

This book contains 270 such drawings, mostly three-views, showing aircraft of particular interest and importance in the history of human flight. Each drawing is accompanied by a photograph of the aircraft, notes on its history and significance, and concise specification data. Some of the photographs are published for the first time; the information is as up-to-date and accurate as many years of careful research can make it.

How does one choose just 270 types of aircraft to illustrate such a story? Clearly, as a start, they must include the famous trailblazers of which everyone has heard - the Vimy of Alcock and Brown, Lindbergh's *Spirit of St. Louis*, the Spitfire, the DC-3 airliner, its modern counterparts like the TriStar and Boeing 747 'Jumbo-jet', the Concorde supersonic airliner, Russia's MiG fighters, America's Bell X-1 which was first to exceed the speed of sound, the Comet jet-liner, Igor Sikorsky's first successful helicopter . . . .

Some 36,000 different designs have flown in our century; so, clearly, the choice must be arbitrary. In some cases a typical machine, not outstanding in itself, must represent a whole generation of different aeroplanes. But the final selection must satisfy the experts and enthusiasts, as well as the general public, and this is where the task becomes really difficult. What, for instance, should come first of all?

While 'searching for odd things' in the Cairo Museum store-rooms recently, Dr Khalil Messiha rediscovered a model bird, made of sycamore wood. Found at Saqqara in 1898, it dates from the third or fourth century BC and has a most un-birdlike vertical tail surface that led Dr Messiha to believe it might be a model glider or sailplane.

Historians of flying who have studied the model consider that it was more likely some kind of weather-vane, pivoted at the top of a mast. It would thus be wrong to begin our highly-factual history of flying more than 2,000 years ago, in Egypt.

There are stories of 'bird-men', like Britain's King Bladud, who tried to fly with the aid of feathered wings at least as early as the time when the Egyptian bird model was carved. Most seem to have shared the fate of Bladud who, according to ancient texts, broke his neck in a crash-landing on the temple of Apollo in Trinavantum, which we now call London.

Another inhabitant of these islands, the scientist-monk Roger Bacon, recorded the earliest known constructive thoughts on flying machines in the thirteenth century. No drawings of these devices remain, although Bacon assures those who read his *Secrets of Art and Nature* that he had met personally the inventor of 'Engines for flying, a man sitting in the midst thereof, by turning about an instrument which moves artificial wings made to beat the air, much after the fashion of a bird's flight.'

In contrast, we do have drawings of the man-powered flying machines devised by the great sixteenth-century Italian master-mind Leonardo da Vinci; but none of them ever left the ground. So our record begins, as it must, on 21 November 1783 when Jean-François Pilâtre de Rozier and François Laurent, Marquis d'Arlandes, travelled 7½ miles over Paris in a Montgolfier hot-air balloon. They stayed aloft for 25 minutes only because the Marquis, firmly under the thumb of de Rozier, dashed to and fro dousing fires in the fabric envelope started by the burning brazier which supplied the hot-air lifting force.

Just seventy years later Sir George Cayley built a glider in which his elderly coachman was flown across a valley on his Yorkshire estate. More terrified than gratified by the experience, the coachman is reported to have shouted in broad Yorkshire dialect: 'Please, Sir George, I wish to give notice. I was hired to drive and not to fly.'

Throughout the second half of the nineteenth century, a succession of inspired men tried to find a means not only of getting airborne but staying up and going wherever they wished. Henson, du Temple, Mozhaiski, Ader, Maxim were all hampered by the lack of a suitable lightweight engine, and it was left to Otto Lilienthal and his unpowered gliders to demonstrate conclusively that man could fly on artificial wings. Providing such proof cost him his life, without regrets, for his last words were 'Sacrifices must be made.'

The Wright brothers did not share such sentiments. From the start they approached the business of flying with a mixture of science and certainty. They were convinced that they could perfect a practical aeroplane by beginning where Lilienthal left off, with gliders, and then fitting one of the newly-available petrol engines. They succeeded within four years, though no-one believed them at first.

It took a World War to prove that the first fragile flying machines of wood, wire and canvas were more than playthings for lunatics. Aeroplanes became more powerful, more reliable, and began carrying guns and bombs. The men who flew them were regarded as heroes rather than candidates for a mental home. And when the fighting stopped those same men showed that aeroplanes could now go anywhere, even over the Atlantic, non-stop.

Ordinary men and women, while admiring supermen, seldom have any ambition to join them. So another World War had to come and go, two decades later, before the idea of mass air travel became acceptable.

Today millions of people fly annually, in armchair comfort, over the route that was so hazardous for Alcock and Brown in 1919. BOAC has become the first airline to order aircraft in which its passengers will fly at supersonic speed. A dozen astronauts have already walked on the Moon, and America is planning to build shuttle craft that will ferry men, supplies and satellites into Earth orbit as routine.

Within the covers of this book the reader can follow all the stages of this incredible journey, from the first wind-blown hop over Paris out into the dark emptiness of space. This is, surely, the achievement for which our century will be remembered, until the very end of time.

AIRCRAFT IDENTIFICATION GUIDE

MONTGOLFIER HOT-AIR BALLOON

Lifting agent: approx 77,700 cu ft (2,200 m³) of hot air, generated by burning straw inside the base of the balloon
Diameter: approx 49 ft (14.95 m)
Height: approx 75 ft (22.75 m)
Gross weight: approx 1,730 lb (785 kg)
Flight of 21 November 1783: of approx 25 minutes duration, covering a distance of 7½ miles (12 km) and reaching a height of over 3,280 ft (1,000 m)

The first public demonstration of a *montgolfière* was at Annonay on 4 June 1783. Details above apply to the balloon in which Jean-François Pilâtre de Rozier and his passenger, François Laurent, Marquis d'Arlandes, made the first human aerial voyage in history. The balloon, made of linen coated with alum to reduce the risk of combustion, took off from the garden of the Château de la Muette in Paris, landing at Butte-aux-Cailles some 25 minutes later.

HENSON AERIAL STEAM CARRIAGE

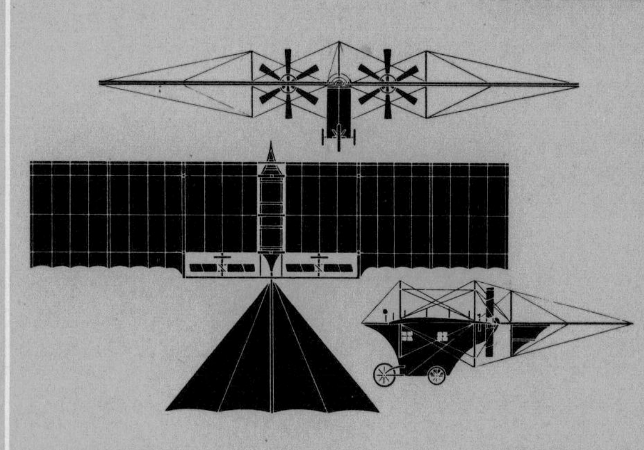

Powered by: One 25-30 hp Henson steam engine, driving two 10 ft (3.05 m) diameter six-blade pusher propellers
Wing span: 150 ft 0 in (45.72 m)
Wing chord: 30 ft 0 in (9.14 m)
Wing area: 4,500 sq ft (418.1 m²)
Horizontal tail area: 1,500 sq ft (139.4 m²)
Length: approx 84 ft 9 in (25.83 m)
Gross weight: approx 3,000 lb (1,360 kg)
Accommodation: Crew of 1, plus provision for passengers or cargo
The data above are for the full-size aircraft designed by William Samuel Henson (1812-1888). The 20 ft (6.10 m) span model tested in 1844-47 has a wing area of 70 sq ft (6.5 m²), tail area of 10 sq ft (0.9 m²) and a weight (including engine) of 25-28 lb (11.3-12.7 kg). The engine drives four-blade propellers of 3 ft (0.91 m) diameter.

GIFFARD DIRIGIBLE AIRSHIP

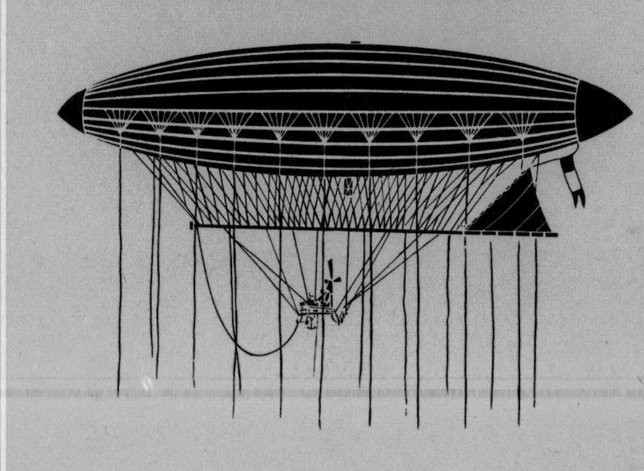

Powered by: One 3 hp Giffard steam engine
Diameter: 39.4 ft (12 m)
Length: 144.4 ft (44 m)
Capacity: 88,300 cu ft (2,500 m³) of gas
Average speed: 5 mph (8 km/h)
Accommodation: Crew of 1
Best journey: Approx 17 miles (28 km) from the Hippodrome, Paris, to Elancourt, near Trappes
First flight: 24 September 1852
Henri Giffard (1825-1882) made his first venture into aeronautics in 1847 with a project for a steam-driven helicopter. His chief claim to fame is his achievement of the first practical steerable lighter-than-air craft, but in later years he concentrated on the building of ever-larger captive balloons. One, shown at the Paris *Exposition* in 1878, was 180 ft (55 m) high, 118 ft (36 m) in diameter, and could lift 50 people at a time. During the course of the *Exposition* over 35,000 people are said to have ridden in it.

Montgolfier balloon launched on
19 September 1783 carrying a sheep,
a duck and a cock

Artist's impression of the Aerial Steam
Carriage in flight over the Pyramids

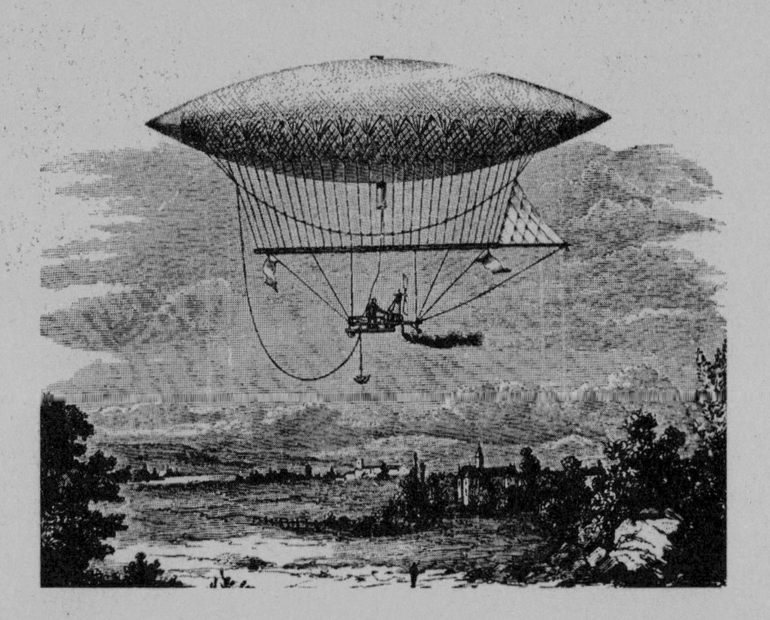

Giffard 3-hp steam-engined airship

CAYLEY MAN-CARRYING GLIDER DESIGN (1852)

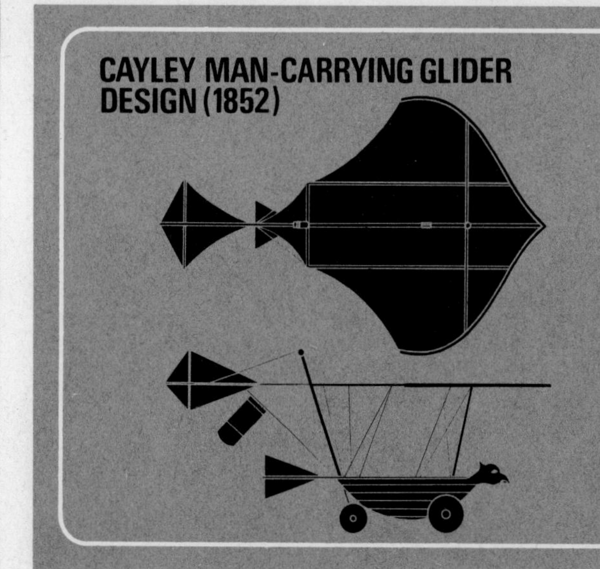

Surface area (main wing): 467 sq ft (43.4 m^2)
Horizontal surface area (rudder): 48 sq ft (4.5 m^2)
Design weight empty: approx 150 lb (68 kg)
Accommodation: Crew of 1
Details of this flying machine designed by Sir George Cayley (1773-1857) appeared in *Mechanics' Magazine* of 25 September 1852, and the silhouette reproduced here is based upon the somewhat simplified illustrations published on that occasion. In fact, as Cayley's text made clear, the wing was intended to have approx 8° of dihedral and to be set at an angle of incidence of about 5°. Cayley called the craft, which was meant to be released in the air from beneath a balloon, a "governable parachute"; though it was in reality a glider. Although never built, it incorporated all except one of the essential design features of a modern aeroplane.

DU TEMPLE MONOPLANE

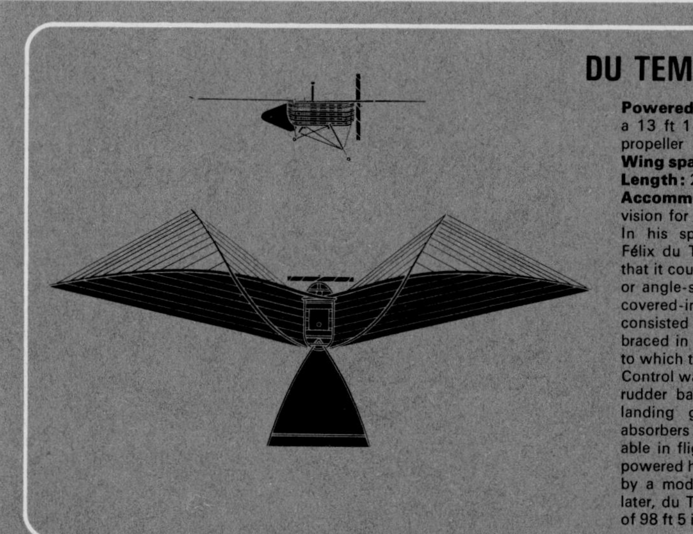

Powered by: One hot-air engine, driving a 13 ft $1\frac{1}{2}$ in (4.00 m) diameter pusher propeller
Wing span: 55 ft 9 in (17.00 m)
Length: 24 ft 1 in (7.35 m)
Accommodation: Crew of 1, plus provision for passengers
In his specification for this aeroplane, Félix du Temple (1823-1890) suggested that it could be built of wood or of tubular or angle-section metal, the nacelle being covered-in or open as desired. The wings consisted of two cross-over main spars, braced in position by a network of cords, to which the fabric covering was attached. Control was exercised by a steering wheel, rudder bar and cables. The three-wheel landing gear was fitted with shock-absorbers and was designed to be retractable in flight. The aircraft, which made a powered hop in about 1874, was preceded by a model weighing 24.7 oz (700 gr); later, du Temple built a wing with a span of 98 ft 5 in (30 m).

MOZHAISKI MONOPLANE

Powered by: One 20 hp steam engine, driving a 13 ft $1\frac{1}{2}$ in (4.00 m) diameter four-blade tractor propeller and one 10 hp steam engine, driving two 11 ft $5\frac{3}{4}$ in (3.50 m) diameter four-blade pusher propellers
Wing span: 74 ft $9\frac{1}{2}$ in (22.80 m)
Wing chord: 46 ft 8 in (14.20 m)
Wing and horizontal tail area: 4,004 sq ft (372 m^2)
Length: 75 ft $5\frac{1}{2}$ in (23.00 m)
Width of fuselage: 4 ft 11 in (1.50 m)
Gross weight: 2,059 lb (934 kg)
Accommodation: Crew of 1, plus provision for passengers
A contemporary of du Temple, the Russian engineer Alexander Fedorovich Mozhaiski (1825-1890) designed this steam-engined monoplane which made a short powered hop in 1884, after running down a slope, with I N Golubev as pilot. It was preceded by tests with various models, of different sizes but similar basic configuration.

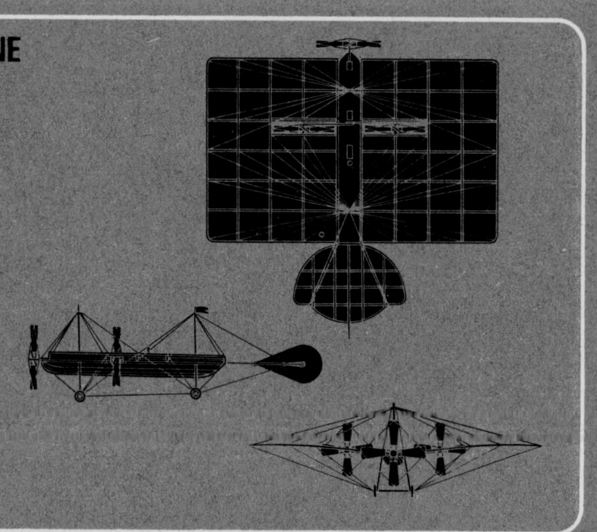

Model of Cayley's boy-carrying glider of 1849

Model of du Temple monoplane in Qantas collection

Artist's impression of the Mozhaiski monoplane *(via Jean Alexander)*

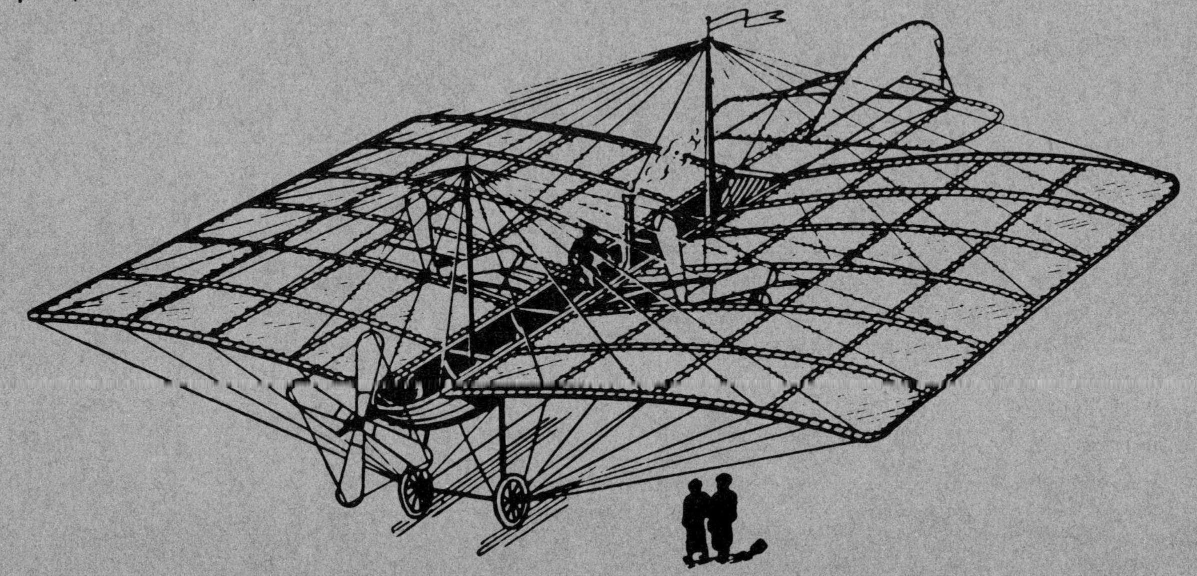

ADER EOLE

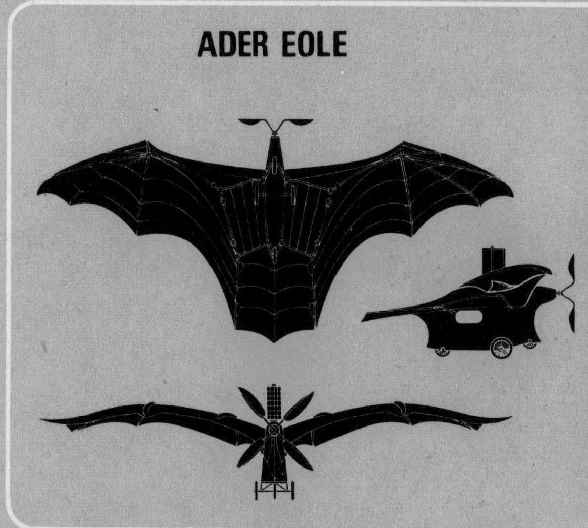

Powered by: One 20 hp Ader four-cylinder steam engine, driving a four-blade tractor propeller of approx 11 ft 6 in (3.50 m) diameter
Wing span: 45 ft 11 in (14.00 m)
Wing area: 301.4 sq ft (28.0 m²)
Length: 21 ft 4 in (6.50 m)
Weight empty: 498 lb (226 kg)
Gross weight: 652 lb (296 kg)
Accommodation: Crew of 1
The Eole was the first aeroplane designed by Clément Ader (1841-1925), and the first man-carrying aeroplane to take off under its own power, without other assistance, and make a short hop-flight. It did so on 9 October 1890, in the grounds of the Château Pereire at Armainvilliers, travelling about 164 ft (50 m) through the air at a height of some 8 in (20 cm) above the ground. Ader's later Avion III (1897) had a 52 ft 6 in (16.00 m) wing span, gross weight of about 882 lb (400 kg), and two 20 hp engines. It failed to fly.

LILIENTHAL 1893 MONOPLANE GLIDER

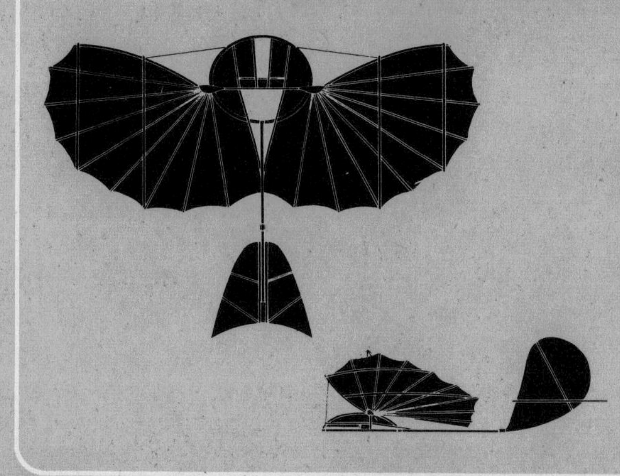

Wing span: 22 ft 11½ in (7.00 m)
Wing area: 150.7 sq ft (14.0 m²)
Wing chord (max): 8 ft 2½ in (2.50 m)
Length: 16 ft 4¾ in (5.00 m)
Weight without pilot: 44 lb (20 kg)
Accommodation: Crew of 1
Otto Lilienthal (1848-1896) made approximately 2,500 successful glides in 1893-96, mostly in monoplane 'hang-gliders' of the type illustrated, in which he flew distances of up to 985 ft (300 m). Prior to this, Lilienthal had built two biplane gliders in 1891 and 1892. His philosophy was well summarised in his own words: 'To design a flying machine is nothing; to build it is not much; to test it is everything'.

MAXIM 1894 BIPLANE

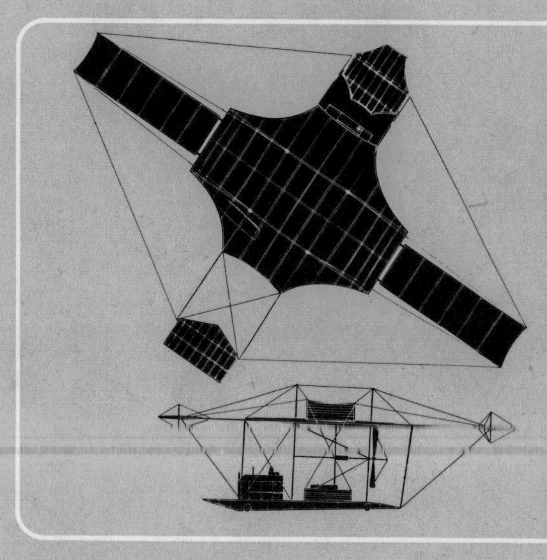

Powered by: Two 180 hp Maxim steam engines, each driving a 17 ft 10 in (5.44 m) diameter two-blade pusher propeller
Wing span: 104 ft 0 in (31.70 m)
Wing/elevator area (total): 4,000 sq ft (371.6 m²)
Length: approx 95 ft 0 in (28.96 m)
Gross weight: 8,000 lb (3,629 kg)
Accommodation: Crew of 4
Sir Hiram Stevens Maxim (1840-1916) began building this huge aeroplane in 1891, describing it as 'a flying machine that would lift itself from the ground'; he did not intend it to fly in the true sense. When tested in 1894, it ran along a railway track until, at a speed slightly above 42 mph (68 km/h), the wheels lifted clear of the track, fouled the guard rails placed to prevent a complete take-off, and the machine had to be brought to a halt. Maxim did not pursue its development further.

Eole model in the Musée de l'Air, Paris
(John W Wood)

Lilienthal biplane glider of 1895

Maxim steam-engined biplane and launching track

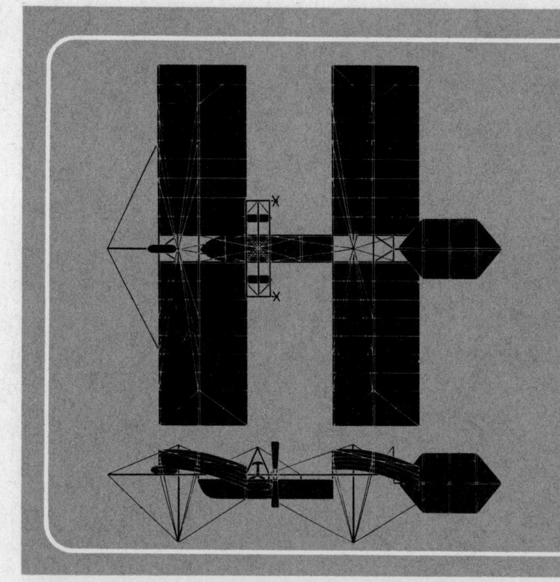

LANGLEY 'AERODROME'

Powered by: One 52 hp Manly five-cylinder radial petrol engine, driving two two-blade outrigged propellers, each of approx 8 ft 9 in (2.67 m) diameter
Wing span: 48 ft 0 in (14.63 m)
Length: approx 54 ft 0 in (16.46 m)
Wing area: 1,040 sq ft (96.6 m²)
Accommodation: Crew of 1
Following his success in 1896 with steam-powered model aircraft, Samuel Pierpont Langley (1834-1906) received financial backing from the US government to build a full-size example of his aeroplane, known as the 'Aerodrome'. It was piloted by Charles Manly, who made two attempts to fly over the Potomac river on 7 October and 8 December 1903; on both occasions it fell into the river, after which the government withdrew its support for the venture.

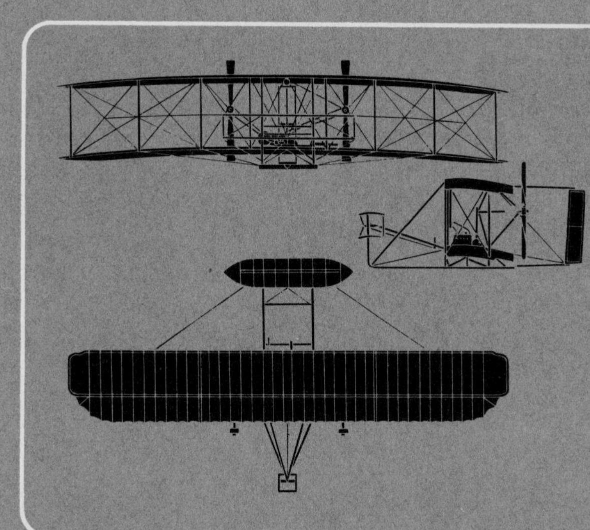

WRIGHT FLYER I

Powered by: One 12 hp Wright four-cylinder water-cooled petrol engine, driving two pusher propellers, each of 8 ft 6 in (2.59 m) diameter
Wing span: 40 ft 4 in (12.29 m)
Length: 21 ft 1 in (6.43 m)
Wing area: 510 sq ft (47.4 m²)
Gross weight: approx 750 lb (340 kg)
Max speed: approx 30 mph (48 km/h) at ground level
Accommodation: Crew of 1
First flight: 17 December 1903
After several years of successful experimenting with biplane gliders, Orville and Wilbur Wright were ready in 1903 to build a powered aeroplane. Before this could fly, they had also to design and build the engine and propellers for it, since none of a suitable kind then existed. Their efforts were rewarded with success on 17 December 1903, when four flights were made, two by each of the brothers.

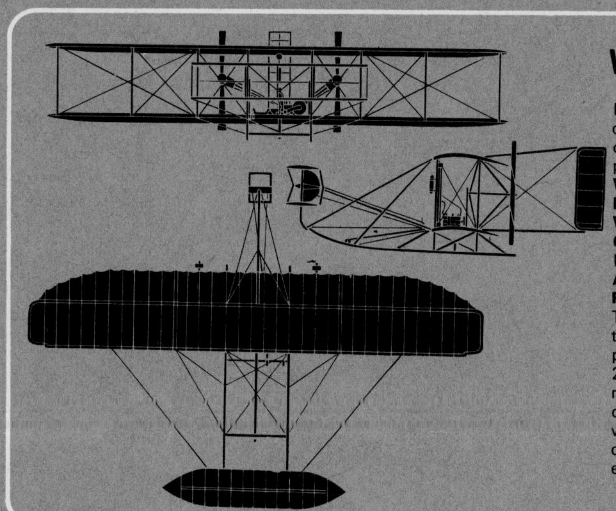

WRIGHT FLYER III

Powered by: One 15-21 hp Wright four-cylinder water-cooled in-line, engine, driving two 8 ft 6 in (2.59 m) diameter pusher propellers
Wing span: 40 ft 6 in (12.34 m)
Length: 28 ft 0 in (8.53 m)
Wing area: 503 sq ft (46.73 m²)
Gross weight: approx 855 lb (388 kg)
Max speed: approx 35 mph (56 km/h)
Accommodation: Crew of 1
First flight: 23 June 1905
The *Flyer* III was the machine regarded by the Wrights themselves as their first fully practical powered aeroplane. Between 23 June and 16 October 1905 it made nearly 50 flights, some of which were well over half an hour in duration. Above all, it was a fully controllable aircraft, which could bank, turn and perform figure-of-eight manoeuvres easily.

Langley 'Aerodrome' ready for launching in 1903

Wright Flyer I on first (unsuccessful) attempt to fly, 14 December 1903

Wright Flyer Type A (1907)

SANTOS-DUMONT 14 bis

Powered by: One 50 hp Antoinette eight-cylinder water-cooled Vee-type engine, driving a two-blade pusher propeller of 8 ft 2½ in (2.50 m) diameter
Wing Span: 36 ft 9 in (11.20 m)
Length: 31 ft 10 in (9.70 m)
Wing area: 559.7 sq ft (52.00 m²)
Gross weight: 661 lb (300 kg)
Speed : approx 25 mph (40 km/h)
Accommodation: Crew of 1
First flight: 13 September 1906 (with 24 hp Antoinette engine)
On its first flight, the 14*bis* covered about 23 ft (7 m) before landing heavily and being damaged. It was repaired and fitted with a 50 hp engine for the October-November 1906 flights, and an octagonal aileron was fitted in each of the outboard wing 'boxes'. Their controls were connected to a body harness worn by the pilot, who leaned to left or right to keep the aeroplane on an even keel.

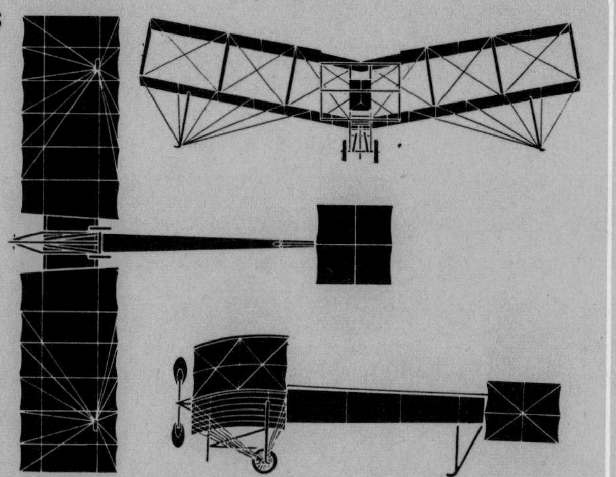

VUIA No1 MONOPLANE

Powered by: One 20 hp modified Serpollet carbonic acid gas engine, driving a 7 ft 2½ in (2.20 m) diameter two-blade propeller
Wing span: 22 ft 11½ in (7.00 m)
Length: 10 ft 6 in (3.20 m)
Wing area: 204.5 sq ft (19.00 m²)
Gross weight: 531 lb (241 kg)
Accommodation: Crew of 1
First flight: 18 March 1906

One of the first Europeans to make a powered flight in his own aeroplane, Traian Vuia is claimed as Romania's first aviator, although at the time of his early flights he was resident in Paris and his birthplace was then a part of the Austro-Hungarian empire. His first aeroplane, built with the assistance of Frenchman Victor Tatin, travelled no more than 78¾ ft (24 m) on its longest hop-flight, but had several novel features, including a variable-incidence wing and an undercarriage with pneumatic tyres. Later Vuia aircraft, although more conventional for their time and (in the case of the No 2 design) fitted with a more reliable engine, did not achieve flights of any great length compared with others of their day.

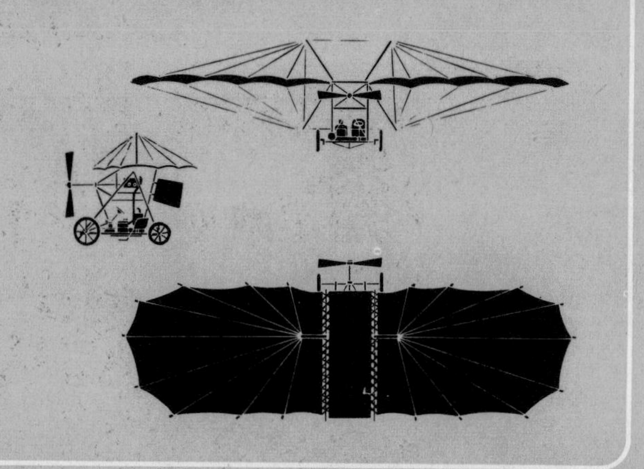

SANTOS-DUMONT DEMOISELLE

Powered by: One 35 hp Darracq-built Dutheil-Chalmers two-cylinder horizontally-opposed water-cooled engine, driving a 6 ft 6¾ in (2.00 m) diameter two-blade Chauvière propeller
Wing span: 16 ft 8¾ in (5.10 m)
Length: 26 ft 3 in (8.00 m)
Wing area: 110 sq ft (10.20 m²)
Gross weight: 315 lb (143 kg)
Speed: 56 mph (90 km/h)
Accommodation: Crew of 1
First flight: 6 March 1909
Alberto Santos Dumont, a pioneer airship builder and the man who made the first officially recognised aeroplane flight in Europe, also gave the world its first practical light aircraft. His little 'No 19', flown in November 1907, made only short hop-flights of up to 656 ft (200 m), but from it was developed the popular and successful Demoiselle series of 1909-10, of which a dozen or more examples were built. The pilot, who sat beneath the wings, wore a harness attached to an upright rod from which wires ran to each wingtip; by moving his body he could 'warp' the wings to control his movements in the air. The data apply to the 'No 20' Demoiselle of 1909.

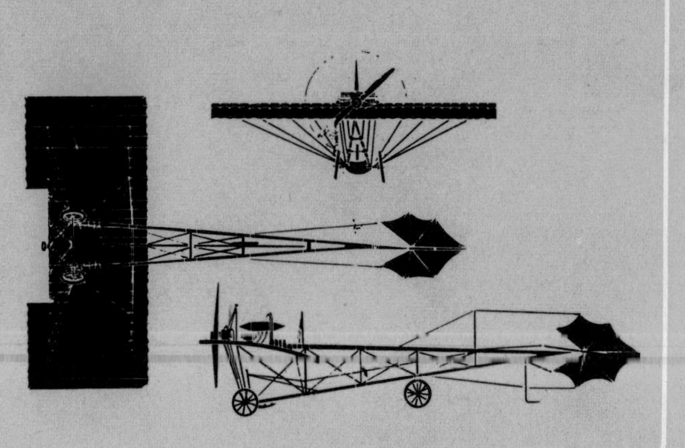

Santos-Dumont 14bis

Vuia 1bis monoplane (1907)

The original 'No 19', prototype of the Demoiselle

ESNAULT-PELTERIE R.E.P. 2bis

Powered by: One 30 hp R.E.P. seven-cylinder air-cooled semi-radial engine, driving a four-blade propeller
Wing span: 28 ft 2½ in (8.60 m)
Length: approx 22 ft 6¾ in (6.85 m)
Height: approx 8 ft 2½ in (2.50 m)
Wing area: 169.5 sq ft (15.75 m²)
Gross weight: 772 lb (350 kg)
Speed: approx 50 mph (80 km/h)
Accommodation: Crew of 1
First flight: 15 February 1909

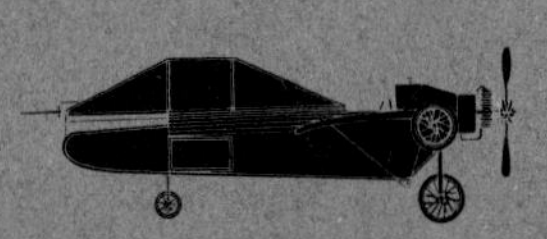

One of the few early pioneers to persevere with the monoplane, Robert Esnault-Pelterie applied to his work the benefits of a sound technical education; had he been more discriminating in some of the lines of research which he pursued his contribution to early aviation would undoubtedly have been greater. Even so, he was the first to apply aileron control to a full-sized aeroplane (a glider, in 1904), the first to use hydraulic wheel brakes, the first to develop an aircraft seat belt; he also designed the engines that powered his early aircraft. The R.E.P.2*bis* represented the culmination of development of his first powered aircraft, and in May 1909 it made its best flight, travelling some 5 miles (8 km). Before the end of the first World War, however, Esnault-Pelterie had transferred his interest to an even more exciting field: that of rocket propulsion and the prospect of space travel.

HENRY FARMAN III

Powered by: One 50 hp Gnome seven-cylinder rotary engine, driving an 8 ft 6½ in (2.60 m) diameter two-blade pusher propeller
Wing span: 32 ft 9¾ in (10.00 m)
Length: 39 ft 4½ in (12.00 m)
Wing area: 430.56 sq ft (40.00 m²)
Gross weight: 1,213 lb (550 kg)
Max speed: 37 mph (60 km/h)
Accommodation: Crew of 1
First flight: 6 April 1909

Henry Farman's Type III biplane, which appeared in 1909, was a marked improvement over the Voisin boxkite aeroplane from which it was developed. At the famous Reims meeting that year it carried off the distance prize with a flight of 112 miles (180 km). In the *Daily Mail*'s London-Manchester race of 1910, both competitors, Louis Paulhan and Claude Grahame-White, flew improved versions of the type illustrated which had slightly longer fuselages and an extension of the upper-wing span to 34 ft 1½ in (10.40 m).

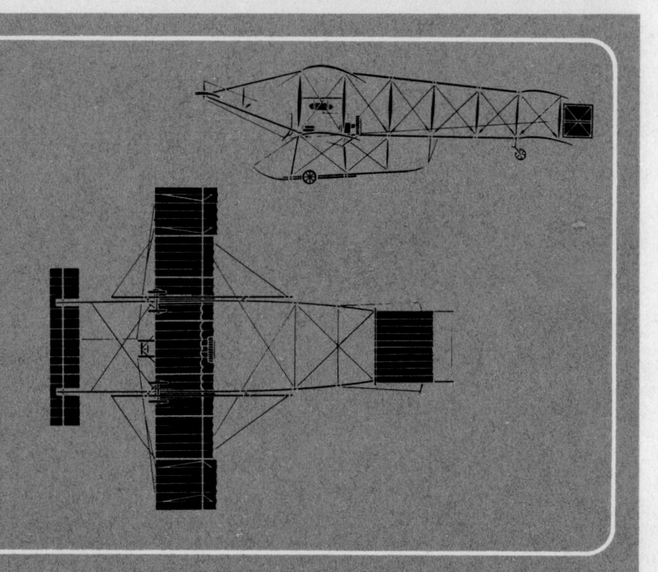

ROE II TRIPLANE

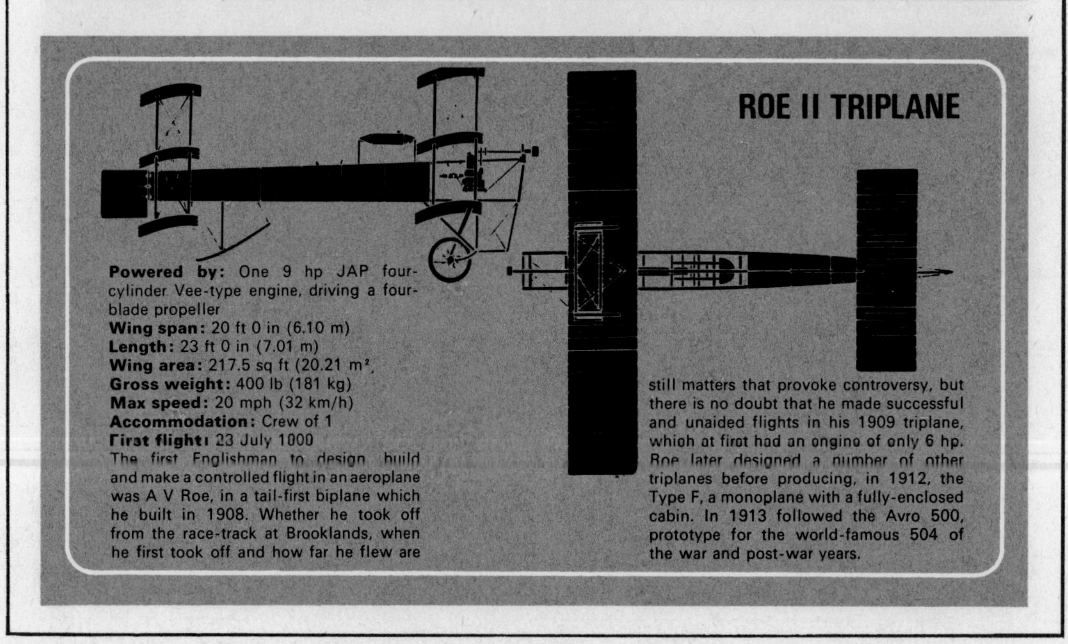

Powered by: One 9 hp JAP four-cylinder Vee-type engine, driving a four-blade propeller
Wing span: 20 ft 0 in (6.10 m)
Length: 23 ft 0 in (7.01 m)
Wing area: 217.5 sq ft (20.21 m²)
Gross weight: 400 lb (181 kg)
Max speed: 20 mph (32 km/h)
Accommodation: Crew of 1
First flight: 23 July 1909

The first Englishman to design, build and make a controlled flight in an aeroplane was A V Roe, in a tail-first biplane which he built in 1908. Whether he took off from the race-track at Brooklands, when he first took off and how far he flew are still matters that provoke controversy, but there is no doubt that he made successful and unaided flights in his 1909 triplane, which at first had an engine of only 6 hp. Roe later designed a number of other triplanes before producing, in 1912, the Type F, a monoplane with a fully-enclosed cabin. In 1913 followed the Avro 500, prototype for the world-famous 504 of the war and post-war years.

R.E.P. monoplane of 1909 (earlier than version shown in silhouette)

Henry Farman biplane flown at Reims (1909)

Roe triplane, December 1909

ANTOINETTE VII

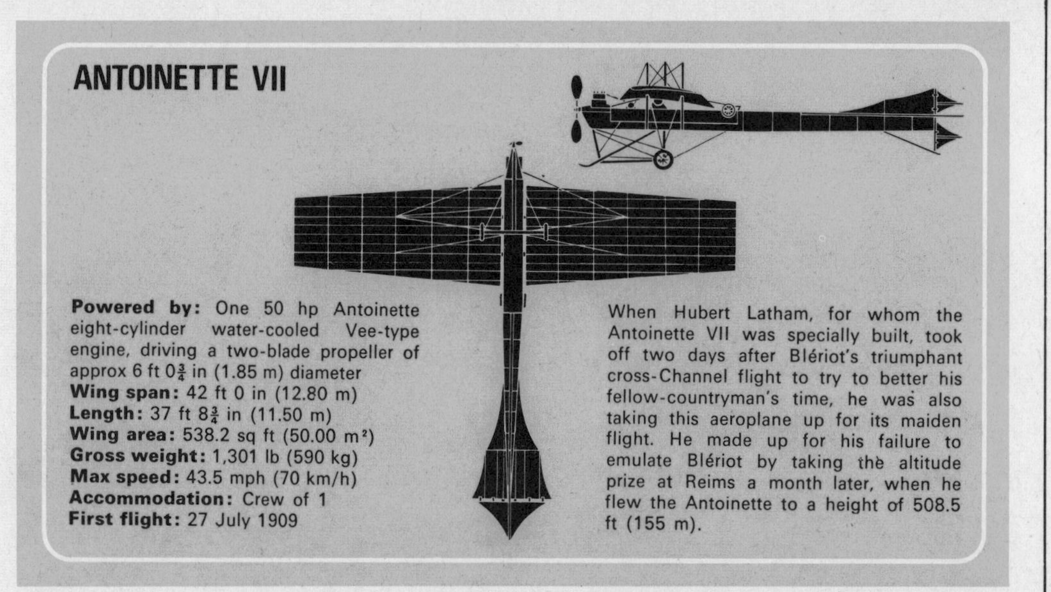

Powered by: One 50 hp Antoinette eight-cylinder water-cooled Vee-type engine, driving a two-blade propeller of approx 6 ft 0¾ in (1.85 m) diameter
Wing span: 42 ft 0 in (12.80 m)
Length: 37 ft 8¾ in (11.50 m)
Wing area: 538.2 sq ft (50.00 m²)
Gross weight: 1,301 lb (590 kg)
Max speed: 43.5 mph (70 km/h)
Accommodation: Crew of 1
First flight: 27 July 1909

When Hubert Latham, for whom the Antoinette VII was specially built, took off two days after Blériot's triumphant cross-Channel flight to try to better his fellow-countryman's time, he was also taking this aeroplane up for its maiden flight. He made up for his failure to emulate Blériot by taking the altitude prize at Reims a month later, when he flew the Antoinette to a height of 508.5 ft (155 m).

BLÉRIOT XI

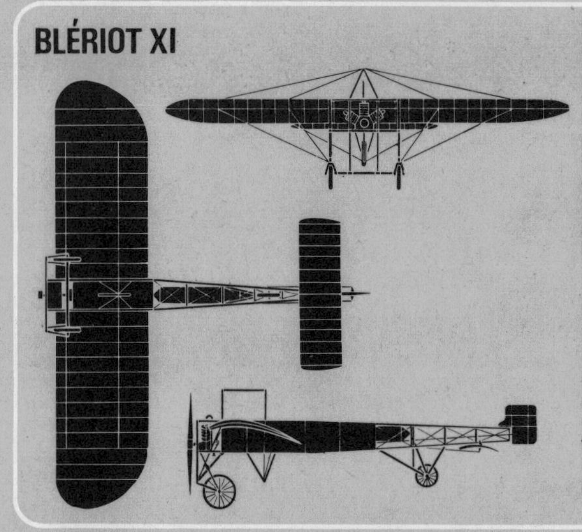

Powered by: One 22/25 hp Anzani three-cylinder air-cooled semi-radial engine, driving a two-blade propeller of 6 ft 6¾ in (2.00 m) diameter
Wing span: 25 ft 7 in (7.80 m)
Length: 26 ft 3 in (8.00 m)
Wing area: 150.7 sq ft (14.00 m²)
Gross weight: 661 lb (300 kg)
Speed: approx 47 mph (75 km/h)
Accommodation: Crew of 1
First flight: 23 January 1909 (with REP engine)

The Blériot XI, for whose design the Frenchman Raymond Saulnier is said to have been partly responsible, originally had a 30 hp REP engine and a kite-shaped dorsal fin, but the fin was later removed and the more efficient Anzani engine installed. On 25 July 1909 Louis Blériot flew from Les Baraques (Calais) to Dover in just over half an hour—an event whose implications had far-reaching effects.

VOISIN 'BIRD OF PASSAGE'

Powered by: One 60 hp ENV Type F eight-cylinder water-cooled Vee-type engine, driving a two-blade pusher propeller of 6 ft 10½ in (2.10 m) diameter
Wing span: 32 ft 9¾ in (10.00 m)
Length: 34 ft 5½ in (10.50 m)
Wing area: 445 sq ft (41.34 m²)
Gross weight: 1,150 lb (522 kg)
Speed: 34 mph (55 km/h)
Accommodation: Crew of 1
First flight: 7 March 1909

This particular Voisin biplane made, unintentionally, a great contribution to aeronautical development. It was ordered by Henry Farman, but the Voisin brothers sold it instead to J T C Moore-Brabazon in England — a piece of 'sharp' business that so incensed Farman that he cancelled his order and started his own aircraft factory, where he developed the Voisin design into a much more efficient and controllable aeroplane. The 'Bird of Passage' was rather smaller than the standard 1909 Voisin, which was 39 ft 4½ in (12.00 m) long and weighed 1,323 lb (600 kg) gross.

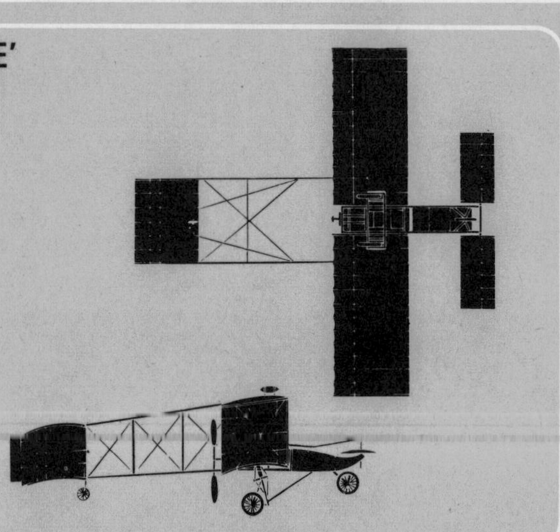

Latham's Antoinette IV, fitted with ailerons, as flown at Reims (1909)

The cross-Channel Blériot, on display at Selfridges, London

Voisin biplane in which Henry Farman flew the first 1-km closed circuit (1908)

CODY 1910 BIPLANE

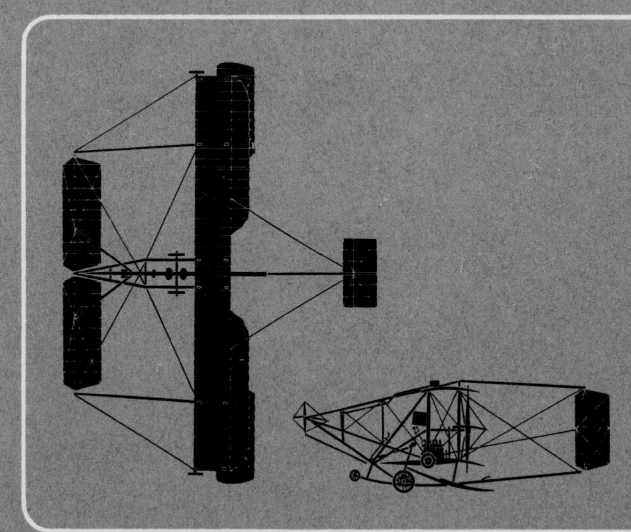

Powered by: One 60 hp ENV Type F eight-cylinder water-cooled Vee-type engine, driving a two-blade pusher propeller of approx 10 ft 0 in (3.05 m) diameter
Wing span: 49 ft 0 in (14.94 m)
Length: 38 ft 6 in (11.73 m)
Wing area: 640 sq ft (59.46 m^2) including ailerons
Gross weight: 2,950 lb (1,338 kg)
Speed: 65 mph (105 km/h)
Accommodation: Crew of 1 plus 1 passenger
The first sustained powered flights in Britain were made by British Army Aeroplane No 1, designed and flown by Samuel Franklin Cody (1861-1913), an American who later acquired British citizenship. From the final version of this aeroplane Cody developed his 1910 biplane to compete for the British Empire Michelin Trophy. After replacing the original Green engine with an ENV, he set new British distance and endurance records before winning the Trophy on the last day of 1910.

FABRE HYDRAVION

Powered by: One 50 hp Gnome seven-cylinder rotary engine, driving a two-blade Chauvière pusher propeller of 8 ft $2\frac{1}{2}$ in (2.50 m) diameter
Wing span: 45 ft 11 in (14.00 m)
Length: 27 ft $10\frac{3}{4}$ in (8.50 m)
Wing area: 183 sq ft (17.00 m^2)
Gross weight: 1,047 lb (475 kg)
Speed: 55 mph (89 km/h)
Accommodation: Crew of 1
First flight: 28 March 1910
The 1910 *Hydravion* was Henri Fabre's second seaplane, his first design of 1909 (with three Anzani engines) having failed to fly. Before 28 March 1910 Fabre had never flown, even as a passenger, yet on his second attempt that day he flew the *Hydravion* for approx 1,640 ft (500 m). On the following day he made a flight of about 3.75 miles (6 km). He abandoned the aircraft after an accident in 1911, but for many years afterward was one of the leading European designers of floats for other water-borne aircraft.

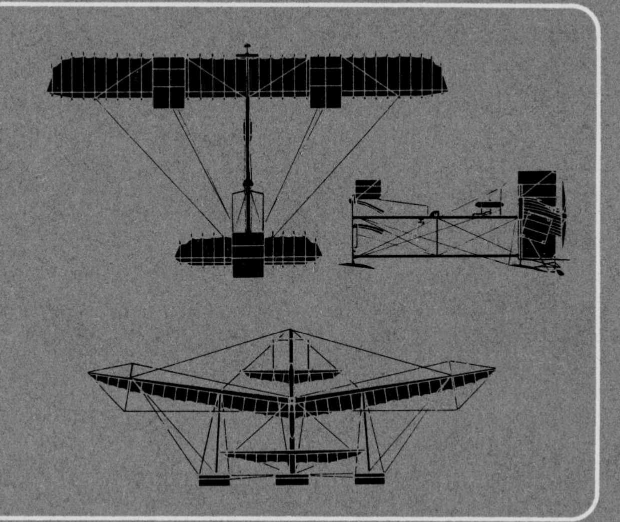

COANDA TURBINE AEROPLANE

Powered by: One 50 hp Clerget four-cylinder in-line engine, driving a centrifugal air compressor in the nose to produce 485 lb (220 kg) thrust
Wing span: 33 ft $9\frac{1}{2}$ in (10.30 m)
Length: 41 ft 0 in (12.50 m)
Height: approx 9 ft 0 in (2.75 m)
Wing area: 352 sq ft (32.70 m^2)
Gross weight: 926 lb (420 kg)
Accommodation: Crew of 1
Whether or not this unique aeroplane ever did more than lurch once, uncontrollably, into the air before coming to an unhappy end, in December 1910, there can be no denying the ingenuity and many talents of its designer, Henri Coanda. Then only 24 years old, he produced not only the world's first full-sized reaction-propelled aeroplane, but gave it such forward-looking structural features as near-cantilever wings and a varnished plywood skin. Some of his later designs were equally ingenious, if less elegant, and included the so-called Coanda Twin, an entry for the 1911 Concours Militaire powered by two outward-facing rotary engines geared to drive a front-turning propeller.

Cody 'Michelin Cup' biplane (1910)

Fabre Hydravion at Monaco (1911)

Coanda turbine aeroplane (1910)

FOKKER SPIN (SPIDER)

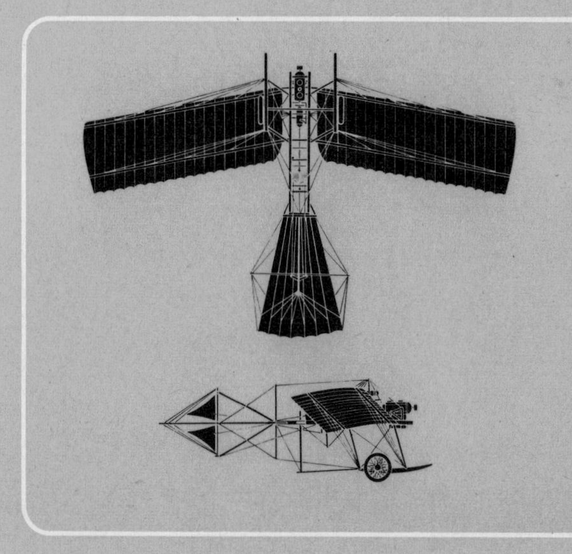

Powered by: One 50 hp Argus four-cylinder in-line engine, driving a two-blade propeller
Wing span: 36 ft 1 in (11.00 m)
Length: 25 ft 5 in (7.75 m)
Wing area: 236.81 sq ft (22.00 m²)
Gross weight: 882 lb (400 kg)
Max speed: 56 mph (90 km/h)
Accommodation: Crew of 1
First flight: August 1911

Anthony Fokker's first 'Spider', built in Germany in association with Jacob Goedecker, was based upon experience gained with two earlier monoplanes built in 1910-11. In 1912 Fokker formed his own company at Johannisthal, near Berlin, where improved versions of the *Spin* were put into production. The initial version, to which the data apply, was the A-1912; the later B-1912 had a 100 hp engine, and a few others were fitted with 70 hp Renaults. Whatever the truth regarding Fokker's ability as a designer, his undoubted skill as a flier contributed much to the pilot appeal of the fighters that he produced for the German Air Force in 1914-18.

ZEPPELIN L.Z. DEUTSCHLAND II

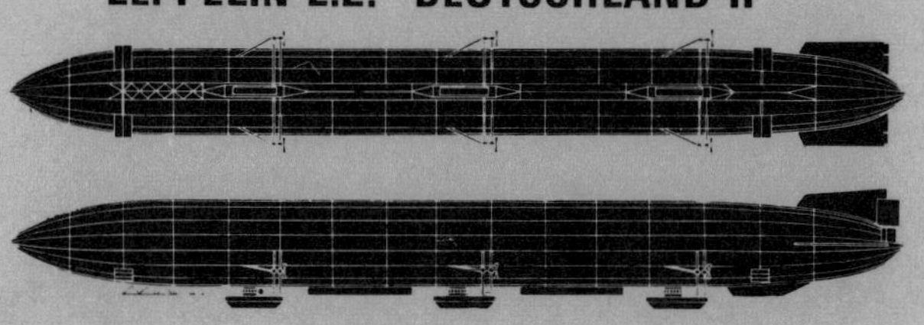

Powered by: Three 115 hp Daimler-Mercedes four-cylinder water-cooled engines, one in each gondola and each driving a pair of outrigged three-blade metal propellers of 12 ft 0 in (3.66 m) diameter
Length: 485 ft 6¾ in (148.0 m)
Max diameter: 45 ft 11 in (14.0 m)
Volume: 529,720 cu ft (15,000 m³)
Gross weight: 36,375 lb (16,500 kg)
Speed: 35 mph (56 km/h)
First flight: 1911

The *Deutschland II* was one of the fleet of Zeppelin rigid airships with which, in 1910, the world's first-ever regular passenger services by air were operated. They had a rigid aluminium framework, divided into compartments each containing a drum-shaped gas 'balloon' and covered overall with a rubberised cotton fabric. After the outbreak of the first World War they were acquired and modified for military service.

AVRO TYPE F

Powered by: One 35 hp Viale five-cylinder air-cooled radial engine, driving a 7 ft 0 in (2.13 m) diameter two-blade propeller
Wing span: 28 ft 0 in (8.53 m)
Length: 23 ft 0 in (7.01 m)
Wing area: 158 sq ft (14.68 m²)
Gross weight: 800 lb (363 kg)
Max speed: 65 mph (105 km/h)
Accommodation: Crew of 1
First flight: 1 May 1912

Although he was not the first to think of the idea, A V Roe must receive credit for building the first aeroplane actually to fly in which the accommodation was completely enclosed. In this he was well ahead of his time, for it was another twenty years before pilots came generally to accept the idea of flying without 'the wind in their faces'. Another novel feature of the Avro F was its Viale engine, which was one of the first to adopt the now-classic radial arrangement of cylinders. Later in 1912 Roe built the Type G, a biplane version somewhat bigger than the F and also having an enclosed cabin; it was one of the most reliable aircraft to take part in the Military Trials held in that year.

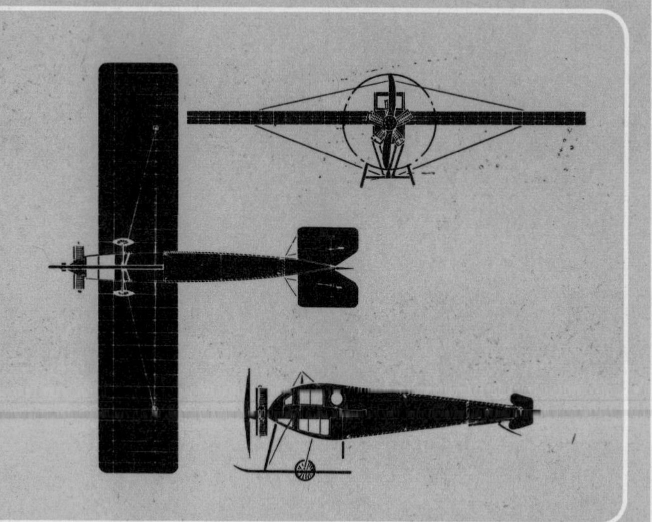

Fokker Spin

Zeppelin LZ.10 Schwaben

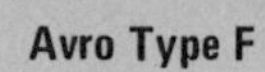

Avro Type F

SHORT TRIPLE TWIN

Powered by: Two 50 hp Gnome seven-cylinder rotary engines, driving one pusher and two tractor two-blade propellers, each of 8 ft 6 in (2.59 m) diameter
Wing span: 34 ft 0 in (10.36 m)
Length: 45 ft 0 in (13.72 m)
Wing area: 435 sq ft (40.41 m²)
Gross weight: 2,100 lb (952 kg)
Max speed: 55 mph (89 km/h)
Accommodation: Crew of 1 and 1 passenger
First flight: 18 September 1911
The Triple Twin, although preceded by such other multi-engined designs as the 1894 Maxim steam-powered aeroplane and Ader's *Avion III*, was the first practical aeroplane to be powered by more than one engine. It was built to the order of Francis McClean, and patents were granted to the Short brothers in 1911 regarding the installation of multiple engines in aircraft. The Tandem Twin had a similar power installation, but with each engine coupled directly to a single propeller, one at the front and one at the rear.

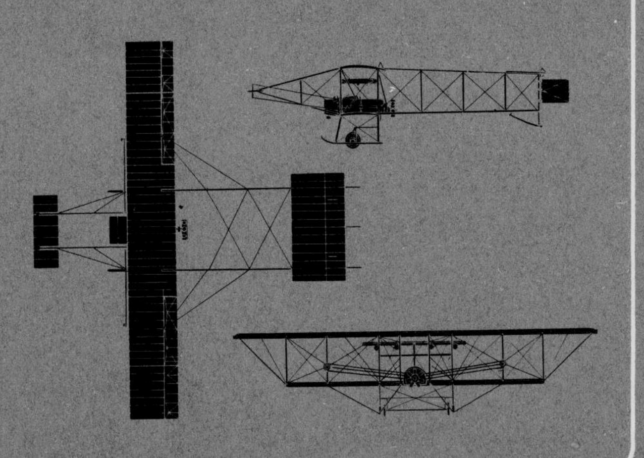

SIKORSKY LE GRAND

Powered by: Four 100 hp Argus four-cylinder in-line piston-engines
Wing span: 91 ft 10¼ in (28.00 m)
Length: 62 ft 4 in (19.00 m)
Gross weight: approx. 9,039 lb (4,100 kg)
Max. speed: approx. 59 mph (95 km/h) at 3,280 ft (1,000 m)
Accommodation: Crew of 2 + 8 passengers
Typical endurance: 1 hr 45 min
First flight: 13 May 1913
The world's first four-engined aeroplane, the Le Grand was built in about six months, and featured such advanced items as a fully-enclosed cabin (with unbreakable glass windows) and dual controls for the crew. It was dismantled in the Autumn of 1913 after having made more than fifty successful flights.

DEPERDUSSIN 1913 RACING MONOPLANE

Powered by: One 160 hp Gnome fourteen-cylinder rotary engine, driving a two-blade propeller of 7 ft 7 in (2.31 m) diameter
Wing span: 21 ft 9¾ in (6.65 m)
Length: 20 ft 0¼ in (6.10 m)
Wing area: 104 sq ft (9.66 m²)
Gross weight: 1,350 lb (612 kg)
Speed: 127 mph (204 km/h)
Accommodation: Crew of 1
The Deperdussin racer is often called the 'monocoque Deperdussin', because of the moulded-plywood fuselage shell developed by its designer, Louis Béchereau, from an idea of the Swedish engineer Ruchonnet. This was not a true monocoque, but it gave the Deperdussin machine a streamlined shape far ahead of its time. With its 'double' Gnome engine — two 80 hp units on a common crankshaft — the 'Dep' was one of the two fastest aircraft in the world prior to the 1914-18 war.

Short Tandem Twin

Sikorsky Le Grand

Deperdussin racing monoplane (1913)

BENOIST FLYING-BOAT

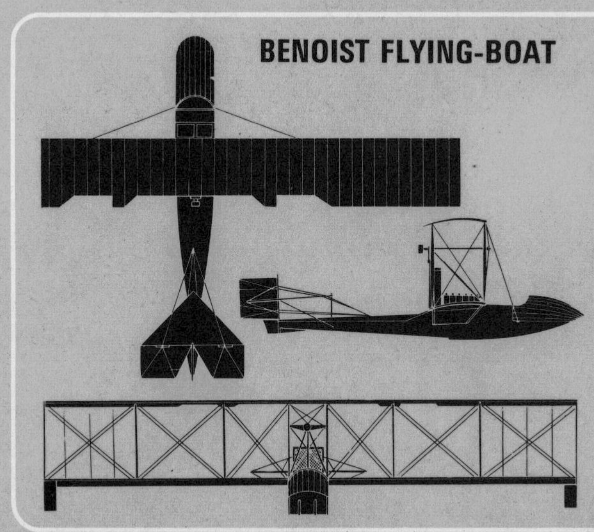

Powered by: One 75 hp Roberts or 70 hp Sturtevant six-cylinder in-line engine, driving a two-blade pusher propeller of approx 7 ft 6 in (2.29 m) diameter
Wing span: 45 ft 0 in (13.72 m)
Length: 26 ft 0 in (7.92 m)
Wing area: approx 400 sq ft (37.16 m²)
Gross weight: approx 1,500 lb (680 kg)
Speed: approx 60-65 mph (97-105 km/h)
Accommodation: Crew of 1 and 1 passenger
First flight: 1913

To this small single-engined flying-boat goes the distinction of inaugurating, on 1 January 1914, the world's first scheduled passenger-carrying service by aeroplane. It seated a pilot and one passenger, who could travel the 22 miles (35.4 km) between Tampa and St Petersburg, Florida, for a fare of five dollars—more if the passenger weighed over 200 lb (90.7 kg). Two trips per day were made, but the operation was not an economic success and ended after only a few months.

VOISIN TYPE 8

Powered by: One 220 hp Peugeot 8Aa eight-cylinder in-line engine, driving a two-blade propeller of approx 9 ft 10 in (3.00 m) diameter
Wing span: 61 ft $8\frac{1}{4}$ in (18.80 m)
Length: 36 ft $1\frac{3}{4}$ in (11.02 m)
Height: 11 ft $5\frac{3}{4}$ in (3.50 m)
Gross weight: 4,101 lb (1,860 kg)
Max speed: 82 mph (132 km/h) at sea level
Endurance: 4 hours
Accommodation: Crew of 2
Armament: 1 or 2 machine-guns and up to 396 lb (180 kg) of bombs
First flight: 1916

Designed in 1914, the Voisin family of 'pusher' military biplanes were more sturdy and effective combat aircraft than their frail appearance suggested. The Voisin Type 1 (Type L) of early 1914 had a 70 hp Gnome rotary engine; it was followed by the Voisin 2 (80 hp Le Rhône), and both types were in service with the French Air Force at the outbreak of the first World War. Most widely used version was the Voisin 3, one of which claimed the first enemy aircraft to be shot down by a French aircraft, on 5 October 1914. The Voisin 8 of 1916, of which more than 1,100 were built, was the second most important version numerically. Duties of the Voisin family included artillery observation, day and night bombing, ground attack, reconnaissance, escort and training.

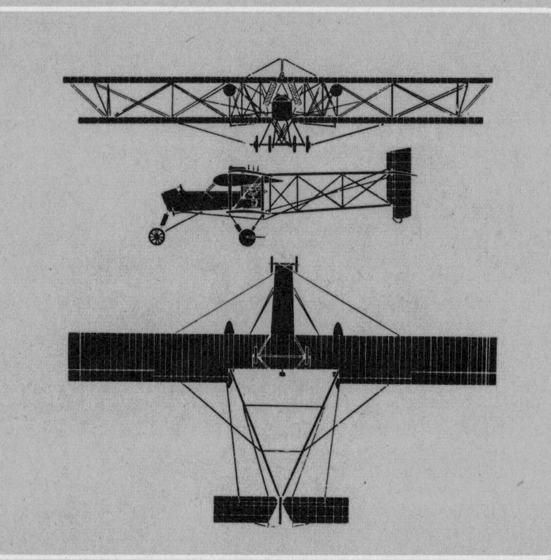

AVRO 504

Powered by: One 100 hp Gnome Monosoupape seven-cylinder rotary engine, driving a two-blade propeller
Wing span: 36 ft 0 in (10.97 m)
Length: 29 ft 5 in (8.97 m)
Wing area: 330 sq ft (30.66 m²)
Gross weight: 1,829 lb (830 kg)
Cruising speed: 75 mph (121 km/h)
Typical range: 225 miles (362 km)
Accommodation: Crew of 1 and 2 passengers
First flight: July 1913

When A V Roe designed the original 504 in 1913, he thought he would be lucky to get an order for six; by the time British production ended in 1932, over 10,000 of these biplanes had been built. Most of them were originally 2-seaters, built during the first World War for training, but after the war, with a third cockpit added, the 504 became one of the most popular circus and joy-riding aircraft of the 1920s. Data apply to the 504K, which had a universal mounting for various types of rotary engine. The last major production model was the Lynx radial-engined 504N, which had a steel-tube fuselage; 598 were built.

Model of Benoist flying-boat in Qantas Collection

Voisin Type 8

Avro 504K

B.E.2c

Powered by: One 90 hp R.A.F. 1a eight-cylinder Vee-type engine, driving a four-blade propeller of 8 ft 10 in (2.69 m) diameter
Wing span: 37 ft 0 in (11.28 m)
Length: 27 ft 3 in (8.31 m)
Wing area: 371 sq ft (34.47 m²)
Gross weight: 2,142 lb (972 kg)
Max speed: 72 mph (116 km/h) at 6,500 ft (1,980 m)
Accommodation: Crew of 2
Armament: One 0.303 in Lewis machine-gun; up to 224 lb (102 kg) of bombs underwing
Endurance: 3 hr 15 min
First flight (B.E.2c): early summer 1914

One of the most striking early examples of the widespread mass-production of aircraft, the B.E.2 series was built by at least 22 British manufacturers, who between them completed well over 3,500 of these biplanes. Despite its unhappy reputation as 'Fokker fodder', the B.E.2c was considerably better in design than earlier B.E. types, due chiefly to the exhaustive test flying of the type by E T Busk of the Royal Aircraft Factory.

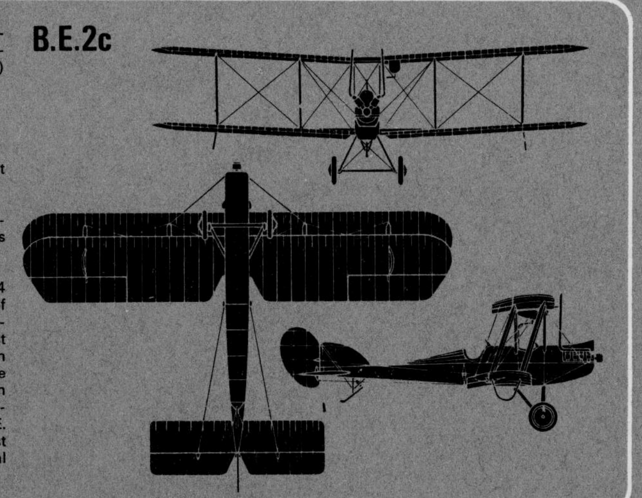

VICKERS F.B.5

Powered by: One 100 hp Gnome Monosoupape nine-cylinder rotary engine, driving a two-blade pusher propeller of approx 9 ft 6 in (2.90 m) diameter
Wing span: 36 ft 6 in (11.13 m)
Length: 27 ft 2 in (8.28 m)
Wing area: 382 sq ft (35.49 m²)
Gross weight: 2,050 lb (930 kg)
Max speed: 70 mph (113 km/h) at 5,000 ft (1,525 m)
Typical endurance: 4 hr
Accommodation: Crew of 2
Armament: One 0.303-in Lewis machine-gun in nose

First production version of what became known as the Vickers 'Gunbus' fighter, the F.B.5 was the outcome of development of the Vickers *Destroyer* biplane (E.F.B.1) first displayed at the Olympia Aero Show in February 1913. At that time no mechanism had been perfected to allow a machine-gun to fire forward past a front-mounted propeller without hitting it, and so the engine was installed at the rear, coupled to a pusher propeller.

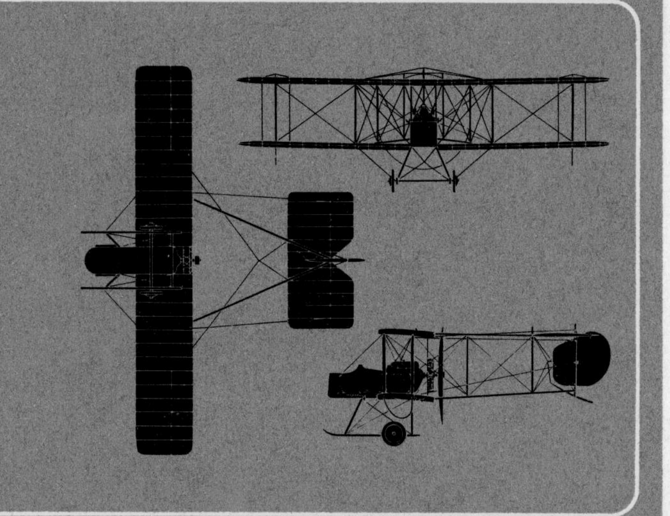

FOKKER E.III

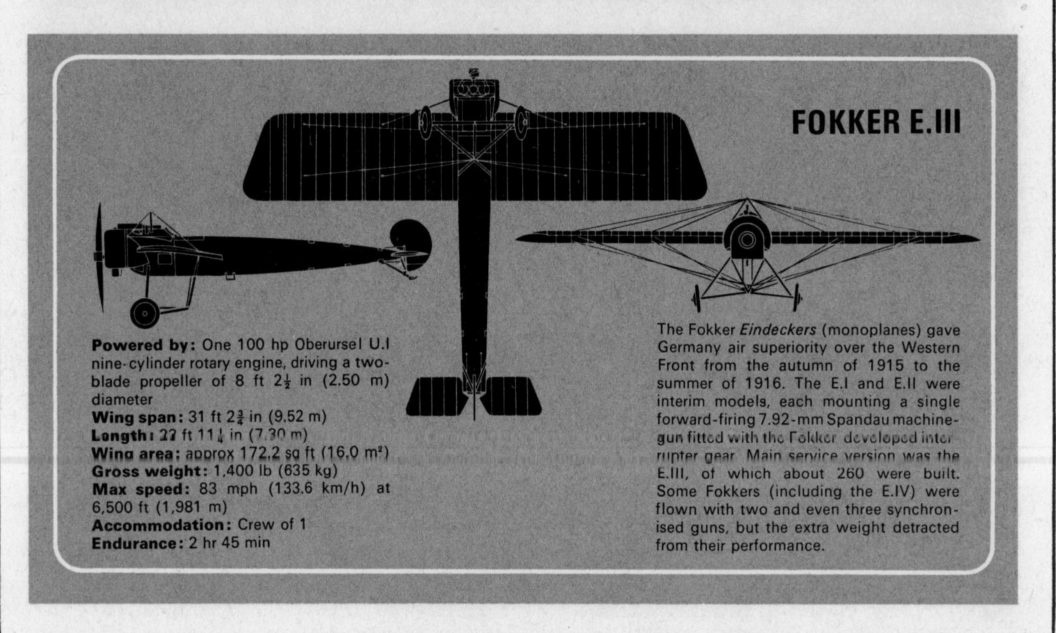

Powered by: One 100 hp Oberursel U.I nine-cylinder rotary engine, driving a two-blade propeller of 8 ft 2½ in (2.50 m) diameter
Wing span: 31 ft 2¾ in (9.52 m)
Length: 2[illegible] ft 11¼ in (7.30 m)
Wing area: approx 172.2 sq ft (16.0 m²)
Gross weight: 1,400 lb (635 kg)
Max speed: 83 mph (133.6 km/h) at 6,500 ft (1,981 m)
Accommodation: Crew of 1
Endurance: 2 hr 45 min

The Fokker *Eindeckers* (monoplanes) gave Germany air superiority over the Western Front from the autumn of 1915 to the summer of 1916. The E.I and E.II were interim models, each mounting a single forward-firing 7.92-mm Spandau machine-gun fitted with the Fokker developed interrupter gear. Main service version was the E.III, of which about 260 were built. Some Fokkers (including the E.IV) were flown with two and even three synchronised guns, but the extra weight detracted from their performance.

B.E.2c

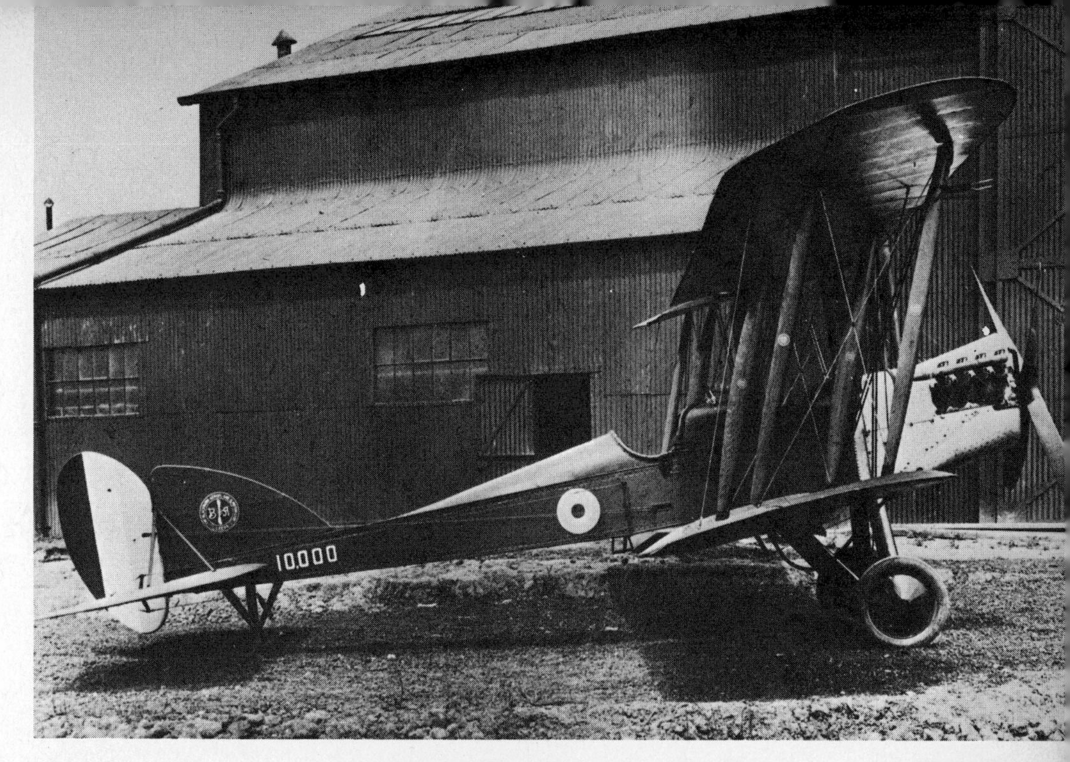

Vickers F.B.5 'Gunbus'

Fokker E.III

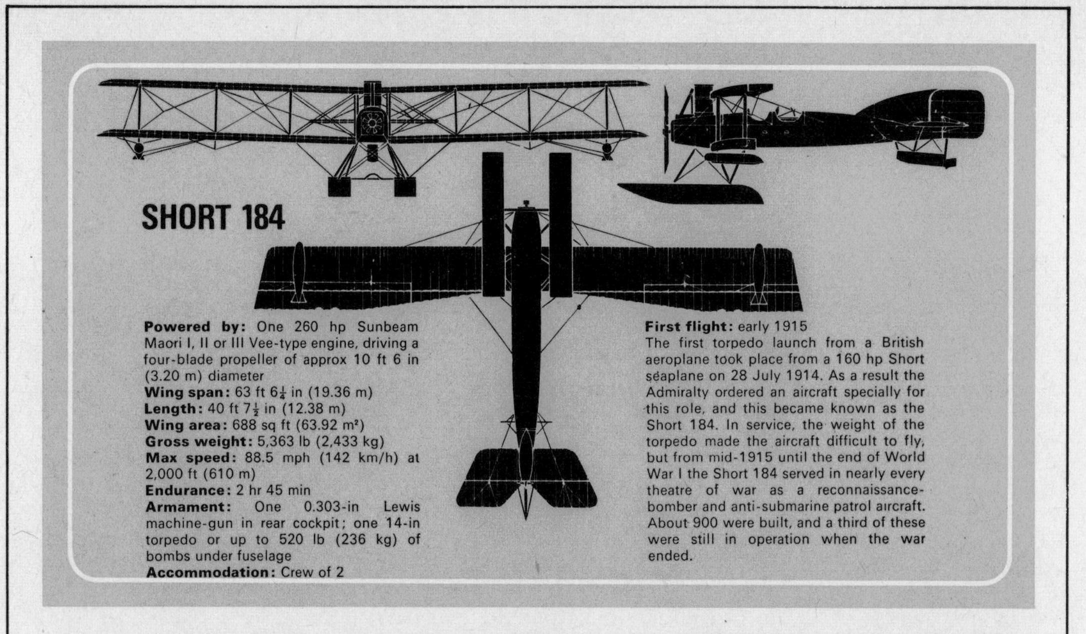

SHORT 184

Powered by: One 260 hp Sunbeam Maori I, II or III Vee-type engine, driving a four-blade propeller of approx 10 ft 6 in (3.20 m) diameter
Wing span: 63 ft 6¼ in (19.36 m)
Length: 40 ft 7½ in (12.38 m)
Wing area: 688 sq ft (63.92 m²)
Gross weight: 5,363 lb (2,433 kg)
Max speed: 88.5 mph (142 km/h) at 2,000 ft (610 m)
Endurance: 2 hr 45 min
Armament: One 0.303-in Lewis machine-gun in rear cockpit; one 14-in torpedo or up to 520 lb (236 kg) of bombs under fuselage
Accommodation: Crew of 2

First flight: early 1915
The first torpedo launch from a British aeroplane took place from a 160 hp Short seaplane on 28 July 1914. As a result the Admiralty ordered an aircraft specially for this role, and this became known as the Short 184. In service, the weight of the torpedo made the aircraft difficult to fly, but from mid-1915 until the end of World War I the Short 184 served in nearly every theatre of war as a reconnaissance-bomber and anti-submarine patrol aircraft. About 900 were built, and a third of these were still in operation when the war ended.

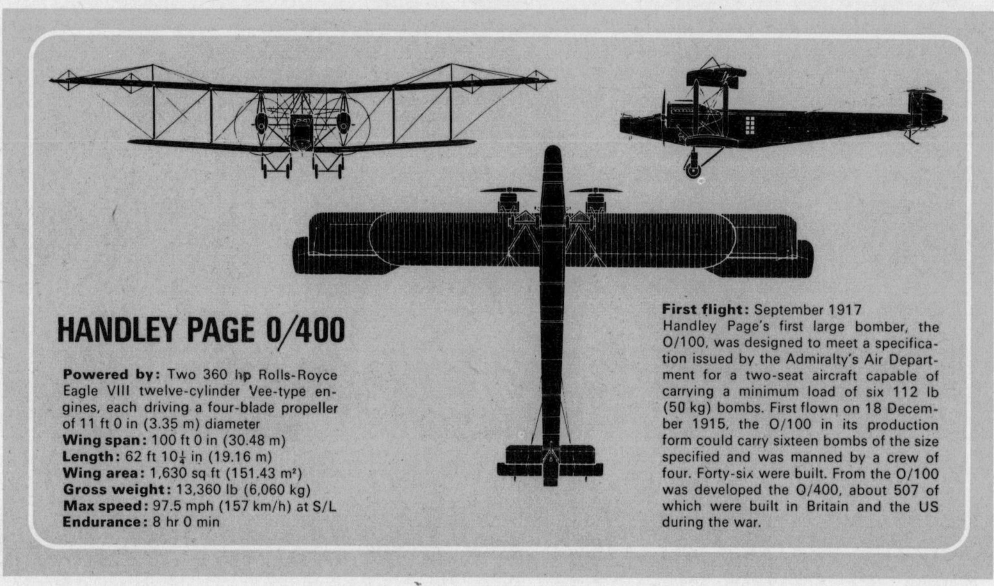

HANDLEY PAGE 0/400

Powered by: Two 360 hp Rolls-Royce Eagle VIII twelve-cylinder Vee-type engines, each driving a four-blade propeller of 11 ft 0 in (3.35 m) diameter
Wing span: 100 ft 0 in (30.48 m)
Length: 62 ft 10¼ in (19.16 m)
Wing area: 1,630 sq ft (151.43 m²)
Gross weight: 13,360 lb (6,060 kg)
Max speed: 97.5 mph (157 km/h) at S/L
Endurance: 8 hr 0 min

First flight: September 1917
Handley Page's first large bomber, the O/100, was designed to meet a specification issued by the Admiralty's Air Department for a two-seat aircraft capable of carrying a minimum load of six 112 lb (50 kg) bombs. First flown on 18 December 1915, the O/100 in its production form could carry sixteen bombs of the size specified and was manned by a crew of four. Forty-six were built. From the O/100 was developed the O/400, about 507 of which were built in Britain and the US during the war.

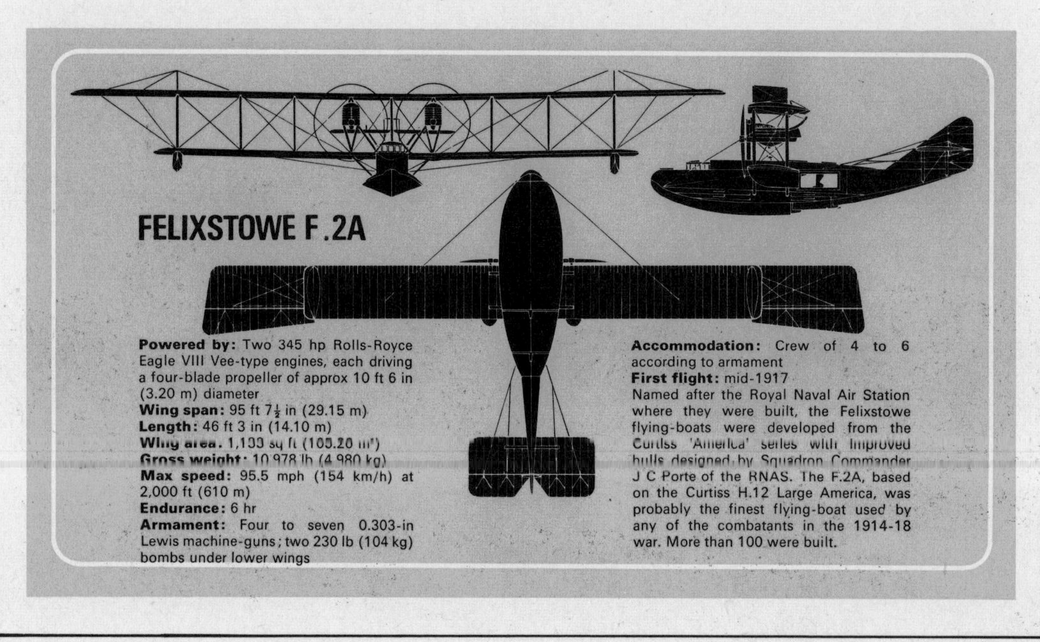

FELIXSTOWE F.2A

Powered by: Two 345 hp Rolls-Royce Eagle VIII Vee-type engines, each driving a four-blade propeller of approx 10 ft 6 in (3.20 m) diameter
Wing span: 95 ft 7½ in (29.15 m)
Length: 46 ft 3 in (14.10 m)
Wing area: 1,133 sq ft (105.26 m²)
Gross weight: 10,978 lb (4,980 kg)
Max speed: 95.5 mph (154 km/h) at 2,000 ft (610 m)
Endurance: 6 hr
Armament: Four to seven 0.303-in Lewis machine-guns; two 230 lb (104 kg) bombs under lower wings
Accommodation: Crew of 4 to 6 according to armament

First flight: mid-1917
Named after the Royal Naval Air Station where they were built, the Felixstowe flying-boats were developed from the Curtiss 'America' series with improved hulls designed by Squadron Commander J C Porte of the RNAS. The F.2A, based on the Curtiss H.12 Large America, was probably the finest flying-boat used by any of the combatants in the 1914-18 war. More than 100 were built.

Short 184

Handley Page O/400, with wings folded

Felixstowe F.2A

JUNKERS J 1

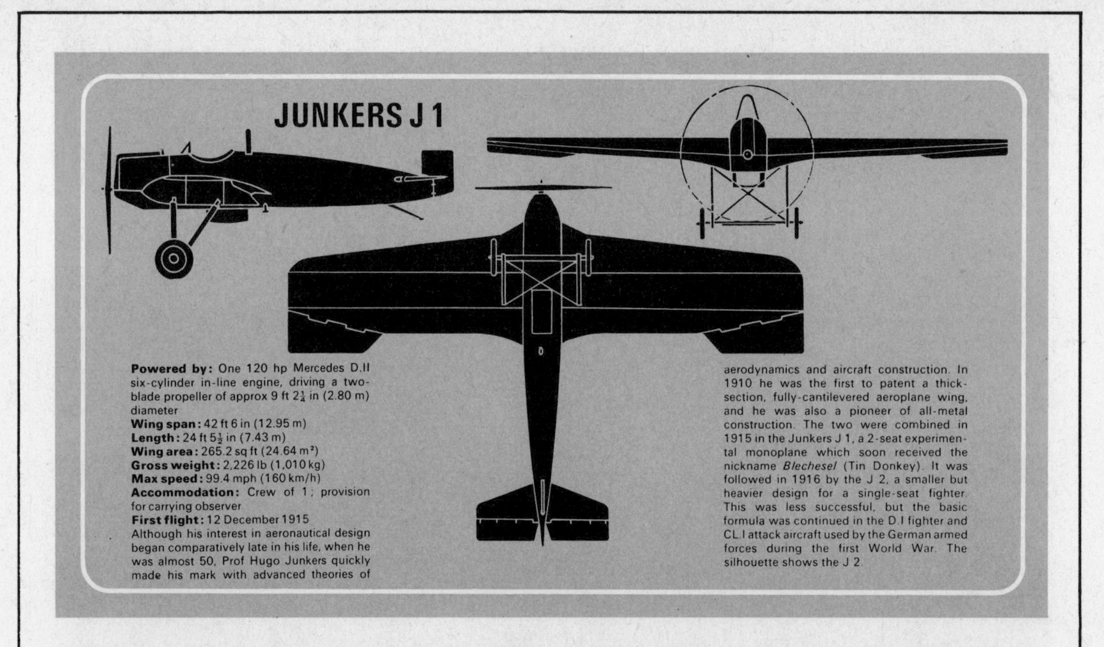

Powered by: One 120 hp Mercedes D.II six-cylinder in-line engine, driving a two-blade propeller of approx 9 ft 2¼ in (2.80 m) diameter
Wing span: 42 ft 6 in (12.95 m)
Length: 24 ft 5½ in (7.43 m)
Wing area: 265.2 sq ft (24.64 m²)
Gross weight: 2,226 lb (1,010 kg)
Max speed: 99.4 mph (160 km/h)
Accommodation: Crew of 1; provision for carrying observer
First flight: 12 December 1915

Although his interest in aeronautical design began comparatively late in his life, when he was almost 50, Prof Hugo Junkers quickly made his mark with advanced theories of aerodynamics and aircraft construction. In 1910 he was the first to patent a thick-section, fully-cantilevered aeroplane wing, and he was also a pioneer of all-metal construction. The two were combined in 1915 in the Junkers J 1, a 2-seat experimental monoplane which soon received the nickname *Blechesel* (Tin Donkey). It was followed in 1916 by the J 2, a smaller but heavier design for a single-seat fighter. This was less successful, but the basic formula was continued in the D.I fighter and CL.I attack aircraft used by the German armed forces during the first World War. The silhouette shows the J 2.

FOKKER D.VII

Powered by: One 160 hp Mercedes D.III six-cylinder in-line engine, driving a two-blade propeller
Wing span: 29 ft 2¼ in (8.90 m)
Length: 22 ft 9¾ in (6.95 m)
Wing area: 220.66 sq ft (20.50 m²)
Gross weight: 1,984 lb (900 kg)
Max speed: 117 mph (189 km/h) at 3,280 ft (1,000 m)
Endurance: 1 hr 30 min
Accommodation: Crew of 1
First flight: January 1918

Indisputably one of the best fighters to appear during the first World War, the Fokker D.VII competed with 30 other aircraft (including six Fokker types) in fighter trials in Germany at the beginning of 1918. It outclassed every other competitor and was immediately ordered into large-scale production, the first examples reaching von Richthofen's squadron at the Front in April 1918. About 1,000 were built before the war ended, and production was continued in Holland after the Armistice, when more than 100 were smuggled out of Germany to prevent their seizure by the Allies.

DE HAVILLAND D.H.9A

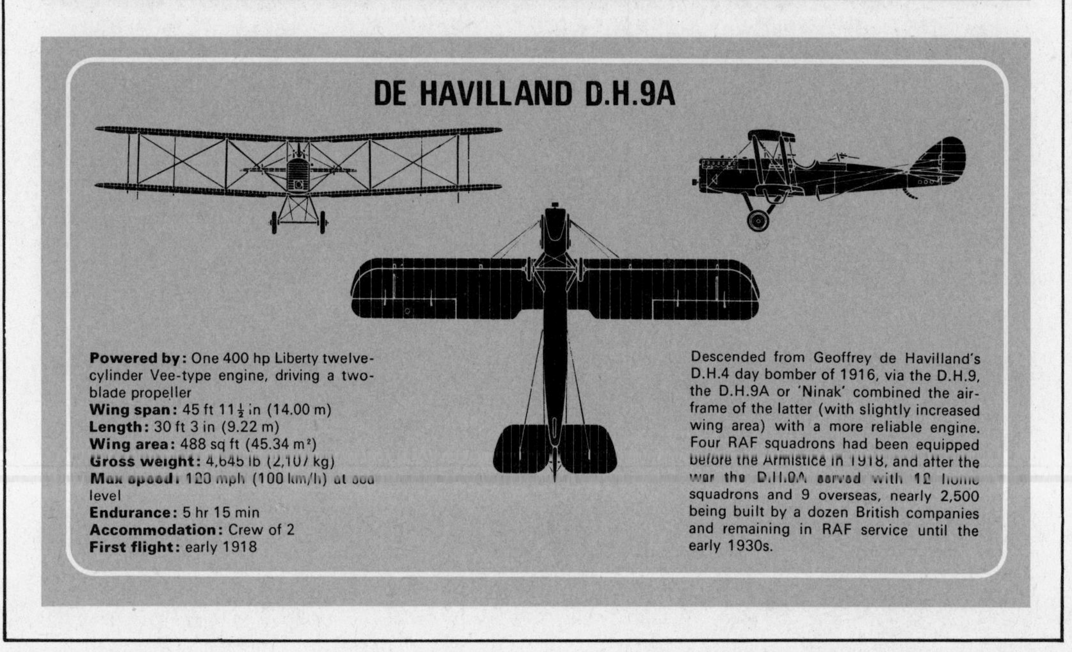

Powered by: One 400 hp Liberty twelve-cylinder Vee-type engine, driving a two-blade propeller
Wing span: 45 ft 11½ in (14.00 m)
Length: 30 ft 3 in (9.22 m)
Wing area: 488 sq ft (45.34 m²)
Gross weight: 4,645 lb (2,107 kg)
Max speed: 120 mph (100 km/h) at sea level
Endurance: 5 hr 15 min
Accommodation: Crew of 2
First flight: early 1918

Descended from Geoffrey de Havilland's D.H.4 day bomber of 1916, via the D.H.9, the D.H.9A or 'Ninak' combined the air-frame of the latter (with slightly increased wing area) with a more reliable engine. Four RAF squadrons had been equipped before the Armistice in 1918, and after the war the D.H.9A served with 12 home squadrons and 9 overseas, nearly 2,500 being built by a dozen British companies and remaining in RAF service until the early 1930s.

Junkers J 1

Fokker D.VII

D.H.9A

VICKERS VIMY

Powered by: Two 360 hp Rolls-Royce Eagle VIII twelve-cylinder Vee-type engines, each driving a four-blade propeller of 10 ft 6 in (3.20 m) diameter
Wing span: 68 ft 0 in (20.73 m)
Length: 43 ft 6½ in (13.27 m)
Wing area: 1,330 sq ft (123.56 m²)
Gross weight (bomber): 12,500 lb (5,670 kg)
Max speed: 103 mph (166 km/h) at S/L
Max range (bomber): 1,880 miles (3,025 km); (trans-Atlantic Vimy): 2,440 miles (3,927 km)
Accommodation: Crew of 2
First flight (bomber): 30 November 1917
The Vimy flown by Alcock and Brown from St John's, Newfoundland, to Clifden, Co Galway, on 14/15 June 1919 was modified from a standard production machine, stripped of its military equipment and carrying 865 Imp gallons (3,932 litres) of fuel instead of the normal 516 gallons (2,346 litres). It completed the 1,890-mile (3,032-km) non-stop trip, despite appalling weather and icing difficulties, in 16 hr 27 min.

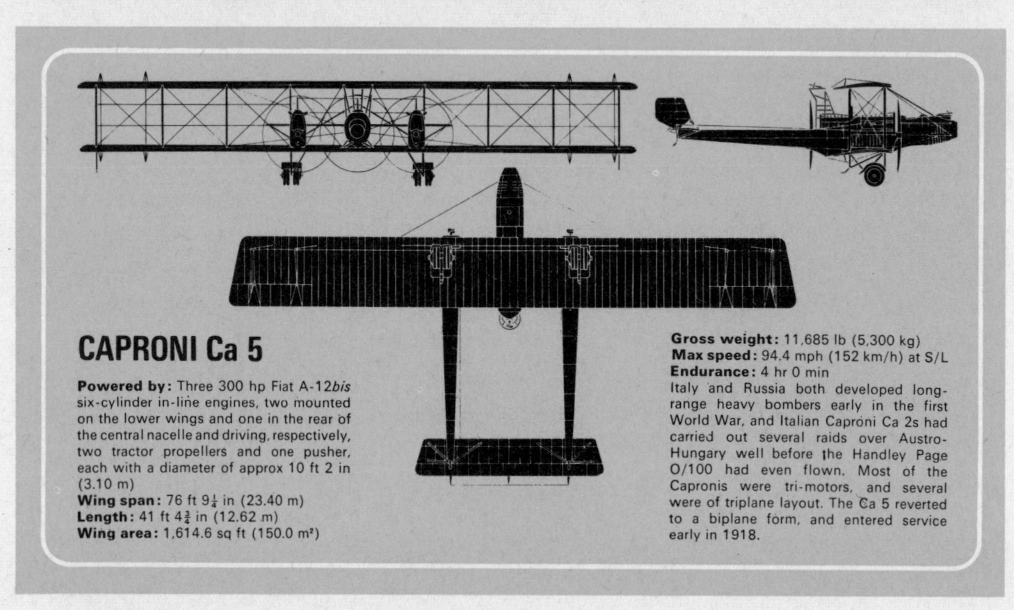

CAPRONI Ca 5

Powered by: Three 300 hp Fiat A-12*bis* six-cylinder in-line engines, two mounted on the lower wings and one in the rear of the central nacelle and driving, respectively, two tractor propellers and one pusher, each with a diameter of approx 10 ft 2 in (3.10 m)
Wing span: 76 ft 9¼ in (23.40 m)
Length: 41 ft 4¾ in (12.62 m)
Wing area: 1,614.6 sq ft (150.0 m²)
Gross weight: 11,685 lb (5,300 kg)
Max speed: 94.4 mph (152 km/h) at S/L
Endurance: 4 hr 0 min
Italy and Russia both developed long-range heavy bombers early in the first World War, and Italian Caproni Ca 2s had carried out several raids over Austro-Hungary well before the Handley Page O/100 had even flown. Most of the Capronis were tri-motors, and several were of triplane layout. The Ca 5 reverted to a biplane form, and entered service early in 1918.

FARMAN F.60 GOLIATH

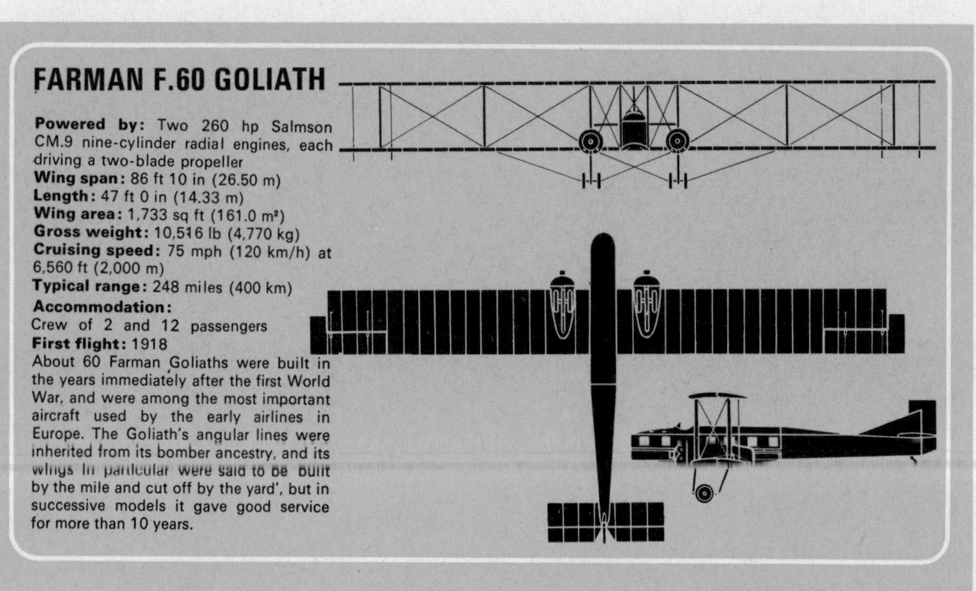

Powered by: Two 260 hp Salmson CM.9 nine-cylinder radial engines, each driving a two-blade propeller
Wing span: 86 ft 10 in (26.50 m)
Length: 47 ft 0 in (14.33 m)
Wing area: 1,733 sq ft (161.0 m²)
Gross weight: 10,516 lb (4,770 kg)
Cruising speed: 75 mph (120 km/h) at 6,560 ft (2,000 m)
Typical range: 248 miles (400 km)
Accommodation:
Crew of 2 and 12 passengers
First flight: 1918
About 60 Farman Goliaths were built in the years immediately after the first World War, and were among the most important aircraft used by the early airlines in Europe. The Goliath's angular lines were inherited from its bomber ancestry, and its wings in particular were said to be built 'by the mile and cut off by the yard', but in successive models it gave good service for more than 10 years.

Vimy flown from England to Australia in 1919 by Ross and Keith Smith

Caproni Ca 5

Farman F.60 Goliath

DE HAVILLAND D.H.4A

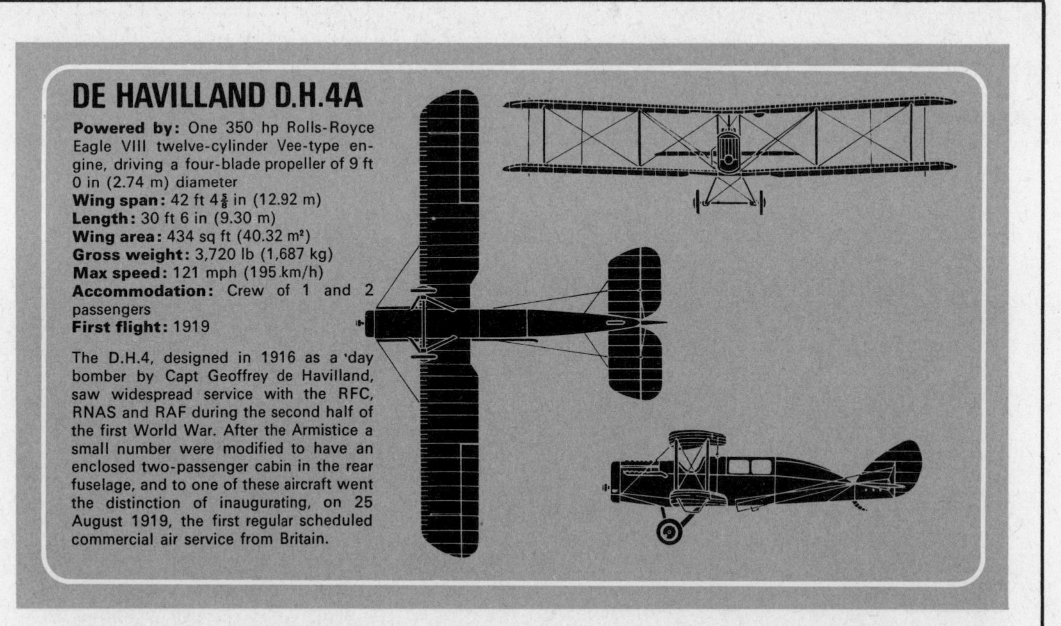

Powered by: One 350 hp Rolls-Royce Eagle VIII twelve-cylinder Vee-type engine, driving a four-blade propeller of 9 ft 0 in (2.74 m) diameter
Wing span: 42 ft 4⅝ in (12.92 m)
Length: 30 ft 6 in (9.30 m)
Wing area: 434 sq ft (40.32 m²)
Gross weight: 3,720 lb (1,687 kg)
Max speed: 121 mph (195 km/h)
Accommodation: Crew of 1 and 2 passengers
First flight: 1919

The D.H.4, designed in 1916 as a day bomber by Capt Geoffrey de Havilland, saw widespread service with the RFC, RNAS and RAF during the second half of the first World War. After the Armistice a small number were modified to have an enclosed two-passenger cabin in the rear fuselage, and to one of these aircraft went the distinction of inaugurating, on 25 August 1919, the first regular scheduled commercial air service from Britain.

FRIEDRICHSHAFEN FF49

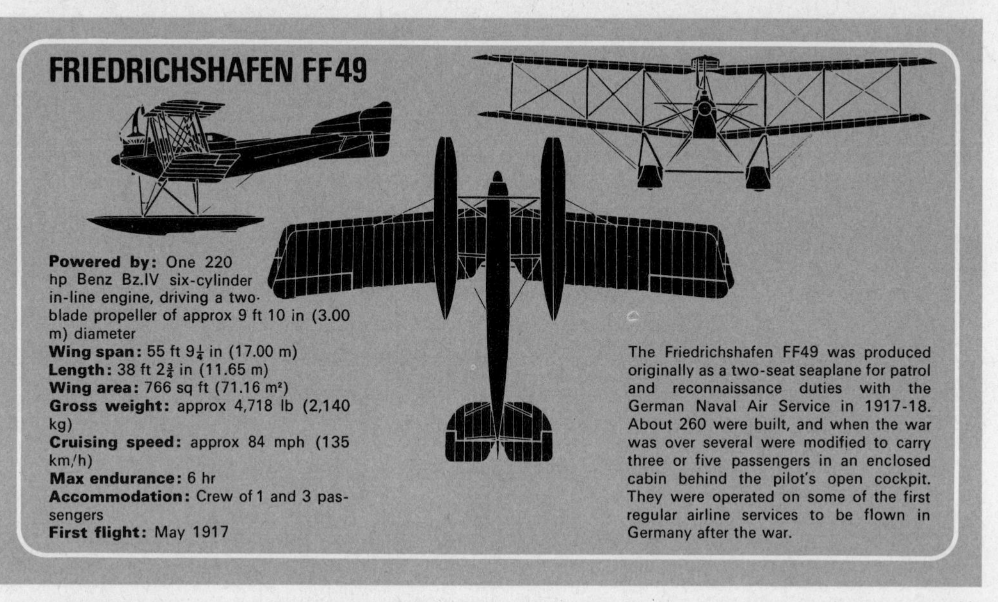

Powered by: One 220 hp Benz Bz.IV six-cylinder in-line engine, driving a two-blade propeller of approx 9 ft 10 in (3.00 m) diameter
Wing span: 55 ft 9¼ in (17.00 m)
Length: 38 ft 2¾ in (11.65 m)
Wing area: 766 sq ft (71.16 m²)
Gross weight: approx 4,718 lb (2,140 kg)
Cruising speed: approx 84 mph (135 km/h)
Max endurance: 6 hr
Accommodation: Crew of 1 and 3 passengers
First flight: May 1917

The Friedrichshafen FF49 was produced originally as a two-seat seaplane for patrol and reconnaissance duties with the German Naval Air Service in 1917-18. About 260 were built, and when the war was over several were modified to carry three or five passengers in an enclosed cabin behind the pilot's open cockpit. They were operated on some of the first regular airline services to be flown in Germany after the war.

HANDLEY PAGE W8b

Powered by: Two 360 hp Rolls-Royce Eagle VIII twelve-cylinder Vee-type engines, each driving a 10 ft 6 in (3.20 m) diameter four-blade propeller
Wing span: 75 ft 0 in (22.86 m)
Length: 60 ft 1 in (18.31 m)
Wing area: 1,456 sq ft (135.26 m²)
Gross weight: 12,500 lb (5,670 kg)
Max speed: 104 mph (167 km/h)
Range: approx 500 miles (800 km)
Accommodation: Crew of 2 and 12 passengers
First flight: 4 December 1919 (W 8)

Following its initial services into Europe with modified O/400 bombers shortly after the first World War, Handley Page Transport operated a series of two- and three-engined developments of the bomber, designated W 8, W 9 and W 10. Best known of these were the trio of W 8bs named *Princess Mary, Prince George* and *Prince Henry,* with which a London-Paris service was started in May 1922. The W 8b can also claim to have been among the first aircraft used to increase man's knowledge of other worlds in space, for one of these aircraft was sent up in June 1927 carrying a photographer to take pictures of an eclipse of the Sun from above the clouds.

D.H.4A

Friedrichshafen FF49 fitted with passenger cabin

Handley Page W8b

JUNKERS F 13

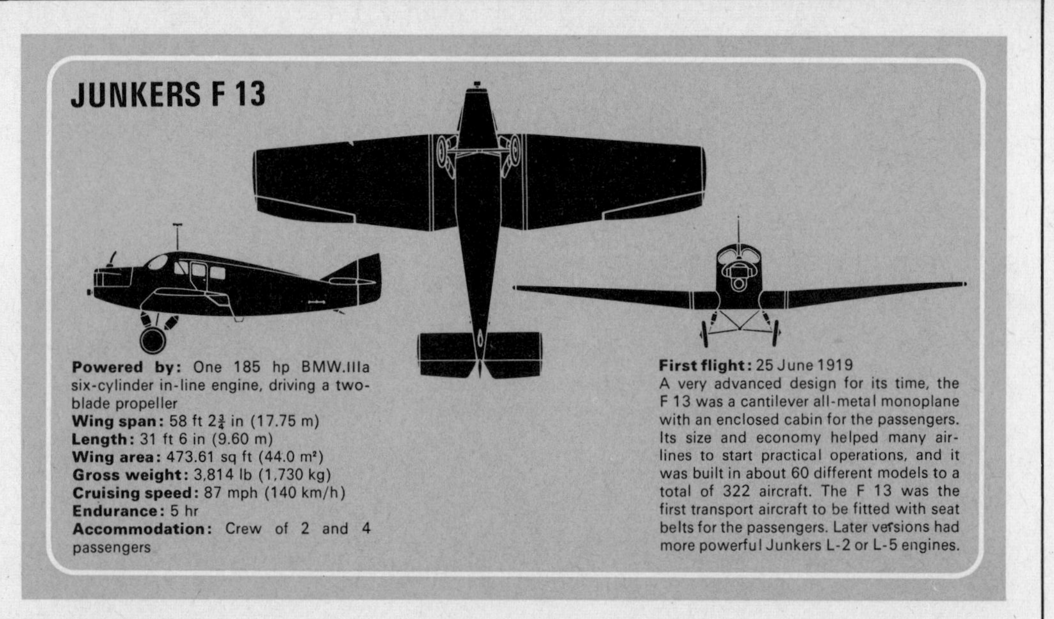

Powered by: One 185 hp BMW.IIIa six-cylinder in-line engine, driving a two-blade propeller
Wing span: 58 ft 2¾ in (17.75 m)
Length: 31 ft 6 in (9.60 m)
Wing area: 473.61 sq ft (44.0 m²)
Gross weight: 3,814 lb (1,730 kg)
Cruising speed: 87 mph (140 km/h)
Endurance: 5 hr
Accommodation: Crew of 2 and 4 passengers
First flight: 25 June 1919

A very advanced design for its time, the F 13 was a cantilever all-metal monoplane with an enclosed cabin for the passengers. Its size and economy helped many airlines to start practical operations, and it was built in about 60 different models to a total of 322 aircraft. The F 13 was the first transport aircraft to be fitted with seat belts for the passengers. Later versions had more powerful Junkers L-2 or L-5 engines.

NAVY-CURTISS NC-4

Powered by: Four 400 hp Liberty 12 twelve-cylinder Vee-type engines (two mounted back-to-back in central nacelle and two singly), each driving a two-blade wooden propeller
Wing span: 126 ft 0 in (38.40 m)
Length: 68 ft 3½ in (20.85 m)
Wing area: 2,380 sq ft (221.11 m²)
Gross weight: 28,500 lb (12,925 kg)
Max speed: 91 mph (146 km/h)
Accommodation: Crew of 5
First flight: 30 April 1919

Four NC (Navy-Curtiss) flying-boats were built, as the result of collaboration between Glenn Curtiss and the US Navy, originally for the purpose of attacking enemy U-boats from the air. The first aircraft (NC-1) did not fly until October 1918, and so the type was too late for war service, but the fourth (NC-4) made aviation history by completing a four-stage crossing of the North Atlantic from Newfoundland to Plymouth between 16-31 May 1919.

DAYTON-WRIGHT RB-1 RACER

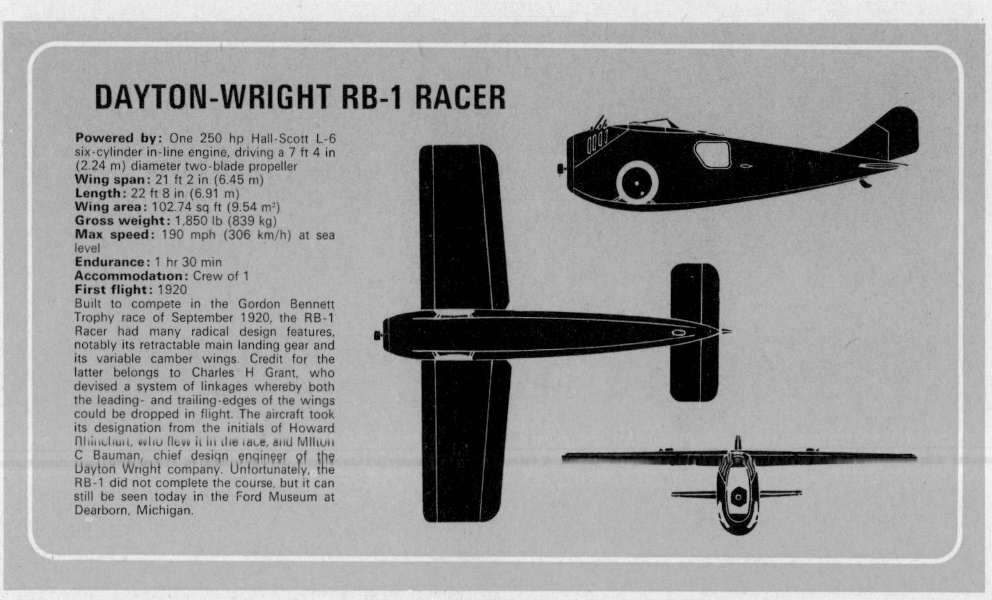

Powered by: One 250 hp Hall-Scott L-6 six-cylinder in-line engine, driving a 7 ft 4 in (2.24 m) diameter two-blade propeller
Wing span: 21 ft 2 in (6.45 m)
Length: 22 ft 8 in (6.91 m)
Wing area: 102.74 sq ft (9.54 m²)
Gross weight: 1,850 lb (839 kg)
Max speed: 190 mph (306 km/h) at sea level
Endurance: 1 hr 30 min
Accommodation: Crew of 1
First flight: 1920

Built to compete in the Gordon Bennett Trophy race of September 1920, the RB-1 Racer had many radical design features, notably its retractable main landing gear and its variable camber wings. Credit for the latter belongs to Charles H Grant, who devised a system of linkages whereby both the leading- and trailing-edges of the wings could be dropped in flight. The aircraft took its designation from the initials of Howard Rhinehart, who flew it in the race, and Milton C Bauman, chief design engineer of the Dayton Wright company. Unfortunately, the RB-1 did not complete the course, but it can still be seen today in the Ford Museum at Dearborn, Michigan.

Junkers F 13

Navy-Curtiss NC-4

Dayton-Wright RB-1 Racer

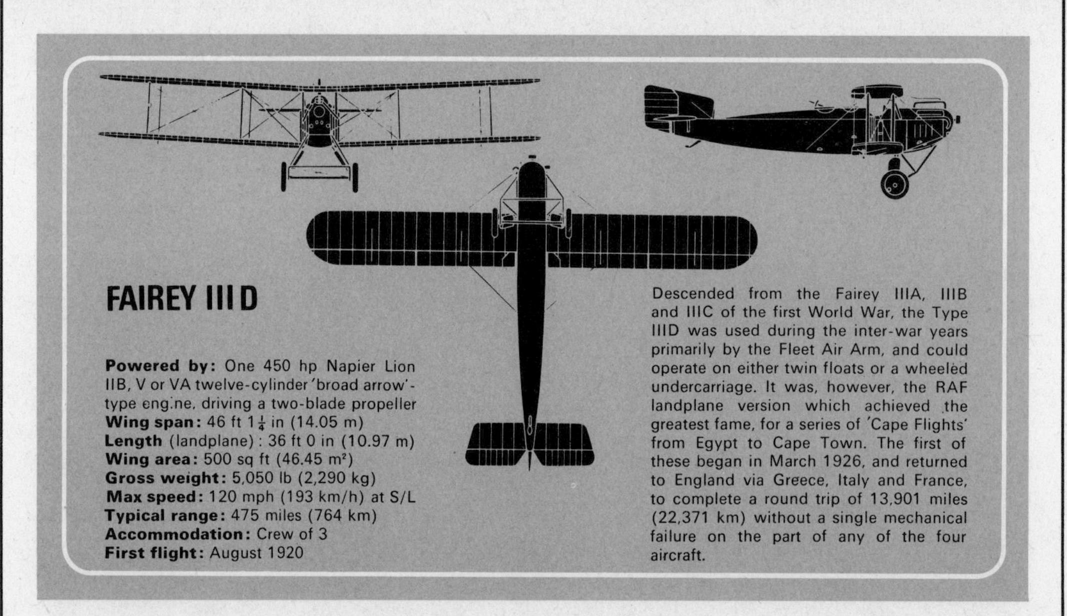

FAIREY IIID

Powered by: One 450 hp Napier Lion IIB, V or VA twelve-cylinder 'broad arrow'-type engine, driving a two-blade propeller
Wing span: 46 ft 1¼ in (14.05 m)
Length (landplane): 36 ft 0 in (10.97 m)
Wing area: 500 sq ft (46.45 m²)
Gross weight: 5,050 lb (2,290 kg)
Max speed: 120 mph (193 km/h) at S/L
Typical range: 475 miles (764 km)
Accommodation: Crew of 3
First flight: August 1920

Descended from the Fairey IIIA, IIIB and IIIC of the first World War, the Type IIID was used during the inter-war years primarily by the Fleet Air Arm, and could operate on either twin floats or a wheeled undercarriage. It was, however, the RAF landplane version which achieved the greatest fame, for a series of 'Cape Flights' from Egypt to Cape Town. The first of these began in March 1926, and returned to England via Greece, Italy and France, to complete a round trip of 13,901 miles (22,371 km) without a single mechanical failure on the part of any of the four aircraft.

VICKERS VERNON

Powered by: Two 375 hp Rolls-Royce Eagle VIII Vee-type piston-engines (later 450 hp Napier Lion 'broad-arrow' type)
Wing span: 68 ft 1 in (20.75 m)
Length: 42 ft 8 in (13.00 m)
Gross weight: 12,544 lb (5,690 kg)
Max speed: 118 mph (190 km/h) at S/L with Lion engines
Accommodation: Crew of 3 plus 11 passengers
Typical range: 320 miles (515 km) at 80 mph (128 km/h)
First flight: 1921

A development of the wartime Vimy bomber, the Vernon served from 1922-26 with Nos 45 and 70 Squadrons of the RAF in India, Cyprus and Iraq. Apart from its role in the evacuation of sick British troops from Iraq in 1922, the Vernon was the chief transport aircraft used on the celebrated Cairo-Baghdad air mail service in the mid-1920s. Sixty were built.

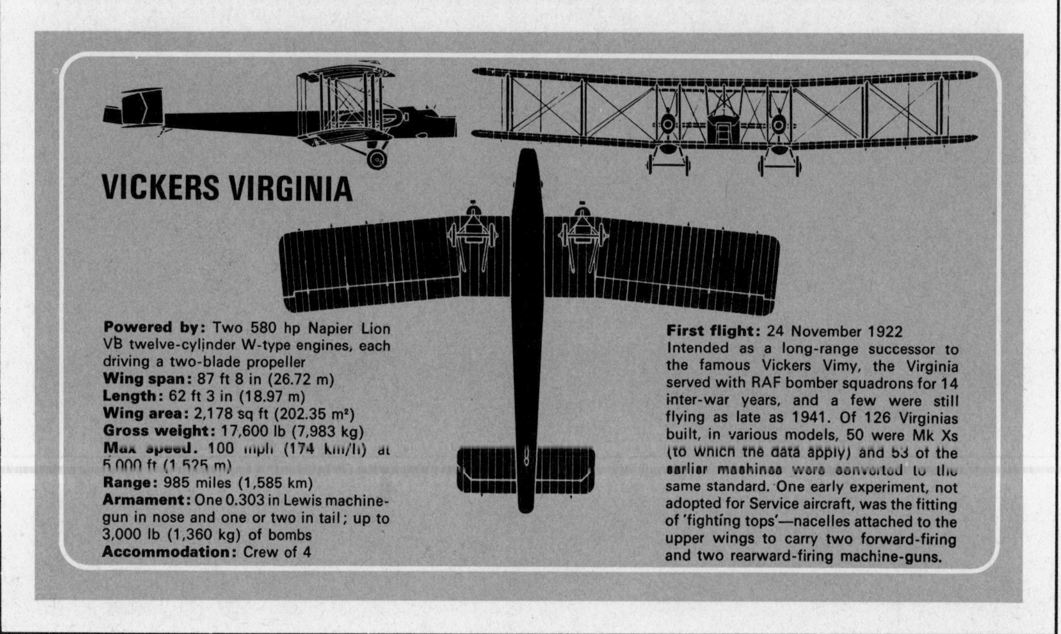

VICKERS VIRGINIA

Powered by: Two 580 hp Napier Lion VB twelve-cylinder W-type engines, each driving a two-blade propeller
Wing span: 87 ft 8 in (26.72 m)
Length: 62 ft 3 in (18.97 m)
Wing area: 2,178 sq ft (202.35 m²)
Gross weight: 17,600 lb (7,983 kg)
Max speed: 100 mph (174 km/h) at 5,000 ft (1,525 m)
Range: 985 miles (1,585 km)
Armament: One 0.303 in Lewis machine-gun in nose and one or two in tail; up to 3,000 lb (1,360 kg) of bombs
Accommodation: Crew of 4
First flight: 24 November 1922

Intended as a long-range successor to the famous Vickers Vimy, the Virginia served with RAF bomber squadrons for 14 inter-war years, and a few were still flying as late as 1941. Of 126 Virginias built, in various models, 50 were Mk Xs (to which the data apply) and 53 of the earlier machines were converted to the same standard. One early experiment, not adopted for Service aircraft, was the fitting of 'fighting tops'—nacelles attached to the upper wings to carry two forward-firing and two rearward-firing machine-guns.

Fairey IIID

Vickers Vernon

Vickers Virginia

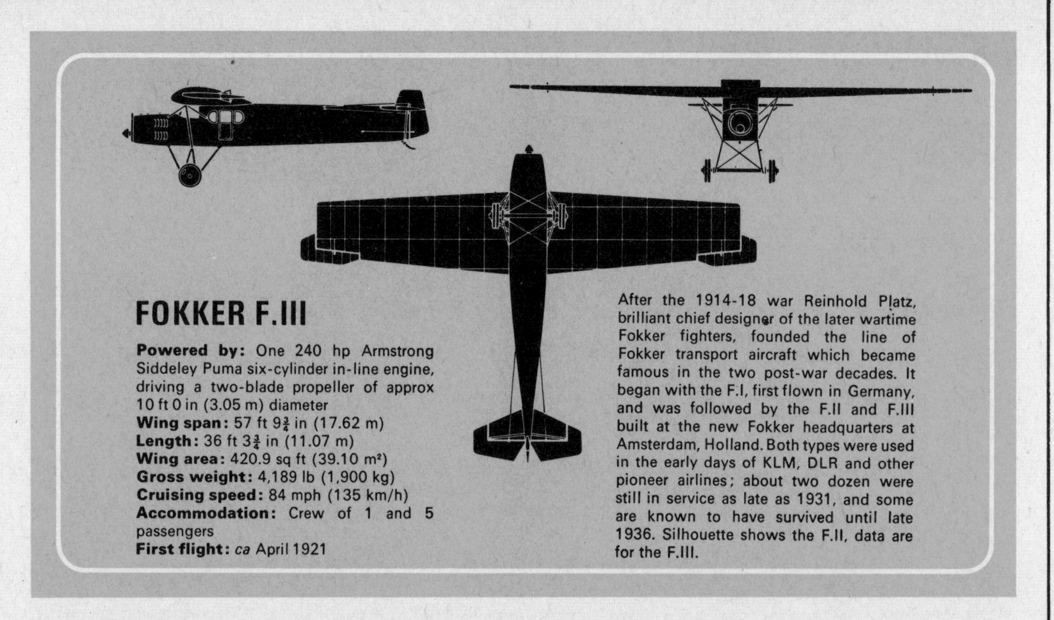

FOKKER F.III

Powered by: One 240 hp Armstrong Siddeley Puma six-cylinder in-line engine, driving a two-blade propeller of approx 10 ft 0 in (3.05 m) diameter
Wing span: 57 ft 9¾ in (17.62 m)
Length: 36 ft 3¾ in (11.07 m)
Wing area: 420.9 sq ft (39.10 m^2)
Gross weight: 4,189 lb (1,900 kg)
Cruising speed: 84 mph (135 km/h)
Accommodation: Crew of 1 and 5 passengers
First flight: *ca* April 1921

After the 1914-18 war Reinhold Platz, brilliant chief designer of the later wartime Fokker fighters, founded the line of Fokker transport aircraft which became famous in the two post-war decades. It began with the F.I, first flown in Germany, and was followed by the F.II and F.III built at the new Fokker headquarters at Amsterdam, Holland. Both types were used in the early days of KLM, DLR and other pioneer airlines; about two dozen were still in service as late as 1931, and some are known to have survived until late 1936. Silhouette shows the F.II, data are for the F.III.

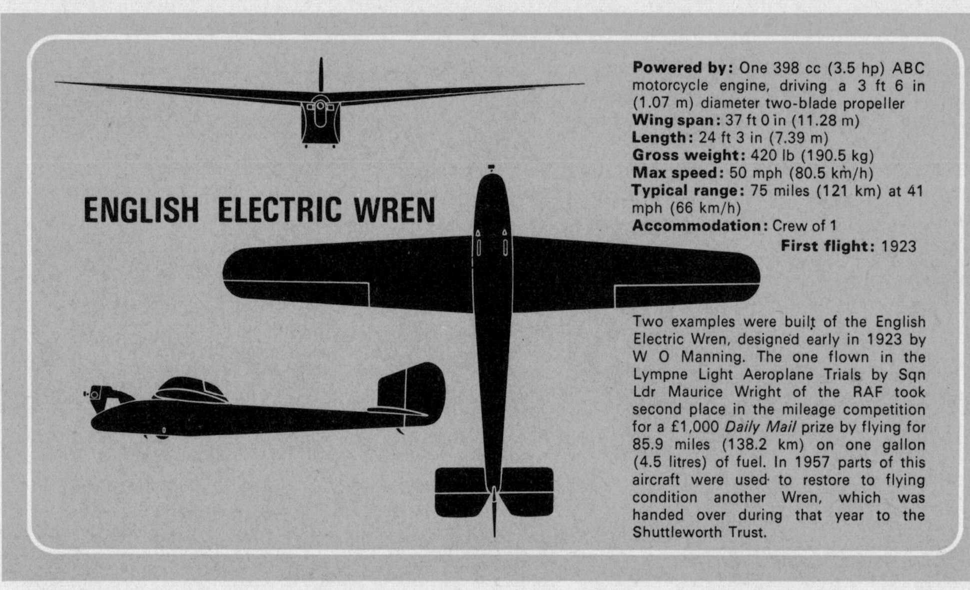

ENGLISH ELECTRIC WREN

Powered by: One 398 cc (3.5 hp) ABC motorcycle engine, driving a 3 ft 6 in (1.07 m) diameter two-blade propeller
Wing span: 37 ft 0 in (11.28 m)
Length: 24 ft 3 in (7.39 m)
Gross weight: 420 lb (190.5 kg)
Max speed: 50 mph (80.5 km/h)
Typical range: 75 miles (121 km) at 41 mph (66 km/h)
Accommodation: Crew of 1
First flight: 1923

Two examples were built of the English Electric Wren, designed early in 1923 by W O Manning. The one flown in the Lympne Light Aeroplane Trials by Sqn Ldr Maurice Wright of the RAF took second place in the mileage competition for a £1,000 *Daily Mail* prize by flying for 85.9 miles (138.2 km) on one gallon (4.5 litres) of fuel. In 1957 parts of this aircraft were used to restore to flying condition another Wren, which was handed over during that year to the Shuttleworth Trust.

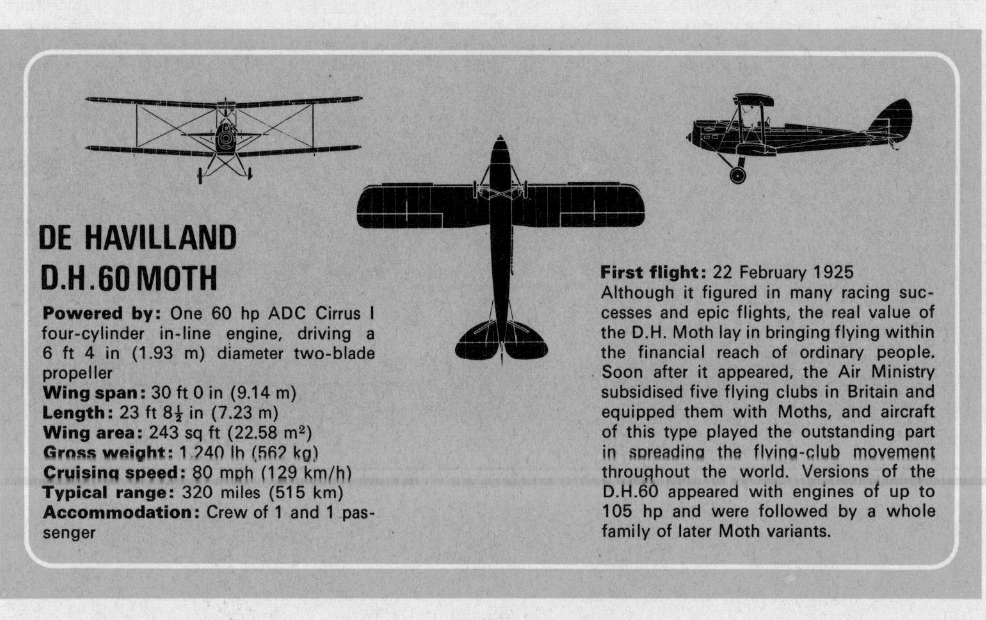

DE HAVILLAND D.H.60 MOTH

Powered by: One 60 hp ADC Cirrus I four-cylinder in-line engine, driving a 6 ft 4 in (1.93 m) diameter two-blade propeller
Wing span: 30 ft 0 in (9.14 m)
Length: 23 ft 8½ in (7.23 m)
Wing area: 243 sq ft (22.58 m^2)
Gross weight: 1,240 lb (562 kg)
Cruising speed: 80 mph (129 km/h)
Typical range: 320 miles (515 km)
Accommodation: Crew of 1 and 1 passenger
First flight: 22 February 1925

Although it figured in many racing successes and epic flights, the real value of the D.H. Moth lay in bringing flying within the financial reach of ordinary people. Soon after it appeared, the Air Ministry subsidised five flying clubs in Britain and equipped them with Moths, and aircraft of this type played the outstanding part in spreading the flying-club movement throughout the world. Versions of the D.H.60 appeared with engines of up to 105 hp and were followed by a whole family of later Moth variants.

Fokker F.III

English Electric Wren

D.H.60G Gipsy Moth

HANDLEY PAGE W10

Powered by: Two 450 hp Napier Lion twelve-cylinder water-cooled engines, each driving a four-blade propeller of approx 10 ft 6 in (3.20 m) diameter
Wing span: 75 ft 0 in (22.86 m)
Length: 59 ft 4 in (18.08 m)
Wing area: 1,456 sq ft (135.26 m²)
Gross weight: 13,780 lb (6,250 kg)
Max speed: 112 mph (180 km/h) at S/L
Accommodation: Crew of 2 and 14 passengers
First flight: 10 February 1926
To replace the converted O/100 and O/400 bombers used for its early post-war airline services, Handley Page produced its first specialised transport, the twin-engined W 8, which entered service in 1921. Later versions, the W 8e and W 8f Hamilton, had a third engine in the nose to improve their safety and reliability. This concept was developed via the W 9a Hampstead of 1925; but the W 10, built for Imperial Airways a year later, reverted to a twin-engined layout—to its detriment, for two of the four built crashed in the Channel following engine failure.

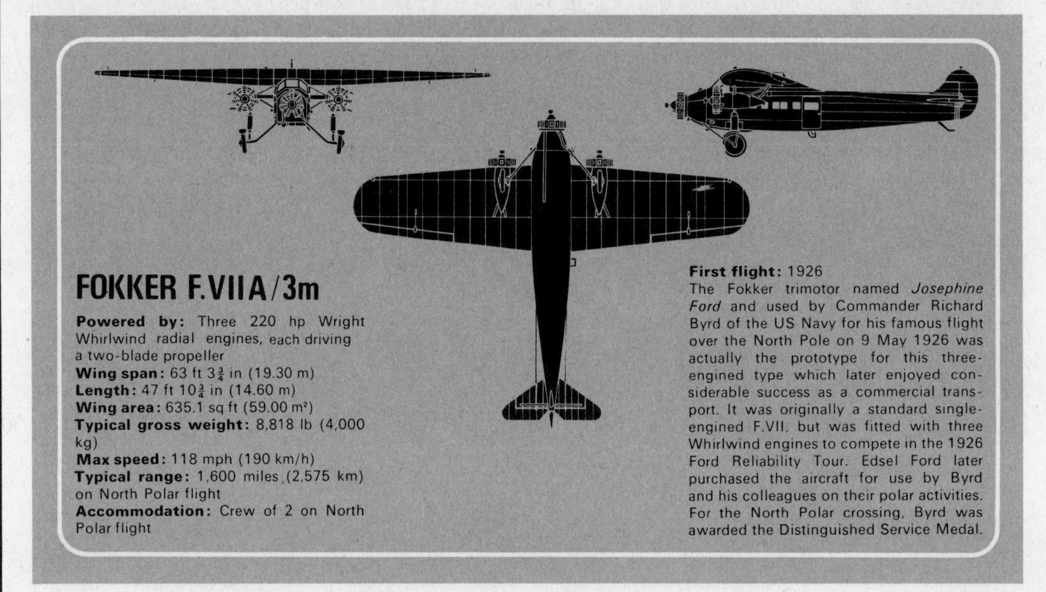

FOKKER F.VIIA/3m

Powered by: Three 220 hp Wright Whirlwind radial engines, each driving a two-blade propeller
Wing span: 63 ft 3¾ in (19.30 m)
Length: 47 ft 10¾ in (14.60 m)
Wing area: 635.1 sq ft (59.00 m²)
Typical gross weight: 8,818 lb (4,000 kg)
Max speed: 118 mph (190 km/h)
Typical range: 1,600 miles (2,575 km) on North Polar flight
Accommodation: Crew of 2 on North Polar flight

First flight: 1926
The Fokker trimotor named *Josephine Ford* and used by Commander Richard Byrd of the US Navy for his famous flight over the North Pole on 9 May 1926 was actually the prototype for this three-engined type which later enjoyed considerable success as a commercial transport. It was originally a standard single-engined F.VII, but was fitted with three Whirlwind engines to compete in the 1926 Ford Reliability Tour. Edsel Ford later purchased the aircraft for use by Byrd and his colleagues on their polar activities. For the North Polar crossing, Byrd was awarded the Distinguished Service Medal.

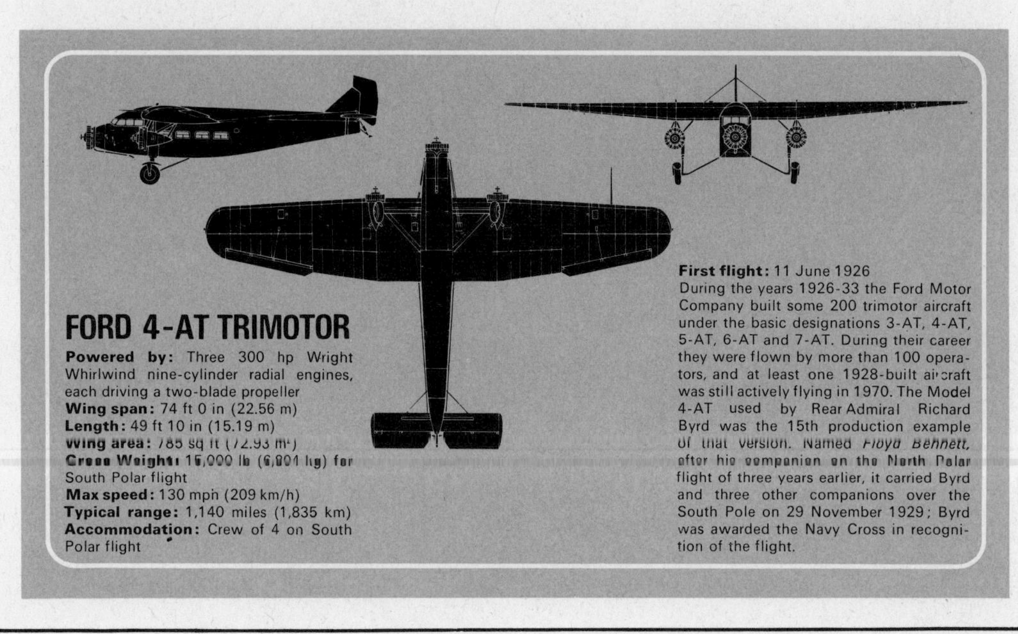

FORD 4-AT TRIMOTOR

Powered by: Three 300 hp Wright Whirlwind nine-cylinder radial engines, each driving a two-blade propeller
Wing span: 74 ft 0 in (22.56 m)
Length: 49 ft 10 in (15.19 m)
Wing area: 785 sq ft (72.93 m²)
Gross Weight: 15,000 lb (6,801 kg) for South Polar flight
Max speed: 130 mph (209 km/h)
Typical range: 1,140 miles (1,835 km)
Accommodation: Crew of 4 on South Polar flight

First flight: 11 June 1926
During the years 1926-33 the Ford Motor Company built some 200 trimotor aircraft under the basic designations 3-AT, 4-AT, 5-AT, 6-AT and 7-AT. During their career they were flown by more than 100 operators, and at least one 1928-built aircraft was still actively flying in 1970. The Model 4-AT used by Rear Admiral Richard Byrd was the 15th production example of that version. Named *Floyd Bennett*, after his companion on the North Polar flight of three years earlier, it carried Byrd and three other companions over the South Pole on 29 November 1929; Byrd was awarded the Navy Cross in recognition of the flight.

Handley Page W10

The trans-Polar Fokker tri motor *Josephine Ford*

Byrd's Ford Tri motor *Floyd Bennett* (1929)

GLOSTER GAMECOCK

Powered by: One 425 hp Bristol Jupiter VI nine-cylinder radial engine, driving a two-blade propeller
Wing span: 29 ft 9½ in (9.08 m)
Length: 19 ft 8 in (5.99 m)
Wing area: 264 sq ft (24.53 m²)
Gross weight: 2,863 lb (1,299 kg)
Max speed: 155 mph (249 km/h) at 5,000 ft (1,525 m)
Range: 365 miles (587 km)
Armament: Two 0.303 in Vickers machine-guns in fuselage
Accommodation: Crew of 1
First flight: February 1925

Descended from H P Folland's Gloster Grebe design, which made its public debut at the 1923 RAF Pageant at Hendon, the Gamecock began to enter RAF service two years later. A familiar sight at Hendon in the 1920s, it equipped five fighter squadrons and also served with the Finnish Air Force. It was not an easy aeroplane to master—at least 22 of the 90 Mk Is were lost in spinning or landing accidents—but many other pilots spun the Gamecock successfully and praised highly its excellent handling qualities.

RYAN NYP 'SPIRIT OF ST. LOUIS'

Powered by: One 237 hp Wright J-5C Whirlwind nine-cylinder radial engine, driving a two-blade propeller
Wing span: 46 ft 0 in (14.02 m)
Length: 27 ft 8 in (8.43 m)
Wing area: 319 sq ft (29.64 m²)
Gross weight: 5,250 lb (2,381 kg)
Max speed: 124 mph (200 km/h) with trans-Atlantic fuel
Range: 4,650 miles (7,483 km)
Accommodation: Crew of 1
First flight: 28 April 1927

Charles Lindbergh's 33½-hour flight from New York to Paris was the 13th crossing of the Atlantic by air, and the fifth non-stop crossing; but it was the first between two great cities and the first to be achieved by a solo flier, and won for Lindbergh the $25,000 prize offered by New York hotelier Raymond Orteig. A fortnight later the Bellanca Columbia which Lindbergh had first hoped to fly, piloted by Clarence D Chamberlin, also crossed the Atlantic successfully and flew 300 miles (483 km) further than Lindbergh, into Germany.

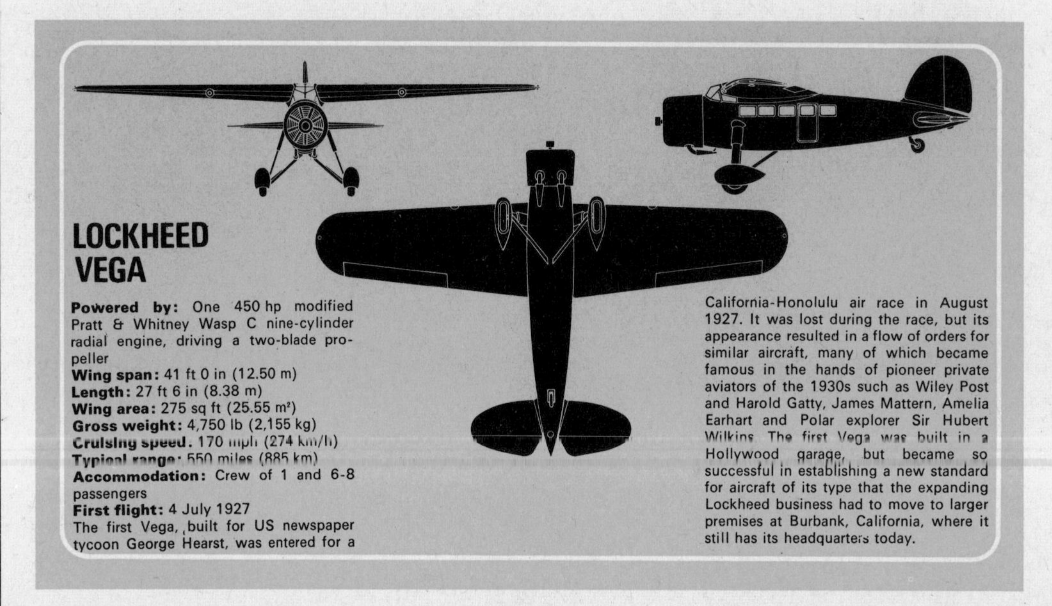

LOCKHEED VEGA

Powered by: One 450 hp modified Pratt & Whitney Wasp C nine-cylinder radial engine, driving a two-blade propeller
Wing span: 41 ft 0 in (12.50 m)
Length: 27 ft 6 in (8.38 m)
Wing area: 275 sq ft (25.55 m²)
Gross weight: 4,750 lb (2,155 kg)
Cruising speed: 170 mph (274 km/h)
Typical range: 550 miles (885 km)
Accommodation: Crew of 1 and 6-8 passengers
First flight: 4 July 1927

The first Vega, built for US newspaper tycoon George Hearst, was entered for a California-Honolulu air race in August 1927. It was lost during the race, but its appearance resulted in a flow of orders for similar aircraft, many of which became famous in the hands of pioneer private aviators of the 1930s such as Wiley Post and Harold Gatty, James Mattern, Amelia Earhart and Polar explorer Sir Hubert Wilkins. The first Vega was built in a Hollywood garage, but became so successful in establishing a new standard for aircraft of its type that the expanding Lockheed business had to move to larger premises at Burbank, California, where it still has its headquarters today.

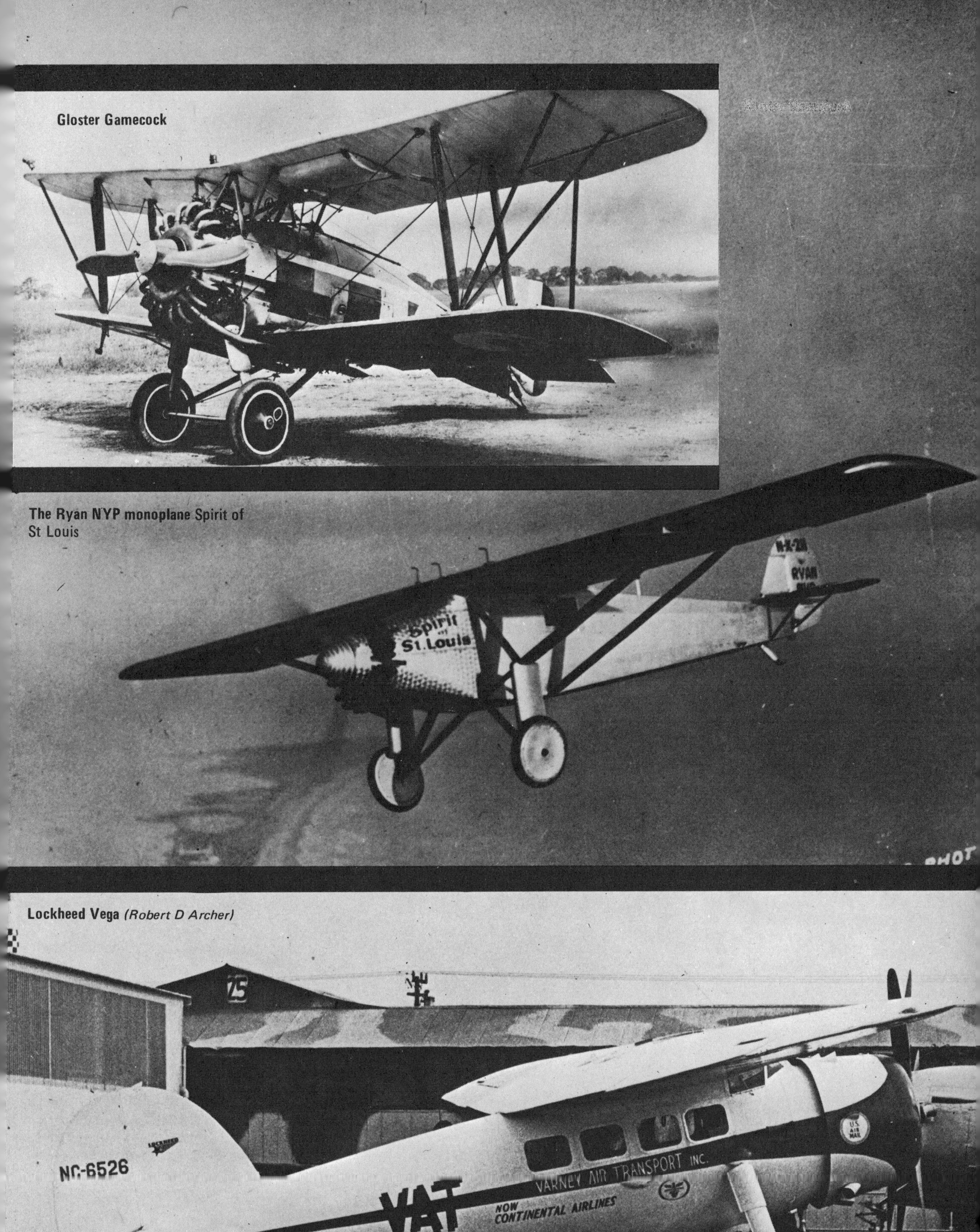

Gloster Gamecock

The Ryan NYP monoplane Spirit of St Louis

Lockheed Vega *(Robert D Archer)*

SUPERMARINE S.4 and S.6B

Powered by: One 700 hp Napier Lion W-type piston-engine
Wing span: 30 ft 6 in (9.30 m)
Length: 27 ft 0 in (8.23 m)
Gross weight: 3,150 lb (1,429 kg)
Max speed: 239 mph (385 km/h) at S/L
Accommodation: Crew of 1
Range at full power: 320 miles (515 km)
First flight: 25 August 1925

The S.4, to which the above data apply, was the first of the family of British Supermarine Schneider Trophy seaplanes, from which were developed the S.5, S.6 and S.6B. The silhouette depicts the S.6B, which was fitted with a 2,300 hp Rolls-Royce "R" engine when it won the Trophy outright in 1931 at an average speed of 340.08 mph (547.29 km/h). Later, with the engine boosted to 2,550 hp, it set a new world seaplane speed record of 407.5 mph (655.81 km/h).

SUPERMARINE S.5 & S.6B

(Silhouette shows S.4)

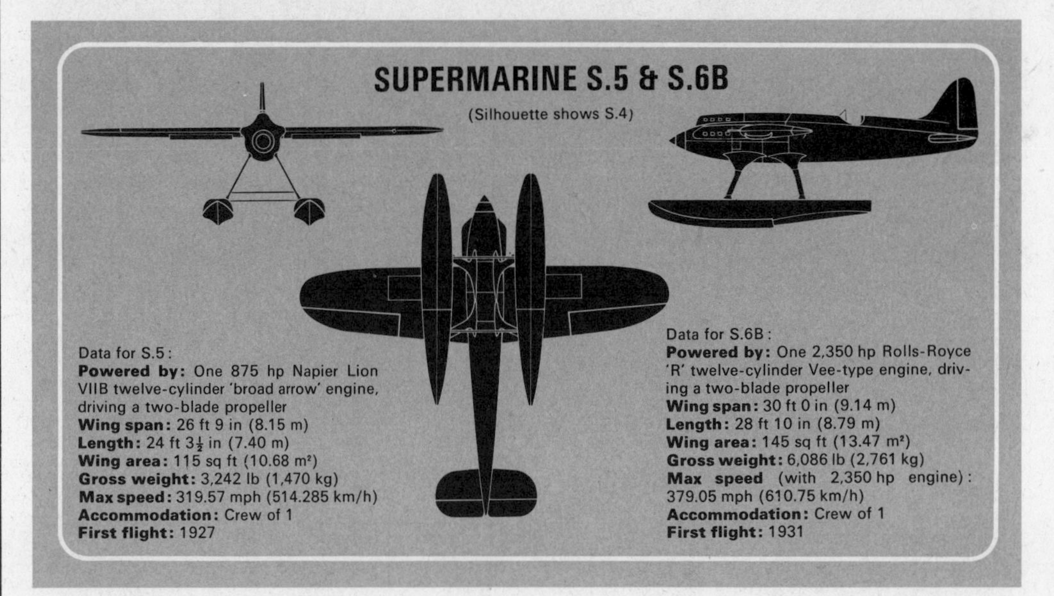

Data for S.5:
Powered by: One 875 hp Napier Lion VIIB twelve-cylinder 'broad arrow' engine, driving a two-blade propeller
Wing span: 26 ft 9 in (8.15 m)
Length: 24 ft 3½ in (7.40 m)
Wing area: 115 sq ft (10.68 m²)
Gross weight: 3,242 lb (1,470 kg)
Max speed: 319.57 mph (514.285 km/h)
Accommodation: Crew of 1
First flight: 1927

Data for S.6B:
Powered by: One 2,350 hp Rolls-Royce 'R' twelve-cylinder Vee-type engine, driving a two-blade propeller
Wing span: 30 ft 0 in (9.14 m)
Length: 28 ft 10 in (8.79 m)
Wing area: 145 sq ft (13.47 m²)
Gross weight: 6,086 lb (2,761 kg)
Max speed (with 2,350 hp engine): 379.05 mph (610.75 km/h)
Accommodation: Crew of 1
First flight: 1931

CIERVA C.8L

Powered by: One 200 hp Armstrong Siddeley Lynx IVC seven-cylinder radial engine, driving a two-blade propeller
Rotor diameter: 39 ft 8 in (12.09 m)
Length of fuselage: 28 ft 6 in (8.69 m)
Gross weight: 2,470 lb (1,120 kg)
Max speed: 100 mph (161 km/h) at S/L
Typical range: 255 miles (410 km)
Accommodation: Crew of 1 and 1 passenger
First flight: 1928

The first successful Cierva Autogiro was the C.4, flown near Madrid on 9 January 1923. It was powered by a 110 hp Le Rhône rotary engine, and succeeded because it had articulated hinges that allowed the rotor blades to 'flap' up and down as they advanced and retreated, so keeping the lift forces in balance. Three C.8L (the L signifying Lynx engine) were built, and one of these—now in the Musée de l'Air in Paris—made the first crossing of the English Channel by a rotating-wing aircraft, on 18 September 1928.

Supermarine S.6

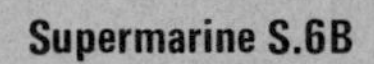
Supermarine S.6B

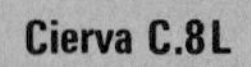
Cierva C.8L

LZ 127 'GRAF ZEPPELIN'

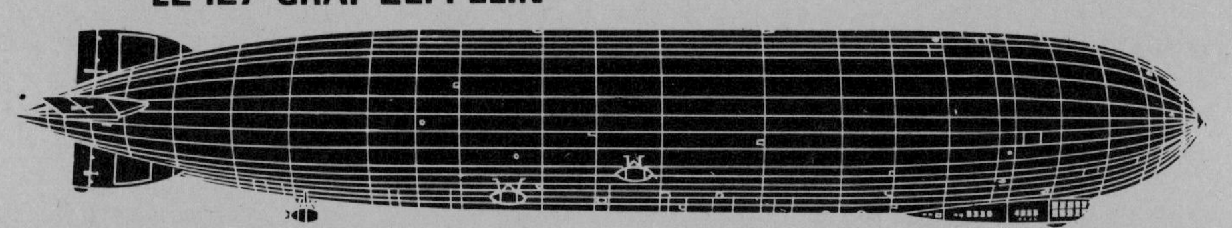

Powered by: Five 550 hp Maybach VL II twelve-cylinder Vee-type engines, each driving a two-blade (later four-blade) propeller
Total gas capacity: 3,708,040 cu ft (105,000 m³), including fuel gas
Length: 776 ft 3 in (236.6 m)
Max diameter: 100 ft 0 in (30.5 m)
Cruising speed: 71.5 mph (115 km/h)
Max endurance: 118 hours with payload of 29,568 lb (13,411 kg)
Accommodation: Crew of 45-50 and 20 passengers
First flight: 18 September 1928

Most successful of all the passenger-carrying German airships, the *Graf Zeppelin* made several hundred flights during the 1930s, of which well over 100 were across the South Atlantic between Friedrichshafen and Pernambuco. A typical year was 1935, when she made 82 trips carrying 1,429 passengers and 14 tons of mail and freight, and covering some 222,016 miles (357,300 km) in more than 3,500 flying hours. Instead of petrol, the *Graf Zeppelin's* engines burned a fuel gas called *Blaugas*, which accounted for about one-third of her total gas capacity; the main gas-bags were filled with hydrogen.

DORNIER Do X

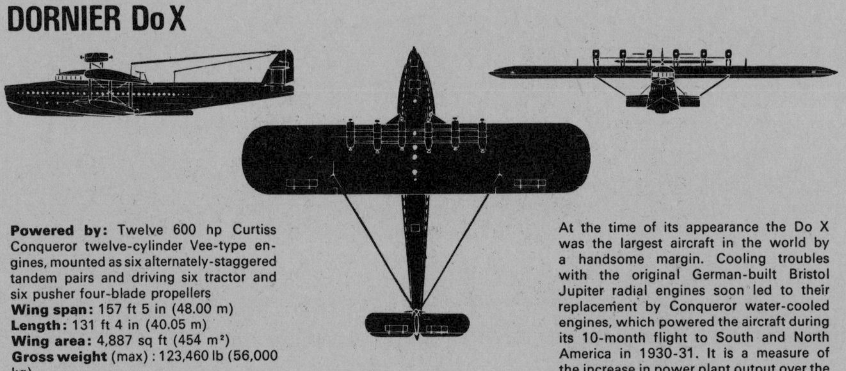

Powered by: Twelve 600 hp Curtiss Conqueror twelve-cylinder Vee-type engines, mounted as six alternately-staggered tandem pairs and driving six tractor and six pusher four-blade propellers
Wing span: 157 ft 5 in (48.00 m)
Length: 131 ft 4 in (40.05 m)
Wing area: 4,887 sq ft (454 m²)
Gross weight (max): 123,460 lb (56,000 kg)
Max speed: 134 mph (216 km/h)
Typical range: 1,055 miles (1,700 km)
Accommodation: Crew of 10 and up to 170 passengers
First flight: 25 July 1929 (with Jupiter engines)

At the time of its appearance the Do X was the largest aircraft in the world by a handsome margin. Cooling troubles with the original German-built Bristol Jupiter radial engines soon led to their replacement by Conqueror water-cooled engines, which powered the aircraft during its 10-month flight to South and North America in 1930-31. It is a measure of the increase in power plant output over the intervening years that the twin-engined Caravelle is currently cleared to operate at exactly the same gross weight as that of the twelve-engined Do X of forty years ago.

JUNKERS G 38

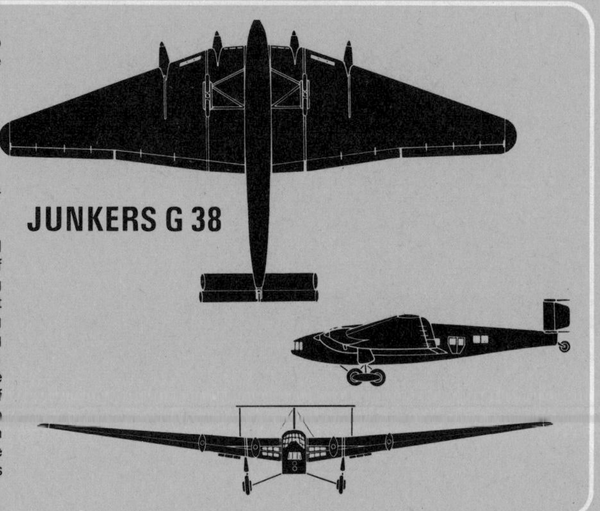

Powered by: Four 750 hp Junkers Jumo 204 diesel engines, each driving a four-blade propeller
Wing span: 144 ft 4¼ in (44.00 m)
Length: 76 ft 1½ in (23.20 m)
Wing area: 3,229.2 sq ft (300.0 m²)
Gross weight: 52,910 lb (24,000 kg)
Cruising speed: 128 mph (208 km/h)
Accommodation: Crew of 7 and 34 passengers
First flight: 6 November 1929

As well as pioneering the use of metal construction and cantilever wings, Prof Hugo Junkers was a firm believer in a 'flying wing' type of aircraft which could carry most of its fuel and payload within the wing structure. The nearest he came to realising this objective was with the G 38 in which six of the 34 passengers were seated in the wing centre-section and could look out of windows in the leading-edge. Only two G 38s were built, but these operated with Deutsche Luft Hansa for several years; one crashed in 1936, and the other was destroyed by RAF bombers during 1940.

The airship Graf Zeppelin

Dornier Do X

Junkers G 38, first aircraft

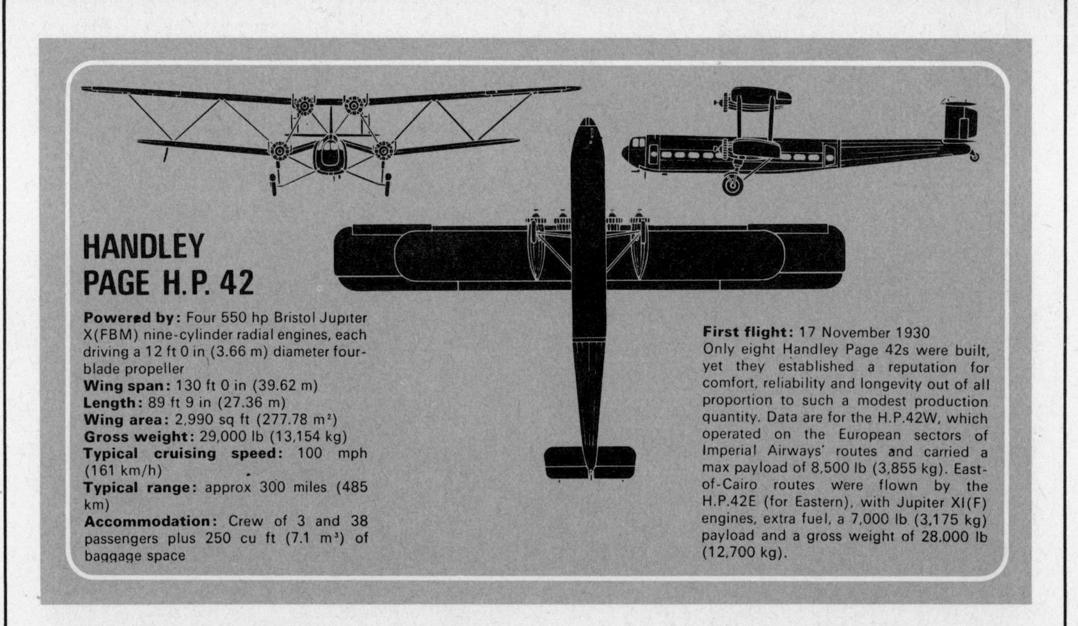

HANDLEY PAGE H.P. 42

Powered by: Four 550 hp Bristol Jupiter X(FBM) nine-cylinder radial engines, each driving a 12 ft 0 in (3.66 m) diameter four-blade propeller
Wing span: 130 ft 0 in (39.62 m)
Length: 89 ft 9 in (27.36 m)
Wing area: 2,990 sq ft (277.78 m²)
Gross weight: 29,000 lb (13,154 kg)
Typical cruising speed: 100 mph (161 km/h)
Typical range: approx 300 miles (485 km)
Accommodation: Crew of 3 and 38 passengers plus 250 cu ft (7.1 m³) of baggage space
First flight: 17 November 1930

Only eight Handley Page 42s were built, yet they established a reputation for comfort, reliability and longevity out of all proportion to such a modest production quantity. Data are for the H.P.42W, which operated on the European sectors of Imperial Airways' routes and carried a max payload of 8,500 lb (3,855 kg). East-of-Cairo routes were flown by the H.P.42E (for Eastern), with Jupiter XI(F) engines, extra fuel, a 7,000 lb (3,175 kg) payload and a gross weight of 28,000 lb (12,700 kg).

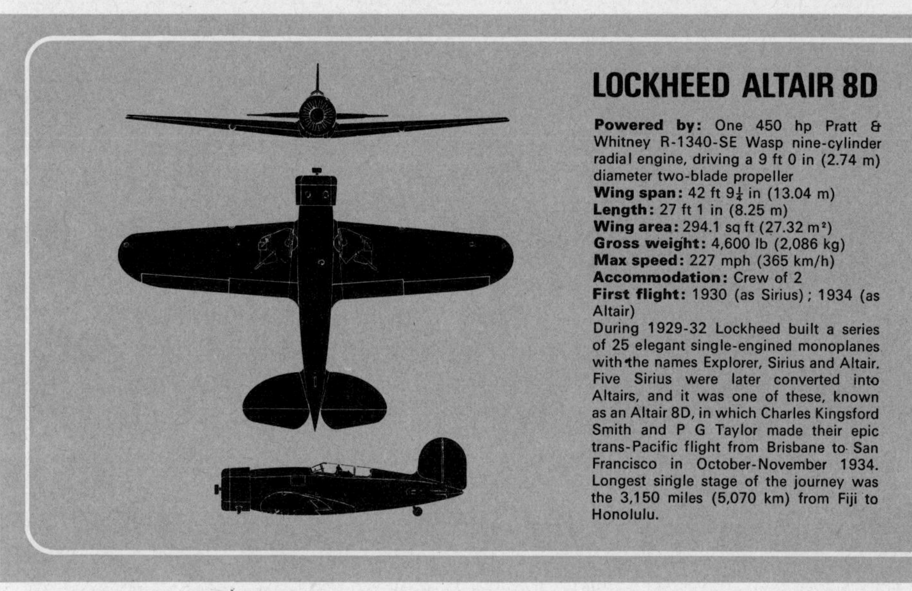

LOCKHEED ALTAIR 8D

Powered by: One 450 hp Pratt & Whitney R-1340-SE Wasp nine-cylinder radial engine, driving a 9 ft 0 in (2.74 m) diameter two-blade propeller
Wing span: 42 ft 9¼ in (13.04 m)
Length: 27 ft 1 in (8.25 m)
Wing area: 294.1 sq ft (27.32 m²)
Gross weight: 4,600 lb (2,086 kg)
Max speed: 227 mph (365 km/h)
Accommodation: Crew of 2
First flight: 1930 (as Sirius); 1934 (as Altair)

During 1929-32 Lockheed built a series of 25 elegant single-engined monoplanes with the names Explorer, Sirius and Altair. Five Sirius were later converted into Altairs, and it was one of these, known as an Altair 8D, in which Charles Kingsford Smith and P G Taylor made their epic trans-Pacific flight from Brisbane to San Francisco in October-November 1934. Longest single stage of the journey was the 3,150 miles (5,070 km) from Fiji to Honolulu.

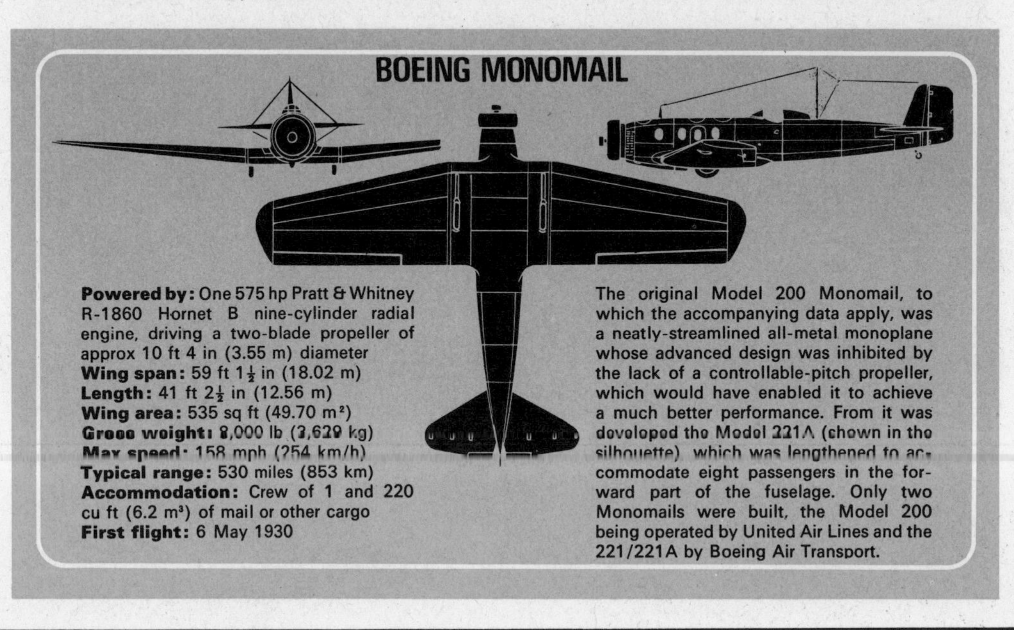

BOEING MONOMAIL

Powered by: One 575 hp Pratt & Whitney R-1860 Hornet B nine-cylinder radial engine, driving a two-blade propeller of approx 10 ft 4 in (3.55 m) diameter
Wing span: 59 ft 1½ in (18.02 m)
Length: 41 ft 2½ in (12.56 m)
Wing area: 535 sq ft (49.70 m²)
Gross weight: 8,000 lb (3,629 kg)
Max speed: 158 mph (254 km/h)
Typical range: 530 miles (853 km)
Accommodation: Crew of 1 and 220 cu ft (6.2 m³) of mail or other cargo
First flight: 6 May 1930

The original Model 200 Monomail, to which the accompanying data apply, was a neatly-streamlined all-metal monoplane whose advanced design was inhibited by the lack of a controllable-pitch propeller, which would have enabled it to achieve a much better performance. From it was developed the Model 221A (shown in the silhouette), which was lengthened to accommodate eight passengers in the forward part of the fuselage. Only two Monomails were built, the Model 200 being operated by United Air Lines and the 221/221A by Boeing Air Transport.

Handley Page H.P.42

Lockheed Altair

Boeing Model 221 Monomail

PZL P.7

Powered by: One 485 hp Polish-built Bristol Jupiter VIIF nine-cylinder radial engine, driving a two-blade propeller
Wing span: 33 ft 9½ in (10.30 m)
Length: 23 ft 6 in (7.16 m)
Wing area: 192.67 sq ft (17.90 m²)
Gross weight: 3,047 lb (1,382 kg)
Max speed: 200 mph (322 km/h) at 16,400 ft (5,000 m)
Range: 435 miles (700 km)
Accommodation: Crew of 1
Armament: Two 0.303 in Vickers machine-guns in forward fuselage
First flight: October 1930

First major production fighter to utilise the gull-wing concept developed by Zygmunt Pulawski, the P.7 entered service with the Polish Air Force at the end of 1932. It remained in service with the PAF, along with the later P.11, until the second World War, and large numbers of the developed P.24 were exported to neighbouring European countries. During 1933, all first-line squadrons of the PAF's four fighter Air Regiments were equipped with the P.7a, so becoming the first fighter force anywhere in the world to be equipped entirely with all-metal monoplanes.

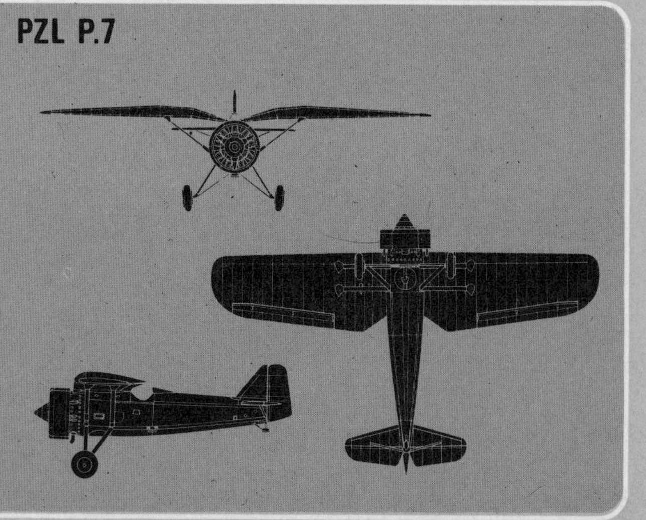

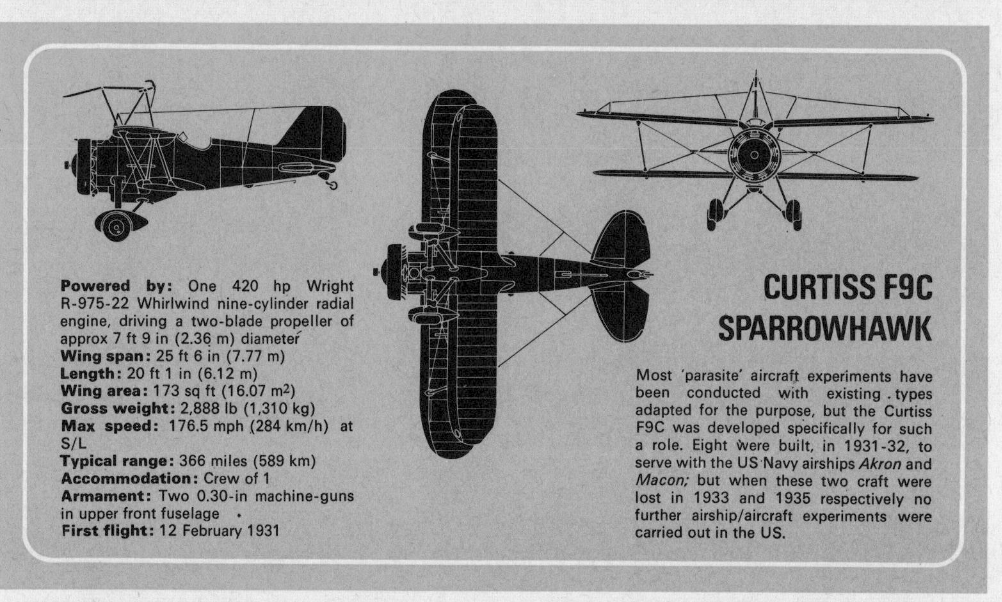

CURTISS F9C SPARROWHAWK

Powered by: One 420 hp Wright R-975-22 Whirlwind nine-cylinder radial engine, driving a two-blade propeller of approx 7 ft 9 in (2.36 m) diameter
Wing span: 25 ft 6 in (7.77 m)
Length: 20 ft 1 in (6.12 m)
Wing area: 173 sq ft (16.07 m²)
Gross weight: 2,888 lb (1,310 kg)
Max speed: 176.5 mph (284 km/h) at S/L
Typical range: 366 miles (589 km)
Accommodation: Crew of 1
Armament: Two 0.30-in machine-guns in upper front fuselage
First flight: 12 February 1931

Most 'parasite' aircraft experiments have been conducted with existing types adapted for the purpose, but the Curtiss F9C was developed specifically for such a role. Eight were built, in 1931-32, to serve with the US Navy airships *Akron* and *Macon;* but when these two craft were lost in 1933 and 1935 respectively no further airship/aircraft experiments were carried out in the US.

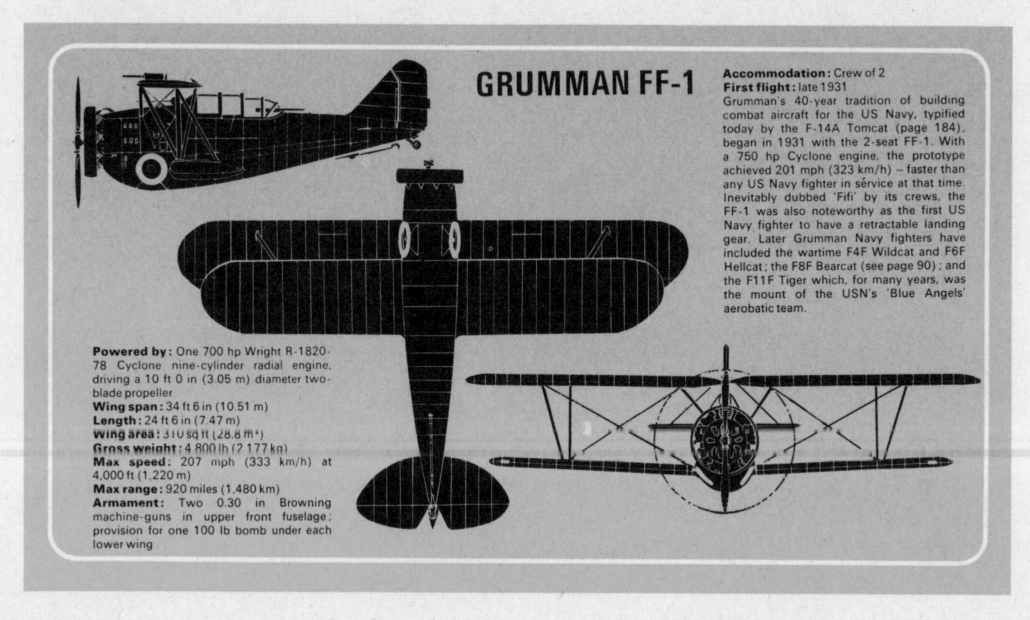

GRUMMAN FF-1

Powered by: One 700 hp Wright R-1820-78 Cyclone nine-cylinder radial engine, driving a 10 ft 0 in (3.05 m) diameter two-blade propeller
Wing span: 34 ft 6 in (10.51 m)
Length: 24 ft 6 in (7.47 m)
Wing area: 310 sq ft (28.8 m²)
Gross weight: 4,800 lb (2,177 kg)
Max speed: 207 mph (333 km/h) at 4,000 ft (1,220 m)
Max range: 920 miles (1,480 km)
Armament: Two 0.30 in Browning machine-guns in upper front fuselage; provision for one 100 lb bomb under each lower wing
Accommodation: Crew of 2
First flight: late 1931

Grumman's 40-year tradition of building combat aircraft for the US Navy, typified today by the F-14A Tomcat (page 184), began in 1931 with the 2-seat FF-1. With a 750 hp Cyclone engine, the prototype achieved 201 mph (323 km/h) – faster than any US Navy fighter in service at that time. Inevitably dubbed 'Fifi' by its crews, the FF-1 was also noteworthy as the first US Navy fighter to have a retractable landing gear. Later Grumman Navy fighters have included the wartime F4F Wildcat and F6F Hellcat; the F8F Bearcat (see page 90); and the F11F Tiger which, for many years, was the mount of the USN's 'Blue Angels' aerobatic team.

PZL P.7A *(J. B. Cynk)*

Curtiss F9C Sparrowhawks

Grumman FF-1

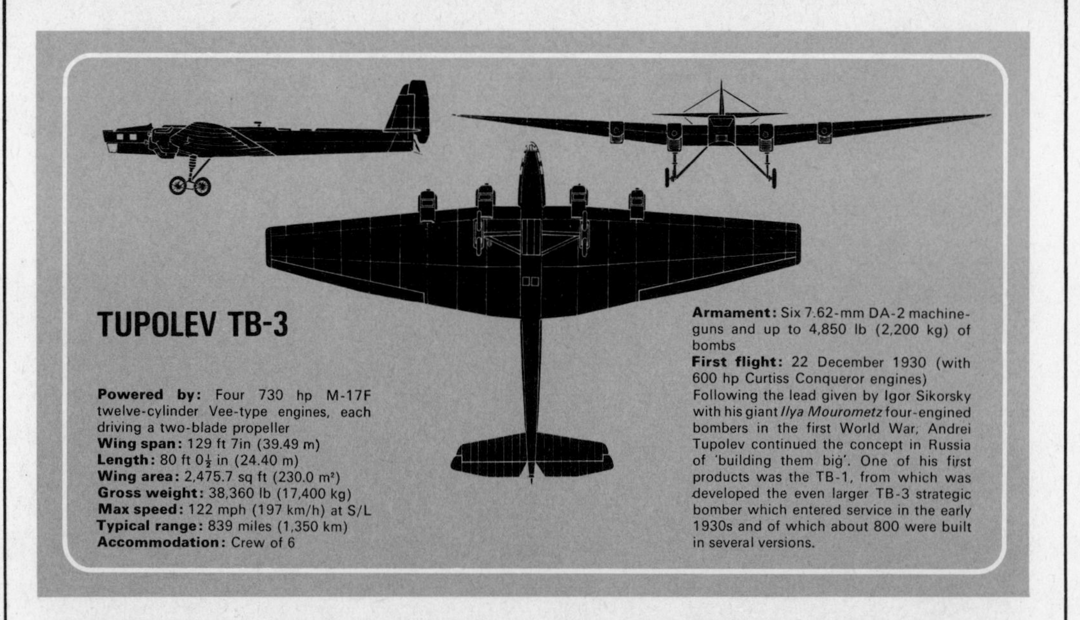

TUPOLEV TB-3

Powered by: Four 730 hp M-17F twelve-cylinder Vee-type engines, each driving a two-blade propeller
Wing span: 129 ft 7in (39.49 m)
Length: 80 ft $0\frac{1}{3}$ in (24.40 m)
Wing area: 2,475.7 sq ft (230.0 m²)
Gross weight: 38,360 lb (17,400 kg)
Max speed: 122 mph (197 km/h) at S/L
Typical range: 839 miles (1,350 km)
Accommodation: Crew of 6

Armament: Six 7.62-mm DA-2 machine-guns and up to 4,850 lb (2,200 kg) of bombs
First flight: 22 December 1930 (with 600 hp Curtiss Conqueror engines)
Following the lead given by Igor Sikorsky with his giant *Ilya Mourometz* four-engined bombers in the first World War, Andrei Tupolev continued the concept in Russia of 'building them big'. One of his first products was the TB-1, from which was developed the even larger TB-3 strategic bomber which entered service in the early 1930s and of which about 800 were built in several versions.

TAYLOR CUB

Powered by: One 35 hp Continental A40 four-cylinder horizontally-opposed engine, driving a two-blade propeller
Wing span: 35 ft 2 in (10.72 m)
Length: 22 ft 6 in (6.86 m)
Wing area: 184 sq ft (17.09 m²)
Gross weight: 925 lb (420 kg)
Cruising speed: 70 mph (113 km/h)
Range: 225 miles (362 km)
Accommodation: Crew of 1 and 1 passenger
First flight: 1931
The best-known light aeroplane ever built, the Cub first appeared in 1931 as a product of the US aircraft company headed by C G Taylor. It was a 2-seat aircraft, and one of the chief reasons for its widespread success was that almost anyone could learn to fly it. When Taylor's former secretary and treasurer, William T Piper, acquired the rights to build and sell the Cub, its sales rose dramatically from 211 in 1935 to 550 in 1936 (its first year as the Piper Cub) and 727 in the following year. When production ended in 1950 a total of 23,512 had been built, many hundreds of which are still flying. The silhouette shows a Piper J-3C-65 Cub. The line continues with the Super Cub (see page 110), which was still in production in 1972.

MACCHI M.C.72

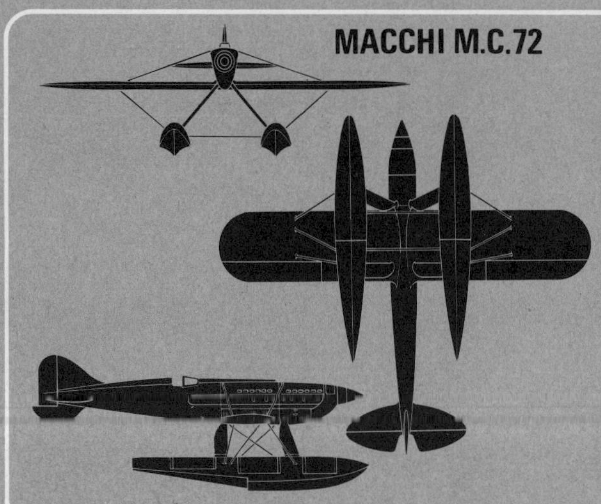

Powered by: One 2,800 hp Fiat A.S.6 twenty-four-cylinder Vee-type engine (two twelve-cylinder A.S.5s mounted in tandem), driving two two-blade contra-rotating propellers
Wing span: 31 ft $1\frac{1}{4}$ in (9.48 m)
Length: 27 ft $3\frac{1}{2}$ in (8.32 m)
Wing area: 161.46 sq ft (15.00 m²)
Gross weight: 6,409 lb (2,907 kg)
Max speed (world record): 440.681 mph (709.209 km/h) in October 1934
Accommodation: Crew of 1
First flight: 1931
The M.C. (Macchi-Castoldi) 72, whose world speed record for seaplanes stood unbeaten for nearly 30 years, was built to compete in the 1931 race for the Schneider Trophy. It was unable to do so due to development problems with its unusual engine installation, the tremendous torque from which drove the aircraft round in circles on the water and prevented it from taking off. The problem was solved eventually by using contra-rotating propellers to cancel out this effect, and the M.C.72's design was vindicated by successive speed records culminating in the figure recorded.

Tupolev TB-3

Early Taylor-built Cub

Macchi M.C. 72

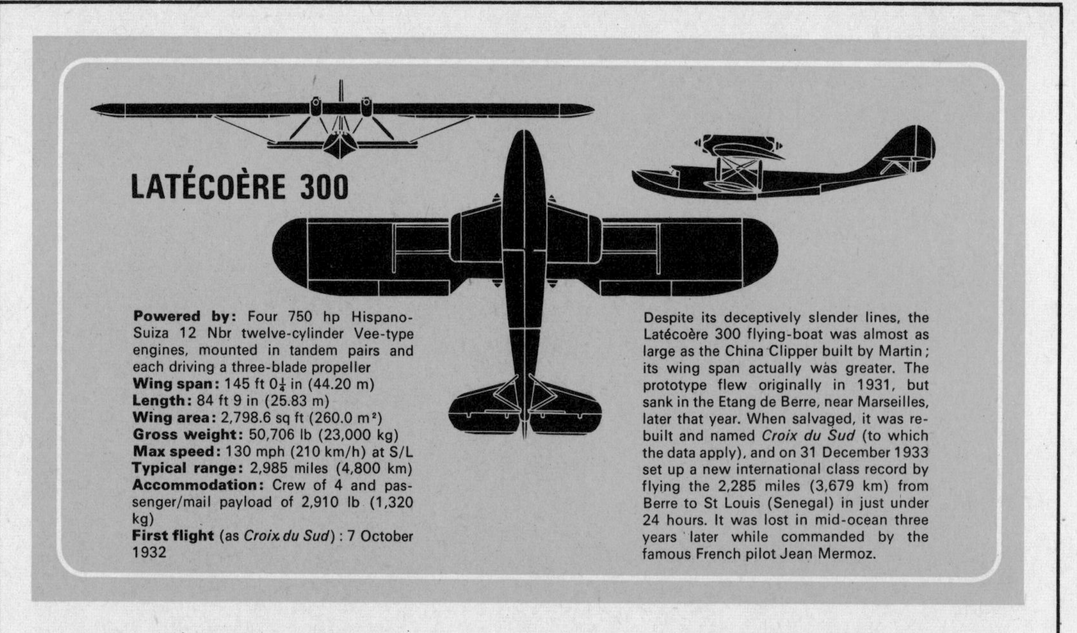

LATÉCOÈRE 300

Powered by: Four 750 hp Hispano-Suiza 12 Nbr twelve-cylinder Vee-type engines, mounted in tandem pairs and each driving a three-blade propeller
Wing span: 145 ft 0¼ in (44.20 m)
Length: 84 ft 9 in (25.83 m)
Wing area: 2,798.6 sq ft (260.0 m²)
Gross weight: 50,706 lb (23,000 kg)
Max speed: 130 mph (210 km/h) at S/L
Typical range: 2,985 miles (4,800 km)
Accommodation: Crew of 4 and passenger/mail payload of 2,910 lb (1,320 kg)
First flight (as *Croix du Sud*) : 7 October 1932

Despite its deceptively slender lines, the Latécoère 300 flying-boat was almost as large as the China Clipper built by Martin; its wing span actually was greater. The prototype flew originally in 1931, but sank in the Etang de Berre, near Marseilles, later that year. When salvaged, it was rebuilt and named *Croix du Sud* (to which the data apply), and on 31 December 1933 set up a new international class record by flying the 2,285 miles (3,679 km) from Berre to St Louis (Senegal) in just under 24 hours. It was lost in mid-ocean three years later while commanded by the famous French pilot Jean Mermoz.

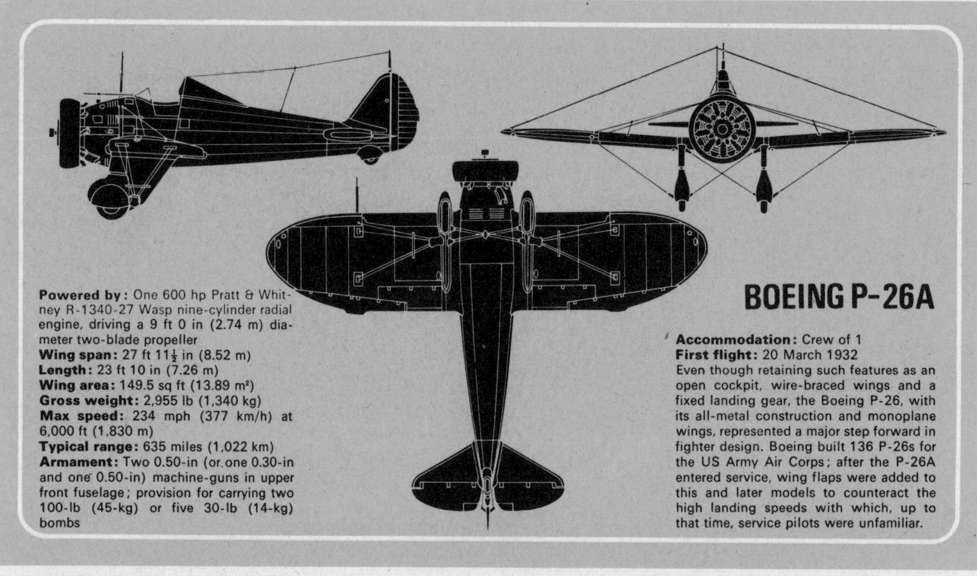

BOEING P-26A

Powered by: One 600 hp Pratt & Whitney R-1340-27 Wasp nine-cylinder radial engine, driving a 9 ft 0 in (2.74 m) diameter two-blade propeller
Wing span: 27 ft 11½ in (8.52 m)
Length: 23 ft 10 in (7.26 m)
Wing area: 149.5 sq ft (13.89 m²)
Gross weight: 2,955 lb (1,340 kg)
Max speed: 234 mph (377 km/h) at 6,000 ft (1,830 m)
Typical range: 635 miles (1,022 km)
Armament: Two 0.50-in (or one 0.30-in and one 0.50-in) machine-guns in upper front fuselage; provision for carrying two 100-lb (45-kg) or five 30-lb (14-kg) bombs
Accommodation: Crew of 1
First flight: 20 March 1932

Even though retaining such features as an open cockpit, wire-braced wings and a fixed landing gear, the Boeing P-26, with its all-metal construction and monoplane wings, represented a major step forward in fighter design. Boeing built 136 P-26s for the US Army Air Corps; after the P-26A entered service, wing flaps were added to this and later models to counteract the high landing speeds with which, up to that time, service pilots were unfamiliar.

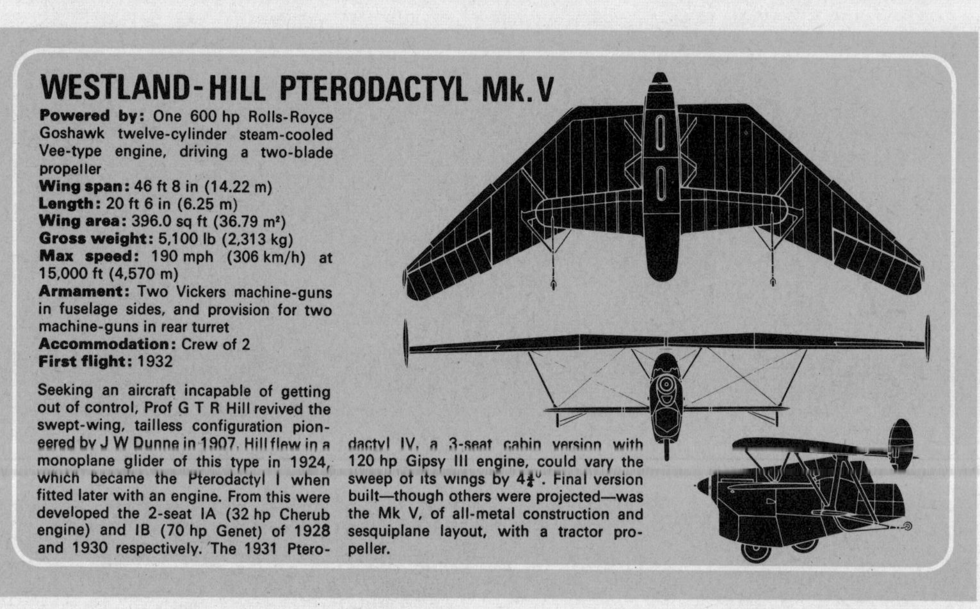

WESTLAND-HILL PTERODACTYL Mk.V

Powered by: One 600 hp Rolls-Royce Goshawk twelve-cylinder steam-cooled Vee-type engine, driving a two-blade propeller
Wing span: 46 ft 8 in (14.22 m)
Length: 20 ft 6 in (6.25 m)
Wing area: 396.0 sq ft (36.79 m²)
Gross weight: 5,100 lb (2,313 kg)
Max speed: 190 mph (306 km/h) at 15,000 ft (4,570 m)
Armament: Two Vickers machine-guns in fuselage sides, and provision for two machine-guns in rear turret
Accommodation: Crew of 2
First flight: 1932

Seeking an aircraft incapable of getting out of control, Prof G T R Hill revived the swept-wing, tailless configuration pioneered by J W Dunne in 1907. Hill flew in a monoplane glider of this type in 1924, which became the Pterodactyl I when fitted later with an engine. From this were developed the 2-seat IA (32 hp Cherub engine) and IB (70 hp Genet) of 1928 and 1930 respectively. The 1931 Pterodactyl IV, a 3-seat cabin version with 120 hp Gipsy III engine, could vary the sweep of its wings by 4½°. Final version built—though others were projected—was the Mk V, of all-metal construction and sesquiplane layout, with a tractor propeller.

Latécoère 300

Boeing P-26B

Westland-Hill Pterodactyl V

GEE BEE R-1 SUPER SPORTSTER

Powered by: One 800 hp Pratt & Whitney Wasp nine-cylinder radial engine, driving a two-blade propeller
Wing span: 25 ft 0 in (7.62 m)
Length: 17 ft 9 in (5.41 m)
Empty weight: 1,840 lb (835 kg)
Gross weight: 3,075 lb (1,395 kg)
Max speed: 296.287 mph (476.741 km/h) on 3 September 1932
Accommodation: Crew of 1
First flight: 13 August 1932
Two Super Sportsters were built. The R-1, which set the speed record shown above, won the 1932 Thompson Trophy race two days later, flown by 'Jimmy' Doolittle. The R-2 (silhouette) had a 550 hp Wasp Junior engine and extra fuel. Both were entered for the 1933 Bendix Trophy contest, R-1 with a 900 hp Hornet engine, its Wasp engine being transferred to R-2; but R-2 withdrew after the crash which destroyed the R-1, and itself crashed later the same year. The salvaged R-1 fuselage and R-2's engine and wings were combined in a new aircraft for the 1935 Bendix race. When this, too, crashed the era of the Gee Bee racers came to an end.

MIGNET POU-DU-CIEL (SKY LOUSE)

Powered by: One 28 hp Carden-modified Ford motor-car engine, driving a two-blade propeller
Wing span: 22 ft 0 in (6.70 m)
Length: 12 ft 3 in (3.73 m)
Wing area: 140 sq ft (13.00 m²)
Gross weight: 551 lb (250 kg)
Max speed: 70 mph (113 km/h)
Accommodation: Crew of 1
Range: 200 miles (320 km)
The original 17 ft (5.18 m) span Pou-du-Ciel designed by Henri Mignet had a variable-incidence front wing and fixed-incidence rear wing, and first flew on 6 September 1933. The 'Pou' achieved almost instant popularity: in Britain alone, over 80 were being built or flying by the Spring of 1936, but several fatal accidents occurred by the end of that year. The first British example, originally flown on 14 July 1935, was later rebuilt by Abbott-Baynes Aircraft Ltd with a longer front wing, which made it safer to fly. The data and silhouette refer to this version.

DE HAVILLAND D.H.88 COMET

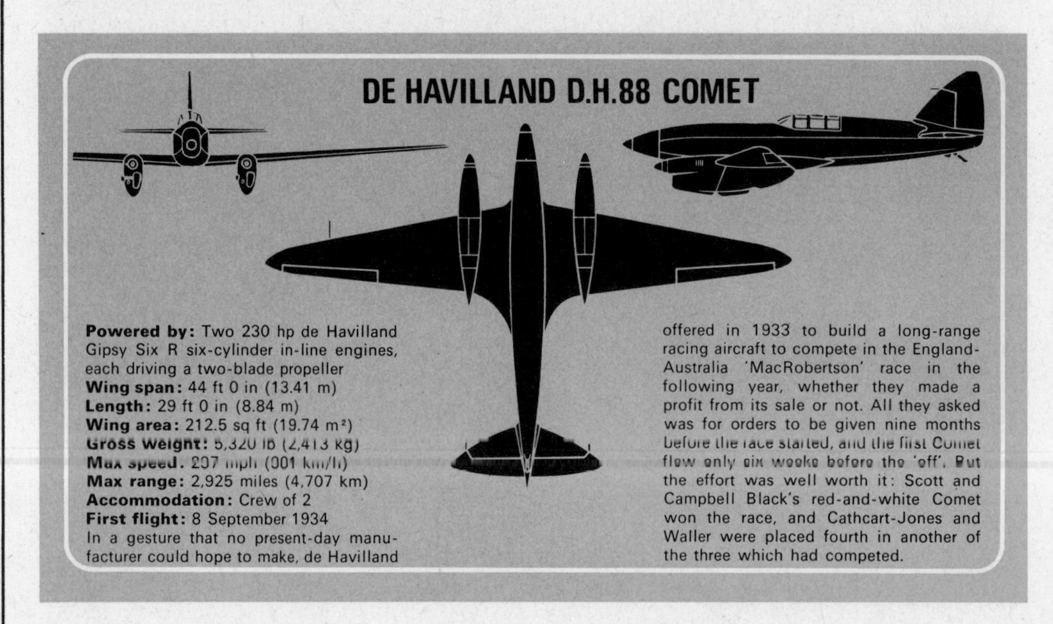

Powered by: Two 230 hp de Havilland Gipsy Six R six-cylinder in-line engines, each driving a two-blade propeller
Wing span: 44 ft 0 in (13.41 m)
Length: 29 ft 0 in (8.84 m)
Wing area: 212.5 sq ft (19.74 m²)
Gross weight: 5,320 lb (2,413 kg)
Max speed: 237 mph (381 km/h)
Max range: 2,925 miles (4,707 km)
Accommodation: Crew of 2
First flight: 8 September 1934
In a gesture that no present-day manufacturer could hope to make, de Havilland offered in 1933 to build a long-range racing aircraft to compete in the England-Australia 'MacRobertson' race in the following year, whether they made a profit from its sale or not. All they asked was for orders to be given nine months before the race started, and the first Comet flew only six weeks before the 'off'. But the effort was well worth it: Scott and Campbell Black's red-and-white Comet won the race, and Cathcart-Jones and Waller were placed fourth in another of the three which had competed.

Gee Bee R-2 Super Sportster

British-built Pou-du-Ciel of the 1930s

D.H. Comet 'MacRobertson' winner, now a museum exhibit

BOEING MODEL 247

Powered by: Two 550 hp Pratt & Whitney R-1340-S1H1G Wasp nine-cylinder radial engines, each driving a 9 ft 8 in (2.95 m) diameter three-blade propeller
Wing span: 74 ft 0 in (22.56 m)
Length: 51 ft 7 in (15.72 m)
Wing area: 836.13 sq ft (167.90 m²)
Gross weight: 13,650 lb (6,192 kg)
Cruising speed: 189 mph (304 km/h) at 12,000 ft (3,658 m)
Typical range: 745 miles (1,200 km)
Accommodation: Crew of 2 and 10 passengers, plus 400 lb (181 kg) of mail
First flight: 8 February 1933

The great revolution in airliner design which heralded the end of the era of 'slow-but-sure' biplanes began with the Boeing Model 247, of which 75 examples were produced. Most of these were either built as, or converted to, Model 247D standard, with modified cockpit windscreens, controllable-pitch propellers and other refinements; the data apply to this version. One specially-modified 247D, flown by Col Roscoe Turner and Clyde Pangborn, came second in the speed division of the 1934 MacRobertson race from London to Melbourne and third in the overall placings.

BOULTON PAUL OVERSTRAND

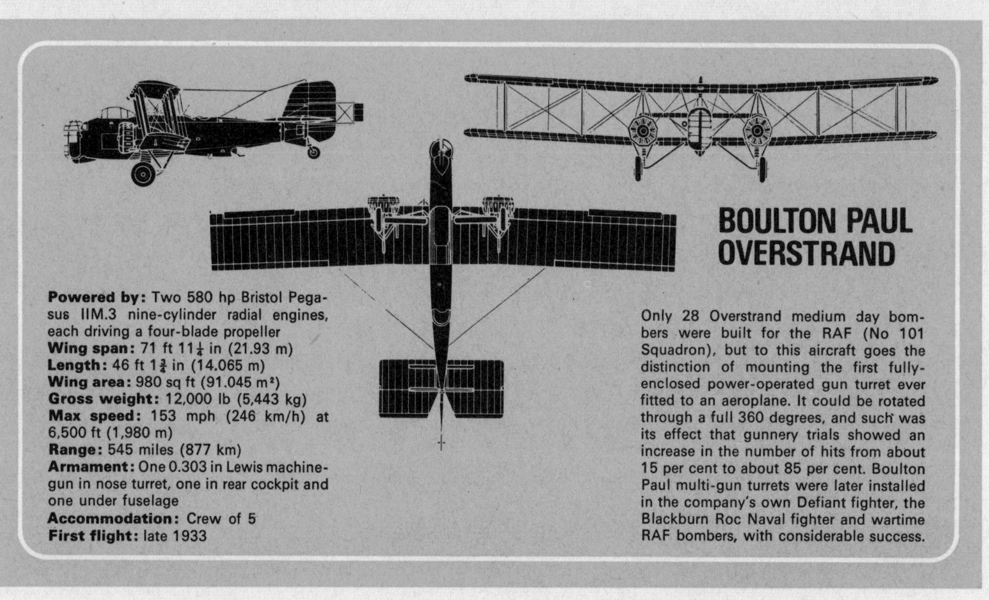

Powered by: Two 580 hp Bristol Pegasus IIM.3 nine-cylinder radial engines, each driving a four-blade propeller
Wing span: 71 ft 11¼ in (21.93 m)
Length: 46 ft 1¾ in (14.065 m)
Wing area: 980 sq ft (91.045 m²)
Gross weight: 12,000 lb (5,443 kg)
Max speed: 153 mph (246 km/h) at 6,500 ft (1,980 m)
Range: 545 miles (877 km)
Armament: One 0.303 in Lewis machine-gun in nose turret, one in rear cockpit and one under fuselage
Accommodation: Crew of 5
First flight: late 1933

Only 28 Overstrand medium day bombers were built for the RAF (No 101 Squadron), but to this aircraft goes the distinction of mounting the first fully-enclosed power-operated gun turret ever fitted to an aeroplane. It could be rotated through a full 360 degrees, and such was its effect that gunnery trials showed an increase in the number of hits from about 15 per cent to about 85 per cent. Boulton Paul multi-gun turrets were later installed in the company's own Defiant fighter, the Blackburn Roc Naval fighter and wartime RAF bombers, with considerable success.

DE HAVILLAND DRAGON RAPIDE

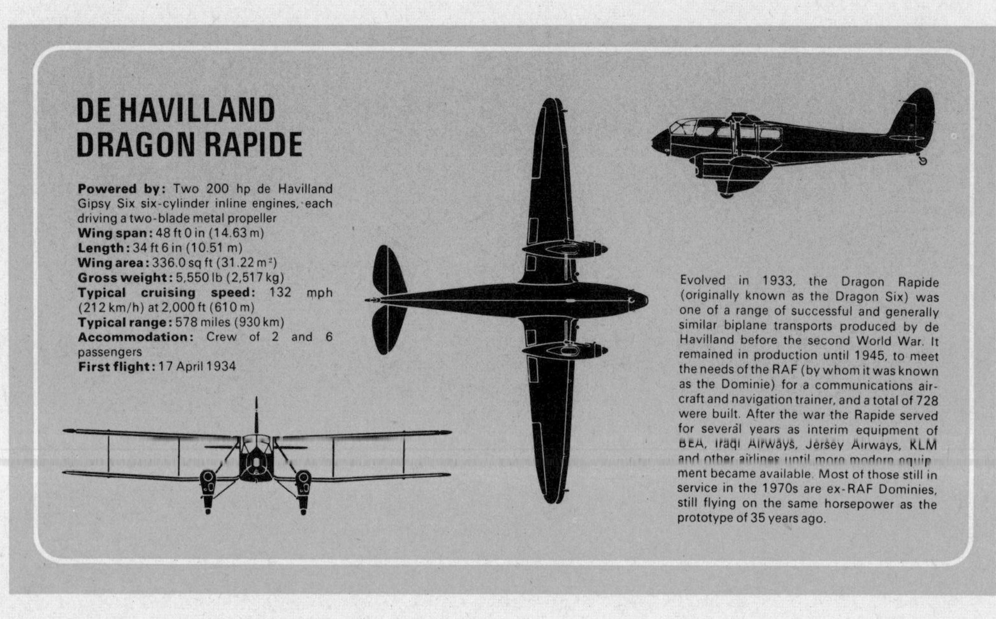

Powered by: Two 200 hp de Havilland Gipsy Six six-cylinder inline engines, each driving a two-blade metal propeller
Wing span: 48 ft 0 in (14.63 m)
Length: 34 ft 6 in (10.51 m)
Wing area: 336.0 sq ft (31.22 m²)
Gross weight: 5,550 lb (2,517 kg)
Typical cruising speed: 132 mph (212 km/h) at 2,000 ft (610 m)
Typical range: 578 miles (930 km)
Accommodation: Crew of 2 and 6 passengers
First flight: 17 April 1934

Evolved in 1933, the Dragon Rapide (originally known as the Dragon Six) was one of a range of successful and generally similar biplane transports produced by de Havilland before the second World War. It remained in production until 1945, to meet the needs of the RAF (by whom it was known as the Dominie) for a communications aircraft and navigation trainer, and a total of 728 were built. After the war the Rapide served for several years as interim equipment of BEA, Iraqi Airways, Jersey Airways, KLM and other airlines until more modern equipment became available. Most of those still in service in the 1970s are ex-RAF Dominies, still flying on the same horsepower as the prototype of 35 years ago.

Boeing Model 247D

Boulton Paul Overstrand

D.H.89 Dragon Rapide

ANT-20 'MAXIM GORKI'

Powered by: Eight 900 hp M-34FRN twelve-cylinder Vee-type engines, three in each wing and two mounted in tandem above the fuselage, and each driving a two-blade propeller of approx 14 ft 9 in (4.50 m) diameter

Wing span: 206 ft 8¼ in (63.00 m)
Length: 107 ft 11¼ in (32.90 m)
Wing area: 5,231.3 sq ft (486.0 m²)
Gross weight: 92,595 lb (42,000 kg)
Cruising speed: 137 mph (220 km/h)
Typical range: 745 miles (1,200 km)
Accommodation: Crew of 23 and up to 40 passengers
First flight: 19 May 1934

The ANT-20, designed by A N Tupolev and built by the TsAGI (Central Aero and Hydrodynamic Institute) in Moscow, can probably claim to be the largest aeroplane ever built for aerial advertising. Electrically-illuminated signs and slogans could be displayed under the wings, and inside the fuselage and wings were a printing press, wireless broadcasting station and cine equipment for disseminating propaganda leaflets, films shows etc. After only one year's flying the *Maxim Gorki* was destroyed on 18 May 1935 in a collision with another aircraft; but a developed version, the ANT-20*bis*, is believed to have served briefly as a conventional transport aircraft from 1940.

TUPOLEV ANT-25

Powered by: One 950 hp M-34R twelve-cylinder Vee-type engine, driving a three-blade propeller
Wing span: 111 ft 6½ in (34.00 m)
Length: 42 ft 11 in (13.08 m)
Wing area: 937.5 sq ft (87.10 m²)
Gross weight: 24,868 lb (11,280 kg)
Max speed: 153 mph (246 km/h)
Range: 8,080 miles (13,000 km)
Accommodation: Crew of 3
First flight: 10 September 1933 (?)

Remarkable for some outstanding long-distance and trans-Polar flights in the mid-1930s, the ANT-25 first captured world attention when, on 10/12 September 1934, it set a new world closed-circuit distance record of 7,711 miles (12,411 km), in which it stayed aloft for 75 hours 2 minutes. Also known as the RD (Rekord Dalnosti, or Long Range Record Aircraft), the aircraft was powered originally by an 874 hp M-34 engine; the data apply to it after the more powerful M-34R had been fitted in 1936. On 18/20 June 1937 the ANT-25 flew non-stop from Moscow to Portland, Washington, via the North Pole in 63 hours 25 minutes, the crew consisting of V P Chkalov, G F Baidukov and A V Belyakov. A month later, on 20/22 July, it flew from Moscow to San Jacinto, California, in 62 hours 17 minutes with M M Gromov, A B Yumashev and S A Danilin as crew, a total distance of 6,306 miles (10,148 km).

DOUGLAS DC-3

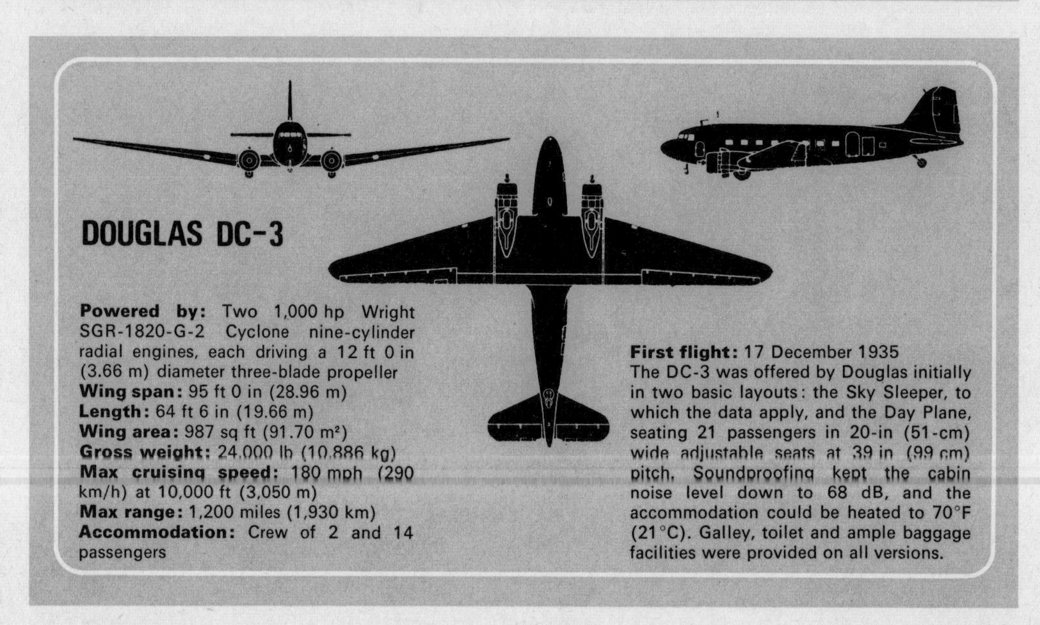

Powered by: Two 1,000 hp Wright SGR-1820-G-2 Cyclone nine-cylinder radial engines, each driving a 12 ft 0 in (3.66 m) diameter three-blade propeller
Wing span: 95 ft 0 in (28.96 m)
Length: 64 ft 6 in (19.66 m)
Wing area: 987 sq ft (91.70 m²)
Gross weight: 24,000 lb (10,886 kg)
Max cruising speed: 180 mph (290 km/h) at 10,000 ft (3,050 m)
Max range: 1,200 miles (1,930 km)
Accommodation: Crew of 2 and 14 passengers
First flight: 17 December 1935

The DC-3 was offered by Douglas initially in two basic layouts: the Sky Sleeper, to which the data apply, and the Day Plane, seating 21 passengers in 20-in (51-cm) wide adjustable seats at 39 in (99 cm) pitch. Soundproofing kept the cabin noise level down to 68 dB, and the accommodation could be heated to 70°F (21°C). Galley, toilet and ample baggage facilities were provided on all versions.

ANT-20 Maxim Gorki *(via Jean Alexander)*

Tupolev ANT-25

Douglas DC-3

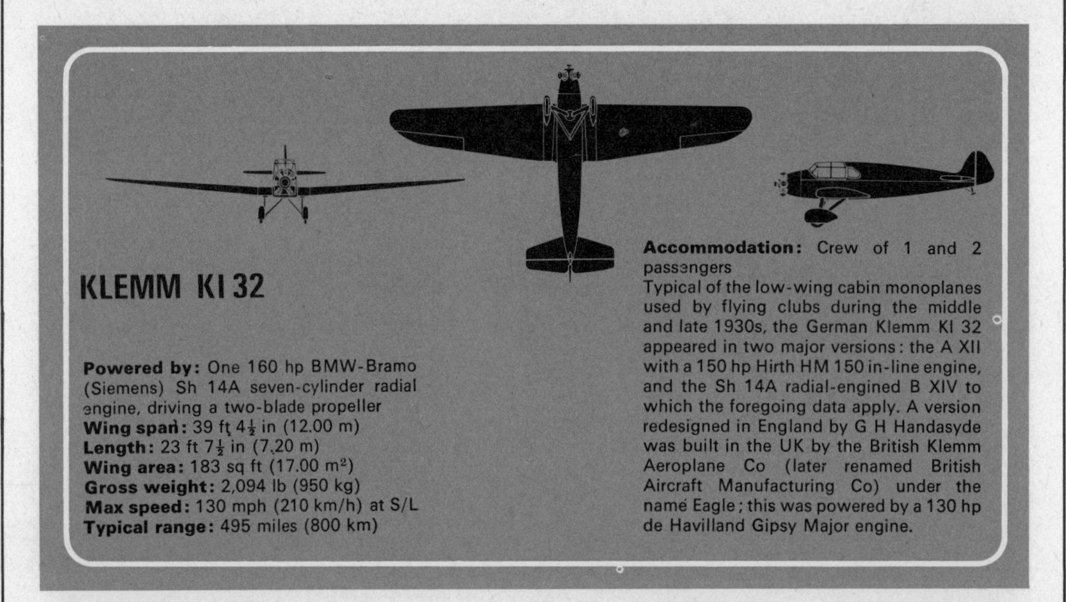

KLEMM Kl 32

Powered by: One 160 hp BMW-Bramo (Siemens) Sh 14A seven-cylinder radial engine, driving a two-blade propeller
Wing span: 39 ft $4\frac{1}{2}$ in (12.00 m)
Length: 23 ft $7\frac{1}{2}$ in (7.20 m)
Wing area: 183 sq ft (17.00 m²)
Gross weight: 2,094 lb (950 kg)
Max speed: 130 mph (210 km/h) at S/L
Typical range: 495 miles (800 km)
Accommodation: Crew of 1 and 2 passengers

Typical of the low-wing cabin monoplanes used by flying clubs during the middle and late 1930s, the German Klemm Kl 32 appeared in two major versions: the A XII with a 150 hp Hirth HM 150 in-line engine, and the Sh 14A radial-engined B XIV to which the foregoing data apply. A version redesigned in England by G H Handasyde was built in the UK by the British Klemm Aeroplane Co (later renamed British Aircraft Manufacturing Co) under the name Eagle; this was powered by a 130 hp de Havilland Gipsy Major engine.

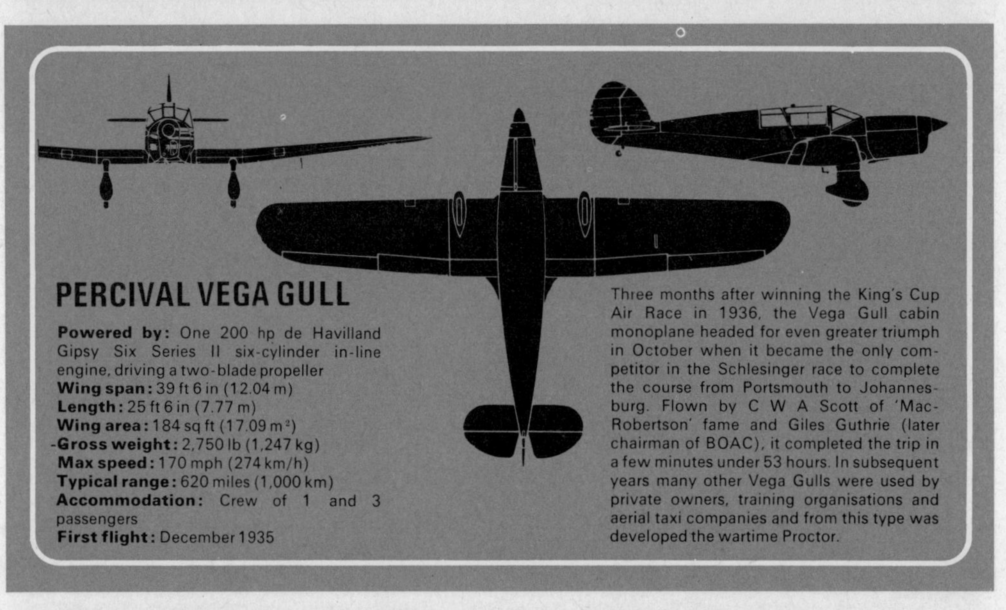

PERCIVAL VEGA GULL

Powered by: One 200 hp de Havilland Gipsy Six Series II six-cylinder in-line engine, driving a two-blade propeller
Wing span: 39 ft 6 in (12.04 m)
Length: 25 ft 6 in (7.77 m)
Wing area: 184 sq ft (17.09 m²)
Gross weight: 2,750 lb (1,247 kg)
Max speed: 170 mph (274 km/h)
Typical range: 620 miles (1,000 km)
Accommodation: Crew of 1 and 3 passengers
First flight: December 1935

Three months after winning the King's Cup Air Race in 1936, the Vega Gull cabin monoplane headed for even greater triumph in October when it became the only competitor in the Schlesinger race to complete the course from Portsmouth to Johannesburg. Flown by C W A Scott of 'MacRobertson' fame and Giles Guthrie (later chairman of BOAC), it completed the trip in a few minutes under 53 hours. In subsequent years many other Vega Gulls were used by private owners, training organisations and aerial taxi companies and from this type was developed the wartime Proctor.

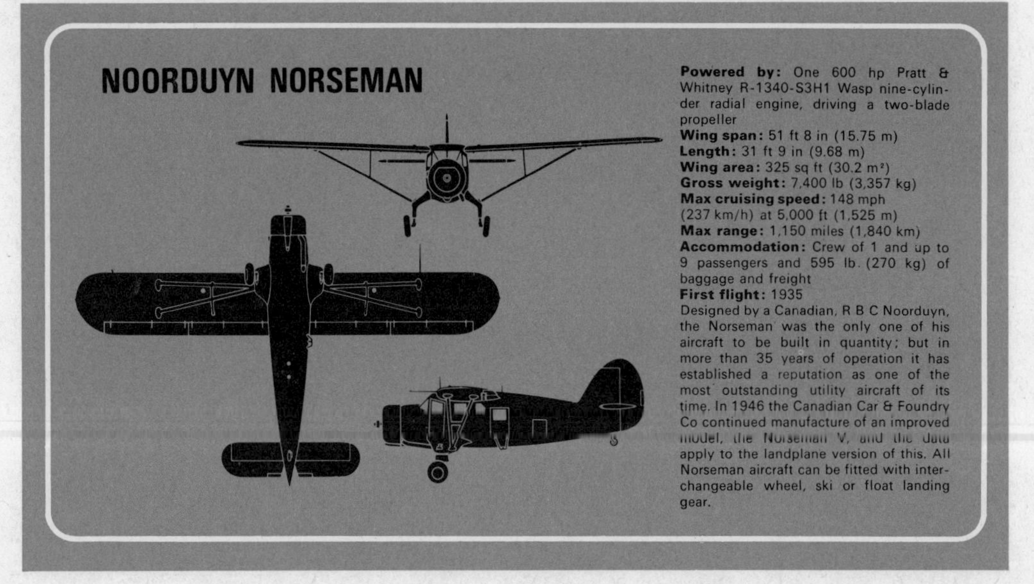

NOORDUYN NORSEMAN

Powered by: One 600 hp Pratt & Whitney R-1340-S3H1 Wasp nine-cylinder radial engine, driving a two-blade propeller
Wing span: 51 ft 8 in (15.75 m)
Length: 31 ft 9 in (9.68 m)
Wing area: 325 sq ft (30.2 m²)
Gross weight: 7,400 lb (3,357 kg)
Max cruising speed: 148 mph (237 km/h) at 5,000 ft (1,525 m)
Max range: 1,150 miles (1,840 km)
Accommodation: Crew of 1 and up to 9 passengers and 595 lb (270 kg) of baggage and freight
First flight: 1935

Designed by a Canadian, R B C Noorduyn, the Norseman was the only one of his aircraft to be built in quantity; but in more than 35 years of operation it has established a reputation as one of the most outstanding utility aircraft of its time. In 1946 the Canadian Car & Foundry Co continued manufacture of an improved model, the Norseman V, and the data apply to the landplane version of this. All Norseman aircraft can be fitted with interchangeable wheel, ski or float landing gear.

B.A. Eagle 2, British de luxe development of the Klemm Kl 32

Percival Vega Gull

Norseman twin-float seaplane

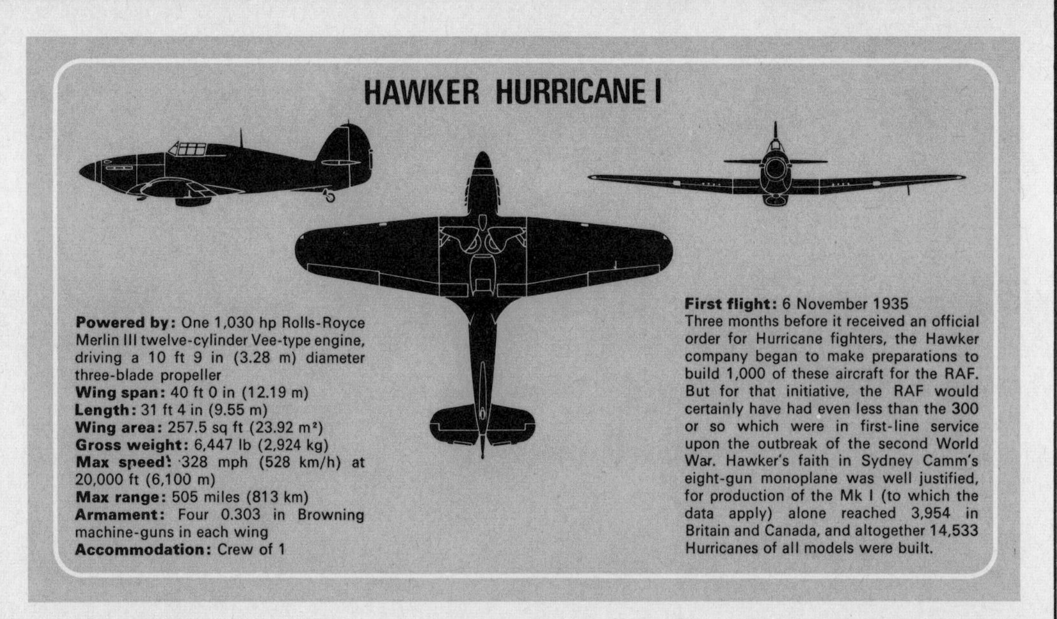

HAWKER HURRICANE I

Powered by: One 1,030 hp Rolls-Royce Merlin III twelve-cylinder Vee-type engine, driving a 10 ft 9 in (3.28 m) diameter three-blade propeller
Wing span: 40 ft 0 in (12.19 m)
Length: 31 ft 4 in (9.55 m)
Wing area: 257.5 sq ft (23.92 m²)
Gross weight: 6,447 lb (2,924 kg)
Max speed: 328 mph (528 km/h) at 20,000 ft (6,100 m)
Max range: 505 miles (813 km)
Armament: Four 0.303 in Browning machine-guns in each wing
Accommodation: Crew of 1
First flight: 6 November 1935

Three months before it received an official order for Hurricane fighters, the Hawker company began to make preparations to build 1,000 of these aircraft for the RAF. But for that initiative, the RAF would certainly have had even less than the 300 or so which were in first-line service upon the outbreak of the second World War. Hawker's faith in Sydney Camm's eight-gun monoplane was well justified, for production of the Mk I (to which the data apply) alone reached 3,954 in Britain and Canada, and altogether 14,533 Hurricanes of all models were built.

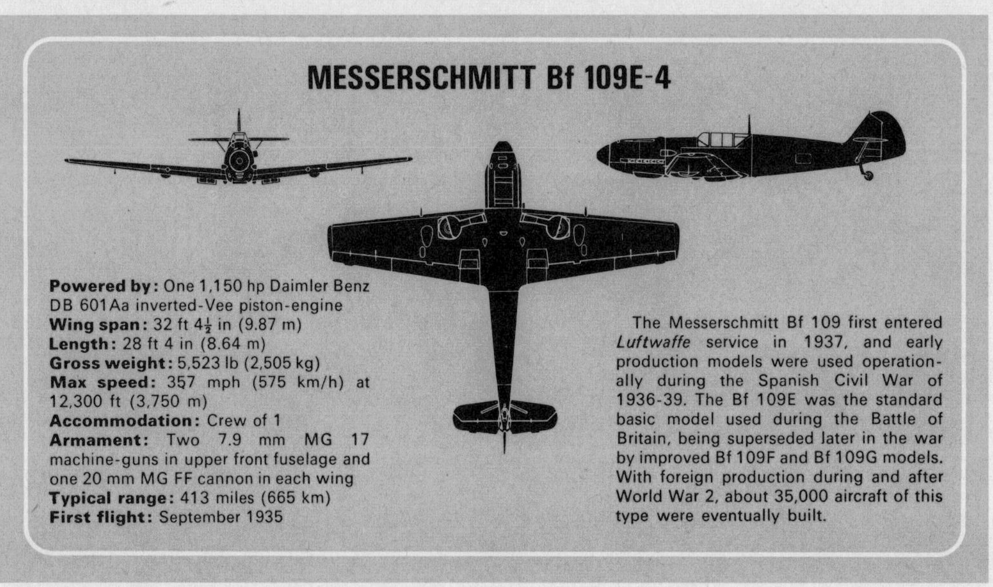

MESSERSCHMITT Bf 109E-4

Powered by: One 1,150 hp Daimler Benz DB 601Aa inverted-Vee piston-engine
Wing span: 32 ft 4½ in (9.87 m)
Length: 28 ft 4 in (8.64 m)
Gross weight: 5,523 lb (2,505 kg)
Max speed: 357 mph (575 km/h) at 12,300 ft (3,750 m)
Accommodation: Crew of 1
Armament: Two 7.9 mm MG 17 machine-guns in upper front fuselage and one 20 mm MG FF cannon in each wing
Typical range: 413 miles (665 km)
First flight: September 1935

The Messerschmitt Bf 109 first entered *Luftwaffe* service in 1937, and early production models were used operationally during the Spanish Civil War of 1936-39. The Bf 109E was the standard basic model used during the Battle of Britain, being superseded later in the war by improved Bf 109F and Bf 109G models. With foreign production during and after World War 2, about 35,000 aircraft of this type were eventually built.

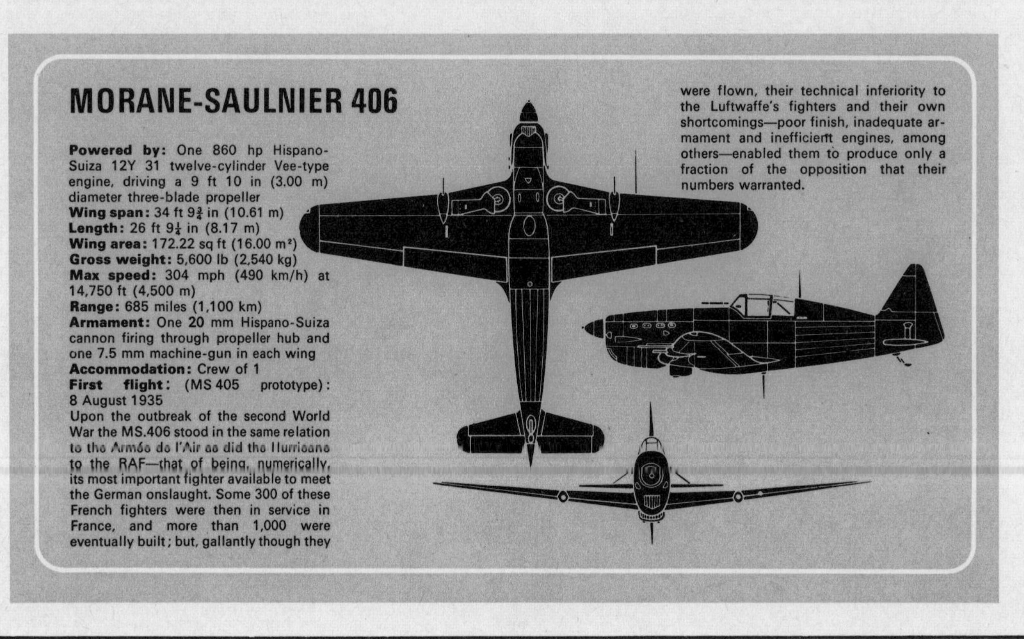

MORANE-SAULNIER 406

Powered by: One 860 hp Hispano-Suiza 12Y 31 twelve-cylinder Vee-type engine, driving a 9 ft 10 in (3.00 m) diameter three-blade propeller
Wing span: 34 ft 9¾ in (10.61 m)
Length: 26 ft 9¼ in (8.17 m)
Wing area: 172.22 sq ft (16.00 m²)
Gross weight: 5,600 lb (2,540 kg)
Max speed: 304 mph (490 km/h) at 14,750 ft (4,500 m)
Range: 685 miles (1,100 km)
Armament: One 20 mm Hispano-Suiza cannon firing through propeller hub and one 7.5 mm machine-gun in each wing
Accommodation: Crew of 1
First flight: (MS 405 prototype): 8 August 1935

Upon the outbreak of the second World War the MS.406 stood in the same relation to the Armée de l'Air as did the Hurricane to the RAF—that of being, numerically, its most important fighter available to meet the German onslaught. Some 300 of these French fighters were then in service in France, and more than 1,000 were eventually built; but, gallantly though they were flown, their technical inferiority to the Luftwaffe's fighters and their own shortcomings—poor finish, inadequate armament and inefficient engines, among others—enabled them to produce only a fraction of the opposition that their numbers warranted.

Hawker Hurricane I

Messerschmitt Bf 109E-3

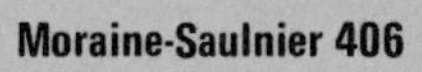

Moraine-Saulnier 406

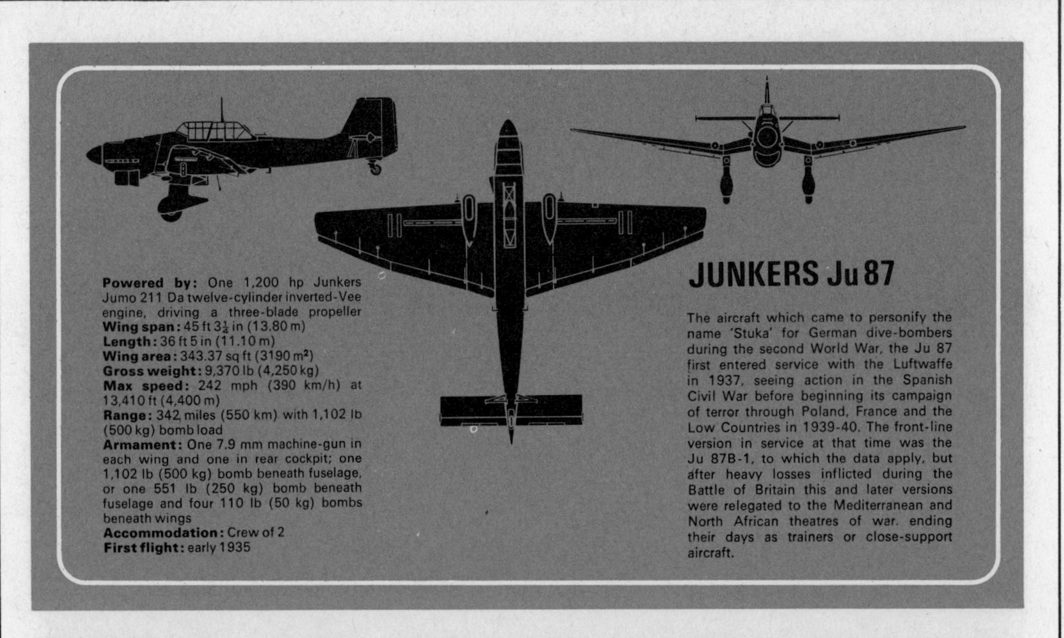

JUNKERS Ju 87

Powered by: One 1,200 hp Junkers Jumo 211 Da twelve-cylinder inverted-Vee engine, driving a three-blade propeller
Wing span: 45 ft 3¼ in (13.80 m)
Length: 36 ft 5 in (11.10 m)
Wing area: 343.37 sq ft (3190 m²)
Gross weight: 9,370 lb (4,250 kg)
Max speed: 242 mph (390 km/h) at 13,410 ft (4,400 m)
Range: 342 miles (550 km) with 1,102 lb (500 kg) bomb load
Armament: One 7.9 mm machine-gun in each wing and one in rear cockpit; one 1,102 lb (500 kg) bomb beneath fuselage, or one 551 lb (250 kg) bomb beneath fuselage and four 110 lb (50 kg) bombs beneath wings
Accommodation: Crew of 2
First flight: early 1935

The aircraft which came to personify the name 'Stuka' for German dive-bombers during the second World War, the Ju 87 first entered service with the Luftwaffe in 1937, seeing action in the Spanish Civil War before beginning its campaign of terror through Poland, France and the Low Countries in 1939-40. The front-line version in service at that time was the Ju 87B-1, to which the data apply, but after heavy losses inflicted during the Battle of Britain this and later versions were relegated to the Mediterranean and North African theatres of war, ending their days as trainers or close-support aircraft.

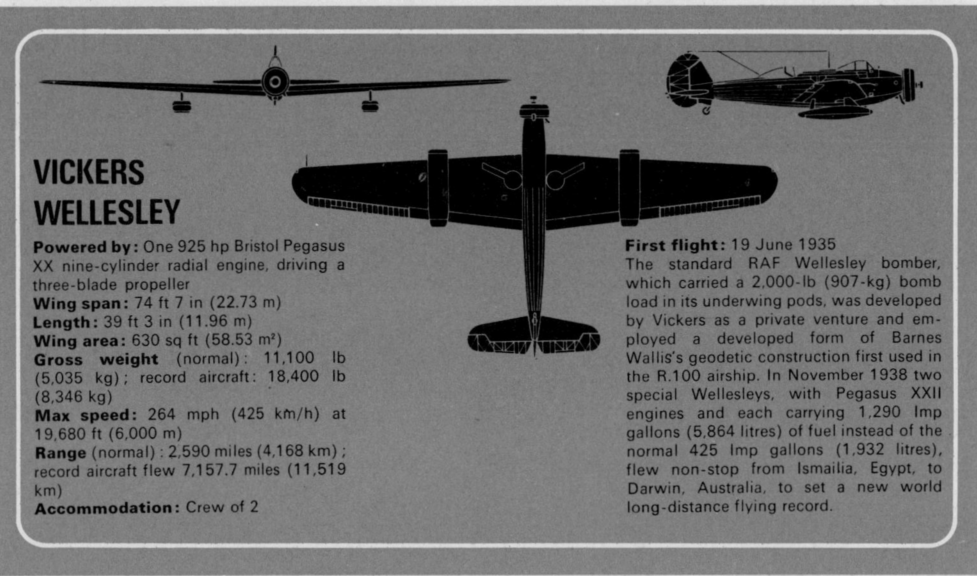

VICKERS WELLESLEY

Powered by: One 925 hp Bristol Pegasus XX nine-cylinder radial engine, driving a three-blade propeller
Wing span: 74 ft 7 in (22.73 m)
Length: 39 ft 3 in (11.96 m)
Wing area: 630 sq ft (58.53 m²)
Gross weight (normal): 11,100 lb (5,035 kg); record aircraft: 18,400 lb (8,346 kg)
Max speed: 264 mph (425 km/h) at 19,680 ft (6,000 m)
Range (normal): 2,590 miles (4,168 km); record aircraft flew 7,157.7 miles (11,519 km)
Accommodation: Crew of 2
First flight: 19 June 1935

The standard RAF Wellesley bomber, which carried a 2,000-lb (907-kg) bomb load in its underwing pods, was developed by Vickers as a private venture and employed a developed form of Barnes Wallis's geodetic construction first used in the R.100 airship. In November 1938 two special Wellesleys, with Pegasus XXII engines and each carrying 1,290 Imp gallons (5,864 litres) of fuel instead of the normal 425 Imp gallons (1,932 litres), flew non-stop from Ismailia, Egypt, to Darwin, Australia, to set a new world long-distance flying record.

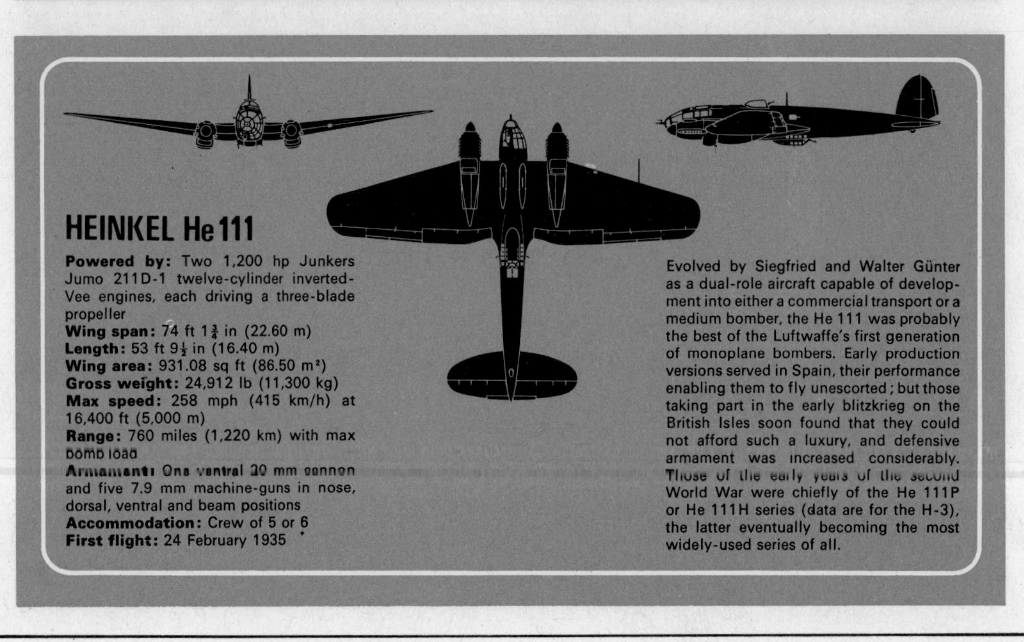

HEINKEL He 111

Powered by: Two 1,200 hp Junkers Jumo 211D-1 twelve-cylinder inverted-Vee engines, each driving a three-blade propeller
Wing span: 74 ft 1¾ in (22.60 m)
Length: 53 ft 9½ in (16.40 m)
Wing area: 931.08 sq ft (86.50 m²)
Gross weight: 24,912 lb (11,300 kg)
Max speed: 258 mph (415 km/h) at 16,400 ft (5,000 m)
Range: 760 miles (1,220 km) with max bomb load
Armament: One ventral 20 mm cannon and five 7.9 mm machine-guns in nose, dorsal, ventral and beam positions
Accommodation: Crew of 5 or 6
First flight: 24 February 1935

Evolved by Siegfried and Walter Günter as a dual-role aircraft capable of development into either a commercial transport or a medium bomber, the He 111 was probably the best of the Luftwaffe's first generation of monoplane bombers. Early production versions served in Spain, their performance enabling them to fly unescorted; but those taking part in the early blitzkrieg on the British Isles soon found that they could not afford such a luxury, and defensive armament was increased considerably. Those of the early years of the second World War were chiefly of the He 111P or He 111H series (data are for the H-3), the latter eventually becoming the most widely-used series of all.

Junkers Ju 87B-1

Vickers Wellesley

Heinkel He 111H-6

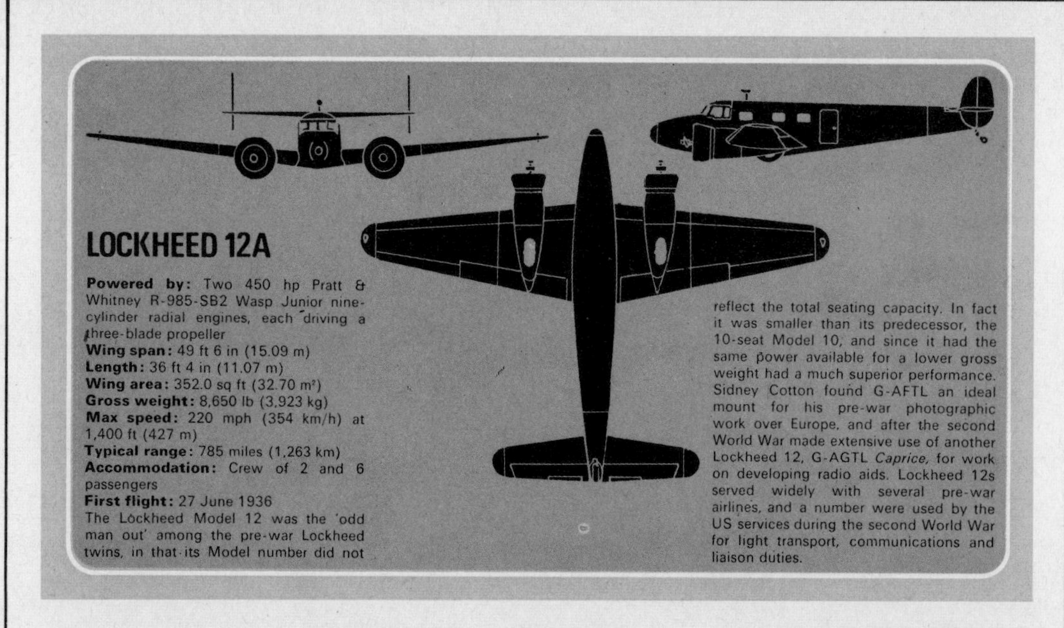

LOCKHEED 12A

Powered by: Two 450 hp Pratt & Whitney R-985-SB2 Wasp Junior nine-cylinder radial engines, each driving a three-blade propeller
Wing span: 49 ft 6 in (15.09 m)
Length: 36 ft 4 in (11.07 m)
Wing area: 352.0 sq ft (32.70 m²)
Gross weight: 8,650 lb (3,923 kg)
Max speed: 220 mph (354 km/h) at 1,400 ft (427 m)
Typical range: 785 miles (1,263 km)
Accommodation: Crew of 2 and 6 passengers
First flight: 27 June 1936

The Lockheed Model 12 was the 'odd man out' among the pre-war Lockheed twins, in that its Model number did not reflect the total seating capacity. In fact it was smaller than its predecessor, the 10-seat Model 10, and since it had the same power available for a lower gross weight had a much superior performance. Sidney Cotton found G-AFTL an ideal mount for his pre-war photographic work over Europe, and after the second World War made extensive use of another Lockheed 12, G-AGTL *Caprice*, for work on developing radio aids. Lockheed 12s served widely with several pre-war airlines, and a number were used by the US services during the second World War for light transport, communications and liaison duties.

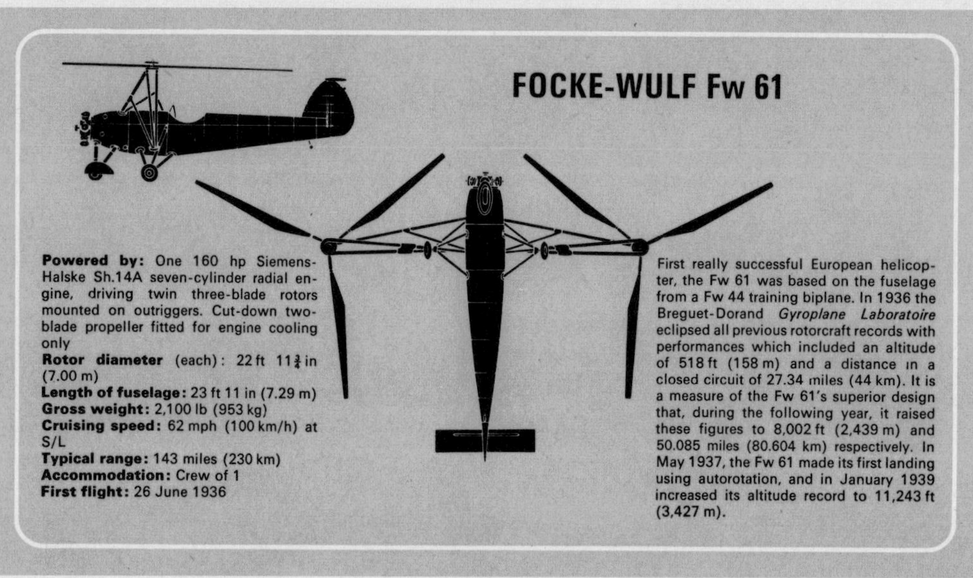

FOCKE-WULF Fw 61

Powered by: One 160 hp Siemens-Halske Sh.14A seven-cylinder radial engine, driving twin three-blade rotors mounted on outriggers. Cut-down two-blade propeller fitted for engine cooling only
Rotor diameter (each): 22 ft 11¾ in (7.00 m)
Length of fuselage: 23 ft 11 in (7.29 m)
Gross weight: 2,100 lb (953 kg)
Cruising speed: 62 mph (100 km/h) at S/L
Typical range: 143 miles (230 km)
Accommodation: Crew of 1
First flight: 26 June 1936

First really successful European helicopter, the Fw 61 was based on the fuselage from a Fw 44 training biplane. In 1936 the Breguet-Dorand *Gyroplane Laboratoire* eclipsed all previous rotorcraft records with performances which included an altitude of 518 ft (158 m) and a distance in a closed circuit of 27.34 miles (44 km). It is a measure of the Fw 61's superior design that, during the following year, it raised these figures to 8,002 ft (2,439 m) and 50.085 miles (80.604 km) respectively. In May 1937, the Fw 61 made its first landing using autorotation, and in January 1939 increased its altitude record to 11,243 ft (3,427 m).

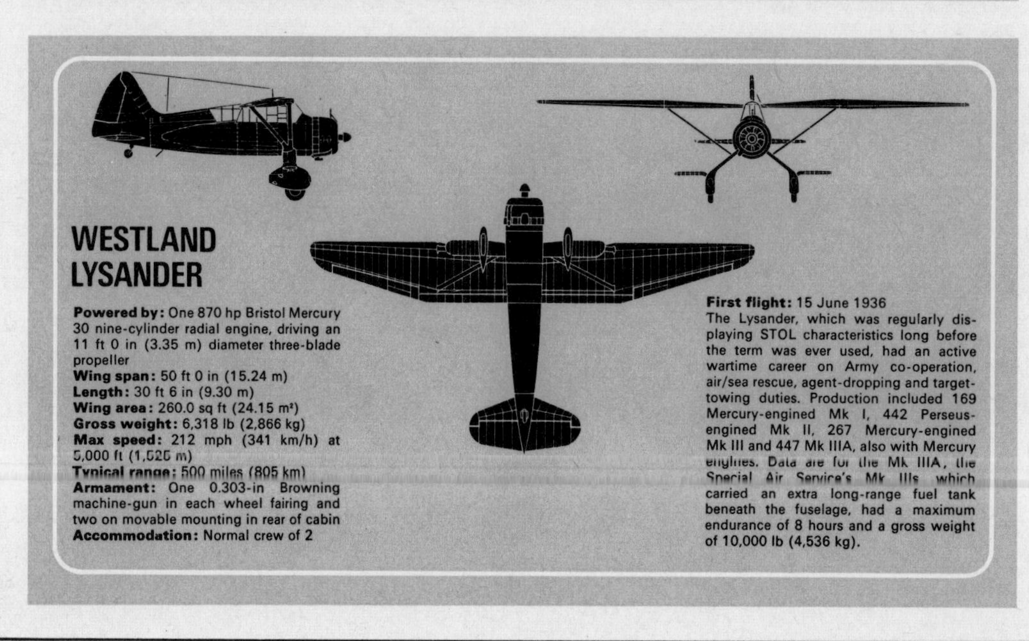

WESTLAND LYSANDER

Powered by: One 870 hp Bristol Mercury 30 nine-cylinder radial engine, driving an 11 ft 0 in (3.35 m) diameter three-blade propeller
Wing span: 50 ft 0 in (15.24 m)
Length: 30 ft 6 in (9.30 m)
Wing area: 260.0 sq ft (24.15 m²)
Gross weight: 6,318 lb (2,866 kg)
Max speed: 212 mph (341 km/h) at 5,000 ft (1,525 m)
Typical range: 500 miles (805 km)
Armament: One 0.303-in Browning machine-gun in each wheel fairing and two on movable mounting in rear of cabin
Accommodation: Normal crew of 2
First flight: 15 June 1936

The Lysander, which was regularly displaying STOL characteristics long before the term was ever used, had an active wartime career on Army co-operation, air/sea rescue, agent-dropping and target-towing duties. Production included 169 Mercury-engined Mk I, 442 Perseus-engined Mk II, 267 Mercury-engined Mk III and 447 Mk IIIA, also with Mercury engines. Data are for the Mk IIIA, the Special Air Service's Mk IIIs which carried an extra long-range fuel tank beneath the fuselage, had a maximum endurance of 8 hours and a gross weight of 10,000 lb (4,536 kg).

Lockheed Model 10 Electra

Focke-Wulf Fw 61, first prototype

Lysander III of the Special Air Service

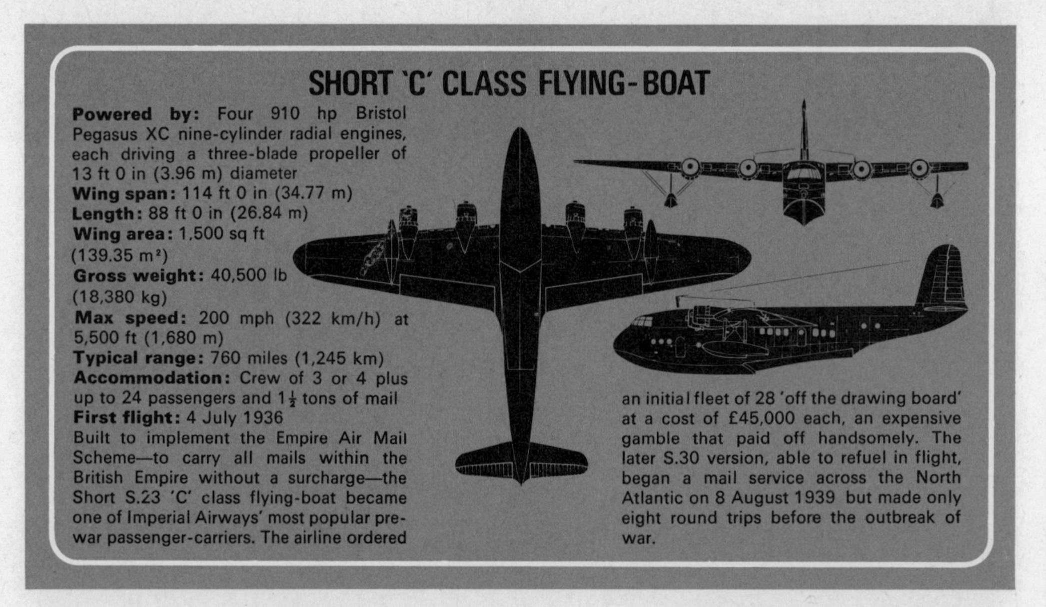

SHORT 'C' CLASS FLYING-BOAT

Powered by: Four 910 hp Bristol Pegasus XC nine-cylinder radial engines, each driving a three-blade propeller of 13 ft 0 in (3.96 m) diameter
Wing span: 114 ft 0 in (34.77 m)
Length: 88 ft 0 in (26.84 m)
Wing area: 1,500 sq ft (139.35 m²)
Gross weight: 40,500 lb (18,380 kg)
Max speed: 200 mph (322 km/h) at 5,500 ft (1,680 m)
Typical range: 760 miles (1,245 km)
Accommodation: Crew of 3 or 4 plus up to 24 passengers and 1½ tons of mail
First flight: 4 July 1936

Built to implement the Empire Air Mail Scheme—to carry all mails within the British Empire without a surcharge—the Short S.23 'C' class flying-boat became one of Imperial Airways' most popular pre-war passenger-carriers. The airline ordered an initial fleet of 28 'off the drawing board' at a cost of £45,000 each, an expensive gamble that paid off handsomely. The later S.30 version, able to refuel in flight, began a mail service across the North Atlantic on 8 August 1939 but made only eight round trips before the outbreak of war.

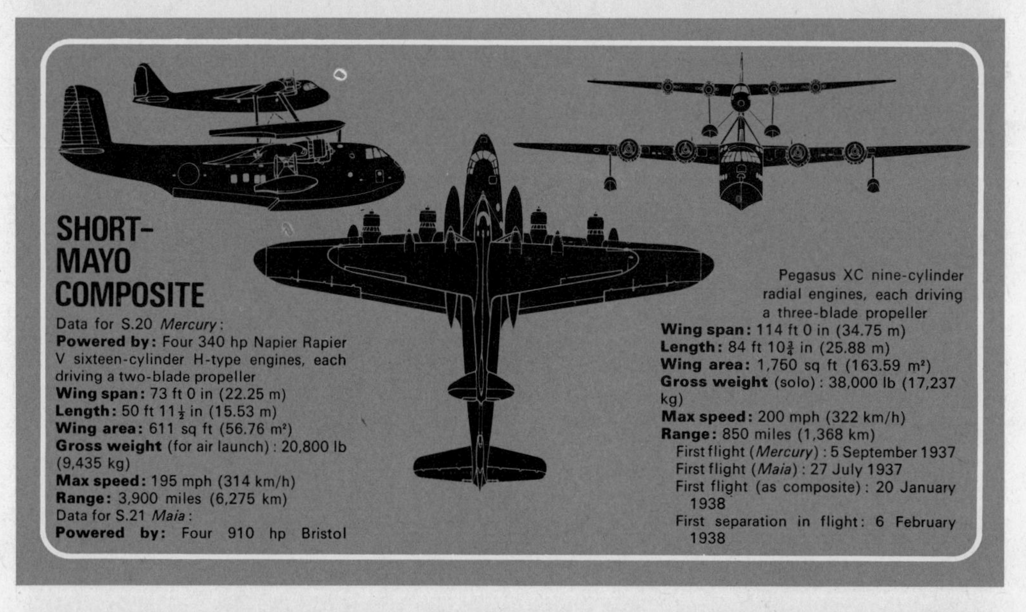

SHORT-MAYO COMPOSITE

Data for S.20 *Mercury*:
Powered by: Four 340 hp Napier Rapier V sixteen-cylinder H-type engines, each driving a two-blade propeller
Wing span: 73 ft 0 in (22.25 m)
Length: 50 ft 11½ in (15.53 m)
Wing area: 611 sq ft (56.76 m²)
Gross weight (for air launch): 20,800 lb (9,435 kg)
Max speed: 195 mph (314 km/h)
Range: 3,900 miles (6,275 km)
Data for S.21 *Maia*:
Powered by: Four 910 hp Bristol Pegasus XC nine-cylinder radial engines, each driving a three-blade propeller
Wing span: 114 ft 0 in (34.75 m)
Length: 84 ft 10¾ in (25.88 m)
Wing area: 1,750 sq ft (163.59 m²)
Gross weight (solo): 38,000 lb (17,237 kg)
Max speed: 200 mph (322 km/h)
Range: 850 miles (1,368 km)
First flight (*Mercury*): 5 September 1937
First flight (*Maia*): 27 July 1937
First flight (as composite): 20 January 1938
First separation in flight: 6 February 1938

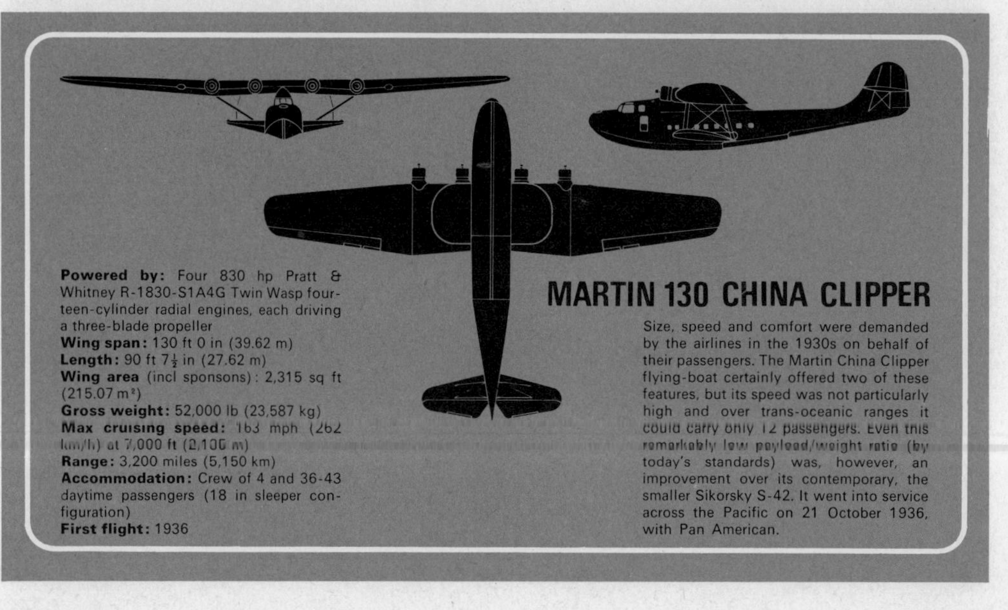

MARTIN 130 CHINA CLIPPER

Powered by: Four 830 hp Pratt & Whitney R-1830-S1A4G Twin Wasp fourteen-cylinder radial engines, each driving a three-blade propeller
Wing span: 130 ft 0 in (39.62 m)
Length: 90 ft 7½ in (27.62 m)
Wing area (incl sponsons): 2,315 sq ft (215.07 m²)
Gross weight: 52,000 lb (23,587 kg)
Max cruising speed: 163 mph (262 km/h) at 7,000 ft (2,100 m)
Range: 3,200 miles (5,150 km)
Accommodation: Crew of 4 and 36-43 daytime passengers (18 in sleeper configuration)
First flight: 1936

Size, speed and comfort were demanded by the airlines in the 1930s on behalf of their passengers. The Martin China Clipper flying-boat certainly offered two of these features, but its speed was not particularly high and over trans-oceanic ranges it could carry only 12 passengers. Even this remarkably low payload/weight ratio (by today's standards) was, however, an improvement over its contemporary, the smaller Sikorsky S-42. It went into service across the Pacific on 21 October 1936, with Pan American.

Short 'C' class flying-boat Canopus
(Flight International)

Short-Mayo Composite aircraft, Mercury and Maia

Martin 130 'China Clipper' of Pan American Airways

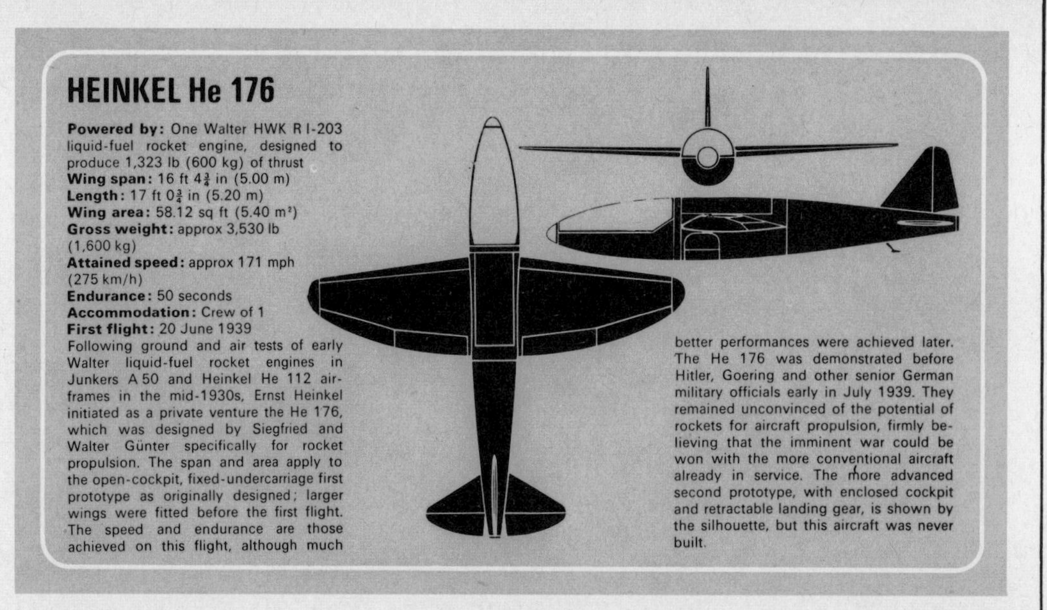

HEINKEL He 176

Powered by: One Walter HWK R I-203 liquid-fuel rocket engine, designed to produce 1,323 lb (600 kg) of thrust
Wing span: 16 ft 4¾ in (5.00 m)
Length: 17 ft 0¾ in (5.20 m)
Wing area: 58.12 sq ft (5.40 m²)
Gross weight: approx 3,530 lb (1,600 kg)
Attained speed: approx 171 mph (275 km/h)
Endurance: 50 seconds
Accommodation: Crew of 1
First flight: 20 June 1939

Following ground and air tests of early Walter liquid-fuel rocket engines in Junkers A 50 and Heinkel He 112 airframes in the mid-1930s, Ernst Heinkel initiated as a private venture the He 176, which was designed by Siegfried and Walter Günter specifically for rocket propulsion. The span and area apply to the open-cockpit, fixed-undercarriage first prototype as originally designed; larger wings were fitted before the first flight. The speed and endurance are those achieved on this flight, although much better performances were achieved later. The He 176 was demonstrated before Hitler, Goering and other senior German military officials early in July 1939. They remained unconvinced of the potential of rockets for aircraft propulsion, firmly believing that the imminent war could be won with the more conventional aircraft already in service. The more advanced second prototype, with enclosed cockpit and retractable landing gear, is shown by the silhouette, but this aircraft was never built.

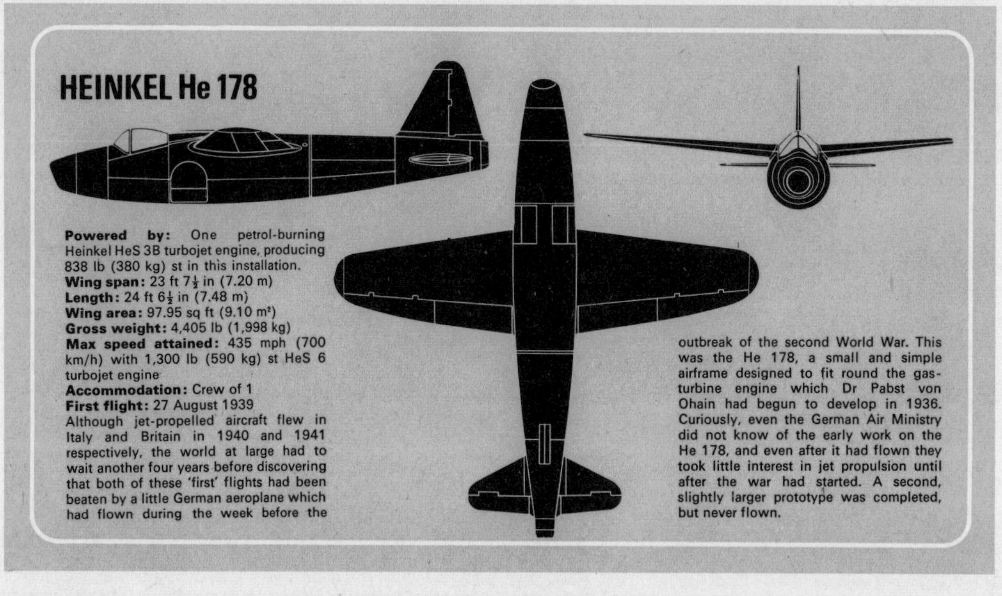

HEINKEL He 178

Powered by: One petrol-burning Heinkel HeS 3B turbojet engine, producing 838 lb (380 kg) st in this installation.
Wing span: 23 ft 7½ in (7.20 m)
Length: 24 ft 6½ in (7.48 m)
Wing area: 97.95 sq ft (9.10 m²)
Gross weight: 4,405 lb (1,998 kg)
Max speed attained: 435 mph (700 km/h) with 1,300 lb (590 kg) st HeS 6 turbojet engine
Accommodation: Crew of 1
First flight: 27 August 1939

Although jet-propelled aircraft flew in Italy and Britain in 1940 and 1941 respectively, the world at large had to wait another four years before discovering that both of these 'first' flights had been beaten by a little German aeroplane which had flown during the week before the outbreak of the second World War. This was the He 178, a small and simple airframe designed to fit round the gas-turbine engine which Dr Pabst von Ohain had begun to develop in 1936. Curiously, even the German Air Ministry did not know of the early work on the He 178, and even after it had flown they took little interest in jet propulsion until after the war had started. A second, slightly larger prototype was completed, but never flown.

GLOSTER E.28/39

Powered by: One 860 lb (390 kg) st Power Jets (Whittle) W.1 centrifugal-flow turbojet engine
Wing span: 29 ft 0 in (8.84 m)
Length: 25 ft 3¾ in (7.72 m)
Wing area: 146.5 sq ft (13.6 m²)
Gross weight: 3,700 lb (1,678 kg)
Max speed: 338 mph (544 km/h) at 15,000 ft (4,570 m)
Accommodation: Crew of 1
First flight: 15 May 1941

The data above apply to the first E.28/39 prototype with original engine. Later, with a 1,700 lb (770 kg) st Power Jets W.2/500 engine, it flew at approx 450 mph (724 km/h). The second prototype, fitted with a Rover W.2B engine of 1,200 lb (544 kg) st, reached a speed of 466 mph (750 km/h) during tests.

Proposed second prototype He 176

Artist's impression of He 178

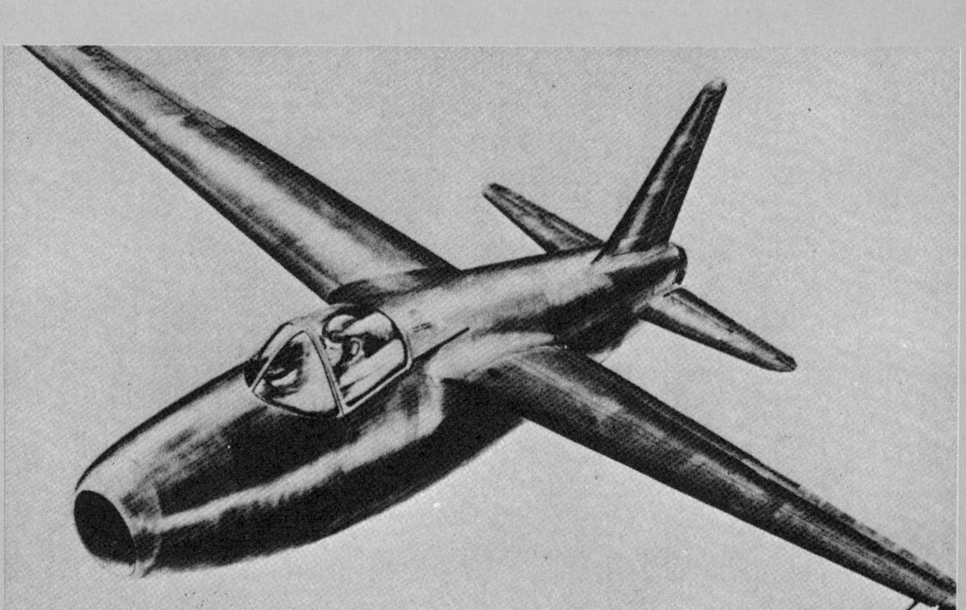

Gloster E.28/39

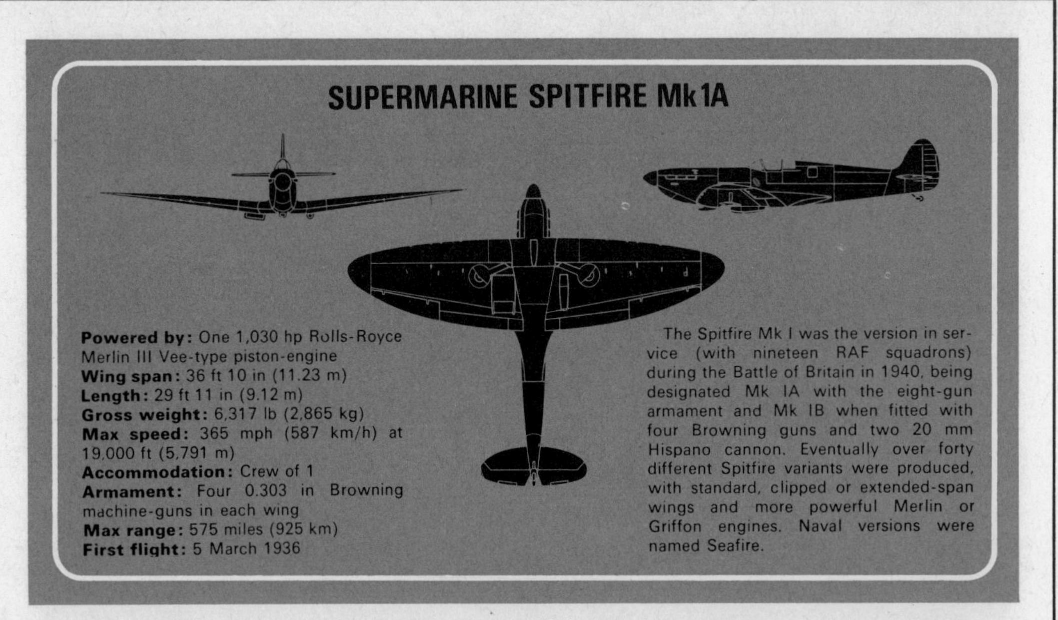

SUPERMARINE SPITFIRE Mk1A

Powered by: One 1,030 hp Rolls-Royce Merlin III Vee-type piston-engine
Wing span: 36 ft 10 in (11.23 m)
Length: 29 ft 11 in (9.12 m)
Gross weight: 6,317 lb (2,865 kg)
Max speed: 365 mph (587 km/h) at 19,000 ft (5,791 m)
Accommodation: Crew of 1
Armament: Four 0.303 in Browning machine-guns in each wing
Max range: 575 miles (925 km)
First flight: 5 March 1936

The Spitfire Mk I was the version in service (with nineteen RAF squadrons) during the Battle of Britain in 1940, being designated Mk IA with the eight-gun armament and Mk IB when fitted with four Browning guns and two 20 mm Hispano cannon. Eventually over forty different Spitfire variants were produced, with standard, clipped or extended-span wings and more powerful Merlin or Griffon engines. Naval versions were named Seafire.

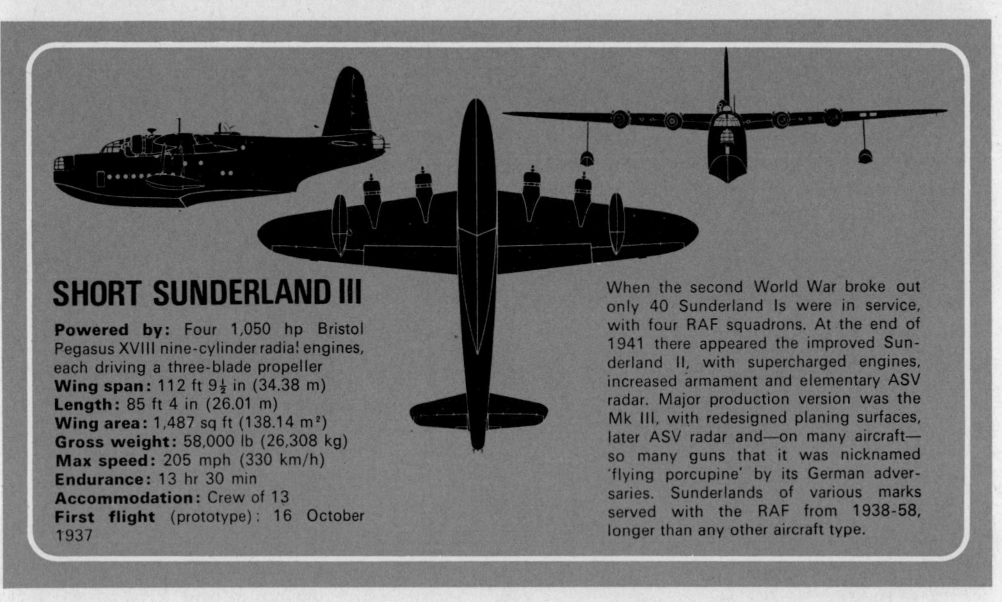

SHORT SUNDERLAND III

Powered by: Four 1,050 hp Bristol Pegasus XVIII nine-cylinder radial engines, each driving a three-blade propeller
Wing span: 112 ft 9½ in (34.38 m)
Length: 85 ft 4 in (26.01 m)
Wing area: 1,487 sq ft (138.14 m^2)
Gross weight: 58,000 lb (26,308 kg)
Max speed: 205 mph (330 km/h)
Endurance: 13 hr 30 min
Accommodation: Crew of 13
First flight (prototype): 16 October 1937

When the second World War broke out only 40 Sunderland Is were in service, with four RAF squadrons. At the end of 1941 there appeared the improved Sunderland II, with supercharged engines, increased armament and elementary ASV radar. Major production version was the Mk III, with redesigned planing surfaces, later ASV radar and—on many aircraft—so many guns that it was nicknamed 'flying porcupine' by its German adversaries. Sunderlands of various marks served with the RAF from 1938-58, longer than any other aircraft type.

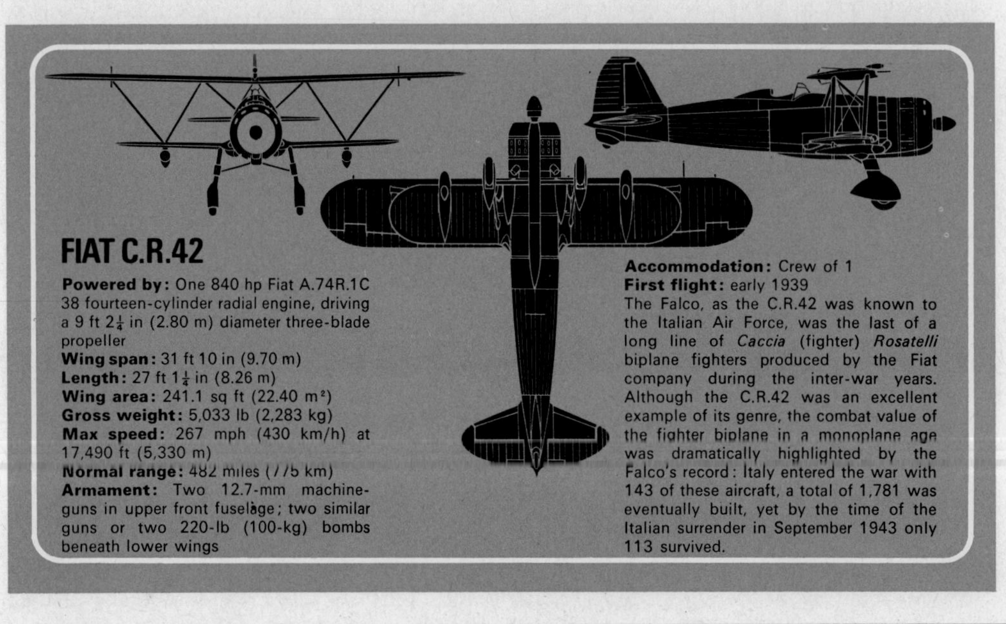

FIAT C.R.42

Powered by: One 840 hp Fiat A.74R.1C 38 fourteen-cylinder radial engine, driving a 9 ft 2¼ in (2.80 m) diameter three-blade propeller
Wing span: 31 ft 10 in (9.70 m)
Length: 27 ft 1¼ in (8.26 m)
Wing area: 241.1 sq ft (22.40 m^2)
Gross weight: 5,033 lb (2,283 kg)
Max speed: 267 mph (430 km/h) at 17,490 ft (5,330 m)
Normal range: 482 miles (775 km)
Armament: Two 12.7-mm machine-guns in upper front fuselage; two similar guns or two 220-lb (100-kg) bombs beneath lower wings
Accommodation: Crew of 1
First flight: early 1939

The Falco, as the C.R.42 was known to the Italian Air Force, was the last of a long line of *Caccia* (fighter) *Rosatelli* biplane fighters produced by the Fiat company during the inter-war years. Although the C.R.42 was an excellent example of its genre, the combat value of the fighter biplane in a monoplane age was dramatically highlighted by the Falco's record: Italy entered the war with 143 of these aircraft, a total of 1,781 was eventually built, yet by the time of the Italian surrender in September 1943 only 113 survived.

Supermarine Spitfire I

Short Sunderland V

Fiat C.R.42

BOEING B-17 FLYING FORTRESS

Powered by: Four 1,200 hp Wright R-1820-97 Cyclone nine-cylinder radial engines, each driving an 11 ft 7 in (3.53 m) diameter three-blade propeller
Wing span: 103 ft 9¾ in (31.63 m)

Length: 74 ft 8⅞ in (22.78 m)
Wing area: 1,420.0 sq ft (131.92 m²)
Gross weight: 55,000 lb (24,948 kg)
Range: 1,300 miles (2,090 km) with 6,000-lb (2,722-kg) bomb load
Armament: Eight or nine 0.50-in Browning machine-guns—two each in forward dorsal, ventral and tail turrets, one each in nose, rear dorsal (optional) and beam positions; max short-range bomb load of 12,800 lb (5,806 kg) internally and 8,000 lb (3,629 kg) externally

Accommodation: Crew of 10
First flight: 28 July 1935
From the original Model 299 prototype to the final in-service models, total engine power of the Flying Fortress increased by 60 per cent, and progressive additions to the defensive armament reflected the heavy losses incurred over Europe before adequate fighter escort was provided for Eighth Air Force bombers carrying out daylight attacks. Data are for the B-17F version; the final production model, the B-17G, had two extra guns in a 'chin' turret, a feature added later to many of the B-17Fs in service.

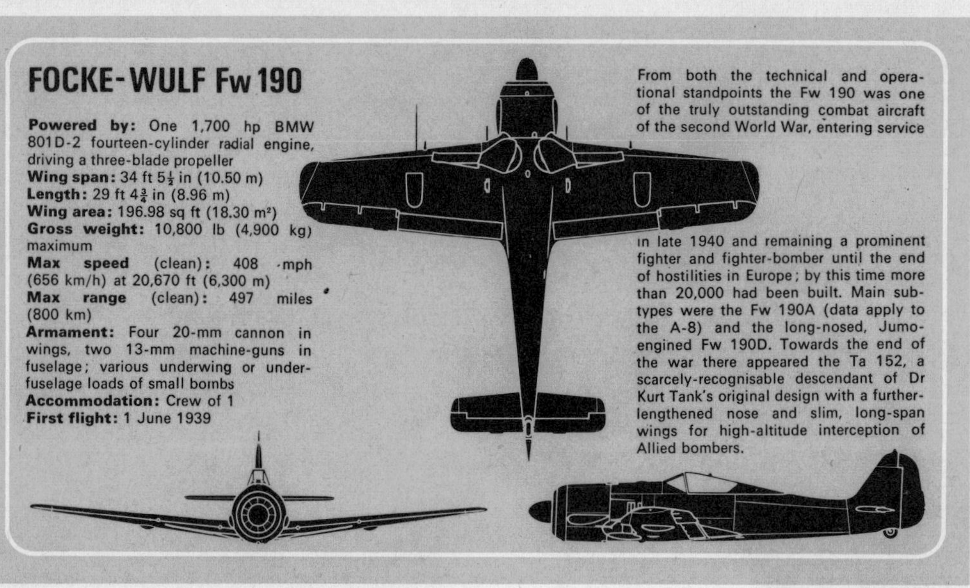

FOCKE-WULF Fw 190

Powered by: One 1,700 hp BMW 801D-2 fourteen-cylinder radial engine, driving a three-blade propeller
Wing span: 34 ft 5⅓ in (10.50 m)
Length: 29 ft 4⅔ in (8.96 m)
Wing area: 196.98 sq ft (18.30 m²)
Gross weight: 10,800 lb (4,900 kg) maximum
Max speed (clean): 408 mph (656 km/h) at 20,670 ft (6,300 m)
Max range (clean): 497 miles (800 km)
Armament: Four 20-mm cannon in wings, two 13-mm machine-guns in fuselage; various underwing or under-fuselage loads of small bombs
Accommodation: Crew of 1
First flight: 1 June 1939

From both the technical and operational standpoints the Fw 190 was one of the truly outstanding combat aircraft of the second World War, entering service in late 1940 and remaining a prominent fighter and fighter-bomber until the end of hostilities in Europe; by this time more than 20,000 had been built. Main subtypes were the Fw 190A (data apply to the A-8) and the long-nosed, Jumo-engined Fw 190D. Towards the end of the war there appeared the Ta 152, a scarcely-recognisable descendant of Dr Kurt Tank's original design with a further-lengthened nose and slim, long-span wings for high-altitude interception of Allied bombers.

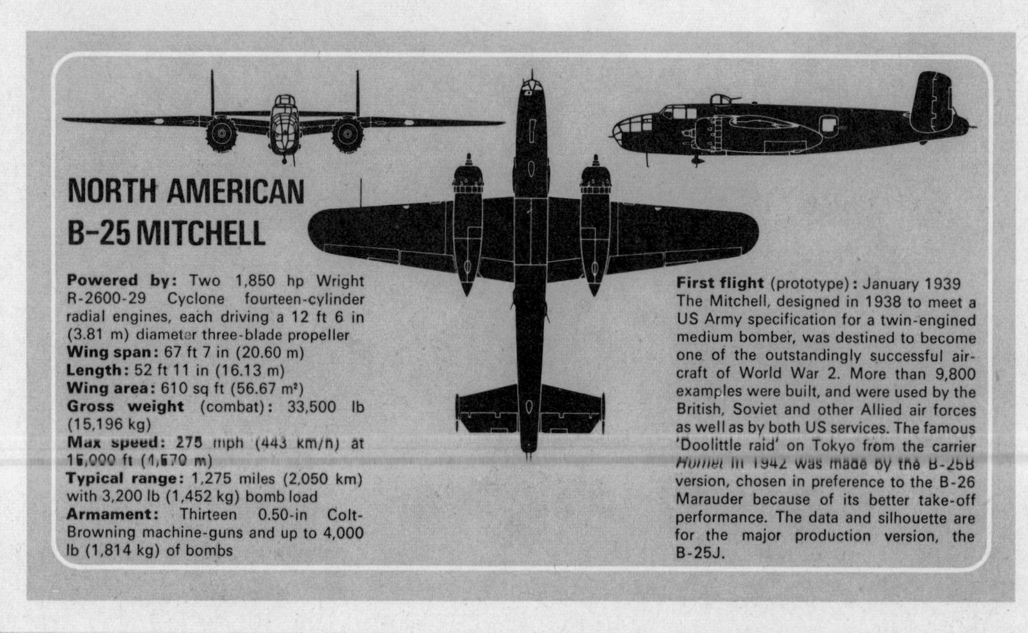

NORTH AMERICAN B-25 MITCHELL

Powered by: Two 1,850 hp Wright R-2600-29 Cyclone fourteen-cylinder radial engines, each driving a 12 ft 6 in (3.81 m) diameter three-blade propeller
Wing span: 67 ft 7 in (20.60 m)
Length: 52 ft 11 in (16.13 m)
Wing area: 610 sq ft (56.67 m²)
Gross weight (combat): 33,500 lb (15,196 kg)
Max speed: 275 mph (443 km/h) at 15,000 ft (4,570 m)
Typical range: 1,275 miles (2,050 km) with 3,200 lb (1,452 kg) bomb load
Armament: Thirteen 0.50-in Colt-Browning machine-guns and up to 4,000 lb (1,814 kg) of bombs

First flight (prototype): January 1939
The Mitchell, designed in 1938 to meet a US Army specification for a twin-engined medium bomber, was destined to become one of the outstandingly successful aircraft of World War 2. More than 9,800 examples were built, and were used by the British, Soviet and other Allied air forces as well as by both US services. The famous 'Doolittle raid' on Tokyo from the carrier *Hornet* in 1942 was made by the B-25B version, chosen in preference to the B-26 Marauder because of its better take-off performance. The data and silhouette are for the major production version, the B-25J.

Boeing B-17F Flying Fortress

Focke-Wulf Fw 190G-3

North American B-25H Mitchell

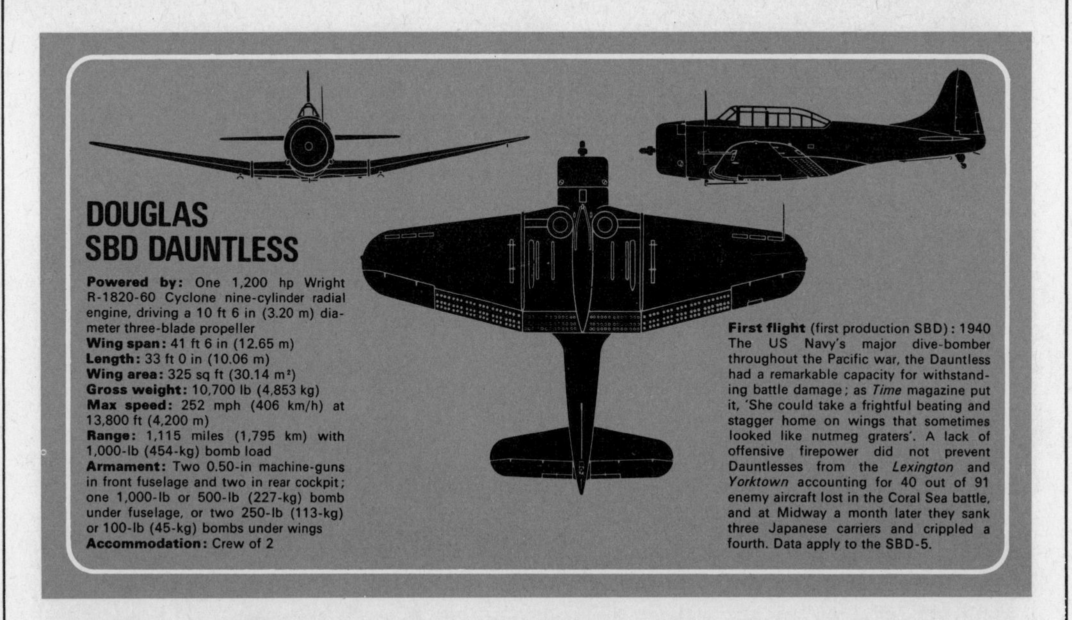

DOUGLAS SBD DAUNTLESS

Powered by: One 1,200 hp Wright R-1820-60 Cyclone nine-cylinder radial engine, driving a 10 ft 6 in (3.20 m) diameter three-blade propeller
Wing span: 41 ft 6 in (12.65 m)
Length: 33 ft 0 in (10.06 m)
Wing area: 325 sq ft (30.14 m²)
Gross weight: 10,700 lb (4,853 kg)
Max speed: 252 mph (406 km/h) at 13,800 ft (4,200 m)
Range: 1,115 miles (1,795 km) with 1,000-lb (454-kg) bomb load
Armament: Two 0.50-in machine-guns in front fuselage and two in rear cockpit; one 1,000-lb or 500-lb (227-kg) bomb under fuselage, or two 250-lb (113-kg) or 100-lb (45-kg) bombs under wings
Accommodation: Crew of 2

First flight (first production SBD): 1940
The US Navy's major dive-bomber throughout the Pacific war, the Dauntless had a remarkable capacity for withstanding battle damage; as *Time* magazine put it, 'She could take a frightful beating and stagger home on wings that sometimes looked like nutmeg graters'. A lack of offensive firepower did not prevent Dauntlesses from the *Lexington* and *Yorktown* accounting for 40 out of 91 enemy aircraft lost in the Coral Sea battle, and at Midway a month later they sank three Japanese carriers and crippled a fourth. Data apply to the SBD-5.

CHANCE VOUGHT F4U CORSAIR

Powered by: One 2,100 hp Pratt & Whitney R-2800-18W Double Wasp eighteen-cylinder radial engine, driving a 13 ft 2 in (4.01 m) diameter four-blade propeller
Wing span: 41 ft 0 in (12.50 m)
Length: 33 ft 8 in (10.26 m)
Wing area: 314 sq ft (29.17 m²)
Gross weight: 14,670 lb (6,654 kg)
Max speed: 446 mph (718 km/h) at 26,200 ft (8,535 m)
Range: 1,005 miles (1,617 km)
Armament: Six 0.50-in machine-guns in wings; two 1,000-lb (454-kg) bombs under fuselage
Accommodation: Crew of 1

First flight: 29 May 1940
First production US warplane to exceed 400 mph (644 km/h) in level flight, the Corsair became operational in the Pacific war from February 1943, subsequently serving with units of the US Navy, US Marine Corps, Fleet Air Arm and Royal New Zealand Air Force. Its distinctive engine note and high 'kill ratio' over enemy aircraft quickly earned it the nickname 'Whistling Death' from its Japanese opponents. The data and silhouette apply to the last major wartime variant, the F4U-4, but in all the Corsair remained in production for an 11-year period during which 12,571 of these fighters were built.

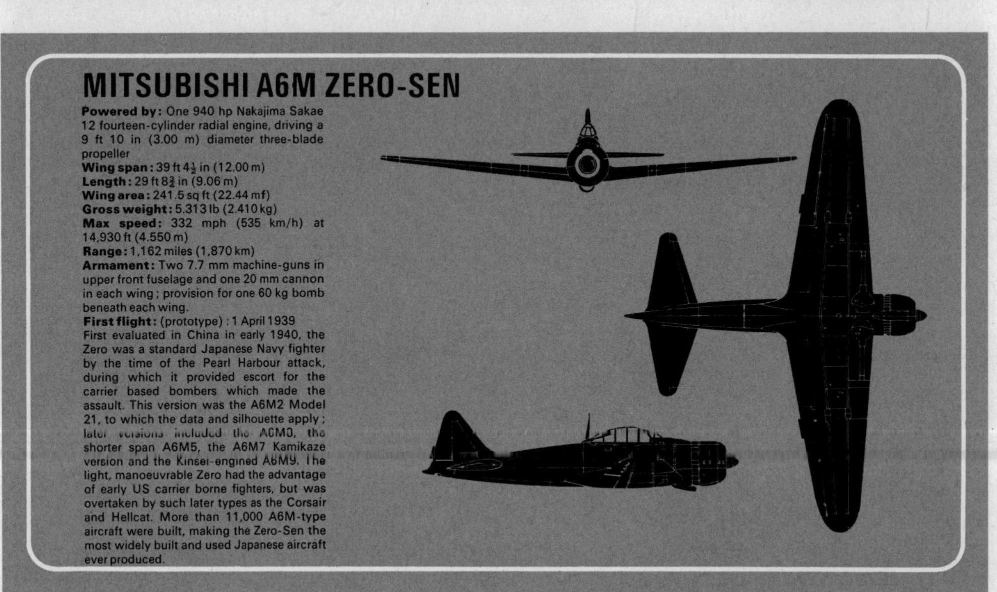

MITSUBISHI A6M ZERO-SEN

Powered by: One 940 hp Nakajima Sakae 12 fourteen-cylinder radial engine, driving a 9 ft 10 in (3.00 m) diameter three-blade propeller
Wing span: 39 ft 4½ in (12.00 m)
Length: 29 ft 8¾ in (9.06 m)
Wing area: 241.5 sq ft (22.44 mf)
Gross weight: 5.313 lb (2.410 kg)
Max speed: 332 mph (535 km/h) at 14,930 ft (4.550 m)
Range: 1,162 miles (1,870 km)
Armament: Two 7.7 mm machine-guns in upper front fuselage and one 20 mm cannon in each wing; provision for one 60 kg bomb beneath each wing.
First flight: (prototype): 1 April 1939
First evaluated in China in early 1940, the Zero was a standard Japanese Navy fighter by the time of the Pearl Harbour attack, during which it provided escort for the carrier based bombers which made the assault. This version was the A6M2 Model 21, to which the data and silhouette apply; later versions included the A6M3, the shorter span A6M5, the A6M7 Kamikaze version and the Kinsei-engined A6M9. The light, manoeuvrable Zero had the advantage of early US carrier borne fighters, but was overtaken by such later types as the Corsair and Hellcat. More than 11,000 A6M-type aircraft were built, making the Zero-Sen the most widely built and used Japanese aircraft ever produced.

Douglas SBD Dauntless

Chance Vought F4U-1D Corsair
(Charles E Brown)

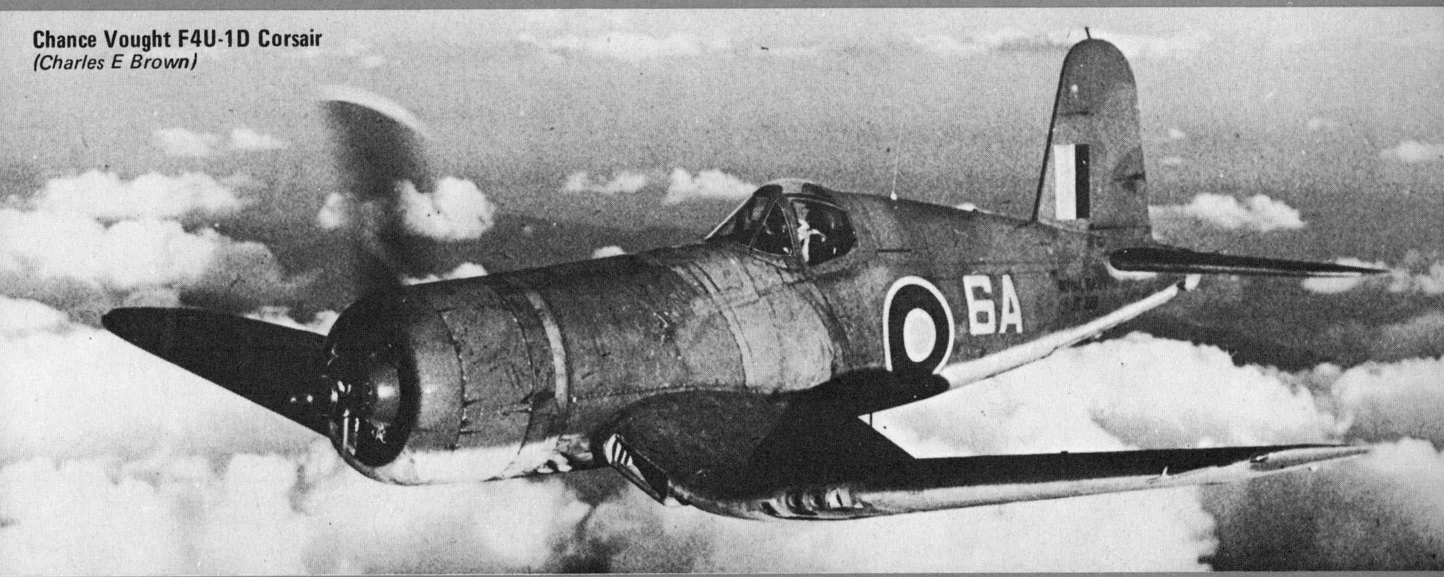

Mitsubishi A6M2 Zero-Sen, captured aircraft

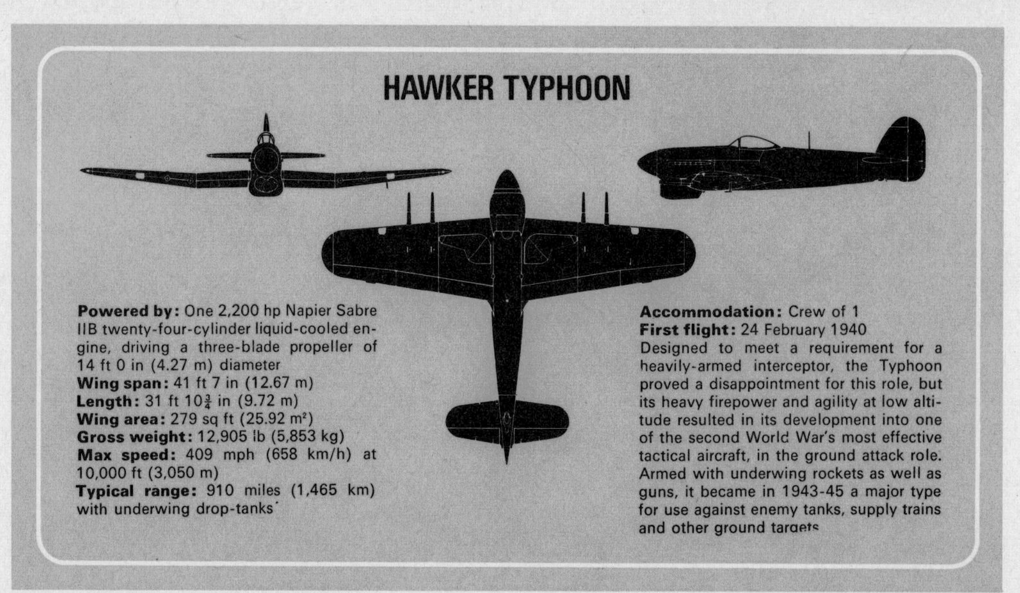

HAWKER TYPHOON

Powered by: One 2,200 hp Napier Sabre IIB twenty-four-cylinder liquid-cooled engine, driving a three-blade propeller of 14 ft 0 in (4.27 m) diameter
Wing span: 41 ft 7 in (12.67 m)
Length: 31 ft 10¾ in (9.72 m)
Wing area: 279 sq ft (25.92 m²)
Gross weight: 12,905 lb (5,853 kg)
Max speed: 409 mph (658 km/h) at 10,000 ft (3,050 m)
Typical range: 910 miles (1,465 km) with underwing drop-tanks

Accommodation: Crew of 1
First flight: 24 February 1940
Designed to meet a requirement for a heavily-armed interceptor, the Typhoon proved a disappointment for this role, but its heavy firepower and agility at low altitude resulted in its development into one of the second World War's most effective tactical aircraft, in the ground attack role. Armed with underwing rockets as well as guns, it became in 1943-45 a major type for use against enemy tanks, supply trains and other ground targets

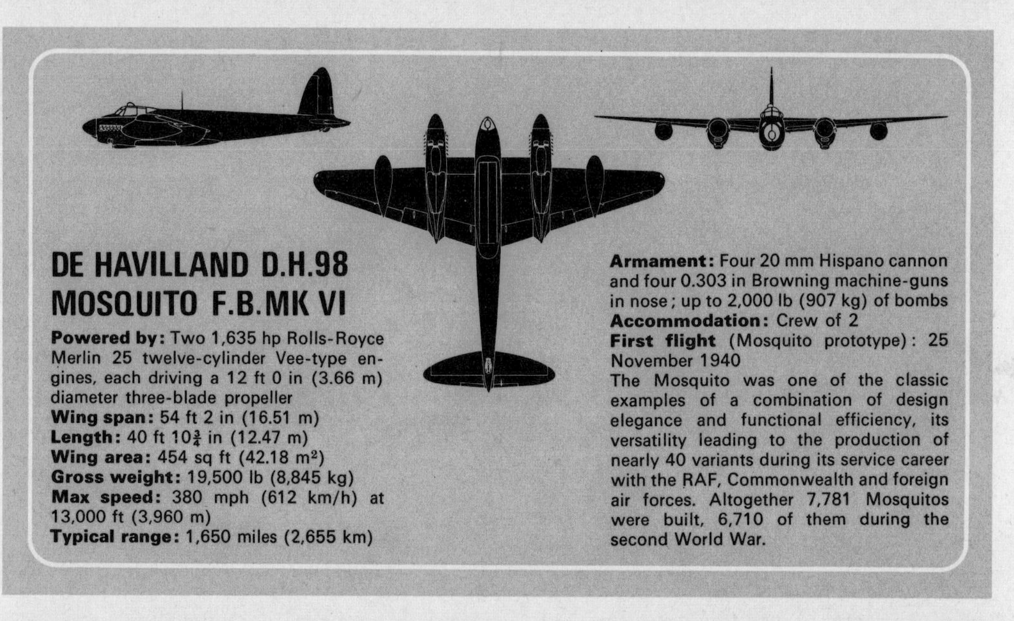

DE HAVILLAND D.H.98 MOSQUITO F.B.MK VI

Powered by: Two 1,635 hp Rolls-Royce Merlin 25 twelve-cylinder Vee-type engines, each driving a 12 ft 0 in (3.66 m) diameter three-blade propeller
Wing span: 54 ft 2 in (16.51 m)
Length: 40 ft 10¾ in (12.47 m)
Wing area: 454 sq ft (42.18 m²)
Gross weight: 19,500 lb (8,845 kg)
Max speed: 380 mph (612 km/h) at 13,000 ft (3,960 m)
Typical range: 1,650 miles (2,655 km)

Armament: Four 20 mm Hispano cannon and four 0.303 in Browning machine-guns in nose; up to 2,000 lb (907 kg) of bombs
Accommodation: Crew of 2
First flight (Mosquito prototype): 25 November 1940
The Mosquito was one of the classic examples of a combination of design elegance and functional efficiency, its versatility leading to the production of nearly 40 variants during its service career with the RAF, Commonwealth and foreign air forces. Altogether 7,781 Mosquitos were built, 6,710 of them during the second World War.

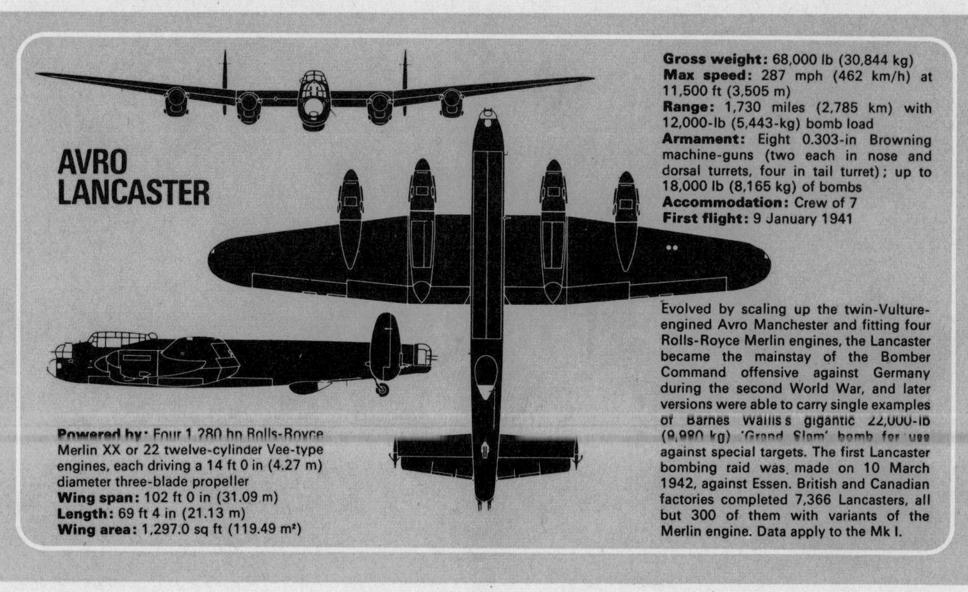

AVRO LANCASTER

Powered by: Four 1,280 hp Rolls-Royce Merlin XX or 22 twelve-cylinder Vee-type engines, each driving a 14 ft 0 in (4.27 m) diameter three-blade propeller
Wing span: 102 ft 0 in (31.09 m)
Length: 69 ft 4 in (21.13 m)
Wing area: 1,297.0 sq ft (119.49 m²)
Gross weight: 68,000 lb (30,844 kg)
Max speed: 287 mph (462 km/h) at 11,500 ft (3,505 m)
Range: 1,730 miles (2,785 km) with 12,000-lb (5,443-kg) bomb load
Armament: Eight 0.303-in Browning machine-guns (two each in nose and dorsal turrets, four in tail turret); up to 18,000 lb (8,165 kg) of bombs
Accommodation: Crew of 7
First flight: 9 January 1941

Evolved by scaling up the twin-Vulture-engined Avro Manchester and fitting four Rolls-Royce Merlin engines, the Lancaster became the mainstay of the Bomber Command offensive against Germany during the second World War, and later versions were able to carry single examples of Barnes Wallis's gigantic 22,000-lb (9,980 kg) 'Grand Slam' bomb for use against special targets. The first Lancaster bombing raid was made on 10 March 1942, against Essen. British and Canadian factories completed 7,366 Lancasters, all but 300 of them with variants of the Merlin engine. Data apply to the Mk I.

Hawker Typhoon IB

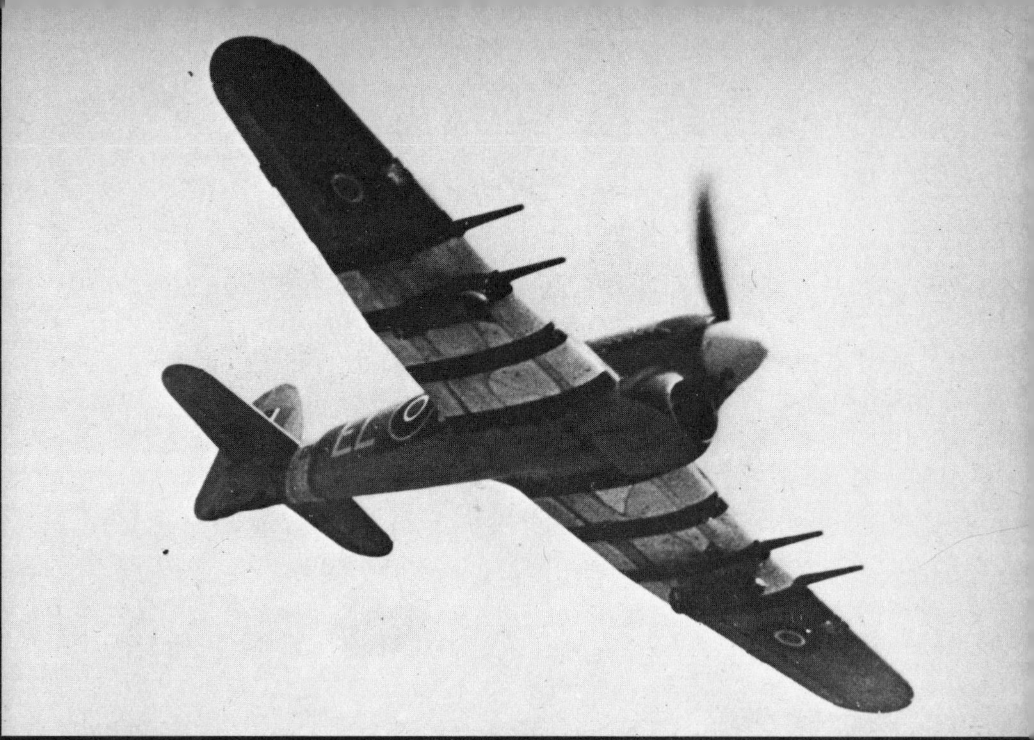

de Havilland Mosquito IV

Avro Lancaster I

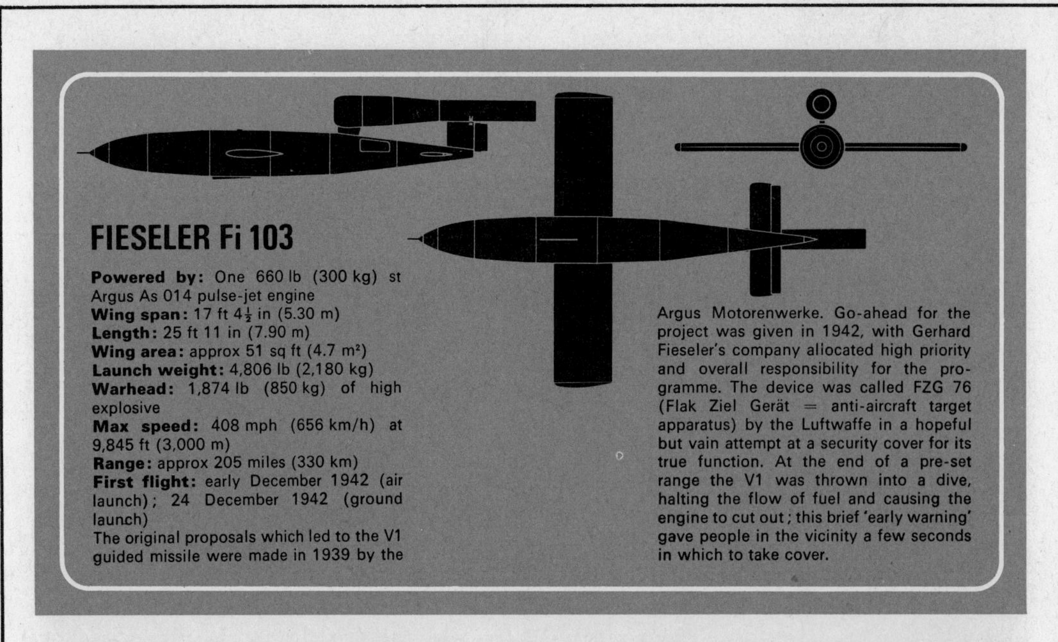

FIESELER Fi 103

Powered by: One 660 lb (300 kg) st Argus As 014 pulse-jet engine
Wing span: 17 ft 4½ in (5.30 m)
Length: 25 ft 11 in (7.90 m)
Wing area: approx 51 sq ft (4.7 m²)
Launch weight: 4,806 lb (2,180 kg)
Warhead: 1,874 lb (850 kg) of high explosive
Max speed: 408 mph (656 km/h) at 9,845 ft (3,000 m)
Range: approx 205 miles (330 km)
First flight: early December 1942 (air launch); 24 December 1942 (ground launch)

The original proposals which led to the V1 guided missile were made in 1939 by the Argus Motorenwerke. Go-ahead for the project was given in 1942, with Gerhard Fieseler's company allocated high priority and overall responsibility for the programme. The device was called FZG 76 (Flak Ziel Gerät = anti-aircraft target apparatus) by the Luftwaffe in a hopeful but vain attempt at a security cover for its true function. At the end of a pre-set range the V1 was thrown into a dive, halting the flow of fuel and causing the engine to cut out; this brief 'early warning' gave people in the vicinity a few seconds in which to take cover.

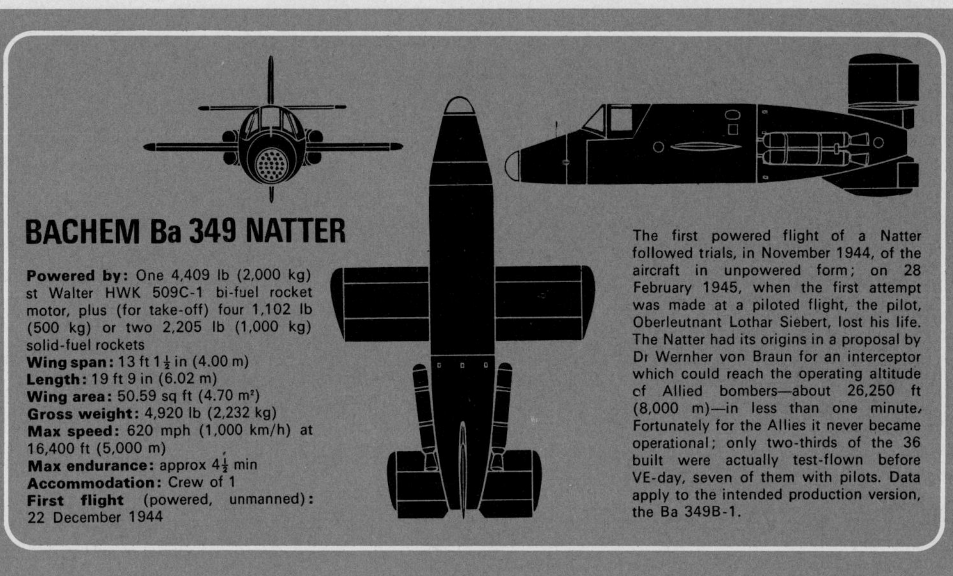

BACHEM Ba 349 NATTER

Powered by: One 4,409 lb (2,000 kg) st Walter HWK 509C-1 bi-fuel rocket motor, plus (for take-off) four 1,102 lb (500 kg) or two 2,205 lb (1,000 kg) solid-fuel rockets
Wing span: 13 ft 1½ in (4.00 m)
Length: 19 ft 9 in (6.02 m)
Wing area: 50.59 sq ft (4.70 m²)
Gross weight: 4,920 lb (2,232 kg)
Max speed: 620 mph (1,000 km/h) at 16,400 ft (5,000 m)
Max endurance: approx 4½ min
Accommodation: Crew of 1
First flight (powered, unmanned): 22 December 1944

The first powered flight of a Natter followed trials, in November 1944, of the aircraft in unpowered form; on 28 February 1945, when the first attempt was made at a piloted flight, the pilot, Oberleutnant Lothar Siebert, lost his life. The Natter had its origins in a proposal by Dr Wernher von Braun for an interceptor which could reach the operating altitude of Allied bombers—about 26,250 ft (8,000 m)—in less than one minute. Fortunately for the Allies it never became operational; only two-thirds of the 36 built were actually test-flown before VE-day, seven of them with pilots. Data apply to the intended production version, the Ba 349B-1.

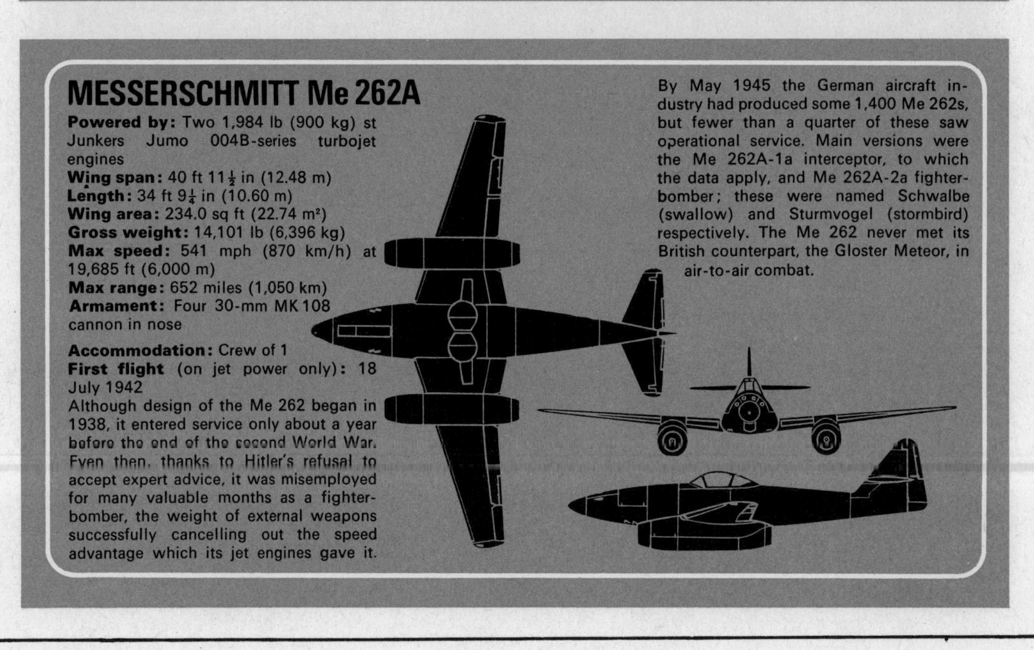

MESSERSCHMITT Me 262A

Powered by: Two 1,984 lb (900 kg) st Junkers Jumo 004B-series turbojet engines
Wing span: 40 ft 11½ in (12.48 m)
Length: 34 ft 9½ in (10.60 m)
Wing area: 234.0 sq ft (22.74 m²)
Gross weight: 14,101 lb (6,396 kg)
Max speed: 541 mph (870 km/h) at 19,685 ft (6,000 m)
Max range: 652 miles (1,050 km)
Armament: Four 30-mm MK 108 cannon in nose
Accommodation: Crew of 1
First flight (on jet power only): 18 July 1942

Although design of the Me 262 began in 1938, it entered service only about a year before the end of the second World War. Even then, thanks to Hitler's refusal to accept expert advice, it was misemployed for many valuable months as a fighter-bomber, the weight of external weapons successfully cancelling out the speed advantage which its jet engines gave it.

By May 1945 the German aircraft industry had produced some 1,400 Me 262s, but fewer than a quarter of these saw operational service. Main versions were the Me 262A-1a interceptor, to which the data apply, and Me 262A-2a fighter-bomber; these were named Schwalbe (swallow) and Sturmvogel (stormbird) respectively. The Me 262 never met its British counterpart, the Gloster Meteor, in air-to-air combat.

V1 'flying bomb'

Bachem Ba 349 Natter on its launching ramp

Messerschmitt Me 262A-1a

BOEING B-29 SUPERFORTRESS

Powered by: Four 2,200 hp Wright R-3350-57 or -83 Double Cyclone eighteen-cylinder radial engines, each driving a four-blade propeller
Wing span: 141 ft 3 in (43.05 m)
Length: 120 ft 1 in (36.60 m)
Wing area: 1,739 sq ft (161.56 m²)
Gross weight: 138,500 lb (62,823 kg)
Max speed: 400 mph (644 km/h) at 30,000 ft (9,145 m)
Range: 2,300 miles (3,700 km)
Accommodation: Crew of 10
First flight (XB-29) : 21 September 1942

During the course of its long and effective career, the B-29 Superfortress could claim a number of impressive 'firsts' of one kind or another. Not least among these was the fact that it was the first aircraft to go into wide-scale service as a flight refuelling tanker: to fulfil this role for the post-war United States Air Force, 92 Superfortresses were converted as KB-29M hose tankers and an additional 116 as KB-29P 'flying boom' tankers. Data apply to the latter version.

GLOSTER METEOR I

Powered by: Two 1,700 lb (771 kg) st Rolls-Royce W.2B/23 Welland Series 1 turbojet engines
Wing span: 43 ft 0 in (13.11 m)
Length: 41 ft 3 in (12.57 m)
Wing area: 374.0 sq ft (34.75 m²)
Gross weight: 11,755 lb (5,332 kg)
Max speed: 420 mph (676 km/h) at 30,000 ft (9,145 m)
Endurance: 1 hr 15 min
Armament: Four 20-mm Hispano cannon in nose
Accommodation: Crew of 1
First flight: 5 March 1943

The Meteor fighter was designed to Air Ministry Specification F.9/40, the first official British requirement to be issued for a single-seat interceptor powered by gas-turbine engines. After completing eight prototypes, Gloster built 20 examples of the Mk I, of which 16 were delivered to the RAF. Their first operational success came on 4 August 1944, when Meteors from No 616 Squadron destroyed two V1 flying bombs over southern England—the first of many of these weapons to be brought down by the new fighters. Major wartime version was the Mk III (280 built), most of which had more powerful Rolls-Royce Derwent engines, giving them a maximum speed of 493 mph (793 km/h) at 30,000 ft (9,145 m). The silhouette shows the Mk III.

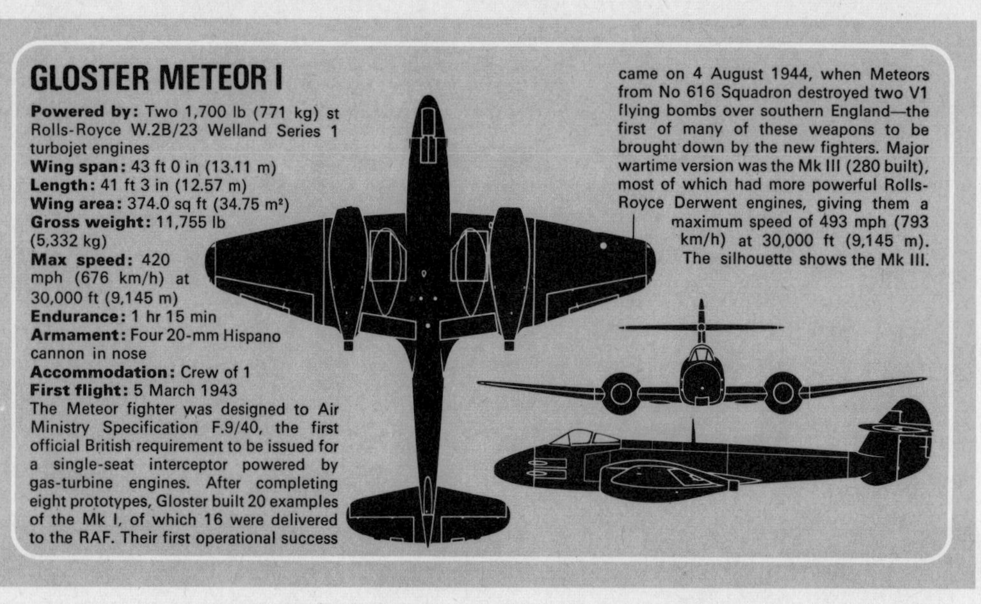

GRUMMAN F8F-2 BEARCAT

Powered by: One 2,500 hp Pratt & Whitney R-2800-34W Double Wasp radial piston-engine
Wing span: 35 ft 10 in (10.92 m)
Length: 28 ft 3 in (8.61 m)
Gross weight: 9,390 lb (4,259 kg)
Max speed: 447 mph (719 km/h) at 28,000 ft (8,534 m)
Accommodation: Crew of 1
Armament: Two 0.50-in Colt-Browning machine-guns in each wing; provision for two 1,000 lb (454 kg) bombs underwing
Typical range: 1,650 miles (2,655 km)
First flight: 21 August 1944

So outstanding was the Bearcat fighter that over 2,000 were ordered within two months of its first flight, though end-of-war cancellations reduced the total actually built to 1,268. They equipped 28 US Navy squadrons, and in 1954 those used by the French in Indochina became the first combat aircraft of the present Vietnam Air Force. Data are for the standard F8F-2; Darryl Greenamyer's specially-stripped Bearcat (shown in silhouette), which broke the 30-year-old World Speed Record on 16 August 1969, reached an average of 483.041 mph (777.384 km/h).

Boeing B-29A Superfortress

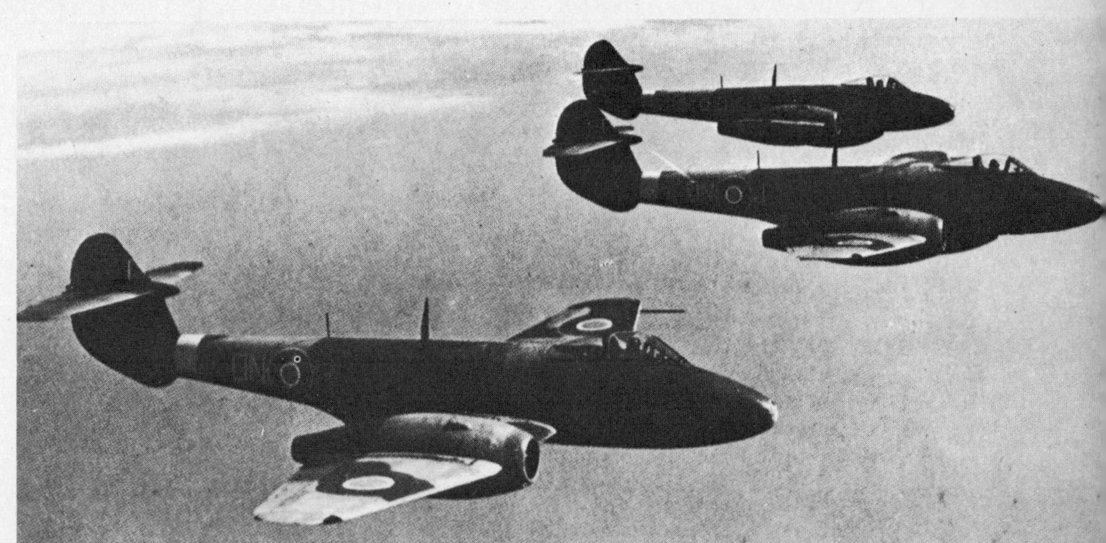

Gloster Meteor Mk IIIs

Grumman F8F-2 Bearcat

DOUGLAS DC-4

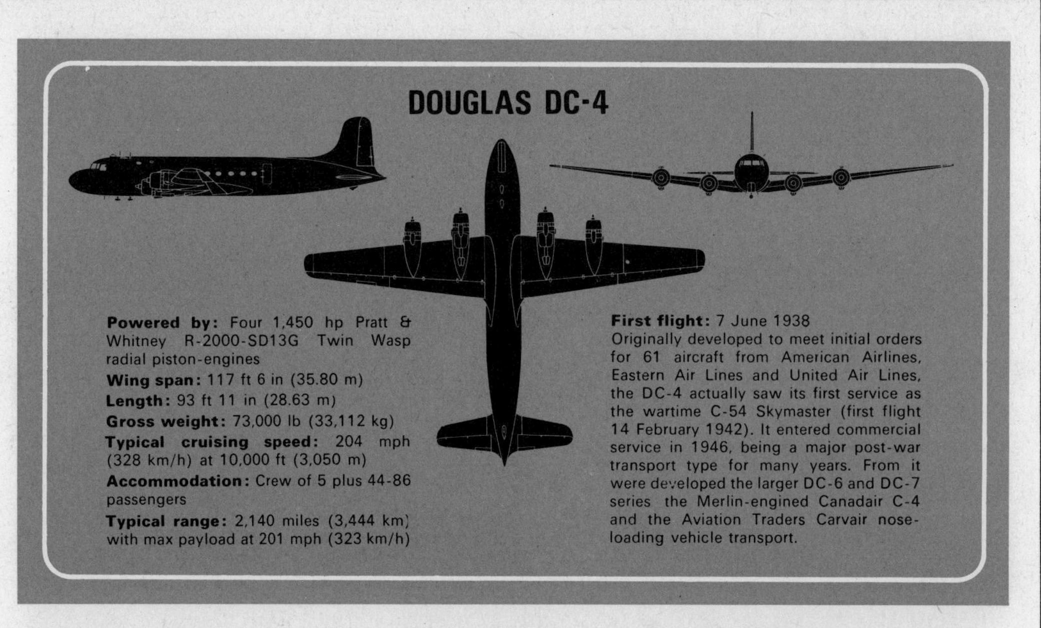

Powered by: Four 1,450 hp Pratt & Whitney R-2000-SD13G Twin Wasp radial piston-engines
Wing span: 117 ft 6 in (35.80 m)
Length: 93 ft 11 in (28.63 m)
Gross weight: 73,000 lb (33,112 kg)
Typical cruising speed: 204 mph (328 km/h) at 10,000 ft (3,050 m)
Accommodation: Crew of 5 plus 44-86 passengers
Typical range: 2,140 miles (3,444 km) with max payload at 201 mph (323 km/h)

First flight: 7 June 1938
Originally developed to meet initial orders for 61 aircraft from American Airlines, Eastern Air Lines and United Air Lines, the DC-4 actually saw its first service as the wartime C-54 Skymaster (first flight 14 February 1942). It entered commercial service in 1946, being a major post-war transport type for many years. From it were developed the larger DC-6 and DC-7 series the Merlin-engined Canadair C-4 and the Aviation Traders Carvair nose-loading vehicle transport.

AVRO YORK

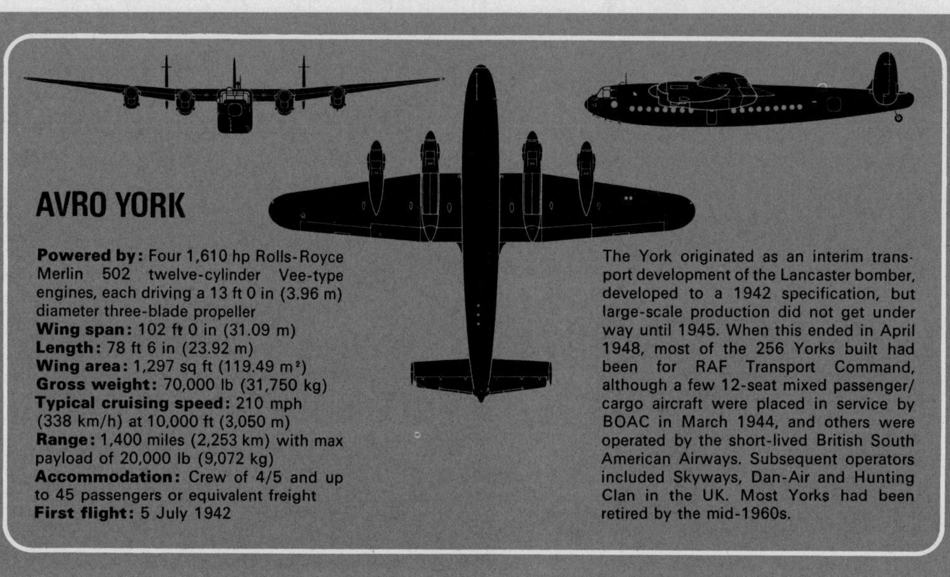

Powered by: Four 1,610 hp Rolls-Royce Merlin 502 twelve-cylinder Vee-type engines, each driving a 13 ft 0 in (3.96 m) diameter three-blade propeller
Wing span: 102 ft 0 in (31.09 m)
Length: 78 ft 6 in (23.92 m)
Wing area: 1,297 sq ft (119.49 m²)
Gross weight: 70,000 lb (31,750 kg)
Typical cruising speed: 210 mph (338 km/h) at 10,000 ft (3,050 m)
Range: 1,400 miles (2,253 km) with max payload of 20,000 lb (9,072 kg)
Accommodation: Crew of 4/5 and up to 45 passengers or equivalent freight
First flight: 5 July 1942

The York originated as an interim transport development of the Lancaster bomber, developed to a 1942 specification, but large-scale production did not get under way until 1945. When this ended in April 1948, most of the 256 Yorks built had been for RAF Transport Command, although a few 12-seat mixed passenger/cargo aircraft were placed in service by BOAC in March 1944, and others were operated by the short-lived British South American Airways. Subsequent operators included Skyways, Dan-Air and Hunting Clan in the UK. Most Yorks had been retired by the mid-1960s.

LOCKHEED CONSTELLATION

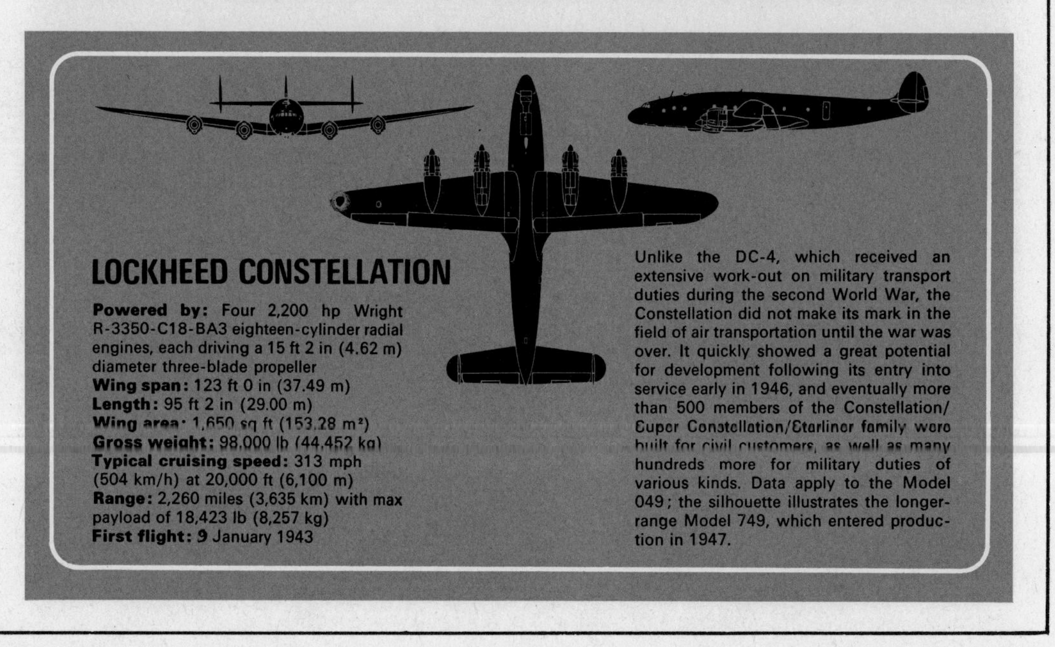

Powered by: Four 2,200 hp Wright R-3350-C18-BA3 eighteen-cylinder radial engines, each driving a 15 ft 2 in (4.62 m) diameter three-blade propeller
Wing span: 123 ft 0 in (37.49 m)
Length: 95 ft 2 in (29.00 m)
Wing area: 1,650 sq ft (153.28 m²)
Gross weight: 98,000 lb (44,452 kg)
Typical cruising speed: 313 mph (504 km/h) at 20,000 ft (6,100 m)
Range: 2,260 miles (3,635 km) with max payload of 18,423 lb (8,257 kg)
First flight: 9 January 1943

Unlike the DC-4, which received an extensive work-out on military transport duties during the second World War, the Constellation did not make its mark in the field of air transportation until the war was over. It quickly showed a great potential for development following its entry into service early in 1946, and eventually more than 500 members of the Constellation/Super Constellation/Starliner family were built for civil customers, as well as many hundreds more for military duties of various kinds. Data apply to the Model 049; the silhouette illustrates the longer-range Model 749, which entered production in 1947.

Douglas DC-4

Avro York

Lockheed Constellation with 'Speedpak' ventral freight container

VICKERS VIKING

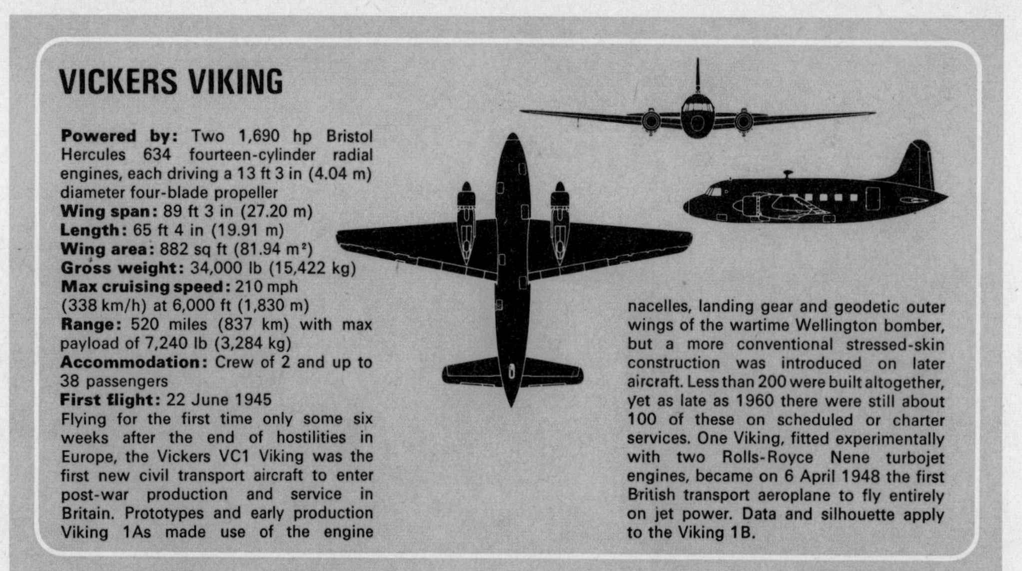

Powered by: Two 1,690 hp Bristol Hercules 634 fourteen-cylinder radial engines, each driving a 13 ft 3 in (4.04 m) diameter four-blade propeller
Wing span: 89 ft 3 in (27.20 m)
Length: 65 ft 4 in (19.91 m)
Wing area: 882 sq ft (81.94 m²)
Gross weight: 34,000 lb (15,422 kg)
Max cruising speed: 210 mph (338 km/h) at 6,000 ft (1,830 m)
Range: 520 miles (837 km) with max payload of 7,240 lb (3,284 kg)
Accommodation: Crew of 2 and up to 38 passengers
First flight: 22 June 1945

Flying for the first time only some six weeks after the end of hostilities in Europe, the Vickers VC1 Viking was the first new civil transport aircraft to enter post-war production and service in Britain. Prototypes and early production Viking 1As made use of the engine nacelles, landing gear and geodetic outer wings of the wartime Wellington bomber, but a more conventional stressed-skin construction was introduced on later aircraft. Less than 200 were built altogether, yet as late as 1960 there were still about 100 of these on scheduled or charter services. One Viking, fitted experimentally with two Rolls-Royce Nene turbojet engines, became on 6 April 1948 the first British transport aeroplane to fly entirely on jet power. Data and silhouette apply to the Viking 1B.

BRISTOL 170 FREIGHTER Mk 32

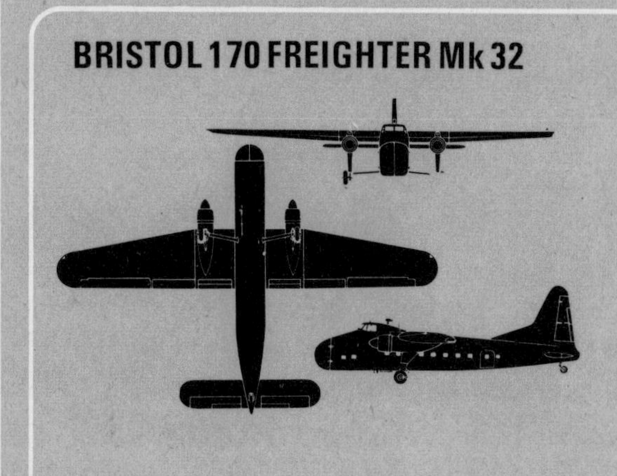

Powered by: Two 1,980 hp Bristol Siddeley Hercules 734 fourteen-cylinder radial air-cooled engines, each driving a four-blade propeller of 14 ft 0 in (4.27 m) diameter
Wing span: 108 ft 0 in (32.92 m)
Length: 73 ft 8 in (22.45 m)
Wing area: 1,487 sq ft (138.14 m²)
Gross weight: 44,000 lb (19,958 kg)
Cruising speed: 164 mph (264 km/h) at 5,000 ft (1,524 m)
Typical range: 820 miles (1,320 km) with 12,000 lb (5,443 kg) payload
Accommodation: Crew of 3 plus 12-20 passengers and up to 3 cars
First flight: 2 December 1945

The original short-nosed Bristol 170 was designed in 1944-45 as a military freighter and ambulance and was remodelled for civil use after the second World War. Initially it was produced as a freighter and as a 32-seat passenger transport known as the Wayfarer. On 13 July 1948 it flew the first cross-Channel car ferry for Silver City Airways, the role in which it was primarily employed for the rest of its career.

BEECHCRAFT BONANZA

Powered by: One 285 hp Continental IO-520-B six-cylinder horizontally-opposed engine, driving a 7 ft 0 in (2.13 m) diameter two-blade metal propeller
Wing span: 33 ft 5½ in (10.20 m)
Length: 26 ft 4½ in (8.04 m)
Wing area: 181.0 sq ft (16.80 m²)
Gross weight: 3,400 lb (1,542 kg)
Max cruising speed: 203 mph (327 km/h) at 6,500 ft (1,980 m)
Typical range: 600 miles (965 km)
Accommodation: Crew of 1 and up to 5 passengers
First flight: 22 December 1945

In continuous production since 1947, the little Beechcraft Bonanza, with its distinctive 'butterfly' Vee tail, is one of the longest-lived private aircraft still being sold; in 1971 total sales were close to the 10,000 mark and showed little sign of abating: ample evidence that its name was well chosen! Engine power has been steadily advanced from the 165 hp of the original prototype, and interior furnishings, baggage capacity and other features have been improved to keep the Bonanza competitive against the almost bewildering variety of rival aircraft that have appeared during its more than 20 years of production life. In addition to this prodigious production, the Bonanza also provided the foundation for the design of the conventional-tailed T-34 Mentor, for many years a primary trainer for the US and foreign services.

Vickers Viking

Bristol Freighter Mk 32

Beechcraft Model V35B Bonanza

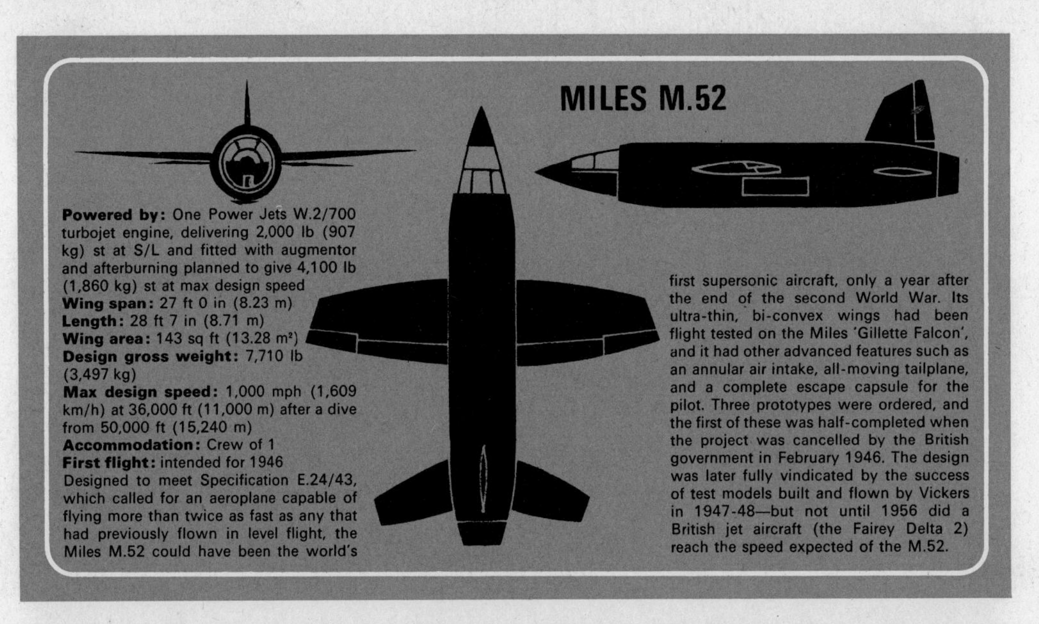

MILES M.52

Powered by: One Power Jets W.2/700 turbojet engine, delivering 2,000 lb (907 kg) st at S/L and fitted with augmentor and afterburning planned to give 4,100 lb (1,860 kg) st at max design speed
Wing span: 27 ft 0 in (8.23 m)
Length: 28 ft 7 in (8.71 m)
Wing area: 143 sq ft (13.28 m²)
Design gross weight: 7,710 lb (3,497 kg)
Max design speed: 1,000 mph (1,609 km/h) at 36,000 ft (11,000 m) after a dive from 50,000 ft (15,240 m)
Accommodation: Crew of 1
First flight: intended for 1946

Designed to meet Specification E.24/43, which called for an aeroplane capable of flying more than twice as fast as any that had previously flown in level flight, the Miles M.52 could have been the world's first supersonic aircraft, only a year after the end of the second World War. Its ultra-thin, bi-convex wings had been flight tested on the Miles 'Gillette Falcon', and it had other advanced features such as an annular air intake, all-moving tailplane, and a complete escape capsule for the pilot. Three prototypes were ordered, and the first of these was half-completed when the project was cancelled by the British government in February 1946. The design was later fully vindicated by the success of test models built and flown by Vickers in 1947-48—but not until 1956 did a British jet aircraft (the Fairey Delta 2) reach the speed expected of the M.52.

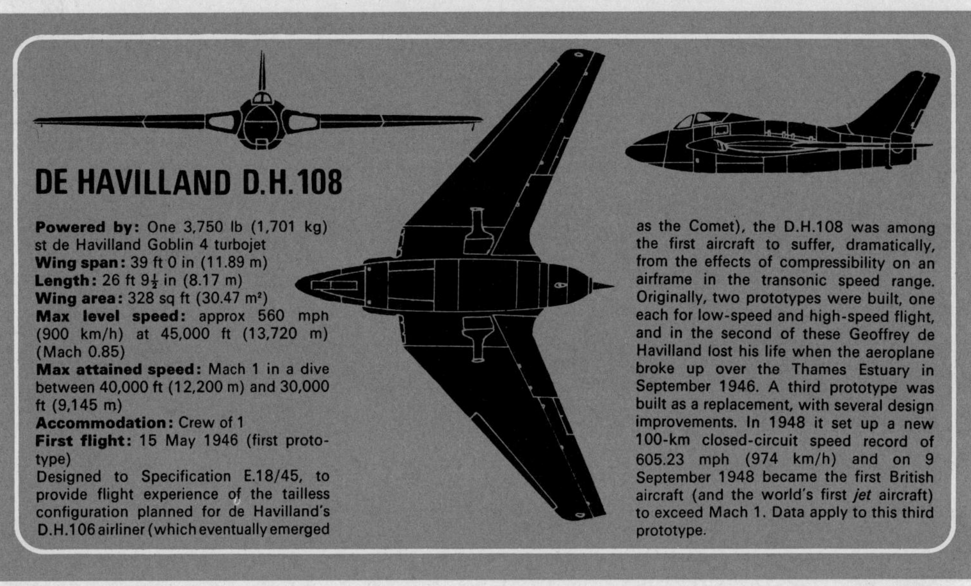

DE HAVILLAND D.H.108

Powered by: One 3,750 lb (1,701 kg) st de Havilland Goblin 4 turbojet
Wing span: 39 ft 0 in (11.89 m)
Length: 26 ft 9½ in (8.17 m)
Wing area: 328 sq ft (30.47 m²)
Max level speed: approx 560 mph (900 km/h) at 45,000 ft (13,720 m) (Mach 0.85)
Max attained speed: Mach 1 in a dive between 40,000 ft (12,200 m) and 30,000 ft (9,145 m)
Accommodation: Crew of 1
First flight: 15 May 1946 (first prototype)

Designed to Specification E.18/45, to provide flight experience of the tailless configuration planned for de Havilland's D.H.106 airliner (which eventually emerged as the Comet), the D.H.108 was among the first aircraft to suffer, dramatically, from the effects of compressibility on an airframe in the transonic speed range. Originally, two prototypes were built, one each for low-speed and high-speed flight, and in the second of these Geoffrey de Havilland lost his life when the aeroplane broke up over the Thames Estuary in September 1946. A third prototype was built as a replacement, with several design improvements. In 1948 it set up a new 100-km closed-circuit speed record of 605.23 mph (974 km/h) and on 9 September 1948 became the first British aircraft (and the world's first *jet* aircraft) to exceed Mach 1. Data apply to this third prototype.

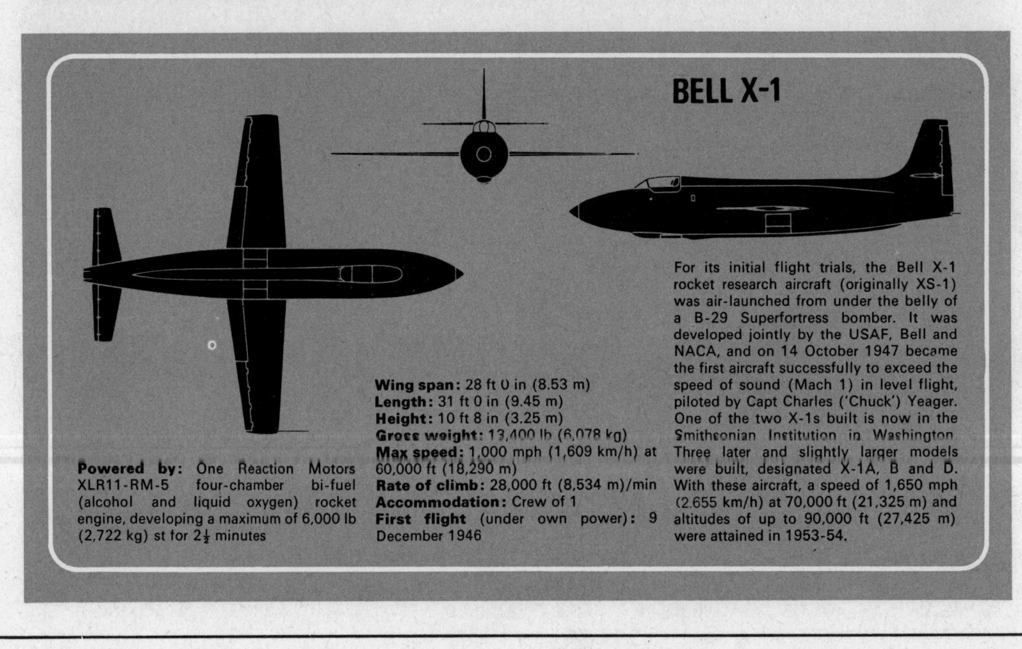

BELL X-1

Powered by: One Reaction Motors XLR11-RM-5 four-chamber bi-fuel (alcohol and liquid oxygen) rocket engine, developing a maximum of 6,000 lb (2,722 kg) st for 2½ minutes
Wing span: 28 ft 0 in (8.53 m)
Length: 31 ft 0 in (9.45 m)
Height: 10 ft 8 in (3.25 m)
Gross weight: 13,400 lb (6,078 kg)
Max speed: 1,000 mph (1,609 km/h) at 60,000 ft (18,290 m)
Rate of climb: 28,000 ft (8,534 m)/min
Accommodation: Crew of 1
First flight (under own power): 9 December 1946

For its initial flight trials, the Bell X-1 rocket research aircraft (originally XS-1) was air-launched from under the belly of a B-29 Superfortress bomber. It was developed jointly by the USAF, Bell and NACA, and on 14 October 1947 became the first aircraft successfully to exceed the speed of sound (Mach 1) in level flight, piloted by Capt Charles ('Chuck') Yeager. One of the two X-1s built is now in the Smithsonian Institution in Washington. Three later and slightly larger models were built, designated X-1A, B and D. With these aircraft, a speed of 1,650 mph (2,655 km/h) at 70,000 ft (21,325 m) and altitudes of up to 90,000 ft (27,425 m) were attained in 1953-54.

Model of the Miles M.52

Third prototype de Havilland D.H.108

One of the original pair of Bell X-1s

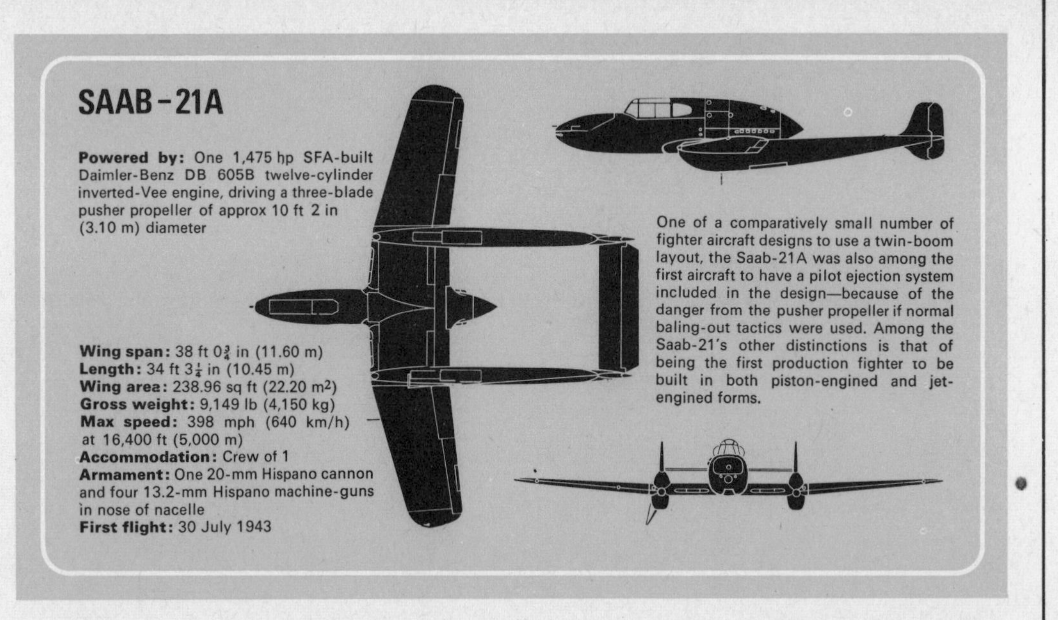

SAAB-21A

Powered by: One 1,475 hp SFA-built Daimler-Benz DB 605B twelve-cylinder inverted-Vee engine, driving a three-blade pusher propeller of approx 10 ft 2 in (3.10 m) diameter

Wing span: 38 ft 0¾ in (11.60 m)
Length: 34 ft 3¼ in (10.45 m)
Wing area: 238.96 sq ft (22.20 m²)
Gross weight: 9,149 lb (4,150 kg)
Max speed: 398 mph (640 km/h) at 16,400 ft (5,000 m)
Accommodation: Crew of 1
Armament: One 20-mm Hispano cannon and four 13.2-mm Hispano machine-guns in nose of nacelle
First flight: 30 July 1943

One of a comparatively small number of fighter aircraft designs to use a twin-boom layout, the Saab-21A was also among the first aircraft to have a pilot ejection system included in the design—because of the danger from the pusher propeller if normal baling-out tactics were used. Among the Saab-21's other distinctions is that of being the first production fighter to be built in both piston-engined and jet-engined forms.

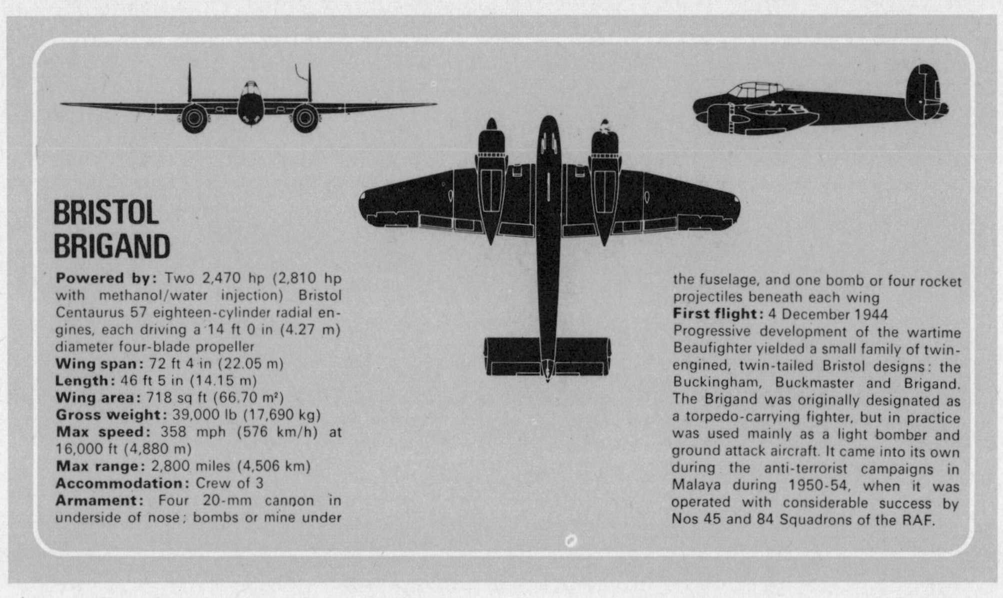

BRISTOL BRIGAND

Powered by: Two 2,470 hp (2,810 hp with methanol/water injection) Bristol Centaurus 57 eighteen-cylinder radial engines, each driving a 14 ft 0 in (4.27 m) diameter four-blade propeller
Wing span: 72 ft 4 in (22.05 m)
Length: 46 ft 5 in (14.15 m)
Wing area: 718 sq ft (66.70 m²)
Gross weight: 39,000 lb (17,690 kg)
Max speed: 358 mph (576 km/h) at 16,000 ft (4,880 m)
Max range: 2,800 miles (4,506 km)
Accommodation: Crew of 3
Armament: Four 20-mm cannon in underside of nose; bombs or mine under the fuselage, and one bomb or four rocket projectiles beneath each wing
First flight: 4 December 1944

Progressive development of the wartime Beaufighter yielded a small family of twin-engined, twin-tailed Bristol designs: the Buckingham, Buckmaster and Brigand. The Brigand was originally designated as a torpedo-carrying fighter, but in practice was used mainly as a light bomber and ground attack aircraft. It came into its own during the anti-terrorist campaigns in Malaya during 1950-54, when it was operated with considerable success by Nos 45 and 84 Squadrons of the RAF.

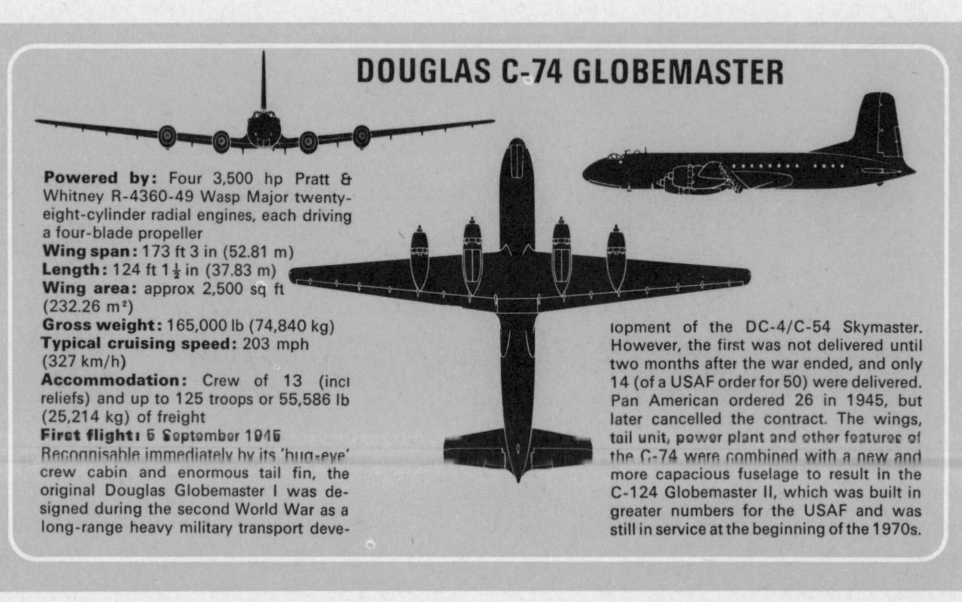

DOUGLAS C-74 GLOBEMASTER

Powered by: Four 3,500 hp Pratt & Whitney R-4360-49 Wasp Major twenty-eight-cylinder radial engines, each driving a four-blade propeller
Wing span: 173 ft 3 in (52.81 m)
Length: 124 ft 1½ in (37.83 m)
Wing area: approx 2,500 sq ft (232.26 m²)
Gross weight: 165,000 lb (74,840 kg)
Typical cruising speed: 203 mph (327 km/h)
Accommodation: Crew of 13 (incl reliefs) and up to 125 troops or 55,586 lb (25,214 kg) of freight
First flight: 5 September 1945

Recognisable immediately by its 'bug-eye' crew cabin and enormous tail fin, the original Douglas Globemaster I was designed during the second World War as a long-range heavy military transport development of the DC-4/C-54 Skymaster. However, the first was not delivered until two months after the war ended, and only 14 (of a USAF order for 50) were delivered. Pan American ordered 26 in 1945, but later cancelled the contract. The wings, tail unit, power plant and other features of the C-74 were combined with a new and more capacious fuselage to result in the C-124 Globemaster II, which was built in greater numbers for the USAF and was still in service at the beginning of the 1970s.

Saab-21A

Bristol Brigand B Mk 1

Douglas C-74 Globemaster I

DOUGLAS A-1 SKYRAIDER

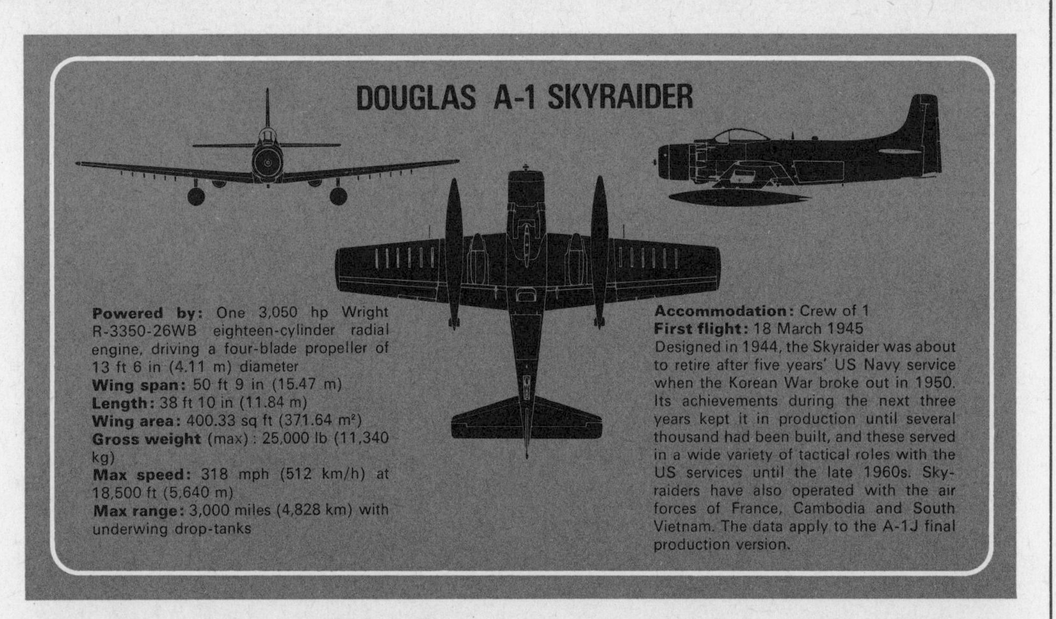

Powered by: One 3,050 hp Wright R-3350-26WB eighteen-cylinder radial engine, driving a four-blade propeller of 13 ft 6 in (4.11 m) diameter
Wing span: 50 ft 9 in (15.47 m)
Length: 38 ft 10 in (11.84 m)
Wing area: 400.33 sq ft (371.64 m²)
Gross weight (max): 25,000 lb (11,340 kg)
Max speed: 318 mph (512 km/h) at 18,500 ft (5,640 m)
Max range: 3,000 miles (4,828 km) with underwing drop-tanks

Accommodation: Crew of 1
First flight: 18 March 1945
Designed in 1944, the Skyraider was about to retire after five years' US Navy service when the Korean War broke out in 1950. Its achievements during the next three years kept it in production until several thousand had been built, and these served in a wide variety of tactical roles with the US services until the late 1960s. Skyraiders have also operated with the air forces of France, Cambodia and South Vietnam. The data apply to the A-1J final production version.

NORTH AMERICAN F-86 SABRE

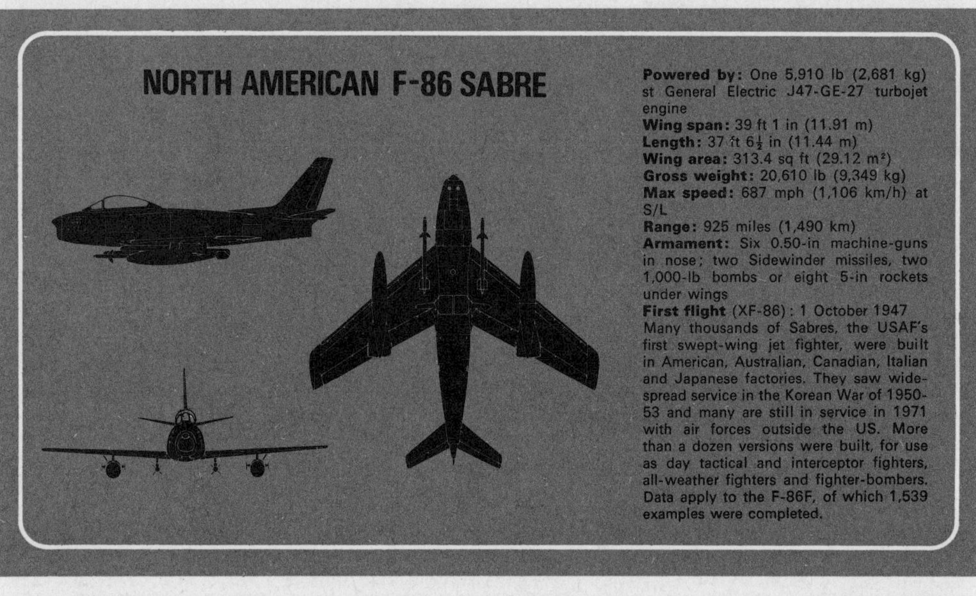

Powered by: One 5,910 lb (2,681 kg) st General Electric J47-GE-27 turbojet engine
Wing span: 39 ft 1 in (11.91 m)
Length: 37 ft 6½ in (11.44 m)
Wing area: 313.4 sq ft (29.12 m²)
Gross weight: 20,610 lb (9,349 kg)
Max speed: 687 mph (1,106 km/h) at S/L
Range: 925 miles (1,490 km)
Armament: Six 0.50-in machine-guns in nose; two Sidewinder missiles, two 1,000-lb bombs or eight 5-in rockets under wings
First flight (XF-86): 1 October 1947
Many thousands of Sabres, the USAF's first swept-wing jet fighter, were built in American, Australian, Canadian, Italian and Japanese factories. They saw widespread service in the Korean War of 1950-53 and many are still in service in 1971 with air forces outside the US. More than a dozen versions were built, for use as day tactical and interceptor fighters, all-weather fighters and fighter-bombers. Data apply to the F-86F, of which 1,539 examples were completed.

MIKOYAN/GUREVICH MiG-15

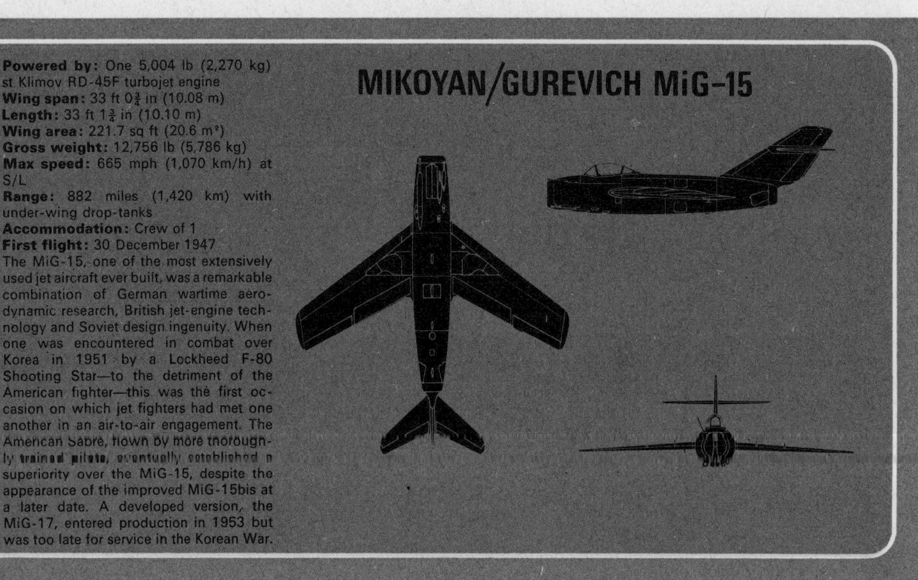

Powered by: One 5,004 lb (2,270 kg) st Klimov RD-45F turbojet engine
Wing span: 33 ft 0¾ in (10.08 m)
Length: 33 ft 1¾ in (10.10 m)
Wing area: 221.7 sq ft (20.6 m²)
Gross weight: 12,756 lb (5,786 kg)
Max speed: 665 mph (1,070 km/h) at S/L
Range: 882 miles (1,420 km) with under-wing drop-tanks
Accommodation: Crew of 1
First flight: 30 December 1947
The MiG-15, one of the most extensively used jet aircraft ever built, was a remarkable combination of German wartime aerodynamic research, British jet-engine technology and Soviet design ingenuity. When one was encountered in combat over Korea in 1951 by a Lockheed F-80 Shooting Star—to the detriment of the American fighter—this was the first occasion on which jet fighters had met one another in an air-to-air engagement. The American Sabre, flown by more thoroughly trained pilots, eventually established a superiority over the MiG-15, despite the appearance of the improved MiG-15bis at a later date. A developed version, the MiG-17, entered production in 1953 but was too late for service in the Korean War.

Douglas A-1J Skyraider

North American F-86A Sabre

MiG-15

BOEING 377 STRATOCRUISER

Powered by: Four 3,500 hp Pratt & Whitney R-4360-B6 Double Wasp radial engines, each driving a four-blade propeller of 16 ft 7 in (5.05 m) diameter
Wing span: 141 ft 3 in (43.05 m)
Length: 110 ft 4 in (33.63 m)
Wing area: 1,769 sq ft (164.3 m²)
Gross weight: 145,800 lb (66,134 kg)
Typical cruising speed: 300 mph (483 km/h) at 25,000 ft (7,620 m)
Typical range: 2,750 miles (4,426 km) with max payload
Accommodation: Crew of 5 and up to 100 passengers
First flight: 8 July 1947

The Stratocruiser was the commercial airline counterpart to the C-97 military transport, itself based on the wings, engines, tail assembly and landing gear of the B-50 Superfortress bomber but with a new 'double-bubble' pressurised fuselage. The internal volume of the new body was sufficient to permit a two-deck passenger cabin with separate bar and lounge, offering a real taste of comfort to trans-Atlantic passengers after the privations of wartime.

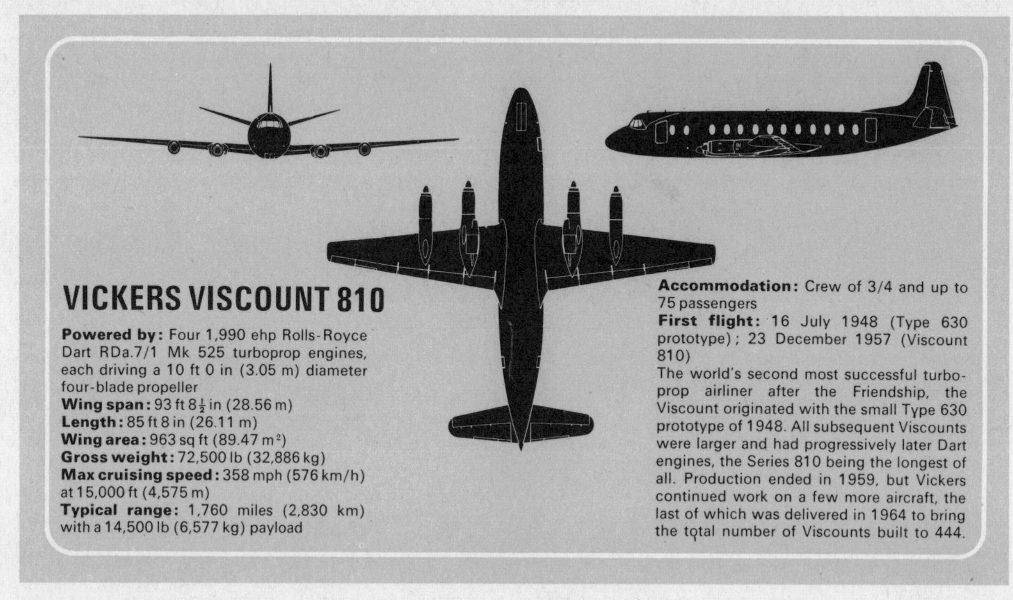

VICKERS VISCOUNT 810

Powered by: Four 1,990 ehp Rolls-Royce Dart RDa.7/1 Mk 525 turboprop engines, each driving a 10 ft 0 in (3.05 m) diameter four-blade propeller
Wing span: 93 ft 8½ in (28.56 m)
Length: 85 ft 8 in (26.11 m)
Wing area: 963 sq ft (89.47 m²)
Gross weight: 72,500 lb (32,886 kg)
Max cruising speed: 358 mph (576 km/h) at 15,000 ft (4,575 m)
Typical range: 1,760 miles (2,830 km) with a 14,500 lb (6,577 kg) payload
Accommodation: Crew of 3/4 and up to 75 passengers
First flight: 16 July 1948 (Type 630 prototype); 23 December 1957 (Viscount 810)

The world's second most successful turboprop airliner after the Friendship, the Viscount originated with the small Type 630 prototype of 1948. All subsequent Viscounts were larger and had progressively later Dart engines, the Series 810 being the longest of all. Production ended in 1959, but Vickers continued work on a few more aircraft, the last of which was delivered in 1964 to bring the total number of Viscounts built to 444.

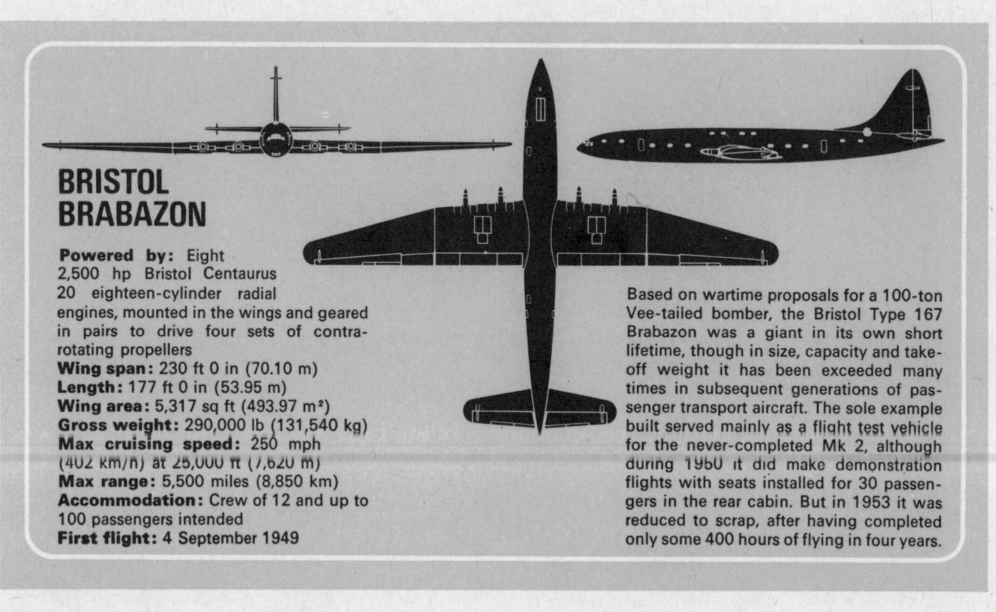

BRISTOL BRABAZON

Powered by: Eight 2,500 hp Bristol Centaurus 20 eighteen-cylinder radial engines, mounted in the wings and geared in pairs to drive four sets of contra-rotating propellers
Wing span: 230 ft 0 in (70.10 m)
Length: 177 ft 0 in (53.95 m)
Wing area: 5,317 sq ft (493.97 m²)
Gross weight: 290,000 lb (131,540 kg)
Max cruising speed: 250 mph (402 km/h) at 25,000 ft (7,620 m)
Max range: 5,500 miles (8,850 km)
Accommodation: Crew of 12 and up to 100 passengers intended
First flight: 4 September 1949

Based on wartime proposals for a 100-ton Vee-tailed bomber, the Bristol Type 167 Brabazon was a giant in its own short lifetime, though in size, capacity and take-off weight it has been exceeded many times in subsequent generations of passenger transport aircraft. The sole example built served mainly as a flight test vehicle for the never-completed Mk 2, although during 1950 it did make demonstration flights with seats installed for 30 passengers in the rear cabin. But in 1953 it was reduced to scrap, after having completed only some 400 hours of flying in four years.

Boeing Stratocruiser

Vickers Viscount Model 757

Bristol Brabazon

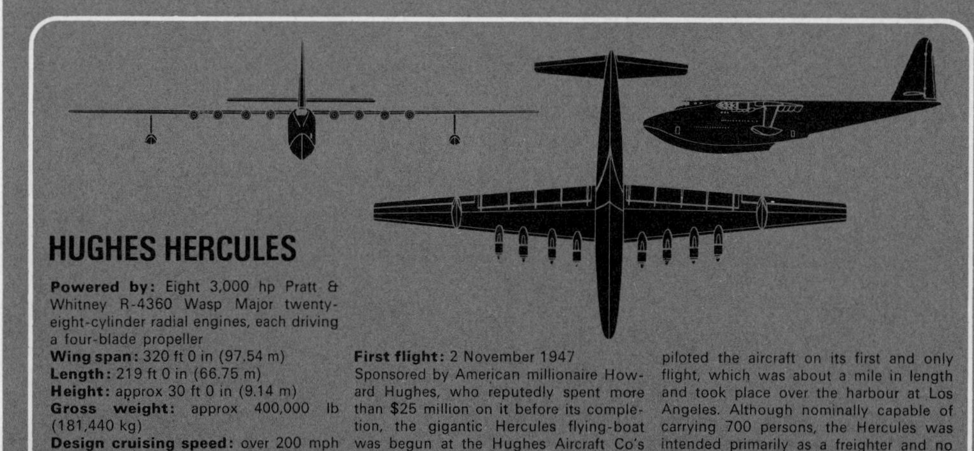

HUGHES HERCULES

Powered by: Eight 3,000 hp Pratt & Whitney R-4360 Wasp Major twenty-eight-cylinder radial engines, each driving a four-blade propeller
Wing span: 320 ft 0 in (97.54 m)
Length: 219 ft 0 in (66.75 m)
Height: approx 30 ft 0 in (9.14 m)
Gross weight: approx 400,000 lb (181,440 kg)
Design cruising speed: over 200 mph (322 km/h)
Accommodation: Crew and up to 700 passengers or equivalent freight
First flight: 2 November 1947
Sponsored by American millionaire Howard Hughes, who reputedly spent more than $25 million on it before its completion, the gigantic Hercules flying-boat was begun at the Hughes Aircraft Co's Culver City plant in 1942, being moved by road to Long Beach, California, for assembly in June 1946. Hughes himself piloted the aircraft on its first and only flight, which was about a mile in length and took place over the harbour at Los Angeles. Although nominally capable of carrying 700 persons, the Hercules was intended primarily as a freighter and no passenger windows were provided. It is preserved inside a huge, closely-guarded hangar.

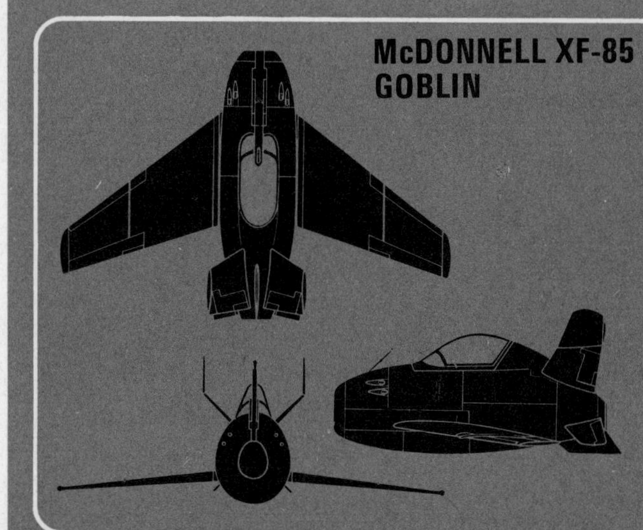

McDONNELL XF-85 GOBLIN

Powered by: One 3,000 lb (1,361 kg) st Westinghouse J34-WE-7 turbojet engine
Wing span: 21 ft 1½ in (6.44 m)
Length: 14 ft 10½ in (4.53 m)
Wing area: 90 sq ft (8.36 m²)
Gross weight: 4,550 lb (2,064 kg)
Max attained speed: 362 mph (583 km/h)
Endurance: approx 30 min
Accommodation: Crew of 1
Armament: Four 0.50-in machine-guns in nose
First flight: 23 August 1948
Conceived during the second World War, two examples were built of the XF-85, one of which is still preserved in the USAF Museum. Only 5 ft 4¾ in (1.64 m) wide and 10 ft 8 in (3.25 m) high with the wings folded, it was intended as a 'parasite' defensive fighter to be carried in the bomb-bay of the Convair B-36. Tests were disappointing, the aircraft falling well below its intended maximum speed of 664 mph (1,068 km/h), and further development was cancelled when long-range versions of more conventional fighters became available.

CHANCE VOUGHT F7U-3 CUTLASS

Powered by: Two 6,100 lb (2,76/ kg) st Westinghouse J46-WE-8A afterburning turbojet engines
Wing span: 38 ft 8 in (11.79 m)
Length: 44 ft 3 in (13.49 m)
Wing area: 496.0 sq ft (46.08 m²)
Gross weight: 31,642 lb (14,352 kg)
Max speed: 680 mph (1,094 km/h) at 10,000 ft (3,050 m)
Range: 660 miles (1,062 km)
Armament: Four 20 mm cannon, and rockets or (F7U-3M) four Sparrow I air-to-air missiles beneath the wings
Accommodation: Crew of 1
First flight: 29 September 1948
Unorthodox designs abound in aviation history. Very few of them achieve production or service status, but one exception was the Cutlass, a carrier-based fighter whose design was based upon research into tailless aircraft by the German Arado company during the second World War. It was also the first US fighter designed from the outset to use afterburning jet engines. Major production version, after a small batch of F7U-1s, was the F7U-3; a reconnaissance version, with lengthened camera nose, was designated F7U-3P. The fighter version was designated F7U-3M when armed with Sparrow missiles.

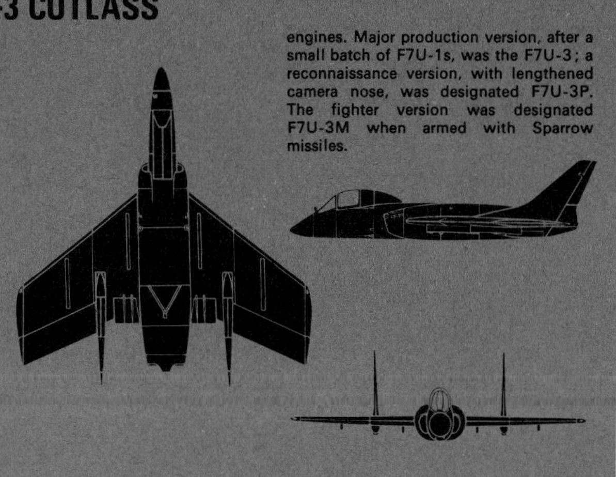

Hughes Hercules

McDonnell XF-85 Goblin

Chance Vought F7U-3 Cutlass

BOEING STRATOJET

Powered by: Six 5,800 lb (2,630 kg) st General Electric J47-GE-23 turbojet engines in underwing pods
Wing span: 116 ft 0 in (35.36 m)
Length: 108 ft 0 in (32.92 m)
Wing area: 1,428 sq ft (132.66 m^2)
Gross weight: 185,000 lb (83,914 kg)
Max speed: 617 mph (993 km/h) at 10,600 ft (3,230 m)
Range: over 3,000 miles (4,830 km)
Armament: Two 0.50-in machine-guns in radar-directed tail mounting; up to 20,000 lb (9,072 kg) of bombs internally
Accommodation: Crew of 3
First flights: 17 December 1947 (XB-47); 26 April 1951 (B-47B)

One aspect of aircraft propulsion which received some attention during the closing years of the second World War was JATO (Jet-Assisted Take-Off), which enabled combat aircraft to use small-size airfields or to take off with much higher gross weights than normal. The relatively low power of early post-war jet engines created a further use for this technique in connection with large aircraft, and America's first swept-wing jet bomber, the B-47 Stratojet, was among those to incorporate built-in JATO units in its early versions. The B-47B, to which the data and silhouette apply, was fitted with eighteen 1,000 lb (454 kg) st rocket units mounted in the fuselage aft of the wings.

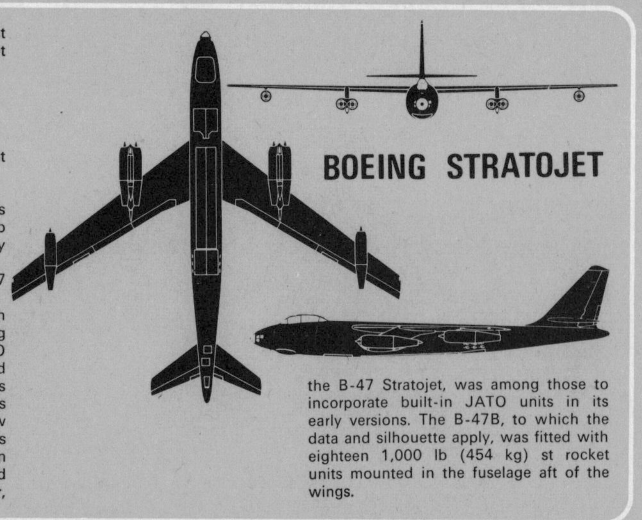

ANTONOV An-2

Powered by: One 1,000 hp Shvetsov ASh-62IR nine-cylinder radial engine, driving a four-blade propeller
Wing span: 59 ft 8½ in (18.18 m)
Length: 42 ft 0 in (12.80 m)
Wing area: 765.3 sq ft (71.10 m^2)
Gross weight: 11,574 lb (5,250 kg)
Max speed: 161 mph (260 km/h) at S/L
Typical range: 560 miles (900 km) with 2,733 lb (1,240 kg) payload
Accommodation: Crew of 2/3 and up to 12 passengers or 3,306 lb (1,500 kg) of cargo
First flight: 1947

More than 5,000 An-2 biplanes were built during 1950-60, serving in both civil and military capacities in every country of the Soviet bloc and in Cuba, Greece, Mali and the Indian sub-continent. It was licence-built in China and is still being built in Poland. Soviet production also included the An-2M, an agricultural version with an enlarged, angular vertical tail. Data apply to the An-2P, the standard general-purpose version; this and other models have been employed for passenger, cargo, agricultural, ambulance, ice and fishery patrol and water bombing duties, and the aircraft can also be used as a glider tug.

DHA-3 DROVER

Powered by: Three 180 hp Lycoming O-360-A1A four-cylinder horizontally-opposed engines, each driving a two-blade propeller
Wing span: 57 ft 0 in (17.37 m)
Length: 36 ft 6 in (11.12 m)
Wing area: 325 sq ft (30.19 m^2)
Gross weight: 6,500 lb (2,948 kg)
Max cruising speed: 140 mph (225 km/h) at 5,000 ft (1,525 m)
Max range: 900 miles (1,450 km)
Accommodation: Crew of 1 or 2, and 2 stretchers with 2 medical attendants, 9 passengers or 1,500 lb (680 kg) of cargo
First flight: 23 January 1948

First aircraft to be designed by the Australian branch of de Havilland, the Drover bush transport was based broadly on the D.H.104 Dove, though it had a three-engined configuration for increased safety while flying over 'outback' areas and more utilitarian lines than its British predecessor. Originally the Drover was powered by 145 hp D.H. Gipsy Major 10 Mk 2 engines, but all Flying Doctor aircraft were converted to Drover 3s in 1960 with Lycomings. Data apply to the latter version, which flew for the first time in May 1960.

Boeing B-47 Stratojet

Antonov An-2

de Havilland Australia Drover with original Gipsy Major engines

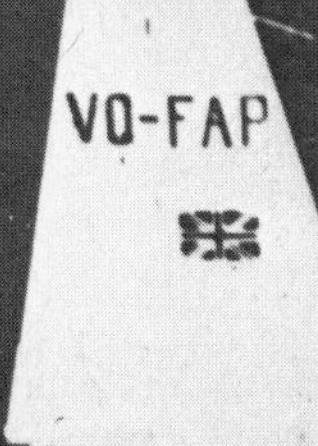

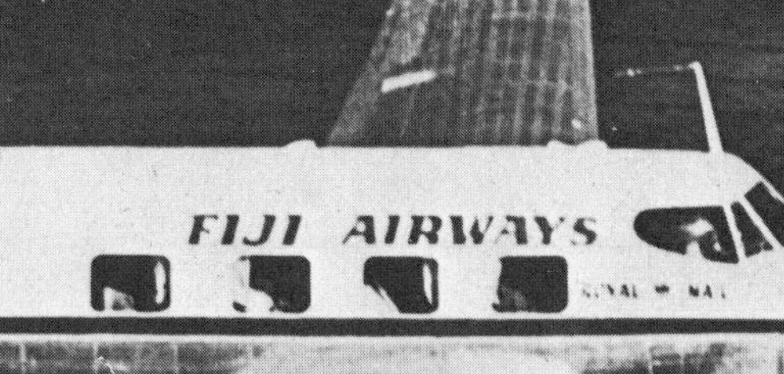

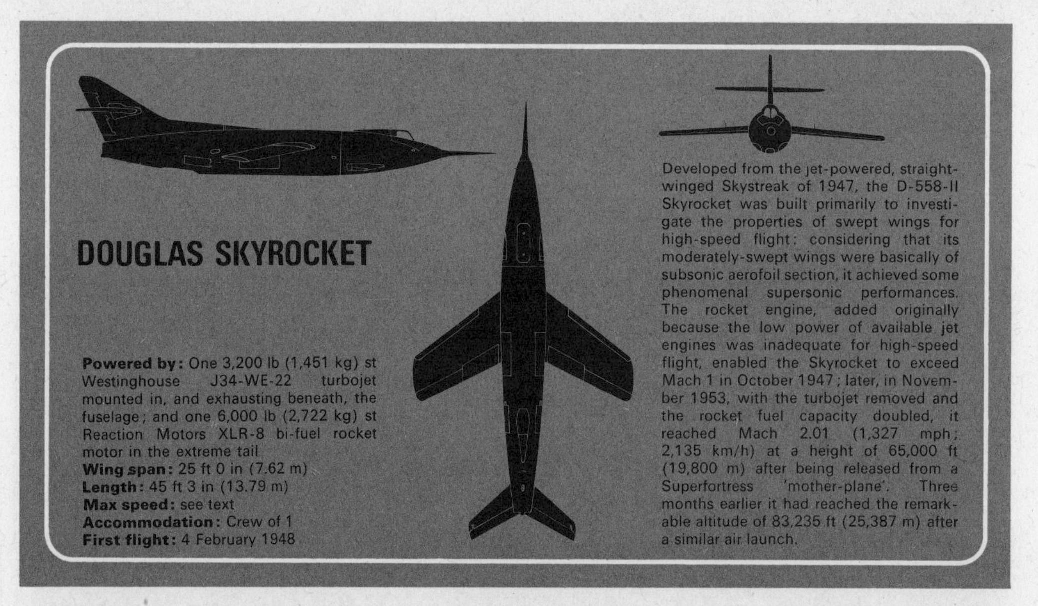

DOUGLAS SKYROCKET

Powered by: One 3,200 lb (1,451 kg) st Westinghouse J34-WE-22 turbojet mounted in, and exhausting beneath, the fuselage; and one 6,000 lb (2,722 kg) st Reaction Motors XLR-8 bi-fuel rocket motor in the extreme tail
Wing span: 25 ft 0 in (7.62 m)
Length: 45 ft 3 in (13.79 m)
Max speed: see text
Accommodation: Crew of 1
First flight: 4 February 1948

Developed from the jet-powered, straight-winged Skystreak of 1947, the D-558-II Skyrocket was built primarily to investigate the properties of swept wings for high-speed flight: considering that its moderately-swept wings were basically of subsonic aerofoil section, it achieved some phenomenal supersonic performances. The rocket engine, added originally because the low power of available jet engines was inadequate for high-speed flight, enabled the Skyrocket to exceed Mach 1 in October 1947; later, in November 1953, with the turbojet removed and the rocket fuel capacity doubled, it reached Mach 2.01 (1,327 mph; 2,135 km/h) at a height of 65,000 ft (19,800 m) after being released from a Superfortress 'mother-plane'. Three months earlier it had reached the remarkable altitude of 83,235 ft (25,387 m) after a similar air launch.

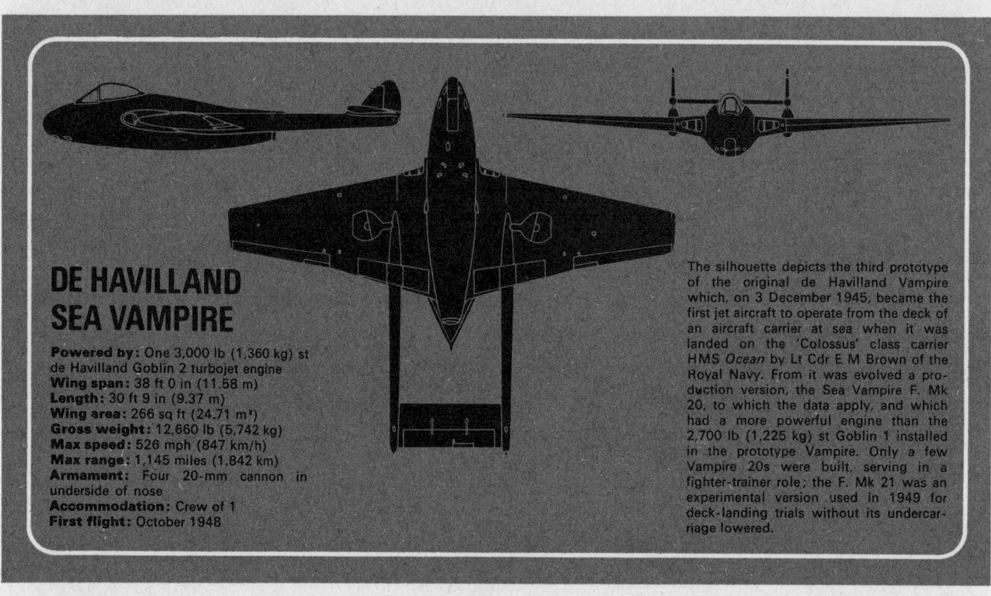

DE HAVILLAND SEA VAMPIRE

Powered by: One 3,000 lb (1,360 kg) st de Havilland Goblin 2 turbojet engine
Wing span: 38 ft 0 in (11.58 m)
Length: 30 ft 9 in (9.37 m)
Wing area: 266 sq ft (24.71 m²)
Gross weight: 12,660 lb (5,742 kg)
Max speed: 526 mph (847 km/h)
Max range: 1,145 miles (1,842 km)
Armament: Four 20-mm cannon in underside of nose
Accommodation: Crew of 1
First flight: October 1948

The silhouette depicts the third prototype of the original de Havilland Vampire which, on 3 December 1945, became the first jet aircraft to operate from the deck of an aircraft carrier at sea when it was landed on the 'Colossus' class carrier HMS *Ocean* by Lt Cdr E M Brown of the Royal Navy. From it was evolved a production version, the Sea Vampire F. Mk 20, to which the data apply, and which had a more powerful engine than the 2,700 lb (1,225 kg) st Goblin 1 installed in the prototype Vampire. Only a few Vampire 20s were built, serving in a fighter-trainer role; the F. Mk 21 was an experimental version used in 1949 for deck-landing trials without its undercarriage lowered.

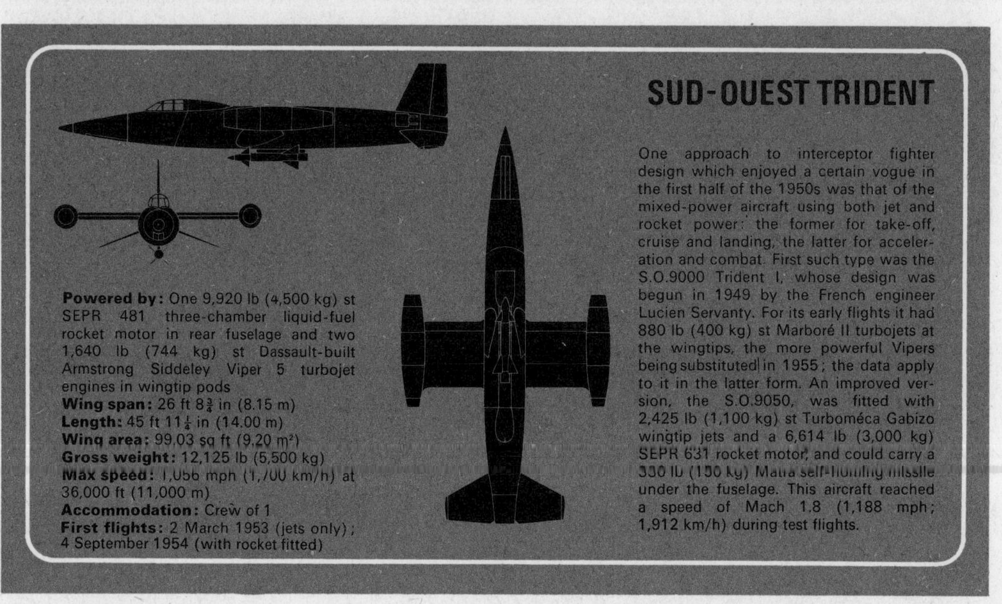

SUD-OUEST TRIDENT

Powered by: One 9,920 lb (4,500 kg) st SEPR 481 three-chamber liquid-fuel rocket motor in rear fuselage and two 1,640 lb (744 kg) st Dassault-built Armstrong Siddeley Viper 5 turbojet engines in wingtip pods
Wing span: 26 ft 8¾ in (8.15 m)
Length: 45 ft 11¼ in (14.00 m)
Wing area: 99.03 sq ft (9.20 m²)
Gross weight: 12,125 lb (5,500 kg)
Max speed: 1,056 mph (1,700 km/h) at 36,000 ft (11,000 m)
Accommodation: Crew of 1
First flights: 2 March 1953 (jets only); 4 September 1954 (with rocket fitted)

One approach to interceptor fighter design which enjoyed a certain vogue in the first half of the 1950s was that of the mixed-power aircraft using both jet and rocket power: the former for take-off, cruise and landing, the latter for acceleration and combat. First such type was the S.O.9000 Trident I, whose design was begun in 1949 by the French engineer Lucien Servanty. For its early flights it had 880 lb (400 kg) st Marboré II turbojets at the wingtips, the more powerful Vipers being substituted in 1955; the data apply to it in the latter form. An improved version, the S.O.9050, was fitted with 2,425 lb (1,100 kg) st Turboméca Gabizo wingtip jets and a 6,614 lb (3,000 kg) SEPR 631 rocket motor, and could carry a 330 lb (150 kg) Matra self-homing missile under the fuselage. This aircraft reached a speed of Mach 1.8 (1,188 mph; 1,912 km/h) during test flights.

Douglas Skyrocket being launched from a B-29 'mother-plane'

Sea Vampire F Mk 20

S.O.9050 Trident II

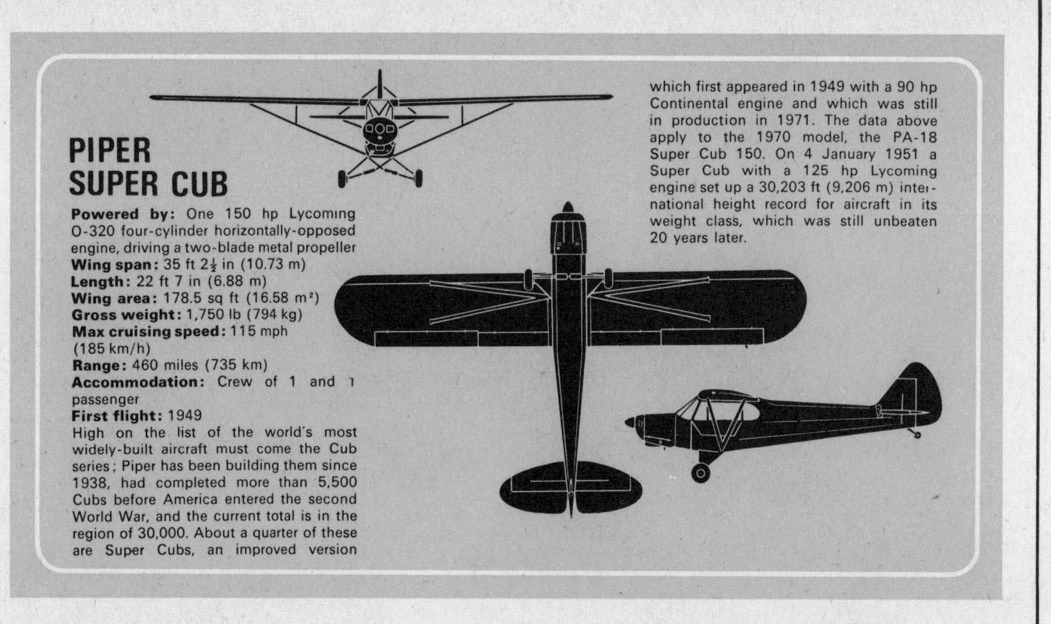

PIPER SUPER CUB

Powered by: One 150 hp Lycoming O-320 four-cylinder horizontally-opposed engine, driving a two-blade metal propeller
Wing span: 35 ft 2½ in (10.73 m)
Length: 22 ft 7 in (6.88 m)
Wing area: 178.5 sq ft (16.58 m^2)
Gross weight: 1,750 lb (794 kg)
Max cruising speed: 115 mph (185 km/h)
Range: 460 miles (735 km)
Accommodation: Crew of 1 and 1 passenger
First flight: 1949

High on the list of the world's most widely-built aircraft must come the Cub series; Piper has been building them since 1938, had completed more than 5,500 Cubs before America entered the second World War, and the current total is in the region of 30,000. About a quarter of these are Super Cubs, an improved version which first appeared in 1949 with a 90 hp Continental engine and which was still in production in 1971. The data above apply to the 1970 model, the PA-18 Super Cub 150. On 4 January 1951 a Super Cub with a 125 hp Lycoming engine set up a 30,203 ft (9,206 m) international height record for aircraft in its weight class, which was still unbeaten 20 years later.

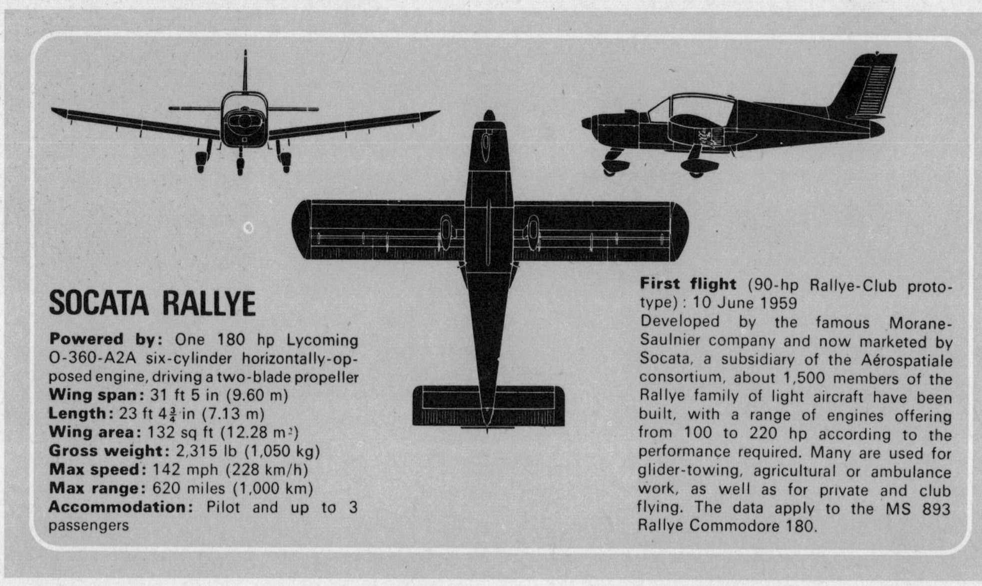

SOCATA RALLYE

Powered by: One 180 hp Lycoming O-360-A2A six-cylinder horizontally-opposed engine, driving a two-blade propeller
Wing span: 31 ft 5 in (9.60 m)
Length: 23 ft 4¾ in (7.13 m)
Wing area: 132 sq ft (12.28 m^2)
Gross weight: 2,315 lb (1,050 kg)
Max speed: 142 mph (228 km/h)
Max range: 620 miles (1,000 km)
Accommodation: Pilot and up to 3 passengers
First flight (90-hp Rallye-Club prototype): 10 June 1959

Developed by the famous Morane-Saulnier company and now marketed by Socata, a subsidiary of the Aérospatiale consortium, about 1,500 members of the Rallye family of light aircraft have been built, with a range of engines offering from 100 to 220 hp according to the performance required. Many are used for glider-towing, agricultural or ambulance work, as well as for private and club flying. The data apply to the MS 893 Rallye Commodore 180.

CESSNA SKYWAGON

Powered by: One 230 hp Continental O - 470 - R six - cylinder horizontally - opposed engine, driving a 6 ft 10 in (2.08 m) diameter two-blade propeller
Wing span: 36 ft 2 in (11.02 m)
Length: 25 ft 9 in (7.85 m)
Wing area: 174.0 sq ft (16.16 m^2)
Gross weight: 2,800 lb (1,270 kg)
Max cruising speed: 162 mph (261 km/h) at 6,500 ft (1,980 m)
Typical range: 695 miles (1,118 km)
Accommodation: Crew of 1 and up to 5 passengers
First flight: early 1953

The family of Cessna single-engined high-wing cabin monoplanes produced since the second World War amounts to tens of thousands of aircraft, which are flown in almost every country in the world. It all started with the two-seat, 85 hp Model 120 which flew for the first time in 1945, and within the next 25 years Cessna had delivered more than 95,000 light aircraft of various shapes and sizes. Of this total, well over 5,000 were Model 180 Skywagons, to which the data and silhouette apply. The name Skywagon is also given to the variously-differing Models 185, 206 and 207.

Piper Super Cub 150

Socata (Morane-Saulnier) MS 892 Rallye

Cessna Model 180 (1965 model)

NORD NORATLAS

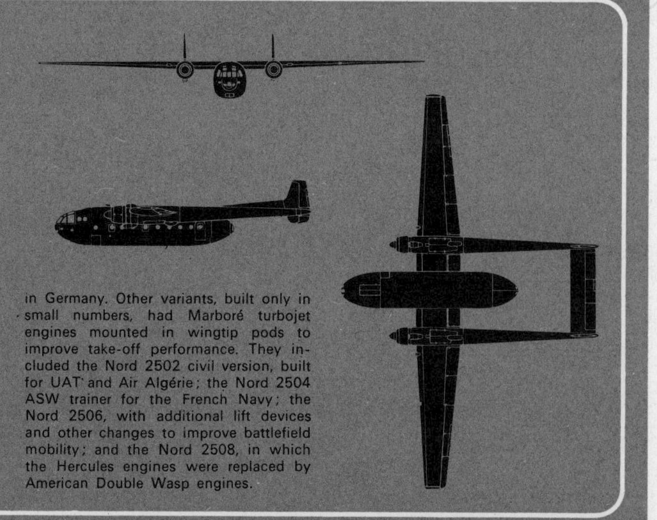

Powered by: Two 2,068 hp SNECMA-built Bristol Hercules 758 fourteen-cylinder radial engines, each driving a four-blade propelle:
Wing span: 106 ft 7½ in (32.50 m)
Length: 72 ft 0½ in (21.96 m)
Wing area: 1,089.3 sq ft (101.2 m²)
Gross weight: 45,415 lb (20,600 kg)
Max cruising speed: 208 mph (335 km/h) at 9,845 ft (3,000 m)
Typical range: 1,550 miles (2,495 km) with 9,920 lb (4,500 kg) payload
Accommodation: Crew of 5 and up to 45 troops or 7½ tons of equipment or cargo
First flights: 10 September 1949 (Nord 2500 with Gnome-Rhône 14R engines); 27 November 1950 (Nord 2501 with Hercules engines)

A standard tactical military transport with the French, German and Israeli air forces since the mid-'fifties, the Noratlas has also served in more recent years with the air arms of Portugal, Niger and Nigeria. Major version was the Nord 2501, of which 200 were built in France and 161 in Germany. Other variants, built only in small numbers, had Marboré turbojet engines mounted in wingtip pods to improve take-off performance. They included the Nord 2502 civil version, built for UAT and Air Algérie; the Nord 2504 ASW trainer for the French Navy; the Nord 2506, with additional lift devices and other changes to improve battlefield mobility; and the Nord 2508, in which the Hercules engines were replaced by American Double Wasp engines.

DASSAULT MYSTÈRE IV-A

Powered by: One 7,716 lb (3,500 kg) st Hispano-Suiza Verdon 350 turbojet engine
Wing span: 36 ft 5¾ in (11.12 m)
Length: 42 ft 1½ in (12.84 m)
Wing area: 344.4 sq ft (32.00 m²)
Gross weight: 18,700 lb (8,482 kg)
Max speed: 696 mph (1,120 km/h) at S/L
Range: 820 miles (1,320 km) with two underwing drop-tanks
Armament: Two 30-mm DEFA cannon (with 150 rpg) and pack of 55 unguided air-to-air rockets in fuselage; two 1,000-lb or four 500-lb bombs, two air-to-air or air-to-surface rocket packs or two napalm containers under the wings
Accommodation: Crew of 1
First flight: 28 September 1952

Developed from France's first production jet fighter, the straight-winged Ouragan, via the interim Mystère II-C, the Mystère IV-A entered service with the French Air Force in 1955. It first fired its guns in anger during the 1956 Suez crisis, both with French squadrons and with the Israeli Air Force, with which it was just beginning to enter service. By the time of the 1967 'six-day war' in the Middle East it had largely been replaced in Israeli service by the Mirage, but in both campaigns it gave a good account of itself against supposedly superior aircraft. Dassault built 421 Mystère IV-As, of which 110 were supplied to India and 60 to Israel.

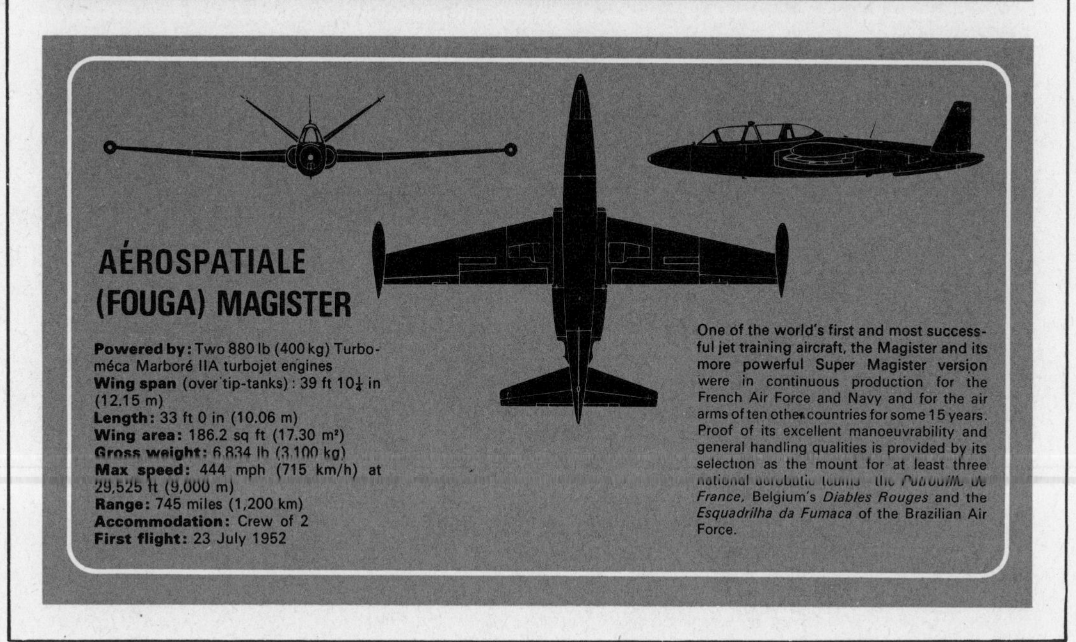

AÉROSPATIALE (FOUGA) MAGISTER

Powered by: Two 880 lb (400 kg) Turbo-méca Marboré IIA turbojet engines
Wing span (over tip-tanks): 39 ft 10¼ in (12.15 m)
Length: 33 ft 0 in (10.06 m)
Wing area: 186.2 sq ft (17.30 m²)
Gross weight: 6,834 lb (3,100 kg)
Max speed: 444 mph (715 km/h) at 29,525 ft (9,000 m)
Range: 745 miles (1,200 km)
Accommodation: Crew of 2
First flight: 23 July 1952

One of the world's first and most successful jet training aircraft, the Magister and its more powerful Super Magister version were in continuous production for the French Air Force and Navy and for the air arms of ten other countries for some 15 years. Proof of its excellent manoeuvrability and general handling qualities is provided by its selection as the mount for at least three national aerobatic teams – the *Patrouille de France*, Belgium's *Diables Rouges* and the *Esquadrilha da Fumaca* of the Brazilian Air Force.

Nord 2501 Noratlas

Dassault Mystère IV-A

Aérospatiale (Fouga) Magister

DE HAVILLAND COMET 1

Powered by: Four 4,450 lb (2,018 kg) st de Havilland Ghost 50 Mk 1 turbojet engines
Wing span: 115 ft 0 in (35.05 m)
Length: 93 ft $1\frac{1}{4}$ in (28.38 m)
Wing area: 2,015 sq ft (187.2 m^2)
Gross weight: 105,000 lb (47,627 kg)
Max cruising speed: 490 mph (788 km/h) at 35,000 ft (10,700 m)
Range: 1,750 miles (2,816 km) with 12,000 lb (5,443 kg) payload
Accommodation: Crew of 4 and 36 passengers
First flight: 27 July 1949

On 2 May 1952, BOAC took one of the boldest steps in airline history by introducing the first scheduled jet passenger services anywhere in the world. Fears that jet airliners would be unprofitable were quickly dispelled, and during its first year of service the Comet 1 operated at an average load factor of over 80 per cent. Then, after almost exactly a year in service, came the first of the tragic and then-unexplained accidents which finally grounded the aircraft in April 1954. It was another $4\frac{1}{2}$ years before the much-modified Comet 4 resumed airline services, by which time the commercial initiative had passed to the United States.

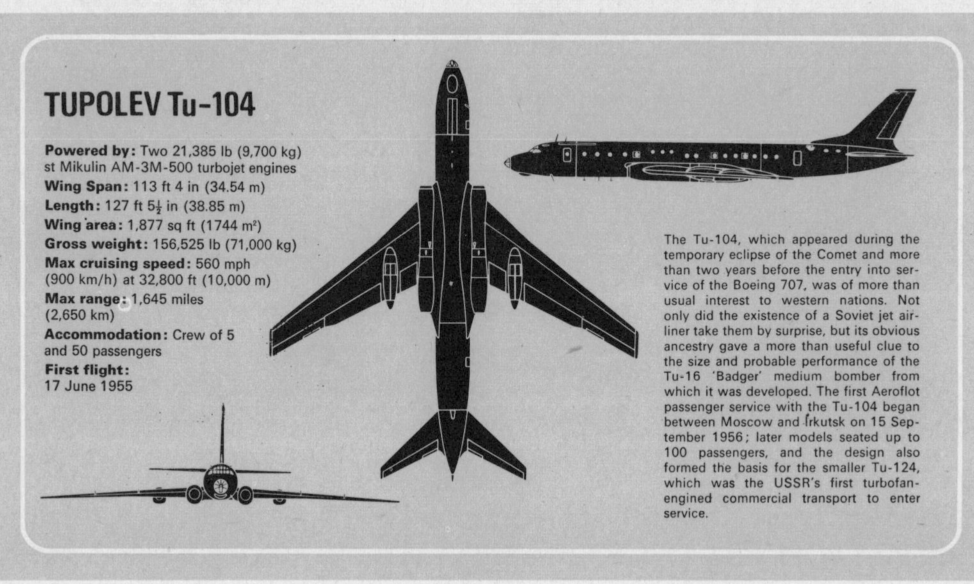

TUPOLEV Tu-104

Powered by: Two 21,385 lb (9,700 kg) st Mikulin AM-3M-500 turbojet engines
Wing Span: 113 ft 4 in (34.54 m)
Length: 127 ft $5\frac{1}{2}$ in (38.85 m)
Wing area: 1,877 sq ft (1744 m^2)
Gross weight: 156,525 lb (71,000 kg)
Max cruising speed: 560 mph (900 km/h) at 32,800 ft (10,000 m)
Max range: 1,645 miles (2,650 km)
Accommodation: Crew of 5 and 50 passengers
First flight: 17 June 1955

The Tu-104, which appeared during the temporary eclipse of the Comet and more than two years before the entry into service of the Boeing 707, was of more than usual interest to western nations. Not only did the existence of a Soviet jet airliner take them by surprise, but its obvious ancestry gave a more than useful clue to the size and probable performance of the Tu-16 'Badger' medium bomber from which it was developed. The first Aeroflot passenger service with the Tu-104 began between Moscow and Irkutsk on 15 September 1956; later models seated up to 100 passengers, and the design also formed the basis for the smaller Tu-124, which was the USSR's first turbofan-engined commercial transport to enter service.

BOEING 707-320B INTERCONTINENTAL

Powered by: Four 18,000 lb st Pratt & Whitney JT3D-3 or -3B turbofan engines
Wing span: 145 ft 9 in (44.42 m)
Length: 152 ft 11 in (46.61 m)
Wing area: 3,010 sq ft (279.64 m^2)
Gross weight: 327,000 lb (148,325 kg)
Max cruising speed: 600 mph (966 km/h) at 25,000 ft (7,620 m)
Typical range: 6,160 miles (9,915 km) with max payload
Accommodation: Crew of 3/4 and up to 189 passengers
First flight: 15 July 1954 (707 prototype); 31 January 1962 (707-320B)

The original Boeing 707 jet transport was intended for service on US domestic routes, although the first route actually flown, in 1958, was across the Atlantic. Two truly intercontinental models of the 707 have appeared, the -320 and the -420, the latter similar except for its Rolls-Royce Conway turbofan engines. The -320 was originally turbojet-powered, but this version has been superseded in production by the fan-engined -320B, which is also available with optional cargo-carrying capability.

de Havilland Comet 1A

Tupolev Tu-104

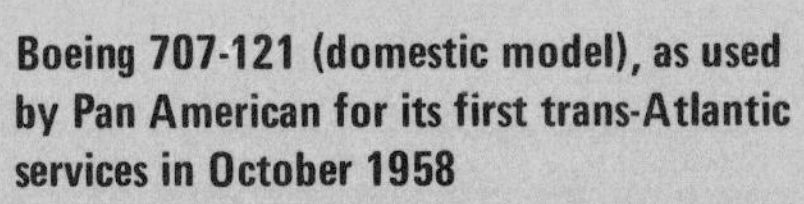
Boeing 707-121 (domestic model), as used by Pan American for its first trans-Atlantic services in October 1958

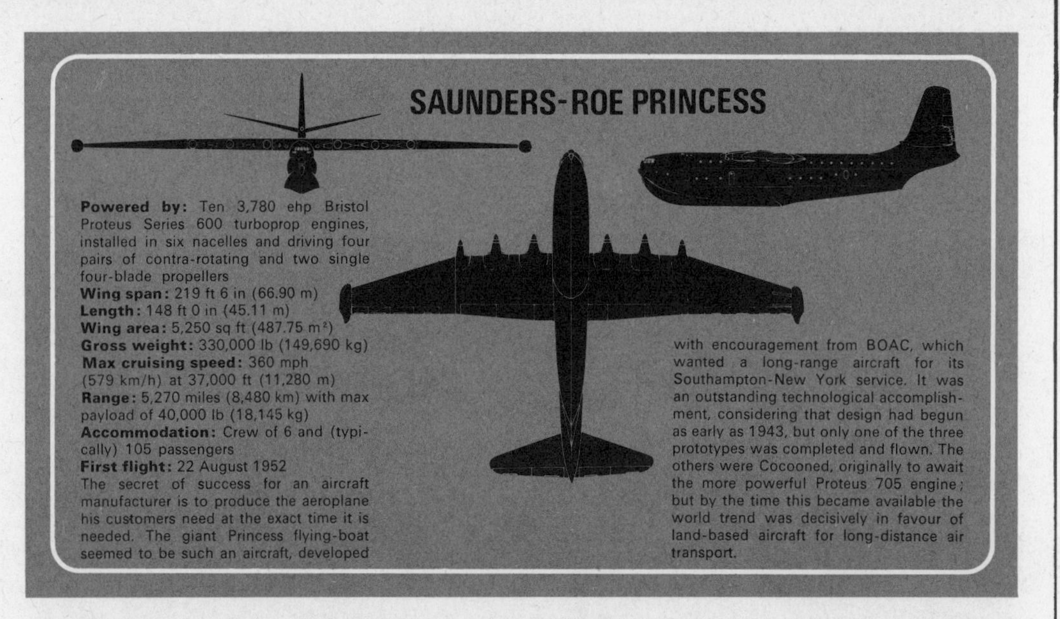

SAUNDERS-ROE PRINCESS

Powered by: Ten 3,780 ehp Bristol Proteus Series 600 turboprop engines, installed in six nacelles and driving four pairs of contra-rotating and two single four-blade propellers
Wing span: 219 ft 6 in (66.90 m)
Length: 148 ft 0 in (45.11 m)
Wing area: 5,250 sq ft (487.75 m²)
Gross weight: 330,000 lb (149,690 kg)
Max cruising speed: 360 mph (579 km/h) at 37,000 ft (11,280 m)
Range: 5,270 miles (8,480 km) with max payload of 40,000 lb (18,145 kg)
Accommodation: Crew of 6 and (typically) 105 passengers
First flight: 22 August 1952

The secret of success for an aircraft manufacturer is to produce the aeroplane his customers need at the exact time it is needed. The giant Princess flying-boat seemed to be such an aircraft, developed with encouragement from BOAC, which wanted a long-range aircraft for its Southampton-New York service. It was an outstanding technological accomplishment, considering that design had begun as early as 1943, but only one of the three prototypes was completed and flown. The others were Cocooned, originally to await the more powerful Proteus 705 engine; but by the time this became available the world trend was decisively in favour of land-based aircraft for long-distance air transport.

BOEING B-52 STRATOFORTRESS

Powered by: Eight 17,000 lb (7,711 kg) st Pratt & Whitney TF33-P-3 turbofan engines
Wing span: 185 ft 0 in (56.42 m)
Length: 156 ft 0 in (47.55 m)
Wing area: 4,000 sq ft (371.6 m²)
Gross weight: 488,000 lb (221,350 kg)
Max speed: approx 660 mph (1,062 km/h) at 20,000 ft (6,100 m)
Max range: 12,500 miles (20,120 km)
Armament: One 20-mm remote-controlled multi-barrel cannon in tail; bombs and Quail diversionary missiles internally; two Hound Dog air-to-surface missiles and ALE-25 diversionary rocket pods under wings
Accommodation: Crew of 6
First flight (YB-52)**:** 15 April 1952

The first operational version of the B-52 entered service in mid-1955, although development of the design had begun ten years earlier, shortly after the end of the war in Europe. It has been continually refined and developed, the major version numerically being the B-52G with greater fuel tankage and range and able to carry Hound Dog stand-off' nuclear weapons. The data apply to the B-52H, the final production version.

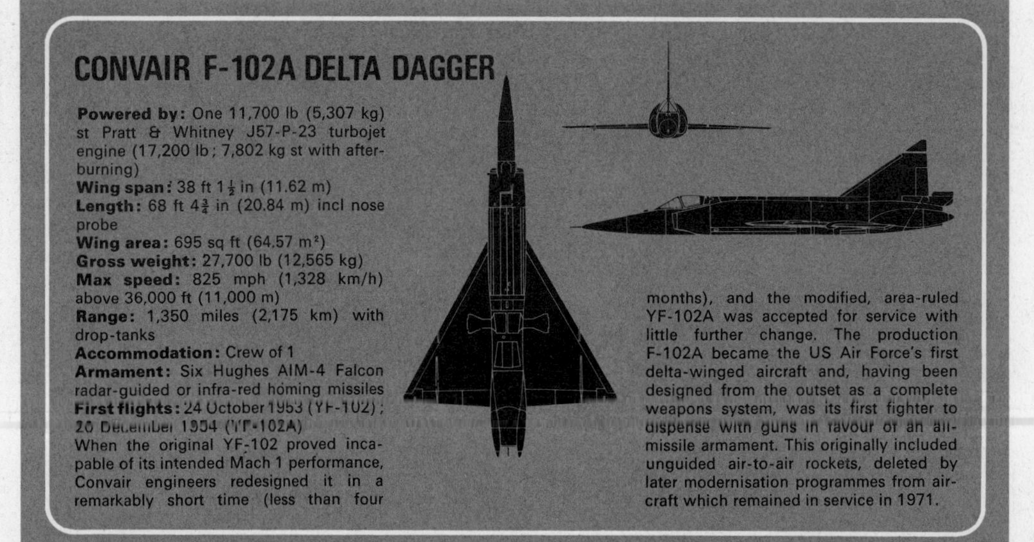

CONVAIR F-102A DELTA DAGGER

Powered by: One 11,700 lb (5,307 kg) st Pratt & Whitney J57-P-23 turbojet engine (17,200 lb; 7,802 kg st with afterburning)
Wing span: 38 ft 1½ in (11.62 m)
Length: 68 ft 4¾ in (20.84 m) incl nose probe
Wing area: 695 sq ft (64.57 m²)
Gross weight: 27,700 lb (12,565 kg)
Max speed: 825 mph (1,328 km/h) above 36,000 ft (11,000 m)
Range: 1,350 miles (2,175 km) with drop-tanks
Accommodation: Crew of 1
Armament: Six Hughes AIM-4 Falcon radar-guided or infra-red homing missiles
First flights: 24 October 1953 (YF-102); 20 December 1954 (YF-102A)

When the original YF-102 proved incapable of its intended Mach 1 performance, Convair engineers redesigned it in a remarkably short time (less than four months), and the modified, area-ruled YF-102A was accepted for service with little further change. The production F-102A became the US Air Force's first delta-winged aircraft and, having been designed from the outset as a complete weapons system, was its first fighter to dispense with guns in favour of an all-missile armament. This originally included unguided air-to-air rockets, deleted by later modernisation programmes from aircraft which remained in service in 1971.

Saunders-Roe Princess

Boeing B-52G Stratofortress, with Hound Dog missiles

Convair F-102A Delta Dagger

MIL Mi-4

Powered by: One 1,700 hp Shvetsov ASh-82V eighteen-cylinder radial engine
Main rotor diameter: 68 ft 11 in (21.00 m)
Length: 55 ft 1 in (16.80 m)
Main rotor disc area: 3,724 sq ft (346.0 m²)
Gross weight: 17,200 lb (7,800 kg)
Max speed: 130 mph (210 km/h) at 4,920 ft (1,500 m)
Typical range: 250 miles (400 km)
Accommodation: Crew of 2 or 3 and up to 14 troops or 16 passengers
First flight: August 1952

A contemporary of the Sikorsky S-55, the Mil Mi-4 follows the classic 'penny-farthing' helicopter layout, with a single main rotor and a tail rotor. The fuselage is of the typical pod-and-boom type, with access to the main cabin via a normal side door or, for bulk loads, through clamshell loading doors at the rear. The Mi-4 has been in production since about 1953, and is a major Soviet 'work-horse' helicopter, used by both military and civil agencies for the transport of passengers and freight and for agricultural duties. It is also the type generally used to recover Soviet cosmonauts returning from journeys into space, picking them up after their landing and flying them back to the cosmodrome.

ROLLS-ROYCE THRUST MEASURING RIG

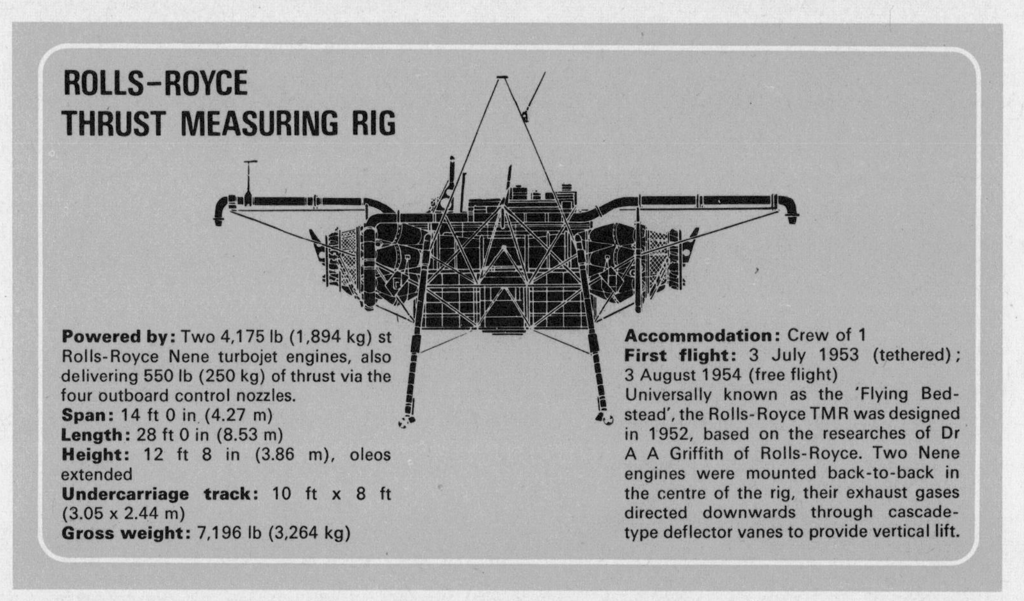

Powered by: Two 4,175 lb (1,894 kg) st Rolls-Royce Nene turbojet engines, also delivering 550 lb (250 kg) of thrust via the four outboard control nozzles.
Span: 14 ft 0 in (4.27 m)
Length: 28 ft 0 in (8.53 m)
Height: 12 ft 8 in (3.86 m), oleos extended
Undercarriage track: 10 ft x 8 ft (3.05 x 2.44 m)
Gross weight: 7,196 lb (3,264 kg)
Accommodation: Crew of 1
First flight: 3 July 1953 (tethered); 3 August 1954 (free flight)

Universally known as the 'Flying Bedstead', the Rolls-Royce TMR was designed in 1952, based on the researches of Dr A A Griffith of Rolls-Royce. Two Nene engines were mounted back-to-back in the centre of the rig, their exhaust gases directed downwards through cascade-type deflector vanes to provide vertical lift.

BELL MODEL 47

Powered by: One 175 hp Franklin 6A-LV-335 six-cylinder horizontally-opposed (but vertically-mounted) engine, driving two-blade main and tail rotors
Main rotor diameter: 35 ft 1½ in (10.71 m)
Length (tail rotor turning): 31 ft 5¼ in (9.58 m)
Main rotor disc area: 965 sq ft (89.65 m²)
Gross weight: 2,100 lb (953 kg)
Max cruising speed: 80 mph (129 km/h)
Range: 200 miles (322 km)
Accommodation: Crew of 1 and 1 passenger
First flight: late 1945

Based on the Bell Model 30 first flown in mid-1943, the Bell 47 received Helicopter Type Certificate No 1 from the American CAA on 8 March 1946 and has been in continuous production ever since, in a multitude of variants. The original version, to which the data apply, had a fully-enclosed fuselage, as do some recent models such as the 47J. More familiar are the 47G series (silhouette shows a 47G-3), with 'goldfish bowl' cabins and openwork rear fuselages. The Bell 47 formed the basis for Bell to become, today, the manufacturer of the greatest number of rotating-wing aircraft in the western world. To date Bell has delivered well over 15,000 helicopters of many different designs, including more commercial helicopters than all other US manufacturers combined.

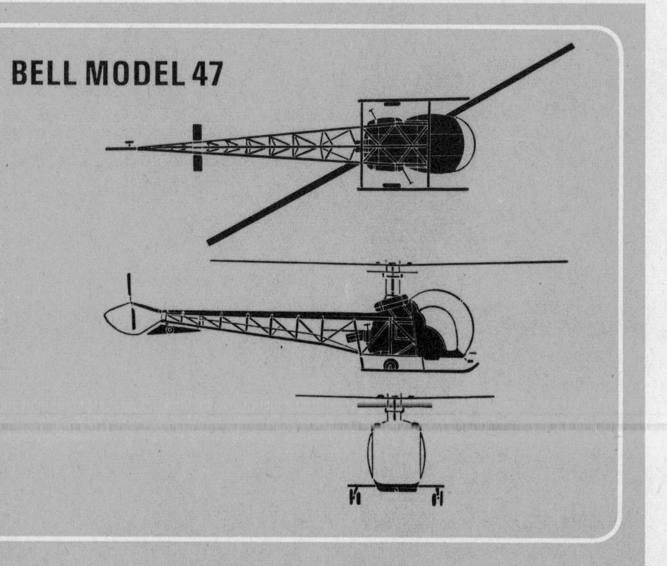

Mil Mi-4, passenger version

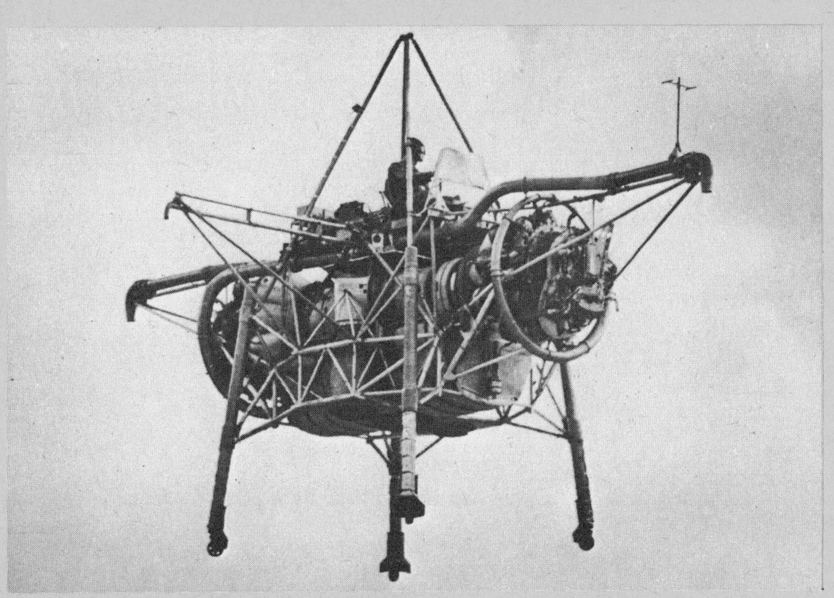

Rolls-Royce Thrust Measuring Rig ('Flying Bedstead')

Bell Model 47G-2

LOCKHEED F-104 STARFIGHTER

Powered by: One 15,800 lb (7,165 kg) st General Electric J79-GE-11A afterburning turbojet engine
Wing span: 21 ft 11 in (6.68 m) without tip-tanks
Length: 54 ft 9 in (16.69 m)
Wing area: 196.1 sq ft (18.22 m²)
Gross weight: 28,779 lb (13,054 kg)
Max speed: 1,450 mph (2,330 km/h) at 36,000 ft (11,000 m) (Mach 2.2)
Radius with max internal fuel: 745 miles (1,200 km)
Accommodation: Crew of 1
First flight: 7 February 1954 (XF-104); 5 October 1960 (F-104G)

Its needle-sharp fuselage and short stubby wings prompted Lockheed to describe the Starfighter, on its first appearance, as 'a missile with a man in it'. In the ensuing decade and a half the F-104 has survived a number of setbacks and proved itself one of the best air superiority fighters of its time, not to mention its useful attack capability. A feature of the original design was the crew escape system, which ejected the pilot (and his companion, in the two-seat versions) downward through the cockpit floor. Data apply to the F-104G version.

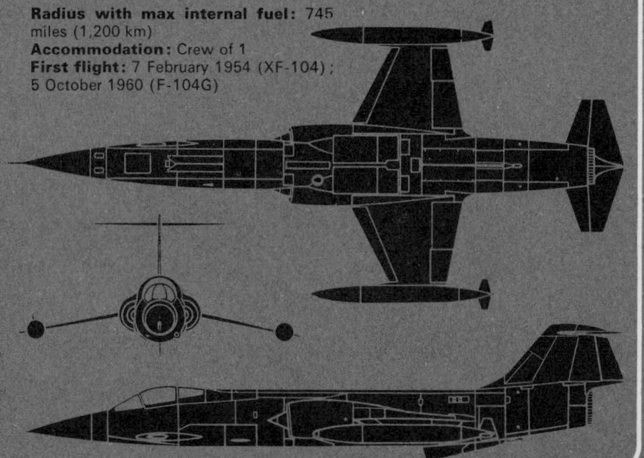

FAIREY DELTA 2

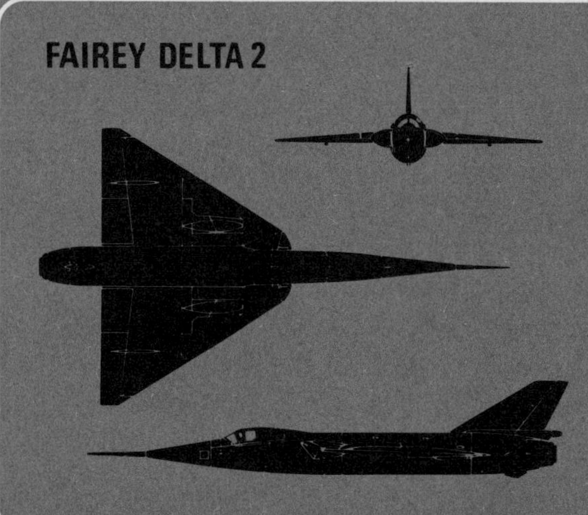

Powered by: One 10,050 lb (4,763 kg) st Rolls-Royce Avon RA.28 turbojet
Wing span: 26 ft 10 in (8.18 m)
Length: 51 ft $7\frac{1}{2}$ in (15.74 m)
Wing area: 360 sq ft (33.45 m²)
Gross weight: 13,400 lb (6,078 kg)
Max speed: 1,188 mph (1,912 km/h) above 36,000 ft (10,975 m)
Max range: 830 miles (1,336 km)
Accommodation: Crew of 1
First flight: 6 October 1954

Last British aircraft to hold the world absolute speed record (1,132 mph=1,822 km/h, set on 10 March 1956), the Fairey Delta 2 was also the first aircraft to raise the record above 1,000 mph (1,609 km/h). Two were built, for high-speed research work; one feature of their design was the drooping nose section, now incorporated in the Concorde and Tu-144 supersonic transports; and one Delta 2 was converted (as the BAC-221) to flight-test a small-scale version of the Concorde's curved-delta wings.

REPUBLIC F-105 THUNDERCHIEF

Powered by: One 26,500 lb (12,030 kg) st Pratt & Whitney J75-P-19W afterburning turbojet engine
Wing span: 34 ft $11\frac{1}{4}$ in (10.65 m)
Length: 67 ft $0\frac{1}{4}$ in (20.43 m)
Wing area: 385 sq ft (35.77 m²)
Gross weight: 52,545 lb (23,814 kg)
Max speed: 1,485 mph (2,390 km/h) at 36,000 ft (11,000 m)
Typical combat radius: 920 miles (1,480 km)
Armament: One 20-mm General Electric Vulcan multi-barrel cannon in fuselage; more than 14,000 lb (6,350 kg) of bombs, rockets, napalm containers or drop-tanks under wings and fuselage.
Accommodation: Crew of 1
First flights: 22 October 1955 (YF-105); 9 June 1959 (F-105D)

One of the most sophisticated aircraft to be thrown into the struggle in Vietnam, the Thunderchief has been called by publicists a 'one-man air force'; to its crews it is known affectionately as the 'Thud'. Major version is the all-weather F-105D (data and silhouette), which entered USAF service in 1960; more than 600 of this model were built. In August 1969 the first example was flown of a modified F-105D, distinguishable by its 'saddleback' dorsal fairing which contains the electronics for a new T-Stick II integral bombing system; about 30 other Thunderchiefs were similarly modernised in 1970.

Lockheed CF-104 Starfighter in Canadian service

Fairey Delta 2, showing drooped nose

Republic F-105D Thunderchief

FIAT G91PAN

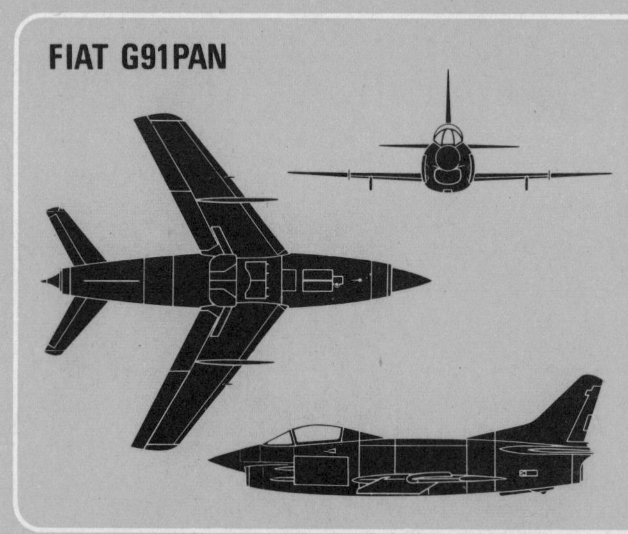

Powered by: One 4,850 lb (2,200 kg) st Bristol Orpheus 801 turbojet engine
Wing span: 28 ft 1 in (8.56 m)
Length: 34 ft 2½ in (10.43 m)
Wing area: 176.74 sq ft (16.42 m²)
Gross weight: 11,880 lb (5,390 kg)
Max speed: 650 mph (1,045 km/h) at 4,925 ft (1,500 m)
Range: 852 miles (1,370 km)
Accommodation: Crew of 1
First flight: 9 August 1956

Winner of a contest launched by NATO in 1954 for a tactical strike/fighter aircraft, the Fiat G91 has since been produced in considerable numbers for the air forces of Italy and Federal Germany. After these had entered service, 16 of the 27 pre-production aircraft were converted in 1964 for Italy's national aerobatic team, the *Pattuglia Acrobatica Nazionale,* under the revised designation G91PAN. These remained in use in 1971; the basic modification consisted of removing the armament, replacing it with ballast to maintain the original gross weight and CG range, and fitting canisters for coloured smoke under the wings.

HAWKER SIDDELEY GNAT TRAINER

Powered by: One 4,400 lb (1,996 kg) st Rolls-Royce (Bristol) Orpheus 101 turbojet engine
Wing span: 24 ft 0 in (7.32 m)
Length: 37 ft 10 in (11.51 m) including nose-probe
Wing area: 175 sq ft (16.26 m²)
Gross weight (normal): 8,250 lb (3,742 kg)
Max speed: 635 mph (1,022 km/h) at 31,000 ft (9,450 m)
Max range: 750 miles (1,200 km) on internal fuel
Accommodation: Crew of 2
First flight: 31 August 1959

The Gnat T. Mk 1 trainer, used by the RAF's 'Red Arrows' aerobatic display team, is probably the best-known participant at almost every air show in Europe. It is also a standard training aircraft of the Royal Air Force, with whom it has been in service since early 1962, and is only slightly different from the single-seat fighter version used by the air forces of Finland and India.

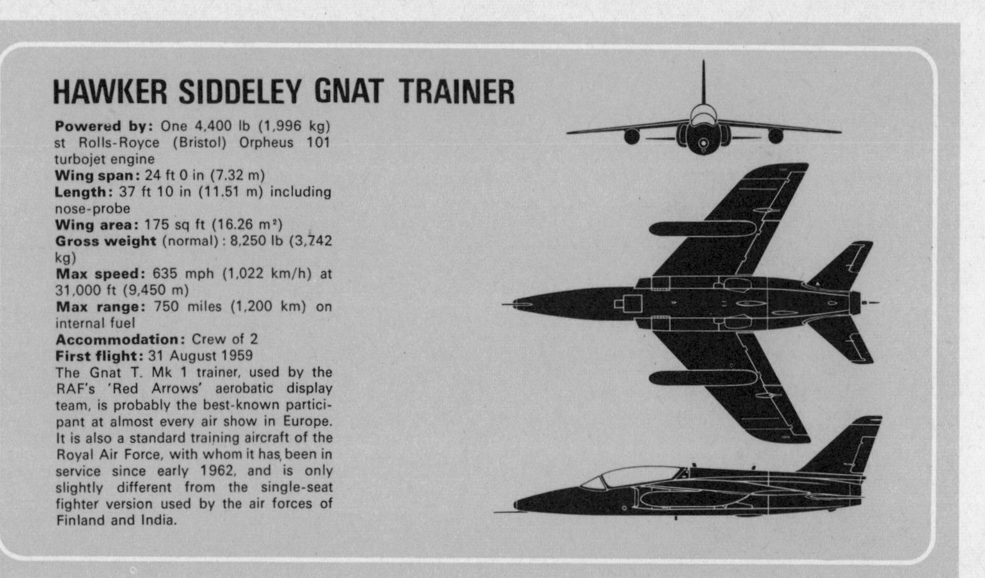

McDONNELL DOUGLAS PHANTOM

Powered by: Two 12,500 lb (5,670 kg) st Rolls-Royce Spey RB.168-25R Mk 201 turbofan engines (21,250 lb; 9,638 kg st with afterburning)
Wing span: 38 ft 5 in (11.70 m)
Length: 57 ft 11 in (17.65 m)
Wing area: 530.0 sq ft (49.24 m²)
Gross weight: 58,000 lb (26.308 kg)
Max speed: 1,386 mph (2,230 km/h) at 36,000 ft (11,000 m)
Typical tactical radius: 550 miles (885 km)
Accommodation: Crew of 2
First flights: 27 May 1958 (XF4H-1 prototype); 27 June 1966 (F-4K)

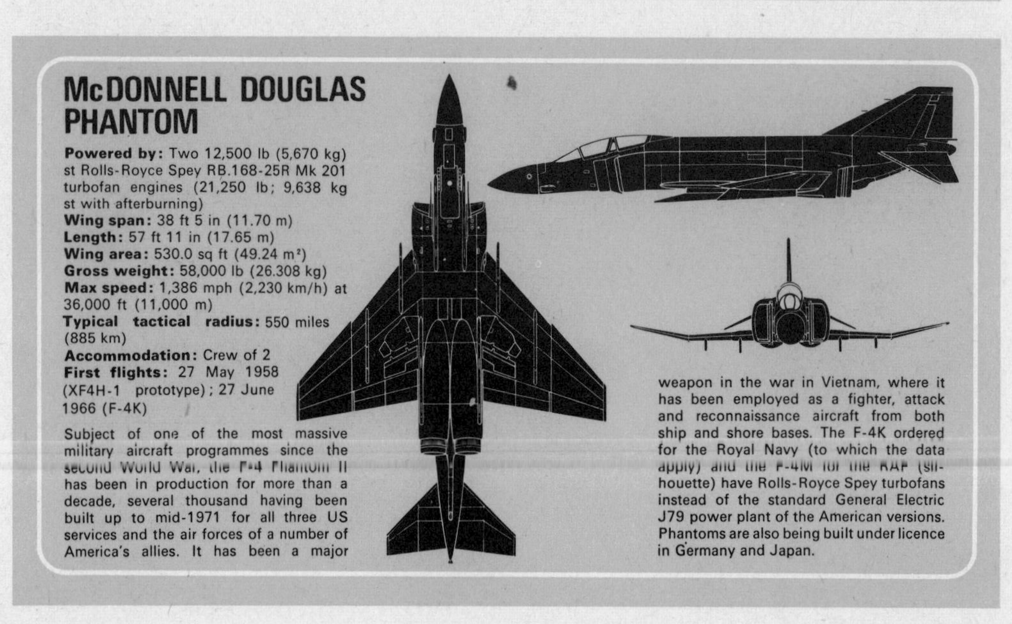

Subject of one of the most massive military aircraft programmes since the second World War, the F-4 Phantom II has been in production for more than a decade, several thousand having been built up to mid-1971 for all three US services and the air forces of a number of America's allies. It has been a major weapon in the war in Vietnam, where it has been employed as a fighter, attack and reconnaissance aircraft from both ship and shore bases. The F-4K ordered for the Royal Navy (to which the data apply) and the F-4M for the RAF (silhouette) have Rolls-Royce Spey turbofans instead of the standard General Electric J79 power plant of the American versions. Phantoms are also being built under licence in Germany and Japan.

Fiat G91PAN

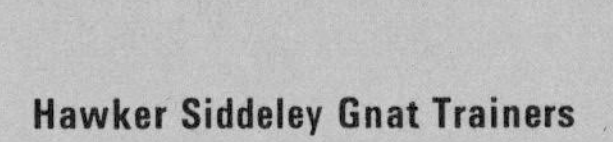

Hawker Siddeley Gnat Trainers

Royal Air Force Phantom FGR Mk 2 (F-4M)

LOCKHEED HC-130H HERCULES

Powered by: Four 4,500 eshp Allison T56-A-15 turboprop engines, each driving a 13 ft 6 in (4.11 m) diameter four-blade propeller
Wing span: 132 ft 7 in (40.41 m)
Length: 98 ft 9 in (30.10 m)
Wing area: 1,745 sq ft (162.12 m²)
Gross weight: 155,000 lb (70,310 kg)
Max speed: 384 mph (618 km/h)
Typical range: 2,450 miles (3,945 km)
Accommodation: Crew of 10
First flights: 23 August 1954 (YC-130); 8 December 1964 (HC-130H)

The Hercules, which has been in continuous production for more than 15 years, is one of the major post-war export successes of the American aircraft industry, which has built many hundreds for the US armed forces and for sale to Australia, Brazil, Canada, Indonesia, Iran, New Zealand, Pakistan, Saudi Arabia, South Africa, Sweden, Turkey and the UK. The 'air snatch' HC-130H, which is used by the USAF's Aerospace Rescue and Recovery Service, has scissor-like folding probes on the nose designed to make pick-ups from the ground or in mid-air by using the probes to engage parachute lines or balloon cables attached to the man or equipment to be recovered.

BOEING EC-135

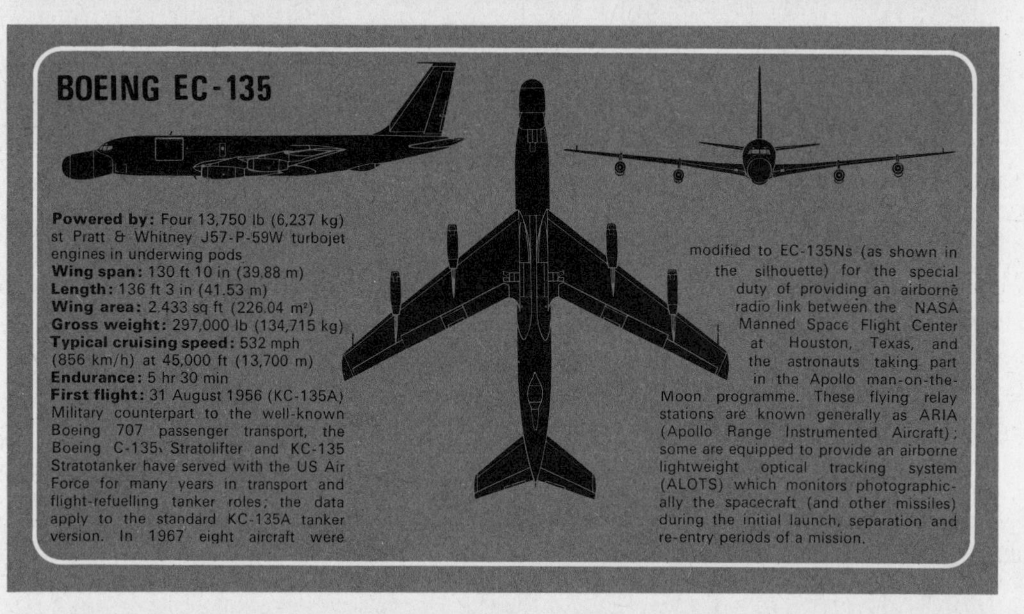

Powered by: Four 13,750 lb (6,237 kg) st Pratt & Whitney J57-P-59W turbojet engines in underwing pods
Wing span: 130 ft 10 in (39.88 m)
Length: 136 ft 3 in (41.53 m)
Wing area: 2,433 sq ft (226.04 m²)
Gross weight: 297,000 lb (134,715 kg)
Typical cruising speed: 532 mph (856 km/h) at 45,000 ft (13,700 m)
Endurance: 5 hr 30 min
First flight: 31 August 1956 (KC-135A)

Military counterpart to the well-known Boeing 707 passenger transport, the Boeing C-135, Stratolifter and KC-135 Stratotanker have served with the US Air Force for many years in transport and flight-refuelling tanker roles; the data apply to the standard KC-135A tanker version. In 1967 eight aircraft were modified to EC-135Ns (as shown in the silhouette) for the special duty of providing an airborne radio link between the NASA Manned Space Flight Center at Houston, Texas, and the astronauts taking part in the Apollo man-on-the-Moon programme. These flying relay stations are known generally as ARIA (Apollo Range Instrumented Aircraft); some are equipped to provide an airborne lightweight optical tracking system (ALOTS) which monitors photographically the spacecraft (and other missiles) during the initial launch, separation and re-entry periods of a mission.

SIKORSKY SH-3A SEA KING

Powered by: Two 1,250 shp General Electric T58-GE-8B turboshaft engines, driving a five-blade main rotor and five-blade tail rotor
Main rotor diameter: 62 ft 0 in (18.90 m)
Length: 72 ft 8 in (22.15 m)
Main rotor disc area: 3,019 sq ft (280.5 m²)
Gross weight: 20,500 lb (9,300 kg)
Cruising speed: 136 mph (219 km/h)
Max range: 625 miles (1,005 km)
Accommodation: Crew of 4 in ASW role; varies in astronaut recovery aircraft according to individual mission
First flight: 11 March 1959

Known to television viewers in all parts of the world as the type of helicopter which stands by to carry out, and to photograph, the recovery of astronauts returning from missions in space, the SH-3A is but one of many variants of Sikorsky's basic S-61 design which first appeared a dozen years ago. These are used by all three US services, and also by the armed forces of Britain, Brazil, Canada, Denmark, Germany, Japan and Italy. Primary function is that of anti-submarine patrol, but other variants are employed for search and rescue or mine countermeasures duties.

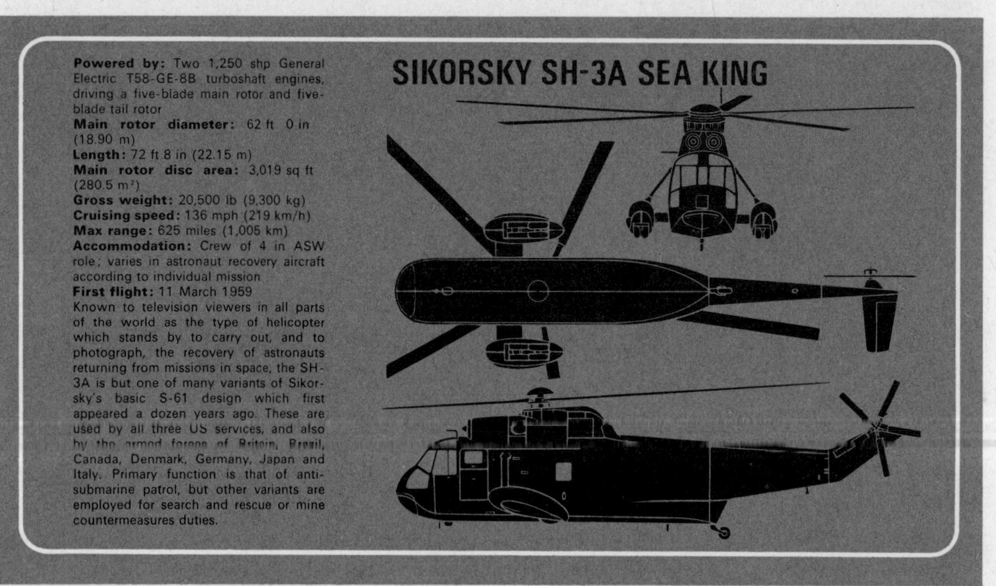

Lockheed C-130E Hercules

Boeing EC-135N airborne relay aircraft for Apollo programme

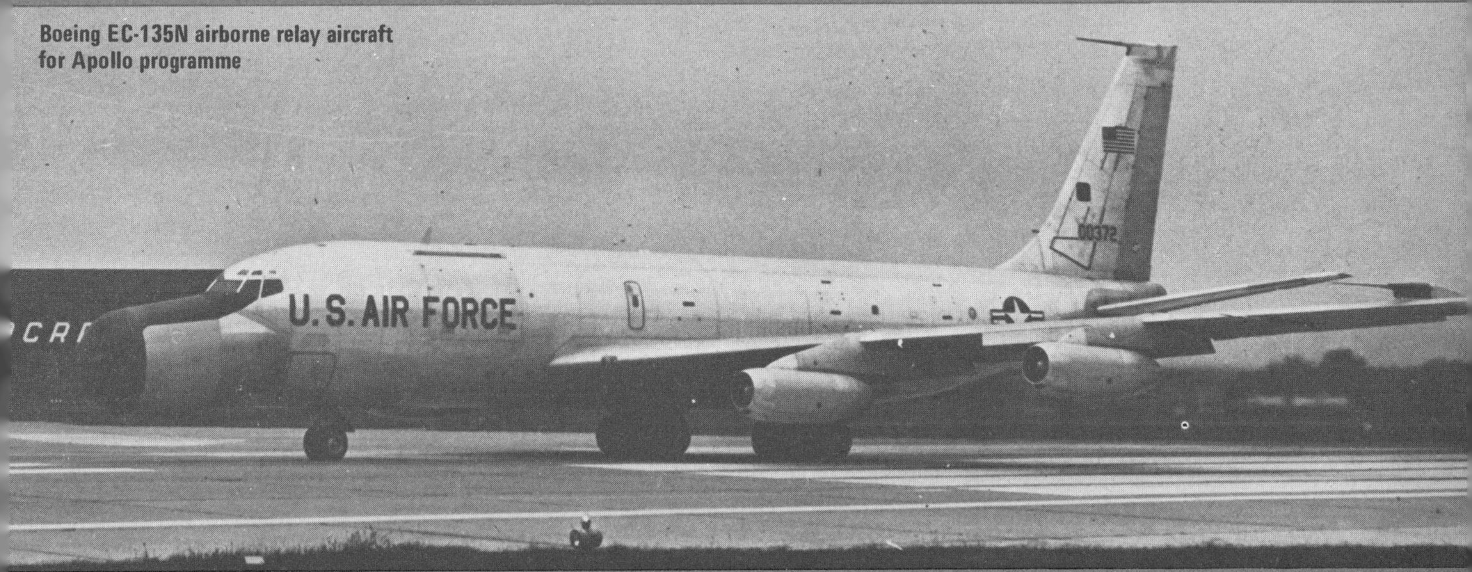

Westland-built Sea King, with dorsal radome

JURCA M.J.2 TEMPÊTE

Powered by: One 65 hp Continental A65 four-cylinder horizontally-opposed air-cooled engine, driving a two-blade propeller
Wing span: 19 ft 8¼ in (6.00 m)
Length: 19 ft 2½ in (5.855 m)
Wing area: 85.90 sq ft (7.98 m^2)
Gross weight: 948 lb (430 kg)
Max speed: 120 mph (193 km/h)
Accommodation: Crew of 1
First flight: 27 June 1956
The Tempête was the first of a wide range of aircraft designs produced for amateur constructors by M Marcel Julea in France. The Tempete will take engines of 65-125 hp, and over 20 were flying or being built in 1970. Other Jurca designs include the two-seat M.J.5 Sirocco and several based on scaling down famous wartime fighters such as the Spitfire, Mustang and Fw 190 to two-thirds or three-quarters their original size.

SMITH DSA-1 MINIPLANE

Powered by: Any 65-125 hp engine. Prototype fitted with a 108 hp Lycoming O-235-C four-cylinder horizontally-opposed air-cooled engine, driving a two-blade propeller of 5 ft 11 in (1.80 m) diameter
Wing span: 17 ft 0 in (5.18 m)
Length: 15 ft 3 in (4.80 m)
Wing area: 100 sq ft (9.29 m^2)
Gross weight: 1,000 lb (454 kg)
Max speed: 135 mph (217 km/h) at S/L
Accommodation: Crew of 1
First flight: October 1956
The designation letters of the Smith Miniplane stand for 'Darn Small Aeroplane', and its popularity is attested by nearly 200 now flying in the US and elsewhere. Marketing of plans of the aircraft has been continued since Frank Smith's death by his wife, Mrs Dorothy Smith, and his son is developing a two-seat version. The details above apply to the prototype.

NIPPER MK III

Powered by: One 1,500 cc (45 hp) Rollason Ardem X four-cylinder horizontally-opposed engine, driving a two-blade propeller
Wing span: 19 ft 8 in (6.00 m)
Length: 15 ft 0 in (4.56 m)
Wing area: 80.70 sq ft (7.50 m^2)
Gross weight: 660 lb (300 kg)
Max speed: 107 mph (173 km/h) at S/L
Normal range: 200 miles (320 km)
Accommodation: Crew of 1
First flight: 2 December 1957
Designed by Mr E O Tips, the Nipper was originally built by Avions Fairey in Belgium as the Tipsy Nipper Mk I, with a 40 hp Pollmann engine. This was succeeded in 1959 by the Nipper Mk II, with a more powerful Stark Stamo engine. Exclusive rights in the Nipper were purchased in 1966 by Nipper Aircraft in the UK, which continues to build this ultra-light single-seater as the Mk III and (with a 1,600 cc engine) Mk IIIA. The Nipper can be fitted with wingtip fuel tanks, which extend its maximum range to 450 miles (720 km).

Jurca Tempêtes

Smith DSA-1 Miniplane *(Robert D Archer)*

Belgian-built Tipsy Nipper

CASSUTT SPECIAL 1

Powered by: One 85 hp Continental C85-8F horizontally-opposed piston-engine, modified to produce 112-115 hp for racing
Wing span: 14 ft 11 in (4.54 m)
Length: 16 ft 0 in (4.88 m)
Gross weight: 730 lb (331 kg)
Max speed: 230 mph (370 km/h)
Accommodation: Crew of 1
Endurance: 3 hr with max fuel load of 15 US gallons (57 litres)

The Cassutt racer was designed and built in 1954 by airline pilot Captain Thomas K Cassutt, who flew it to win the 1958 US championships. In 1959 he produced a slightly smaller version known as the Cassutt Special II. A modified version of the Cassutt I known as the Cassutt 111M, has been built in the UK by Airmark Ltd. and has a 90 hp Rolls-Royce/Continental engine.

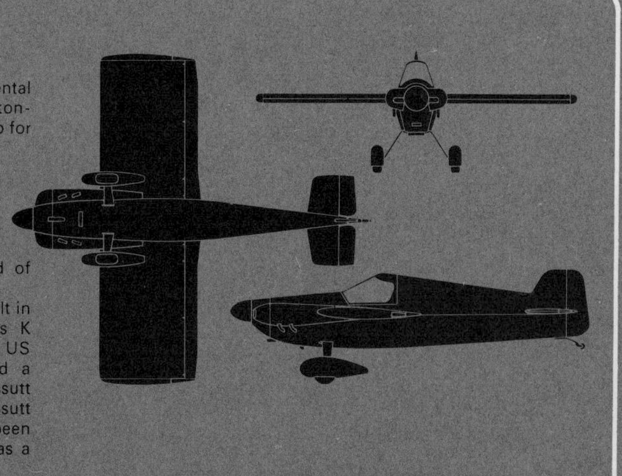

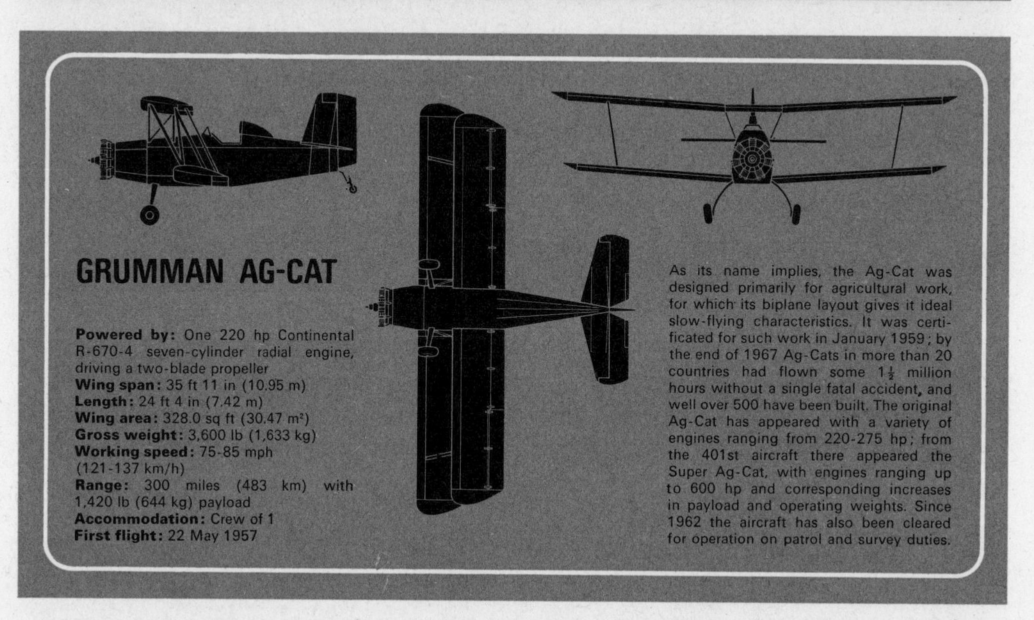

GRUMMAN AG-CAT

Powered by: One 220 hp Continental R-670-4 seven-cylinder radial engine, driving a two-blade propeller
Wing span: 35 ft 11 in (10.95 m)
Length: 24 ft 4 in (7.42 m)
Wing area: 328.0 sq ft (30.47 m²)
Gross weight: 3,600 lb (1,633 kg)
Working speed: 75-85 mph (121-137 km/h)
Range: 300 miles (483 km) with 1,420 lb (644 kg) payload
Accommodation: Crew of 1
First flight: 22 May 1957

As its name implies, the Ag-Cat was designed primarily for agricultural work, for which its biplane layout gives it ideal slow-flying characteristics. It was certificated for such work in January 1959; by the end of 1967 Ag-Cats in more than 20 countries had flown some 1½ million hours without a single fatal accident, and well over 500 have been built. The original Ag-Cat has appeared with a variety of engines ranging from 220-275 hp; from the 401st aircraft there appeared the Super Ag-Cat, with engines ranging up to 600 hp and corresponding increases in payload and operating weights. Since 1962 the aircraft has also been cleared for operation on patrol and survey duties.

PIPER PA-25 PAWNEE

Powered by: One 235 hp (derated) Lycoming O-540-B2B5 six-cylinder horizontally-opposed engine, driving a 7 ft 0 in (2.13 m) diameter two-blade propeller
Wing span: 36 ft 2 in (11.02 m)
Length: 24 ft 8½ in (7.53 m)
Wing area: 183 sq ft (17.0 m²)
Gross weight: 2,900 lb (1,315 kg)
Max cruising speed (duster/sprayer): 100/105 mph (161/169 km/h)
Max range (duster/sprayer): 255/270 miles (410/434 km)
Accommodation: Crew of 1
First flight: 1959

More than 4,000 Pawnees, with engines ranging in power from 150 to 260 hp, were in operation by 1970, making it the most widely-built type of agricultural aircraft outside of the USSR. Its hopper/tank can carry 150 US gallons (568 litres) of liquid or 1,200 lb (544 kg) of dry chemical, and it can be changed over from duster to sprayer (or vice versa) in less than five minutes. Like others of its kind, it has a fuselage designed to fail progressively from the front and other design features devised specially to protect the pilot in the event of a severe crash.

Airmark Cassutt 111M

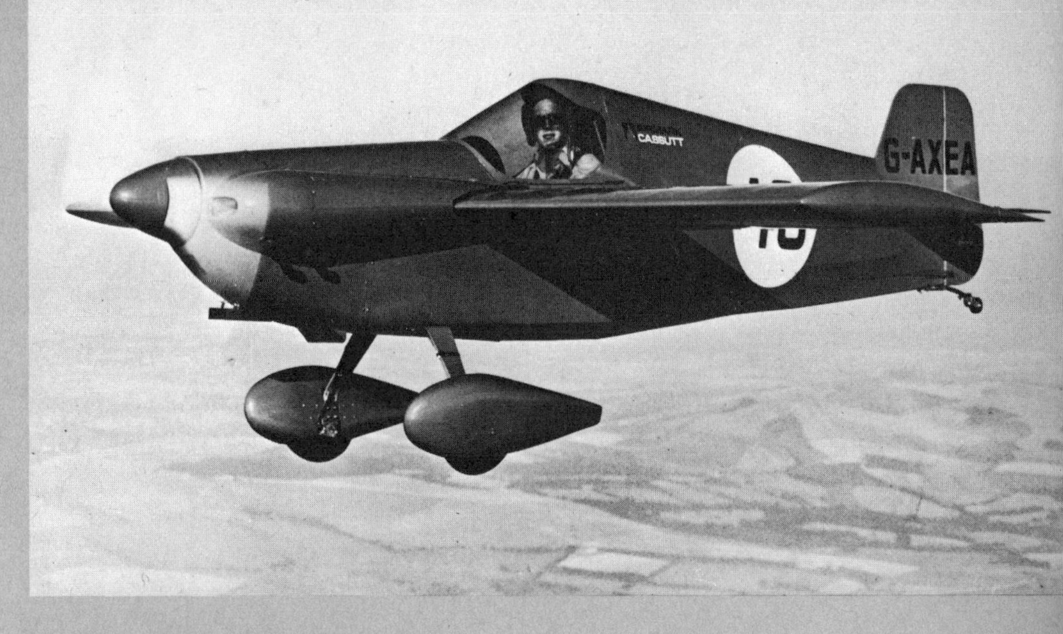

Grumman Super Ag-Cat

Piper PA-25 Pawnee

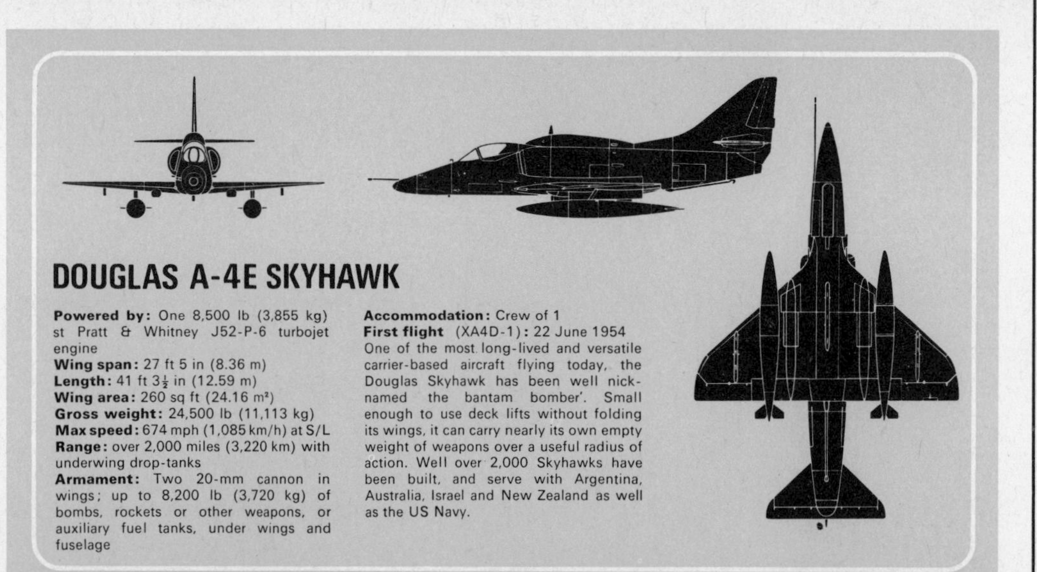

DOUGLAS A-4E SKYHAWK

Powered by: One 8,500 lb (3,855 kg) st Pratt & Whitney J52-P-6 turbojet engine
Wing span: 27 ft 5 in (8.36 m)
Length: 41 ft $3\frac{1}{3}$ in (12.59 m)
Wing area: 260 sq ft (24.16 m²)
Gross weight: 24,500 lb (11,113 kg)
Max speed: 674 mph (1,085 km/h) at S/L
Range: over 2,000 miles (3,220 km) with underwing drop-tanks
Armament: Two 20-mm cannon in wings; up to 8,200 lb (3,720 kg) of bombs, rockets or other weapons, or auxiliary fuel tanks, under wings and fuselage
Accommodation: Crew of 1
First flight (XA4D-1)**:** 22 June 1954

One of the most long-lived and versatile carrier-based aircraft flying today, the Douglas Skyhawk has been well nicknamed 'the bantam bomber'. Small enough to use deck lifts without folding its wings, it can carry nearly its own empty weight of weapons over a useful radius of action. Well over 2,000 Skyhawks have been built, and serve with Argentina, Australia, Israel and New Zealand as well as the US Navy.

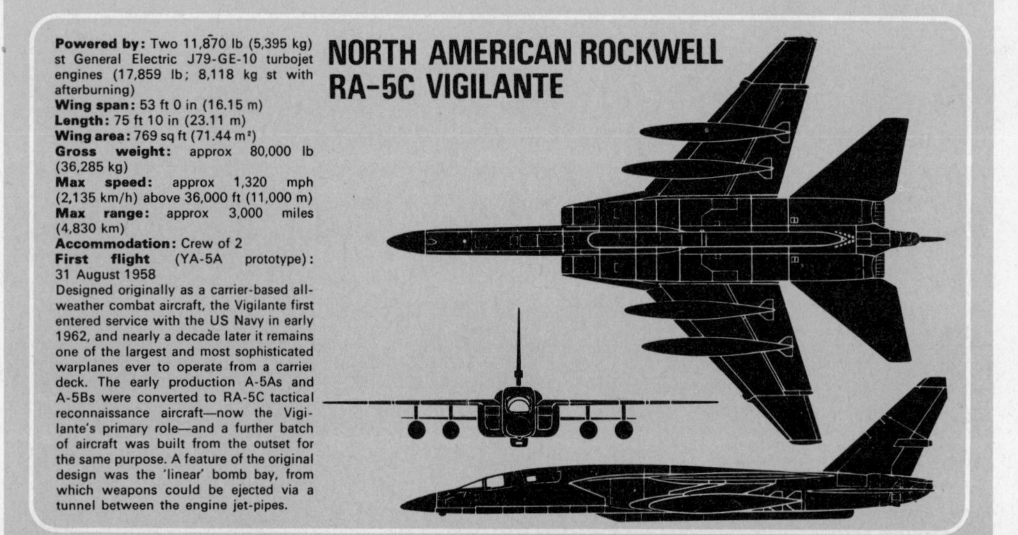

NORTH AMERICAN ROCKWELL RA-5C VIGILANTE

Powered by: Two 11,870 lb (5,395 kg) st General Electric J79-GE-10 turbojet engines (17,859 lb; 8,118 kg st with afterburning)
Wing span: 53 ft 0 in (16.15 m)
Length: 75 ft 10 in (23.11 m)
Wing area: 769 sq ft (71.44 m²)
Gross weight: approx 80,000 lb (36,285 kg)
Max speed: approx 1,320 mph (2,135 km/h) above 36,000 ft (11,000 m)
Max range: approx 3,000 miles (4,830 km)
Accommodation: Crew of 2
First flight (YA-5A prototype)**:** 31 August 1958

Designed originally as a carrier-based all-weather combat aircraft, the Vigilante first entered service with the US Navy in early 1962, and nearly a decade later it remains one of the largest and most sophisticated warplanes ever to operate from a carrier deck. The early production A-5As and A-5Bs were converted to RA-5C tactical reconnaissance aircraft—now the Vigilante's primary role—and a further batch of aircraft was built from the outset for the same purpose. A feature of the original design was the 'linear' bomb bay, from which weapons could be ejected via a tunnel between the engine jet-pipes.

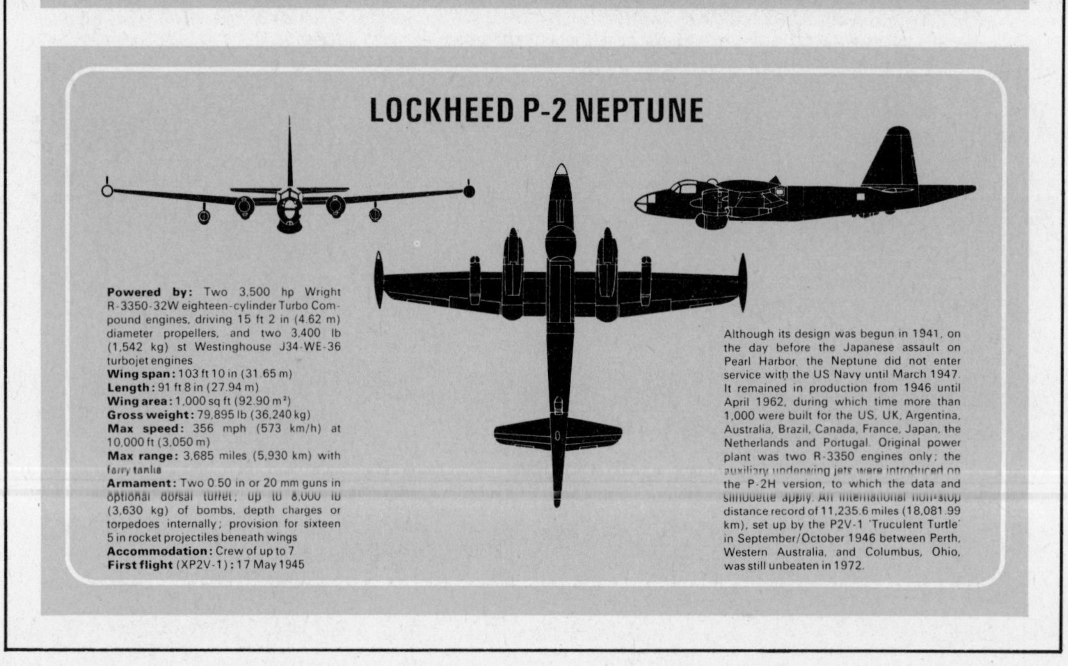

LOCKHEED P-2 NEPTUNE

Powered by: Two 3,500 hp Wright R-3350-32W eighteen-cylinder Turbo Compound engines, driving 15 ft 2 in (4.62 m) diameter propellers, and two 3,400 lb (1,542 kg) st Westinghouse J34-WE-36 turbojet engines
Wing span: 103 ft 10 in (31.65 m)
Length: 91 ft 8 in (27.94 m)
Wing area: 1,000 sq ft (92.90 m²)
Gross weight: 79,895 lb (36,240 kg)
Max speed: 356 mph (573 km/h) at 10,000 ft (3,050 m)
Max range: 3,685 miles (5,930 km) with ferry tanks
Armament: Two 0.50 in or 20 mm guns in optional dorsal turret; up to 8,000 lb (3,630 kg) of bombs, depth charges or torpedoes internally; provision for sixteen 5 in rocket projectiles beneath wings
Accommodation: Crew of up to 7
First flight (XP2V-1)**:** 17 May 1945

Although its design was begun in 1941, on the day before the Japanese assault on Pearl Harbor, the Neptune did not enter service with the US Navy until March 1947. It remained in production from 1946 until April 1962, during which time more than 1,000 were built for the US, UK, Argentina, Australia, Brazil, Canada, France, Japan, the Netherlands and Portugal. Original power plant was two R-3350 engines only; the auxiliary underwing jets were introduced on the P-2H version, to which the data and silhouette apply. An international non-stop distance record of 11,235.6 miles (18,081.99 km), set up by the P2V-1 'Truculent Turtle' in September/October 1946 between Perth, Western Australia, and Columbus, Ohio, was still unbeaten in 1972.

Douglas A-4E Skyhawk

North American Rockwell RA-5C Vigilante

Lockheed P-2E (P2V-5) Neptune

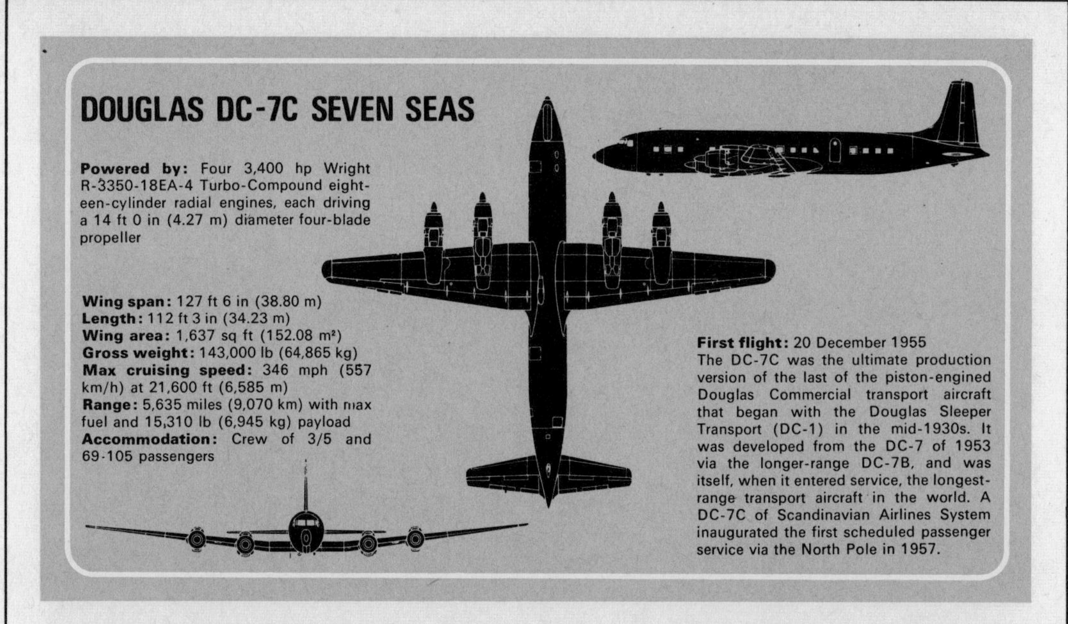

DOUGLAS DC-7C SEVEN SEAS

Powered by: Four 3,400 hp Wright R-3350-18EA-4 Turbo-Compound eighteen-cylinder radial engines, each driving a 14 ft 0 in (4.27 m) diameter four-blade propeller

Wing span: 127 ft 6 in (38.80 m)
Length: 112 ft 3 in (34.23 m)
Wing area: 1,637 sq ft (152.08 m²)
Gross weight: 143,000 lb (64,865 kg)
Max cruising speed: 346 mph (557 km/h) at 21,600 ft (6,585 m)
Range: 5,635 miles (9,070 km) with max fuel and 15,310 lb (6,945 kg) payload
Accommodation: Crew of 3/5 and 69-105 passengers
First flight: 20 December 1955

The DC-7C was the ultimate production version of the last of the piston-engined Douglas Commercial transport aircraft that began with the Douglas Sleeper Transport (DC-1) in the mid-1930s. It was developed from the DC-7 of 1953 via the longer-range DC-7B, and was itself, when it entered service, the longest-range transport aircraft in the world. A DC-7C of Scandinavian Airlines System inaugurated the first scheduled passenger service via the North Pole in 1957.

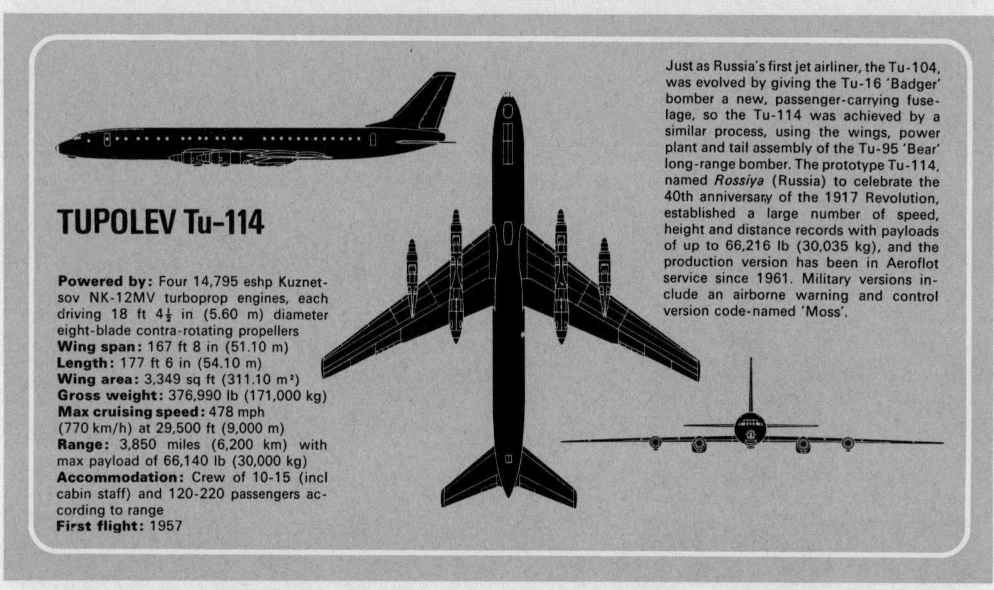

TUPOLEV Tu-114

Powered by: Four 14,795 eshp Kuznetsov NK-12MV turboprop engines, each driving 18 ft 4½ in (5.60 m) diameter eight-blade contra-rotating propellers
Wing span: 167 ft 8 in (51.10 m)
Length: 177 ft 6 in (54.10 m)
Wing area: 3,349 sq ft (311.10 m²)
Gross weight: 376,990 lb (171,000 kg)
Max cruising speed: 478 mph (770 km/h) at 29,500 ft (9,000 m)
Range: 3,850 miles (6,200 km) with max payload of 66,140 lb (30,000 kg)
Accommodation: Crew of 10-15 (incl cabin staff) and 120-220 passengers according to range
First flight: 1957

Just as Russia's first jet airliner, the Tu-104, was evolved by giving the Tu-16 'Badger' bomber a new, passenger-carrying fuselage, so the Tu-114 was achieved by a similar process, using the wings, power plant and tail assembly of the Tu-95 'Bear' long-range bomber. The prototype Tu-114, named *Rossiya* (Russia) to celebrate the 40th anniversary of the 1917 Revolution, established a large number of speed, height and distance records with payloads of up to 66,216 lb (30,035 kg), and the production version has been in Aeroflot service since 1961. Military versions include an airborne warning and control version code-named 'Moss'.

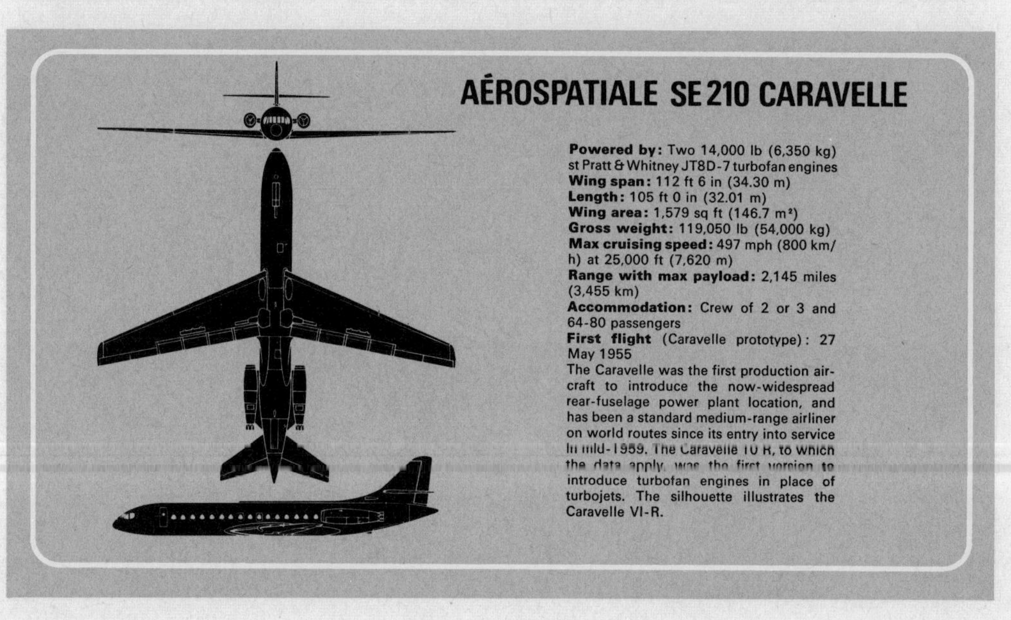

AÉROSPATIALE SE 210 CARAVELLE

Powered by: Two 14,000 lb (6,350 kg) st Pratt & Whitney JT8D-7 turbofan engines
Wing span: 112 ft 6 in (34.30 m)
Length: 105 ft 0 in (32.01 m)
Wing area: 1,579 sq ft (146.7 m²)
Gross weight: 119,050 lb (54,000 kg)
Max cruising speed: 497 mph (800 km/h) at 25,000 ft (7,620 m)
Range with max payload: 2,145 miles (3,455 km)
Accommodation: Crew of 2 or 3 and 64-80 passengers
First flight (Caravelle prototype): 27 May 1955

The Caravelle was the first production aircraft to introduce the now-widespread rear-fuselage power plant location, and has been a standard medium-range airliner on world routes since its entry into service in mid-1959. The Caravelle 10 R, to which the data apply, was the first version to introduce turbofan engines in place of turbojets. The silhouette illustrates the Caravelle VI-R.

Douglas DC-7C

Tupolev Tu-114 *(Novosti)*

Aérospatiale Caravelle VI-R

MIKOYAN MiG-21 PF

Powered by: One 9,840 lb (4,300 kg) Tumanski TDR Mk R-37F turbojet (13,120 lb; 5,950 kg st with afterburning); provision for rocket-assisted take-off
Wing span: 23 ft 5½ in (7.15 m)
Length: approx 52 ft 6 in (16.00 m)
Wing area: 247.6 sq ft (23.00 m²)
Gross weight: approx 20,500 lb (9,300 kg)
Max speed: approx 1,320 mph (2,135 km/h) above 36,000 ft (11,000 m) (Mach 2)
Combat radius: 350 miles (560 km)
Armament: Two underwing pods of unguided rockets or two 'Atoll' air-to-air guided missiles
Accommodation: Crew of 1
First flight: *ca* 1955
The original MiG-21F production version, known to NATO as Fishbed-C, is a day interceptor fighter with a cannon armament in addition to the two underwing 'Atoll' missiles; it is in service with about 20 air forces throughout the world. The MiG-21PF (Fishbed-D) is an all-weather version which dispenses with the fixed guns and has a more powerful R-37F engine and larger nose radar. Improved versions include Fishbed-F, -H and -J, of which the last-named is a multi-mission fighter with four underwing stations and reinforced wings for improved low-level performance. It equipped Soviet Air Force squadrons stationed in the Middle East in 1970.

AERMACCHI M.B.326 GB

Powered by: One 3,410 lb (1,547 kg) st Rolls-Royce Bristol Viper 20 Mk 540 turbojet engine
Wing span: 35 ft 7 in (10.85 m) over tip-tanks
Length: 34 ft 11¼ in (10.65 m)
Wing area: 208.3 sq ft (19.35 m²)
Gross weight: 11,500 lb (5,216 kg)
Max speed: 539 mph (867 km/h) at AUW of 8,680 lb (3,937 kg)
Typical combat radius: 405 miles (650 km)
Armament: Wide variety of bombs, rockets, machine-gun or Minigun pods or missiles on six underwing pylons
Accommodation: Crew of 2
First flight (M.B.326 prototype): 10 December 1957
The original Viper 11-engined M.B.326 has been in service as a basic trainer with the Italian Air Force since 1962, and as a dual-role trainer/ground attack aircraft it also serves with the air forces of Tunisia, Ghana and South Africa. The M.B.326G and GB, which have the more powerful Viper 20 engine, can carry an increased armament load, and have been ordered by the Argentine Navy, Brazilian Air Force and Congolese Air Force. A special single-seat attack version is known as the M.B.326K.

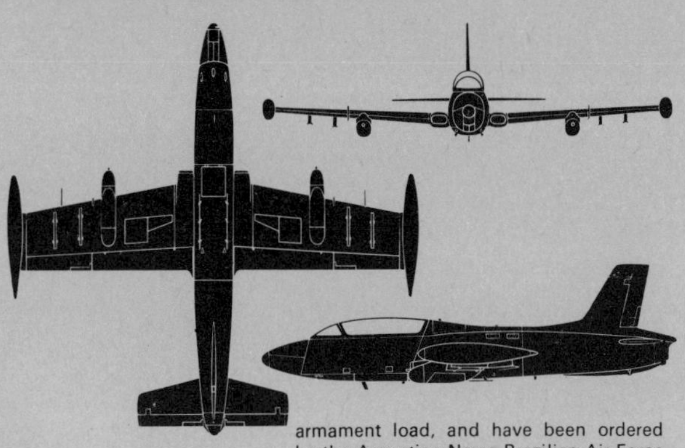

NORTHROP T-38A TALON

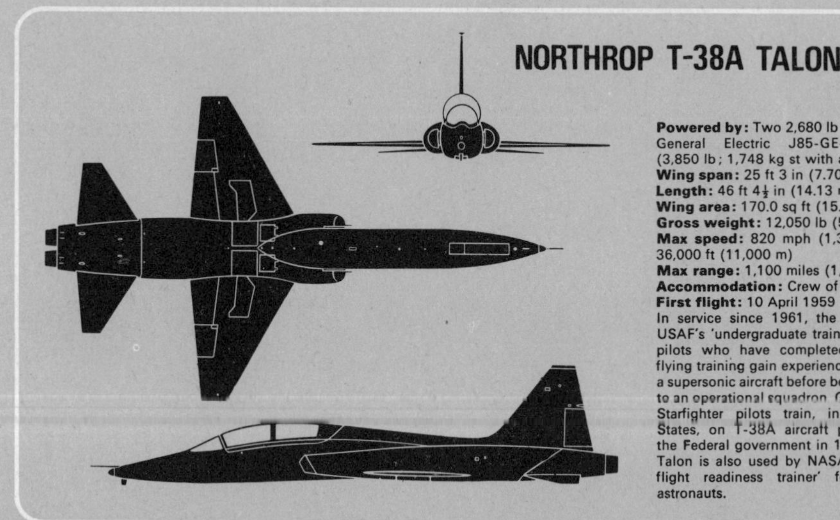

Powered by: Two 2,680 lb (1,216 kg) st General Electric J85-GE-5 turbojets (3,850 lb; 1,748 kg st with afterburning)
Wing span: 25 ft 3 in (7.70 m)
Length: 46 ft 4½ in (14.13 m)
Wing area: 170.0 sq ft (15.79 m²)
Gross weight: 12,050 lb (5,465 kg)
Max speed: 820 mph (1,320 km/h) at 36,000 ft (11,000 m)
Max range: 1,100 miles (1,770 km)
Accommodation: Crew of 2
First flight: 10 April 1959
In service since 1961, the Talon is the USAF's 'undergraduate trainer', on which pilots who have completed their basic flying training gain experience of handling a supersonic aircraft before being allocated to an operational squadron. German F-104 Starfighter pilots train, in the United States, on T-38A aircraft purchased by the Federal government in 1967; and the Talon is also used by NASA as a 'space flight readiness trainer' for American astronauts.

MiG-21PF *(Novosti)*

Aermacchi M.B.326H of the RAAF

Northrop T-38A Talons

LOCKHEED U-2

Powered by: One 11,200 lb (5,080 kg) st Pratt & Whitney J57-P-37A turbojet
Wing span: 80 ft 0 in (24.38 m)
Length: 49 ft 7 in (15.11 m)
Gross weight: 15,850 lb (7,190 kg)
Max speed: 495 mph (797 km/h) at 40,000 ft (12,200 m)
Accommodation: Crew of 1
Armament: None
Typical range: 2,200 miles (3,540 km)
Data above are for the original U-2A version. The later U-2B was fitted with a more powerful J75 turbojet engine, and a two-seat counterpart of this model is designated U-2D. Since the Powers episode in 1960, the U-2 has been used by the USAF chiefly for upper-altitude weather research flying, although it continued to be used for a while for strategic reconnaissance work over Cuba and by the Chinese Nationalist Air Force.

NORTH AMERICAN X-15A-2

Powered by: One 57,000 lb (25,855 kg) st Thiokol (Reaction Motors) XLR99-RM-2 single-chamber liquid-propellant rocket engine
Wing span: 22 ft 0 in (6.70 m)
Length: 52 ft 5 in (15.98 m)
Wing area: 200 sq ft (18.6 m²)
Gross weight: 50,914 lb (23,095 kg) at launch
Max speed: 4,534 mph (7,297 km/h) (Mach 6.72)
Accommodation: Crew of 1
First flight: 8 June 1959

The X-15 research programme, for which three aircraft were built, lasted from 1959 to 1968. During that time the aircraft (one of which was lost in a crash in 1967) flew at hypersonic speeds and at altitudes above the earth that were high enough to qualify their pilots for astronauts' wings. Apart from their direct contribution to the American space programme, the X-15s carried out considerable research into materials for the construction of ultra-high-speed aircraft of the future.

GENERAL DYNAMICS/MARTIN RB-57F

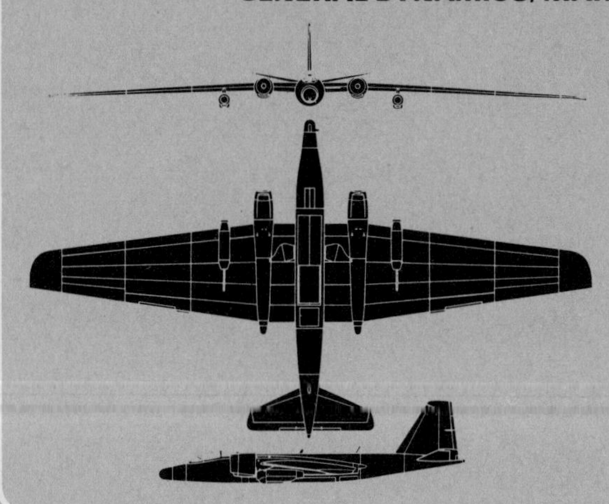

Powered by: Two 18,000 lb (8,165 kg) st Pratt & Whitney TF33-P-11 turbofan engines, and two 3,300 lb (1,500 kg) st P & W J60-P-9 auxiliary turbojets
Wing span: 122 ft 5 in (37.32 m)
Length: 69 ft 0 in (21.03 m)
Accommodation: Crew of 2
Armament: None
Typical endurance: Over 10 hr
First flight: 1964
This much-modified development of the English Electric Canberra tactical bomber is used by the USAF for high-altitude weather reconnaissance and research, including the sampling of the upper air for radioactive particles. Compared with the original Canberra design, the RB-57F has a completely new wing of almost twice the span, an extensively redesigned fuselage and a completely new power plant. It is reported to have a range of up to 4,000 miles (6,435 km) and to be able to cruise at 90-100,000 ft (27,400-30,500 m).

Lockheed U-2B

North American X-15

General Dynamics/Martin RB-57F
(T Matsuzaki)

Powered by: Two 15,400 lb (7,000 kg) st SNECMA Atar 09K afterburning turbojet engines
Wing span: 38 ft 10½ in (11.85 m)
Length: 77 ft 1 in (23.50 m)
Wing area: 840 sq ft (78.0 m²)
Gross weight: 69,665 lb (31,600 kg)
Max speed: 1,450 mph (2,335 km/h) at 36,000 ft (11,000 m)
Max range: 2,000 miles (3,220 km)
Accommodation: Crew of 2
First flight: 17 June 1959

Evolved by scaling up the single-seat Mirage III fighter, the Mirage IV prototype was followed by three pre-series aircraft and a total of 62 production Mirage IV-A twin-engined bombers for the French Air Force's *Force de Frappe*. These have been in service since the mid-1960s as strategic bombers capable of carrying either a nuclear weapon or conventional bombs. The useful radius of some 1,000 miles (1,610 km) can be extended by in-flight refuelling from Boeing C-135F tanker aircraft and, like Britain's Hawker Siddeley Vulcan, the Mirage IV-A has received in-service modifications permitting it to be used for low-level as well as high-level bombing missions.

DASSAULT MIRAGE IV-A

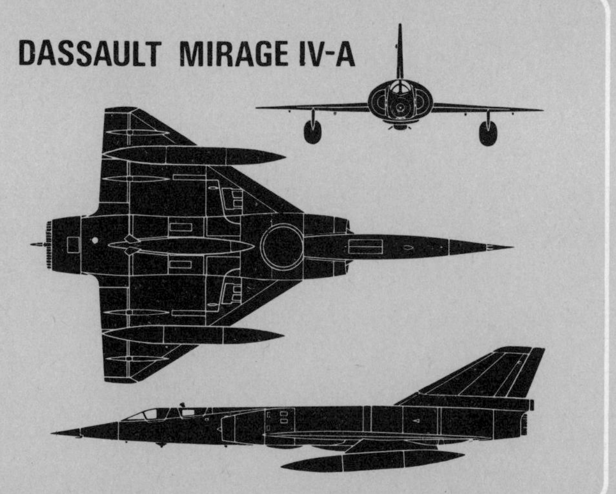

TUPOLEV Tu-22

Powered by: Two 26,000 lb (11,790 kg) st afterburning turbojet engines, mounted side-by-side in pods above the rear fuselage
Wing span: 90 ft 10½ in (27.70 m)
Length: 132 ft 11½ in (40.53 m)
Height: 17 ft 0 in (5.18 m)
Gross weight: 184,970 lb (83,900 kg)
Max speed: 920 mph (1,480 km/h) at 40,000 ft (12,200 m)
Max range: 1,400 miles (2,250 km)
Accommodation: Crew of 2 or 3
First flight: (?) 1960

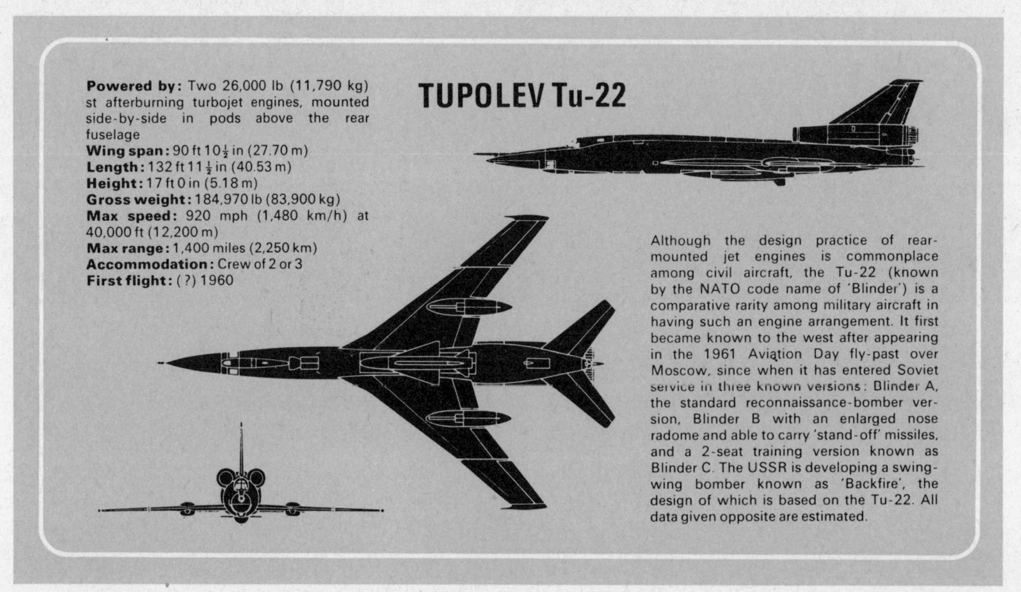

Although the design practice of rear-mounted jet engines is commonplace among civil aircraft, the Tu-22 (known by the NATO code name of 'Blinder') is a comparative rarity among military aircraft in having such an engine arrangement. It first became known to the west after appearing in the 1961 Aviation Day fly-past over Moscow, since when it has entered Soviet service in three known versions: Blinder A, the standard reconnaissance-bomber version, Blinder B with an enlarged nose radome and able to carry 'stand-off' missiles, and a 2-seat training version known as Blinder C. The USSR is developing a swing-wing bomber known as 'Backfire', the design of which is based on the Tu-22. All data given opposite are estimated.

Powered by: One Bristol Siddeley Stentor BSSt.1 twin-chamber liquid-propellant rocket engine
Wing span: 13 ft 0 in (3.96 m)
Foreplane span: 6 ft 6 in (1.98 m)
Length: 35 ft 0 in (10.67 m)
Max diameter: 4 ft 2¼ in (1.28 m)
Warhead: Thermonuclear device
Max speed: approx 1,058 mph (1,703 km/h) (Mach 1.6)
Range: approx 200 miles (320 km)

Developed by Hawker Siddeley Dynamics, the Blue Steel stand-off bomb was first test-launched from Valiant and Vulcan Mk 1 bombers and powered by a 16,000 lb (7,260 kg) st de Havilland Double Spectre rocket engine. Production Blue Steels, with Stentor engines, later became standard armament for the Mk 2 versions of the RAF's Vulcan and Victor strategic bombers, and were still operational with the former type in 1971. The weapon is built mainly of stainless steel and light alloy, and has a self-contained inertial guidance system capable, if necessary, of evasive action on the way to the target.

HSD BLUE STEEL

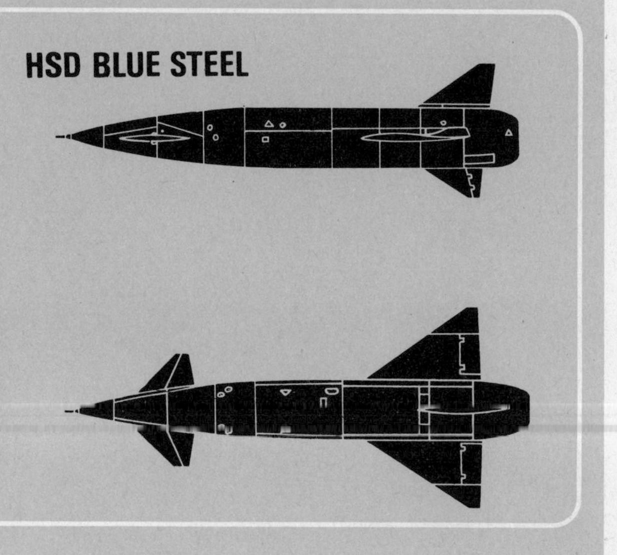

Dassault Mirage IV-A, taking off with JATO rockets

Tupolev Tu-22

Blue Steel missile under the fuselage of a Hawker Siddeley Vulcan B Mk 2 bomber of the RAF

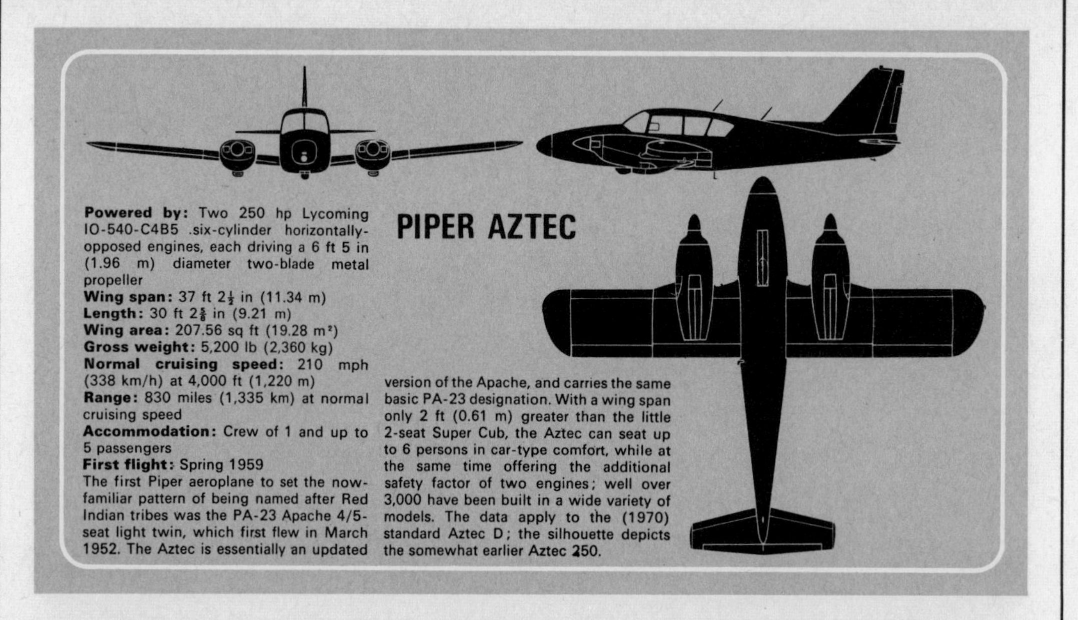

PIPER AZTEC

Powered by: Two 250 hp Lycoming IO-540-C4B5 six-cylinder horizontally-opposed engines, each driving a 6 ft 5 in (1.96 m) diameter two-blade metal propeller
Wing span: 37 ft 2½ in (11.34 m)
Length: 30 ft 2⅜ in (9.21 m)
Wing area: 207.56 sq ft (19.28 m²)
Gross weight: 5,200 lb (2,360 kg)
Normal cruising speed: 210 mph (338 km/h) at 4,000 ft (1,220 m)
Range: 830 miles (1,335 km) at normal cruising speed
Accommodation: Crew of 1 and up to 5 passengers
First flight: Spring 1959

The first Piper aeroplane to set the now-familiar pattern of being named after Red Indian tribes was the PA-23 Apache 4/5-seat light twin, which first flew in March 1952. The Aztec is essentially an updated version of the Apache, and carries the same basic PA-23 designation. With a wing span only 2 ft (0.61 m) greater than the little 2-seat Super Cub, the Aztec can seat up to 6 persons in car-type comfort, while at the same time offering the additional safety factor of two engines; well over 3,000 have been built in a wide variety of models. The data apply to the (1970) standard Aztec D; the silhouette depicts the somewhat earlier Aztec 250.

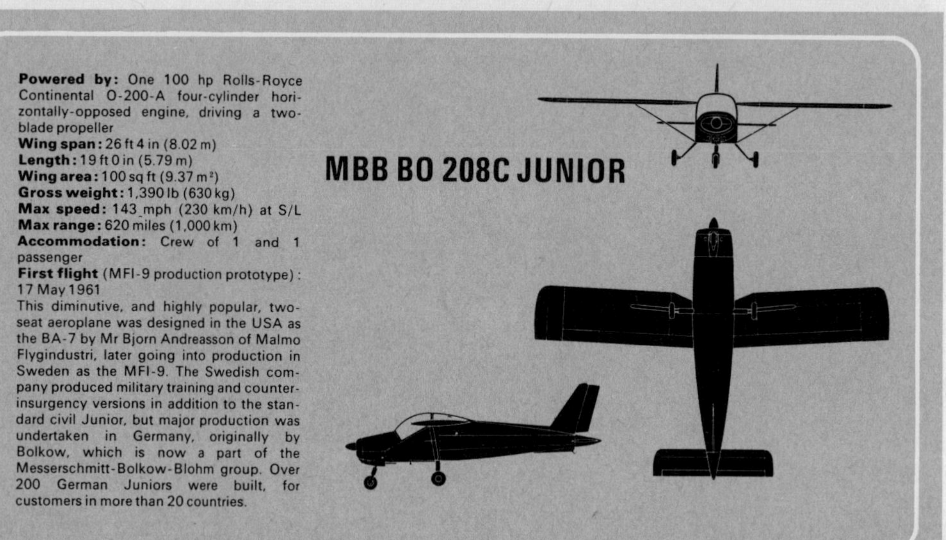

MBB BO 208C JUNIOR

Powered by: One 100 hp Rolls-Royce Continental O-200-A four-cylinder horizontally-opposed engine, driving a two-blade propeller
Wing span: 26 ft 4 in (8.02 m)
Length: 19 ft 0 in (5.79 m)
Wing area: 100 sq ft (9.37 m²)
Gross weight: 1,390 lb (630 kg)
Max speed: 143 mph (230 km/h) at S/L
Max range: 620 miles (1,000 km)
Accommodation: Crew of 1 and 1 passenger
First flight (MFI-9 production prototype): 17 May 1961

This diminutive, and highly popular, two-seat aeroplane was designed in the USA as the BA-7 by Mr Bjorn Andreasson of Malmo Flygindustri, later going into production in Sweden as the MFI-9. The Swedish company produced military training and counter-insurgency versions in addition to the standard civil Junior, but major production was undertaken in Germany, originally by Bolkow, which is now a part of the Messerschmitt-Bolkow-Blohm group. Over 200 German Juniors were built, for customers in more than 20 countries.

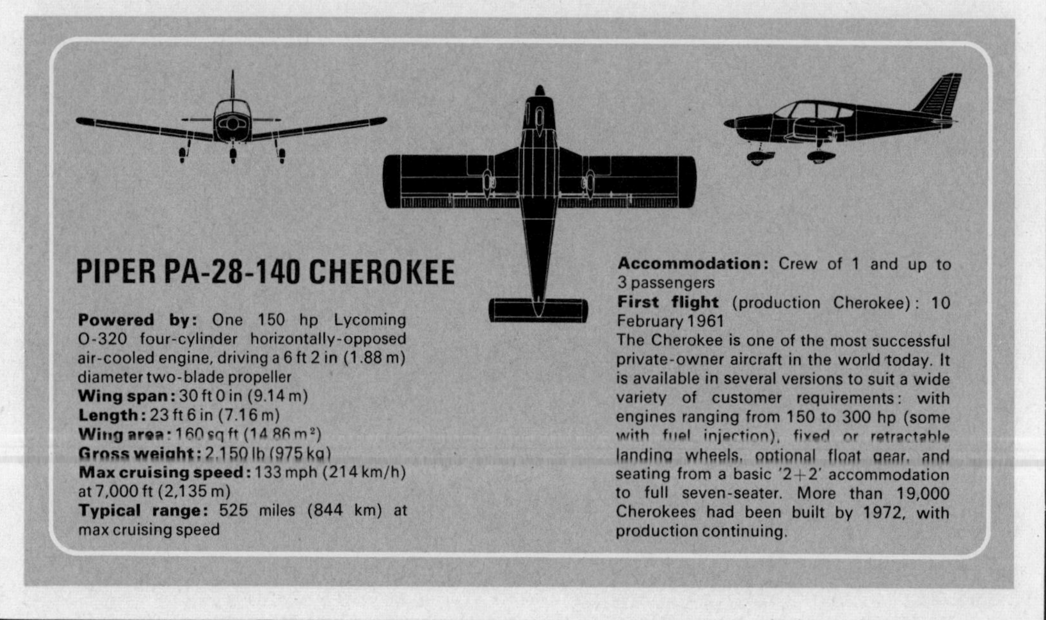

PIPER PA-28-140 CHEROKEE

Powered by: One 150 hp Lycoming O-320 four-cylinder horizontally-opposed air-cooled engine, driving a 6 ft 2 in (1.88 m) diameter two-blade propeller
Wing span: 30 ft 0 in (9.14 m)
Length: 23 ft 6 in (7.16 m)
Wing area: 160 sq ft (14.86 m²)
Gross weight: 2,150 lb (975 kg)
Max cruising speed: 133 mph (214 km/h) at 7,000 ft (2,135 m)
Typical range: 525 miles (844 km) at max cruising speed
Accommodation: Crew of 1 and up to 3 passengers
First flight (production Cherokee): 10 February 1961

The Cherokee is one of the most successful private-owner aircraft in the world today. It is available in several versions to suit a wide variety of customer requirements: with engines ranging from 150 to 300 hp (some with fuel injection), fixed or retractable landing wheels, optional float gear, and seating from a basic '2+2' accommodation to full seven-seater. More than 19,000 Cherokees had been built by 1972, with production continuing.

Piper Aztec D *(James Gilbert)*

MBB BO 208C Junior

Piper Cherokees

CANADAIR FORTY FOUR (CL-44D4)

Powered by: Four 5,730 shp Rolls-Royce Tyne RTy.12 Mk 515/10 turboprop engines, each driving a 16 ft 0 in (4.88 m) diameter four-blade propeller
Wing span: 142 ft 3½ in (43.38 m)
Length: 136 ft 9¾ in (41.70 m)
Wing area: 2,075 sq ft (192.78 m²)
Gross weight: 210,000 lb (95,250 kg)
Typical cruising speed: 373 mph (600 km/h) at 25,000 ft (7,620 m)
Typical range: 4,020 miles (6,470 km) with 37,600 lb (17,055 kg) payload
Accommodation: Crew of 4 and up to 65,200 lb (29,575 kg) of cargo or 189 passengers
First flight: 16 November 1960
First swing-tailed transport aircraft to enter service (in mid-1961, with The Flying Tiger Line), the Canadair Forty Four was developed from the Argus maritime reconnaissance aircraft and Yukon military transport, which in turn derived from the Bristol Britannia turboprop airliner. A later version, the Canadair 400, has a 15 ft (4.57 m) longer fuselage accommodating up to 214 passengers or an equivalent increase in cargo.

AVIATION TRADERS ATL.98 CARVAIR

Powered by: Four 1,450 hp Pratt & Whitney R-2000-7M2 Twin Wasp fourteen-cylinder radial air-cooled engines, each driving a three-blade propeller of 13 ft 1 in (3.99 m) diameter
Wing span: 117 ft 6 in (35.82 m)
Length: 102 ft 7 in (31.27 m)
Wing area: 1,457 sq ft (135.4 m²)
Gross weight: 73,800 lb (33,475 kg)
Max cruising speed: 216 mph (348 km/h) at 10,000 ft (3,050 m)
Typical range: 2,300 miles (3,700 km) with max payload of 19,335 lb (8,770 kg)
Accommodation: Crew of 2 or 3 and up to 85 passengers or 22 passengers and 4 to 6 cars
First flight: 21 June 1961
The Carvair was evolved specifically for car-carrying, by converting the airframe of the Douglas DC-4 airliner. Alterations include a new and longer front fuselage, with a sideways-hinged nose loading door, and an enlarged vertical tail similar to that of the DC-7. It has served with British Air Ferries (its main operator), Aer Lingus, Aviaco of Spain, Compagnie Air Transport of France and Ansett/ANA of Australia.

AERO SPACELINES SUPER GUPPY

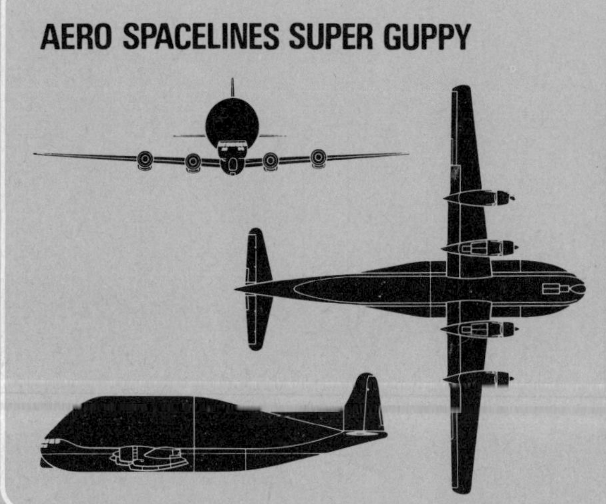

Powered by: Four 7,000 eshp Pratt & Whitney T34-P-7WA turboprop engines, each driving a four-blade propeller
Wing span: 156 ft 3 in (47.63 m)
Length: 141 ft 3 in (43.05 m)
Wing area: 1,769 sq ft (164.35 m²)
Gross weight: 175,000 lb (79,378 kg)
Cruising speed: 300 mph (483 km/h)
Accommodation: Crew of 2 and 50,000 lb (22,680 kg) payload
First flight (Pregnant Guppy): 19 September 1962
Aero Spacelines has developed a small family of 'Guppy' aircraft specially contoured to transport large booster rockets and other outsize pieces of equipment used in the American space programme. First was the Pregnant Guppy of 1962 (as shown in silhouette); this has since been followed by the Super Guppy, Guppy-201, Mini-Guppy and Guppy-101. All are based on the airframe of the Boeing Model 377 Stratocruiser/C-97.

Canadair Forty Four

Aviation Traders Carvair

Aero Spacelines Super Guppy

AÉROSPATIALE SA 318 ALOUETTE II

Powered by: One 530 shp Turboméca Astazou IIA turboshaft engine, driving a three-blade main rotor and two-blade tail rotor

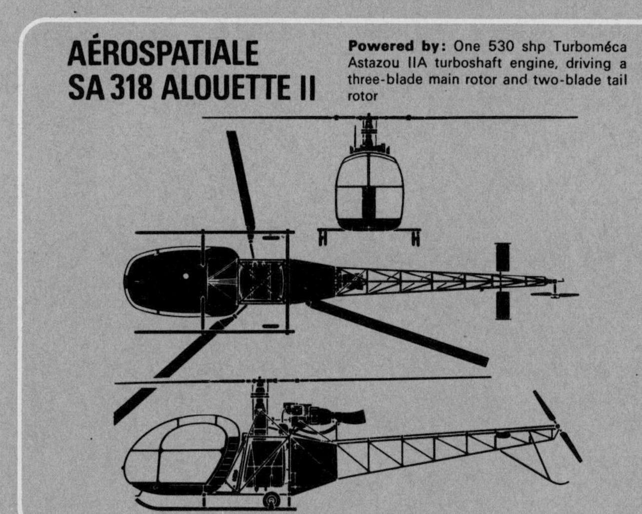

Main rotor diameter: 33 ft 5½ in (10.20 m)
Length of fuselage (tail rotor turning): 31 ft 11¾ in (9.75 m)
Gross weight: 3,630 lb (1,650 kg)
Max cruising speed: 112 mph (180 km/h) at S/L
Typical range: 186 miles (300 km) with 1,058 lb (480 kg) payload
Accommodation: Crew of 1 and 4 passengers
First flight (Alouette II Astazou): 31 January 1961
From the little Sud-Est SE 3130 prototype, first flown on 12 March 1955, the Alouette (lark) was developed to become one of the most successful small 'workhorse' helicopters of the 1960s. Originally developed for an agricultural role, it now performs a great variety of military and civil duties with operators the world over. By 1970 more than 1,200 Alouette IIs had been ordered, plus more than 800 of the larger and more powerful Alouette III. Of these, nearly 1,750 were powered by Artouste turbine engines, but the Astazou is now becomin the standard Alouette power plant. The data apply to this version.

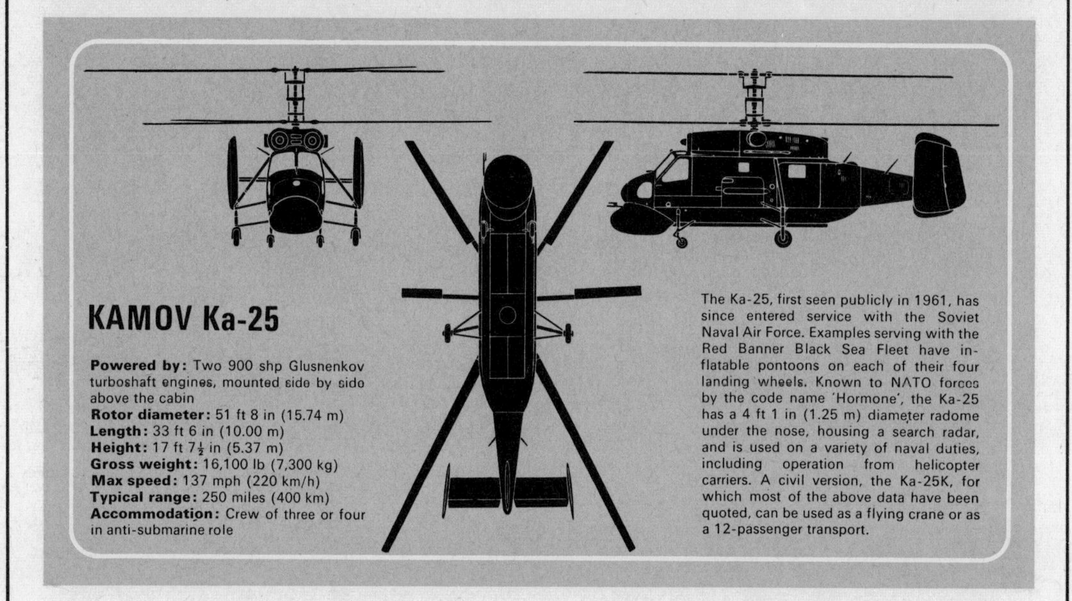

KAMOV Ka-25

Powered by: Two 900 shp Glusnenkov turboshaft engines, mounted side by side above the cabin
Rotor diameter: 51 ft 8 in (15.74 m)
Length: 33 ft 6 in (10.00 m)
Height: 17 ft 7½ in (5.37 m)
Gross weight: 16,100 lb (7,300 kg)
Max speed: 137 mph (220 km/h)
Typical range: 250 miles (400 km)
Accommodation: Crew of three or four in anti-submarine role

The Ka-25, first seen publicly in 1961, has since entered service with the Soviet Naval Air Force. Examples serving with the Red Banner Black Sea Fleet have inflatable pontoons on each of their four landing wheels. Known to NATO forces by the code name 'Hormone', the Ka-25 has a 4 ft 1 in (1.25 m) diameter radome under the nose, housing a search radar, and is used on a variety of naval duties, including operation from helicopter carriers. A civil version, the Ka-25K, for which most of the above data have been quoted, can be used as a flying crane or as a 12-passenger transport.

SIKORSKY S-64 SKYCRANE

Powered by: Two 4,500 shp Pratt & Whitney JFTD12-4A turboshaft engines.
Rotor diameter: 72 ft 0 in (21.95 m).
Length: 70 ft 3 in (21.41 m).
Gross weight: 42,000 lb (19,050 kg).
Max. speed: 127 mph (204 km/h) at sea level.
Accommodation/Payload: Crew of 2 or 3 + up to 90 persons or 17,500 lb (7,937 kg) of cargo in detachable pods, or up to 22,400 lb (10,160 kg) of slung cargo.
Max. range: 253 miles (407 km).
First flight: 9 May 1962.

The S-64 is a "flying crane" helicopter, consisting of a basic skeletal airframe to which can be attached large freight containers or "people pods" for short-haul transportation. In addition to its use by civil operators on a variety of duties, it is also used by the US Army, by whom it is designated CH-54.

Aérospatiale Alouette II Astazou

Kamov Ka-25 of the Soviet Navy

Sikorsky CH-54 (S-64) Skycrane

BREGUET ATLANTIC

Powered by: Two 6,105 ehp Rolls-Royce Tyne RTy.20 Mk 21 turboprop engines, each driving a 16 ft 0 in (4.88 m) diameter four-blade propeller
Wing span: 119 ft 1 in (36.30 m)
Length: 104 ft 2 in (31.75 m)
Wing area: 1,295 sq ft (120.34 m²)
Gross weight: 95,900 lb (43,500 kg)
Cruising speed: 345 mph (556 km/h)
Max range: 5,590 miles (9,000 km)
Accommodation: Crew of 12, plus relief crew for extra-long missions
First flight: 21 October 1961
Built by a six-nation consortium, the Breguet Atlantic maritime patrol aircraft is of basically French design, and was evolved originally to meet the requirements of the French and German Navies. Others are now in service with the Italian and Royal Netherlands Navies, the total programme consisting of 87 production aircraft for the four user nations. The Atlantic, which first entered service in 1965-66 with the French Navy, has a large bay in the fuselage which can carry a wide range of anti-submarine and other weapons,' and can cruise for up to 18 hours at a speed of 195 mph (320 km/h).

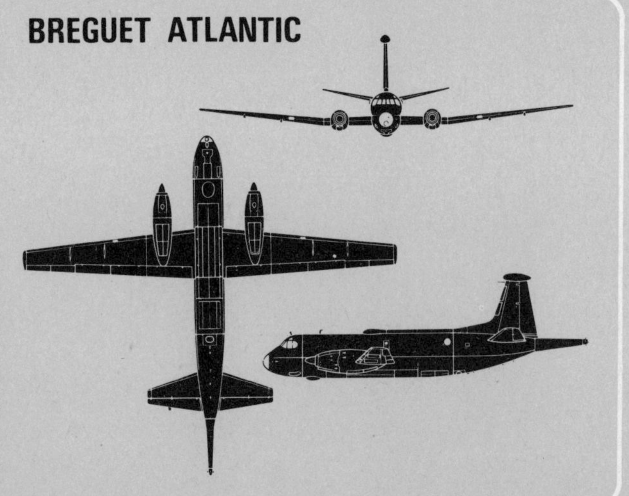

BERIEV Be-12 TCHAIKA (SEAGULL)

Powered by: Two 4,000 shp Ivchenko AI-20D turboprop engines, each driving a four-bladed propeller of approx 16 ft 0 in (4.85 m) diameter
Wing span: 107 ft 11½ in (32.90 m)
Length: 95 ft 9½ in (29.20 m)
Gross weight: 65,035 lb (29,500 kg)
Max speed: 379 mph (610 km/h)
Accommodation: Flight crew of 2 or 3, plus operators for patrol and detection equipment
The dimensions, weight and performance data above are estimated; but amphibian and flying-boat versions of the Be-12 (known also as the M-12), probably stripped of much of their military equipment, have established world records for lifting payload to height (22,266 lb = 10,100 kg), altitude without payload (39,977 ft=12,185 m), speed in a closed circuit (351.290 mph=565.347 km/h) and distance in a closed circuit (666.54 miles= 1,072.698 km). The gull-winged configuration is adopted to raise the engines as far as possible above the water.

SIKORSKY S-61N

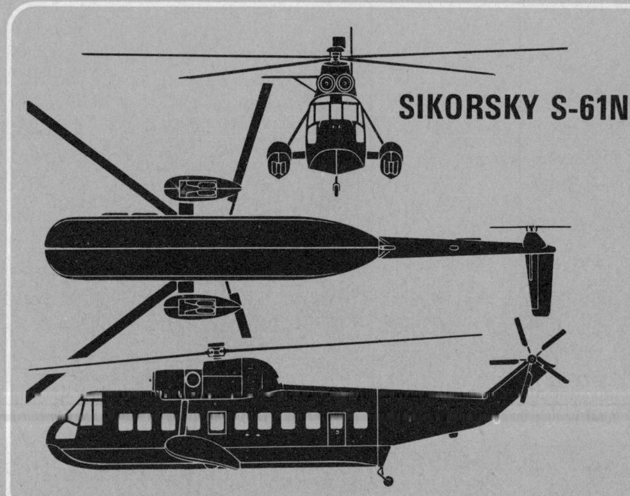

Powered by: Two 1,500 shp General Electric CT58-140-2 turboshaft engines, driving five-blade main and tail rotors
Main rotor diameter: 62 ft 0 in (18.90 m)
Length of fuselage: 72 ft 10 in (22.20 m)
Gross weight: 19,000 lb (8,620 kg)
Average cruising speed: 140 mph (225 km/h)
Accommodation: Crew of 3 and up to 28 passengers
First flight: 7 August 1962
Development of the S-61 helicopter began with the first flight on 11 March 1959 of the XHSS-2 prototype for the US Navy, now in widespread production and service as the Sea King and familiar to television audiences the world over as the pick-up helicopter for returning American astronauts. The commercial passenger-carrying versions use basically the same structure, but have a lengthened fuselage. Main version is the amphibious S-61N, which has a sealed hull and stabilising floats; the S-61L is generally similar but is not amphibious. Data are for the S-61N Mark II; earlier examples had 1,350 shp engines.

Breguet Atlantic

Beriev Be-12 *(Tass)*

Sikorsky S-61N

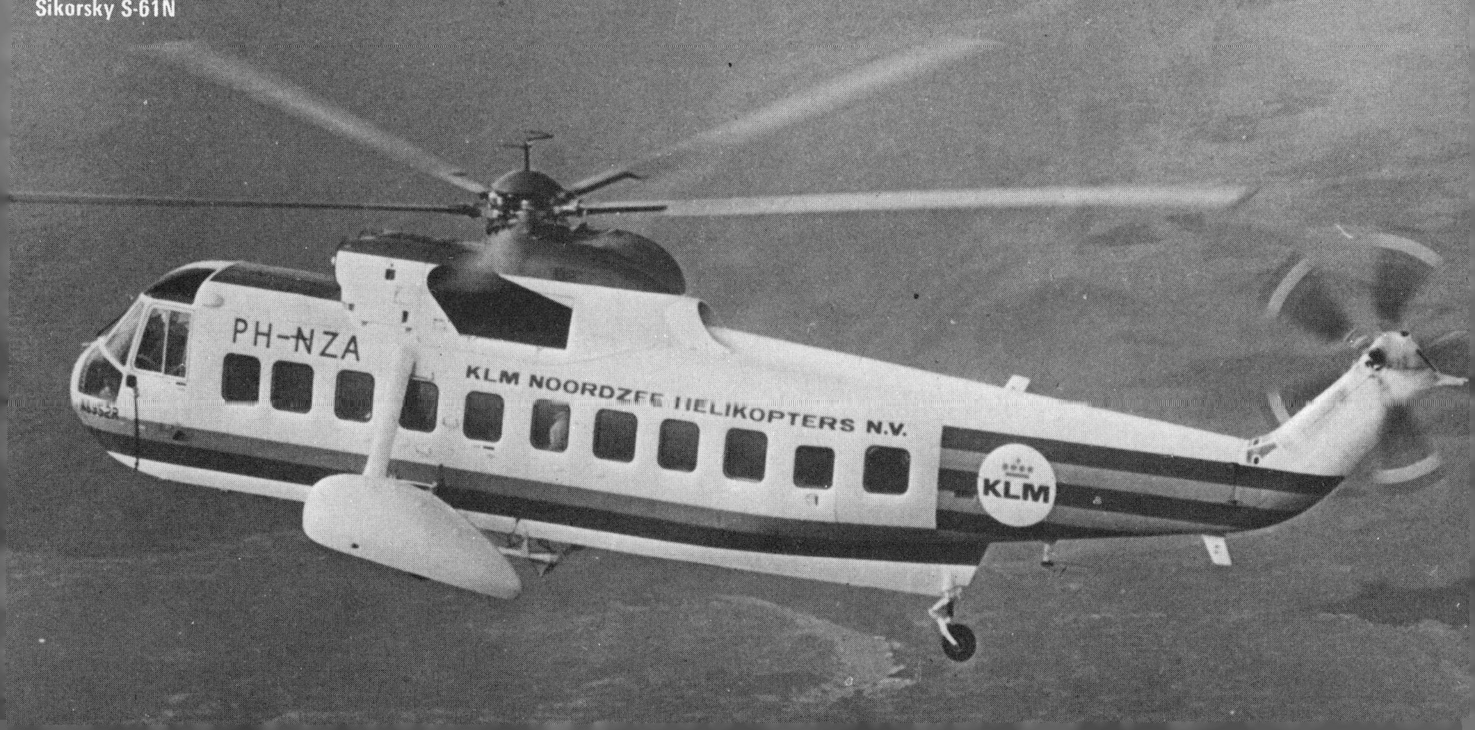

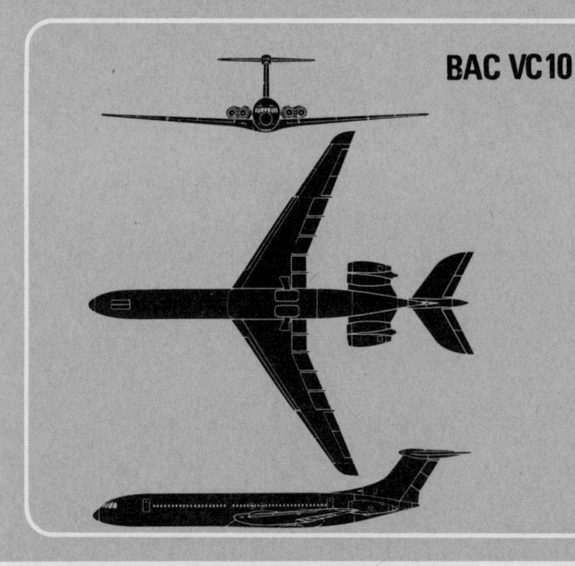

BAC VC10

Powered by: Four 20,370 lb (9,240 kg) st Rolls-Royce Conway RCo.42 turbofan engines
Wing span: 146 ft 2 in (44.55 m)
Length: 158 ft 8 in (48.36 m)
Wing area: 2,851 sq ft (264.9 m²)
Gross weight: 314,000 lb (142,430 kg)
Max cruising speed: 568 mph (914 km/h)
Typical range: 5,040 miles (8,115 km) with max payload
Accommodation: Crew of 3/4 and 109 passengers (BOAC Model 1101)
First flight: 29 June 1962

Tailored closely—too closely, as events proved—to the requirements of BOAC, the VC10 is a classic case of an excellent aeroplane whose world-wide appeal was inhibited by a too-rigid design: only nine of those built were for customers outside Britain. Ironically, its passenger appeal is higher than that of many more commercially-successful types, and in 1970 it was a popular stand-in when BOAC was unable to introduce its Boeing 747s into service because of a trade dispute.

BOEING 727

Powered by: Three 14,000 lb (6,350 kg) st Pratt & Whitney JT8D-7 turbofan engines
Wing span: 108 ft 0 in (32.92 m)
Length: 153 ft 2 in (46.69 m)
Wing area: 1,700 sq ft (157.9 m²)
Gross weight: 172,000 lb (78,015 kg)
Max cruising speed: 595 mph (958 km/h) at 21,600 ft (6,585 m)
Typical range: 1,290 miles (2,076 km)
Accommodation: Crew of 3 and 163-189 passengers
First flight: 9 February 1963 (prototype); 27 July 1967 (727-200)

The Boeing 727, biggest-selling member of the family of Boeing jet transports, is in service with over 50 of the world's airlines, more than 975 having been sold by mid-1972. Originally built as the 727-100 to seat a maximum of 131 passengers, it was quickly followed by a stretched version, the 727-200, to which the silhouette and data apply. This has a 20 ft (6.10 m) longer fuselage than the 727-100 which first went into service with Eastern Air Lines on 1 February 1964.

McDONNELL DOUGLAS DC-9

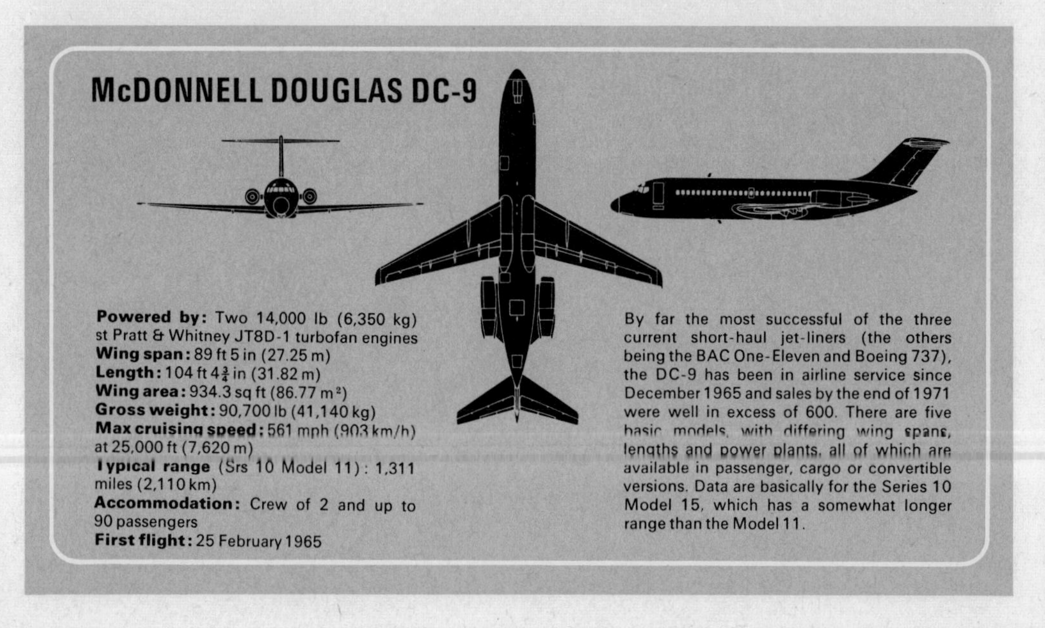

Powered by: Two 14,000 lb (6,350 kg) st Pratt & Whitney JT8D-1 turbofan engines
Wing span: 89 ft 5 in (27.25 m)
Length: 104 ft 4¾ in (31.82 m)
Wing area: 934.3 sq ft (86.77 m²)
Gross weight: 90,700 lb (41,140 kg)
Max cruising speed: 561 mph (903 km/h) at 25,000 ft (7,620 m)
Typical range (Srs 10 Model 11): 1,311 miles (2,110 km)
Accommodation: Crew of 2 and up to 90 passengers
First flight: 25 February 1965

By far the most successful of the three current short-haul jet-liners (the others being the BAC One-Eleven and Boeing 737), the DC-9 has been in airline service since December 1965 and sales by the end of 1971 were well in excess of 600. There are five basic models, with differing wing spans, lengths and power plants, all of which are available in passenger, cargo or convertible versions. Data are basically for the Series 10 Model 15, which has a somewhat longer range than the Model 11.

VC10 C Mk 1 of the Royal Air Force

Boeing 727-100

McDonnell Douglas DC-9 Series 30

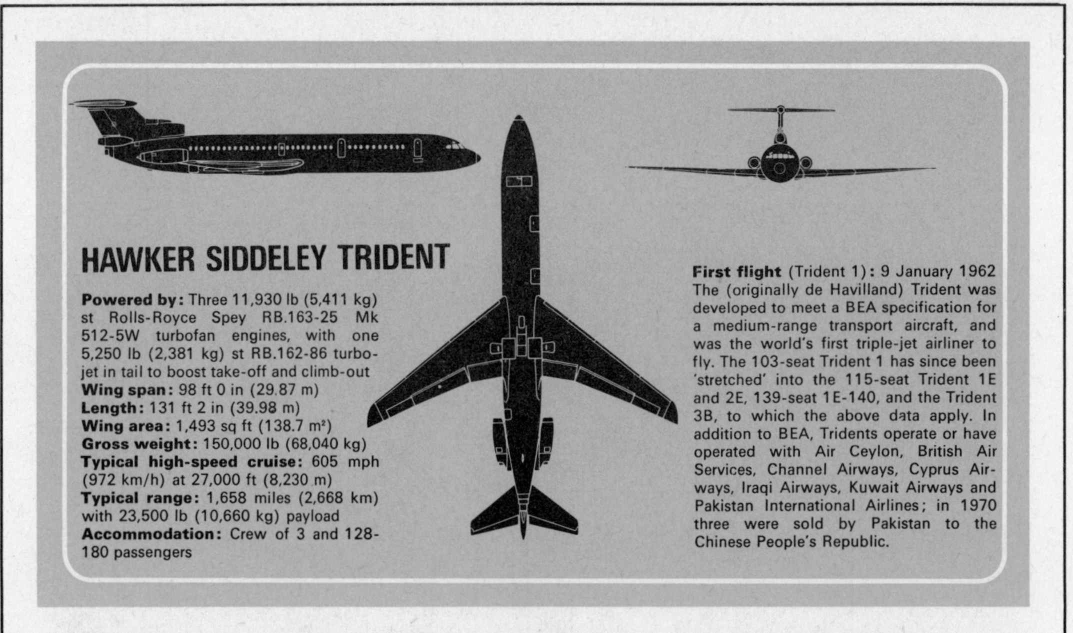

HAWKER SIDDELEY TRIDENT

Powered by: Three 11,930 lb (5,411 kg) st Rolls-Royce Spey RB.163-25 Mk 512-5W turbofan engines, with one 5,250 lb (2,381 kg) st RB.162-86 turbojet in tail to boost take-off and climb-out
Wing span: 98 ft 0 in (29.87 m)
Length: 131 ft 2 in (39.98 m)
Wing area: 1,493 sq ft (138.7 m²)
Gross weight: 150,000 lb (68,040 kg)
Typical high-speed cruise: 605 mph (972 km/h) at 27,000 ft (8,230 m)
Typical range: 1,658 miles (2,668 km) with 23,500 lb (10,660 kg) payload
Accommodation: Crew of 3 and 128-180 passengers

First flight (Trident 1): 9 January 1962
The (originally de Havilland) Trident was developed to meet a BEA specification for a medium-range transport aircraft, and was the world's first triple-jet airliner to fly. The 103-seat Trident 1 has since been 'stretched' into the 115-seat Trident 1E and 2E, 139-seat 1E-140, and the Trident 3B, to which the above data apply. In addition to BEA, Tridents operate or have operated with Air Ceylon, British Air Services, Channel Airways, Cyprus Airways, Iraqi Airways, Kuwait Airways and Pakistan International Airlines; in 1970 three were sold by Pakistan to the Chinese People's Republic.

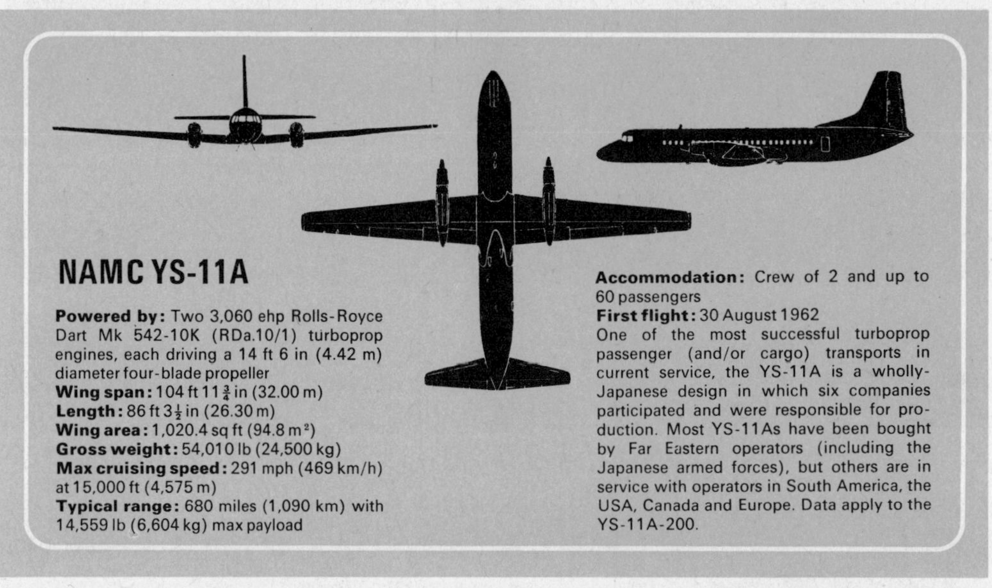

NAMC YS-11A

Powered by: Two 3,060 ehp Rolls-Royce Dart Mk 542-10K (RDa.10/1) turboprop engines, each driving a 14 ft 6 in (4.42 m) diameter four-blade propeller
Wing span: 104 ft 11¾ in (32.00 m)
Length: 86 ft 3½ in (26.30 m)
Wing area: 1,020.4 sq ft (94.8 m²)
Gross weight: 54,010 lb (24,500 kg)
Max cruising speed: 291 mph (469 km/h) at 15,000 ft (4,575 m)
Typical range: 680 miles (1,090 km) with 14,559 lb (6,604 kg) max payload
Accommodation: Crew of 2 and up to 60 passengers
First flight: 30 August 1962
One of the most successful turboprop passenger (and/or cargo) transports in current service, the YS-11A is a wholly-Japanese design in which six companies participated and were responsible for production. Most YS-11As have been bought by Far Eastern operators (including the Japanese armed forces), but others are in service with operators in South America, the USA, Canada and Europe. Data apply to the YS-11A-200.

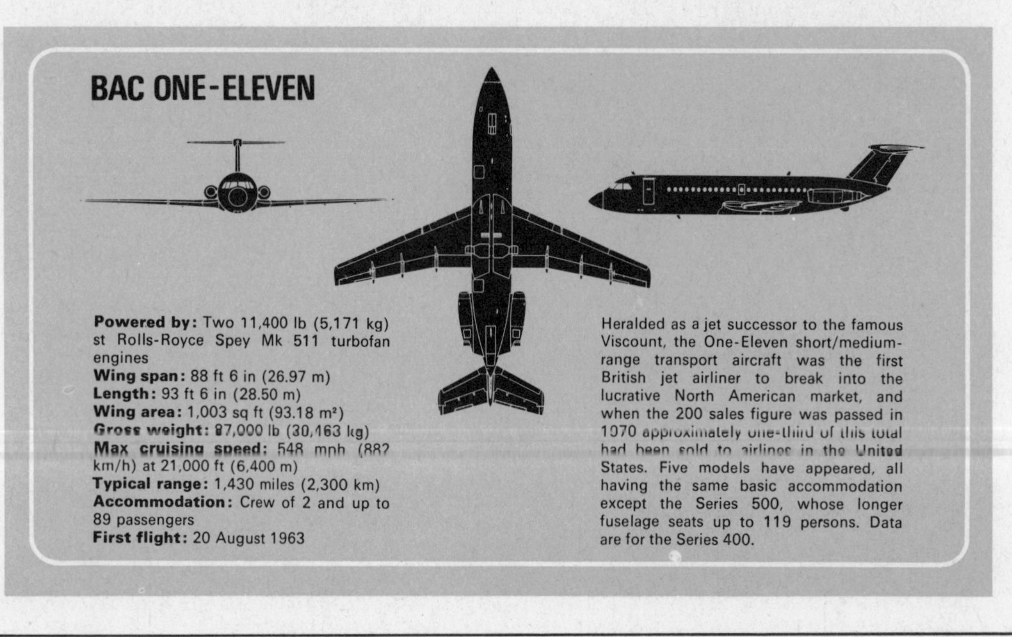

BAC ONE-ELEVEN

Powered by: Two 11,400 lb (5,171 kg) st Rolls-Royce Spey Mk 511 turbofan engines
Wing span: 88 ft 6 in (26.97 m)
Length: 93 ft 6 in (28.50 m)
Wing area: 1,003 sq ft (93.18 m²)
Gross weight: 87,000 lb (30,163 kg)
Max cruising speed: 548 mph (882 km/h) at 21,000 ft (6,400 m)
Typical range: 1,430 miles (2,300 km)
Accommodation: Crew of 2 and up to 89 passengers
First flight: 20 August 1963

Heralded as a jet successor to the famous Viscount, the One-Eleven short/medium-range transport aircraft was the first British jet airliner to break into the lucrative North American market, and when the 200 sales figure was passed in 1970 approximately one-third of this total had been sold to airlines in the United States. Five models have appeared, all having the same basic accommodation except the Series 500, whose longer fuselage seats up to 119 persons. Data are for the Series 400.

Hawker Siddeley Trident 2E

NAMC YS-11A-300

BAC One-Eleven Series 500

HMPAC PUFFIN 1 & 2

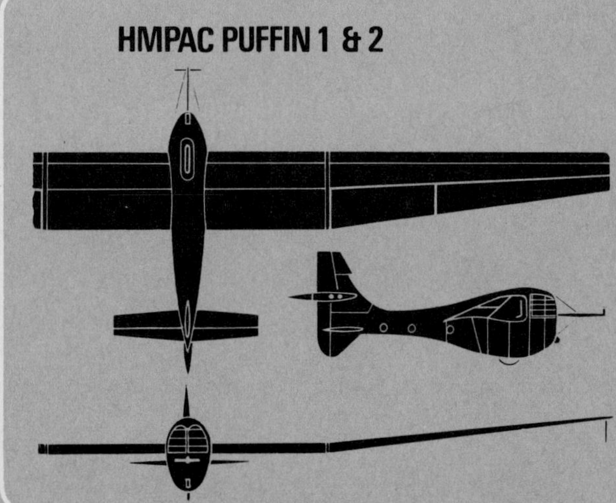

Power system: Pedal drive to two-blade pusher propeller, developing an estimated 0.3 hp for level flight
Wing span (Puffin 2) : 93 ft 0 in (28.35 m)
Length (Puffin 2) : 16 ft 0 in (4.88 m)
Gross weight (Puffin 2): 265 lb (120 kg)
Cruising speed (Puffin 2): 18 mph (29 km/h)
Accommodation: Crew of 1
Best flight (Puffin 1) : 993 yd (908 m) on 2 May 1962
First flight: 16 November 1961 (Puffin 1) ; 31 August 1965 (Puffin 2)
The Puffin man-powered aircraft were built by the Hatfield Man Powered Aircraft Club, an association which in mid-1962 had over 30 members, including a number of apprentices of the de Havilland Technical School at Hatfield. Puffin 1 was completed on 15 November 1961, started its flight trials the following day, and by the end of that year had made flights of up to 700 yd (640 m) in length and turns through 70–80°.

BAC (HUNTING) H 126

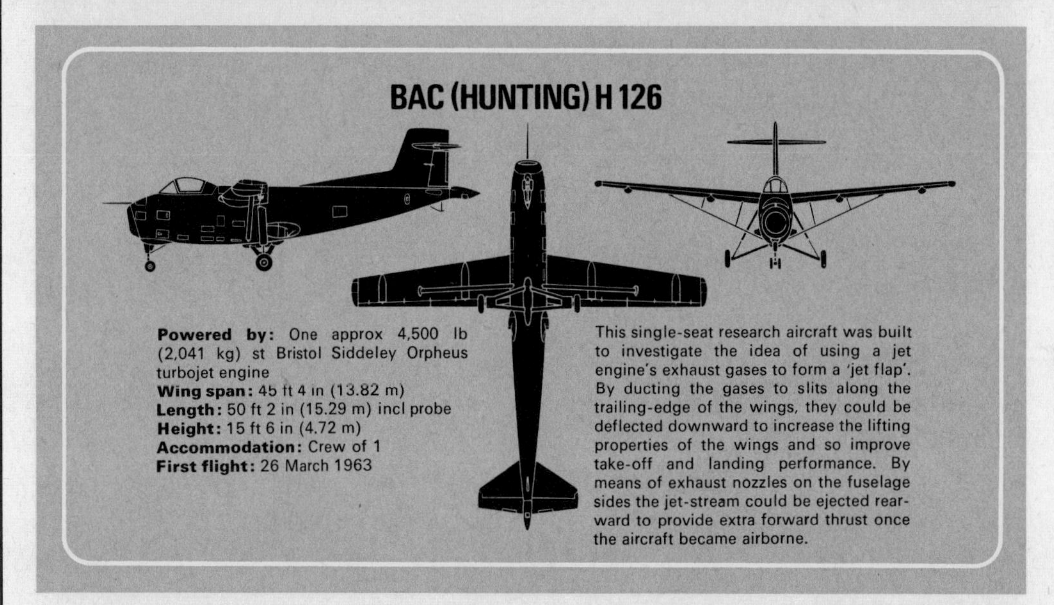

Powered by: One approx 4,500 lb (2,041 kg) st Bristol Siddeley Orpheus turbojet engine
Wing span: 45 ft 4 in (13.82 m)
Length: 50 ft 2 in (15.29 m) incl probe
Height: 15 ft 6 in (4.72 m)
Accommodation: Crew of 1
First flight: 26 March 1963

This single-seat research aircraft was built to investigate the idea of using a jet engine's exhaust gases to form a 'jet flap'. By ducting the gases to slits along the trailing-edge of the wings, they could be deflected downward to increase the lifting properties of the wings and so improve take-off and landing performance. By means of exhaust nozzles on the fuselage sides the jet-stream could be ejected rearward to provide extra forward thrust once the aircraft became airborne.

BAC 221

Powered by: One 10,050 lb (4,559 kg) st Rolls-Royce Avon RA.28R afterburning turbojet engine
Wing span: 25 ft 0 in(7.62 m)
Length: 57 ft 7½ in (17.56 m)
Wing area: approx 500 sq ft (46.5 m²)
Max speed: approx 1,060 mph (1,706 km/h) at 40,000 ft (12,200 m)
Accommodation: Crew of 1
First flight: 1 May 1964
The BAC 221 research aircraft was modified from the airframe of the Fairey F.D.2, the first aircraft to set a world speed record in excess of 1,000 mph (1,609 km/h). Its purpose was to flight test the delta-wing planform designed for the Concorde supersonic transport aircraft. Early Concorde research programmes also included the Handley Page HP 115 slim-delta aircraft, designed to investigate the lower end of the speed range.

Puffin man-powered aircraft

BAC (Hunting) H 126

BAC 221

HAWKER SIDDELEY 125

Powered by: Two 3,360 lb (1,525 kg) st Rolls-Royce Bristol Viper 522 turbojet engines
Wing span: 47 ft 0 in (14.33 m)
Length: 47 ft 5 in (14.45 m)
Wing area: 353 sq ft (32.8 m²)
Gross weight: 23,300 lb (10,568 kg)
Max cruising speed: 510 mph (821 km/h) at 31,000 ft (9,450 m)
Typical range: 1,762 miles (2,835 km)
Accommodation: Crew of 2/3 and up to 12 passengers
First flight: 13 August 1962

One of the two most successful jet executive aircraft produced in Europe, the HS 125 has been in production since 1964 and more than 200 have been sold. These include small batches of the Series 1, 1A, 1B and 3; and 20 Srs 2s equipped as Dominie navigation trainers for the Royal Air Force. The data apply to the current Series 400, which since 1970 has been marketed in the United States as the Beechcraft Hawker BH 125.

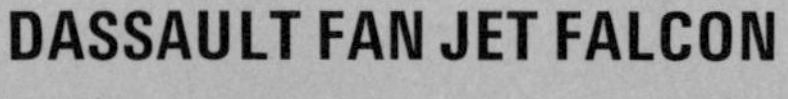

DASSAULT FAN JET FALCON

Powered by: Two 4,315 lb (1,957 kg) st General Electric CF700-2D-2 turbofan engines
Wing span: 53 ft 6 in (16.30 m)
Length: 56 ft 3 in (17.15 m)
Wing area: 441.3 sq ft (41.00 m²)
Gross weight: 28,660 lb (13,000 kg)
Max cruising speed: 536 mph (862 km/h) at 25,000 ft (7,620 m)
Typical range: 2,190 miles (3,520 km) with 8 passengers
Accommodation: Crew of 2 and 8-10 passengers
First flight: 4 May 1963

Known by the dual names of Mystère 20 and Falcon 20, this attractive twin rear engined executive transport is one of the most successful yet to appear, more than 280 having been sold by early 1972. The prototype was powered by turbojet engines for its first flight, but just over a year later was refitted with turbofans, which are standard on production aircraft, and have resulted in the name 'Fan Jet Falcon' bestowed by Pan American's Business Jets Division, the sales agency for the western hemisphere. About three-quarters of the total sales have been in this area. Data apply to the Falcon Series F, which was introduced in 1969 and has additional high-lift devices to improve airfield performance

YAKOVLEV Yak-40

Powered by: Three 3,306 lb (1,500 kg) st Ivchenko AI-25 turbofan engines
Wing span: 82 ft 0¼ in (25.00 m)
Length: 66 ft 9½ in (20.36 m)
Wing area: 735 sq ft (70.0 m²)
Gross weight: 30,200 lb (13,700 kg)
Max cruising speed: 342 mph (550 km/h)
Typical range: 620 miles (1,000 km) with normal payload of 5,070 lb (2,300 kg)
Accommodation: Crew of 2 and 24-40 passengers
First flight: 21 October 1966

Designed as a short-haul feeder-liner and air ambulance for use on 'several thousand of Aeroflot's routes within the Soviet Union, the Yak-40 is yet another type in the long list of 'DC-3 replacement' aircraft. Of attractive appearance, it has three small rear-mounted turbofan engines which enable it to take off and land within 1,600 ft (500 m), and it can operate from grass airfields. Several hundred have been built since production started in 1967; the latest version has a thrust reverser on the centre engine and can seat a maximum of 40 passengers.

Hawker Siddeley 125 Series 400

Dassault Mystère 20/Falcon 20 of the Canadian Armed Forces

Yak-40 *(Flight International)*

TRANSALL C-160

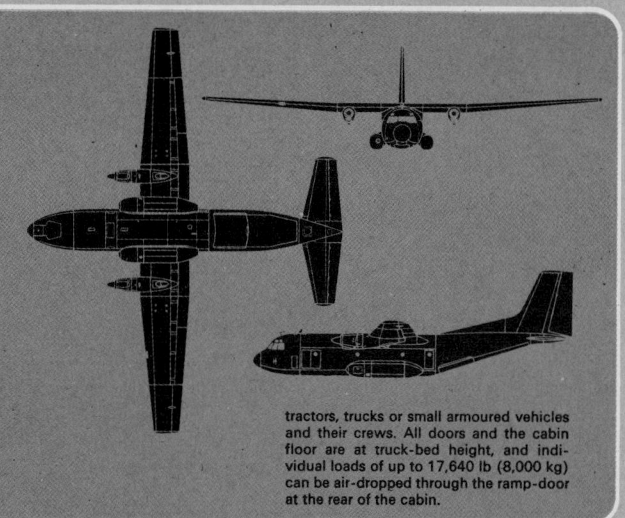

Powered by: Two 6,100 eshp Rolls-Royce Tyne RTy.20 Mk 22 turboprop engines, each driving an 18 ft 0 in (5.49 m) diameter four-blade propeller
Wing span: 131 ft 3 in (40.00 m)
Length: 106 ft 3½ in (32.40 m)
Wing area: 1,722.7 sq ft (160.1 m^2)
Gross weight: 108,250 lb (49,100 kg)
Max cruising speed: 319 mph (513 km/h) at 18,050 ft (5,500 m)
Range: 2,832 miles (4,558 km) with 17,640 lb (8,000 kg) payload
Accommodation: Crew of 4 and max payload of 35,270 lb (16,000 kg)
First flight: 25 February 1963

This large twin-engined military transport originated in 1959 as a joint Franco-German programme, the name Transall being a contraction of *Trans*porter *All*ianz. Fifty C-160Fs are being built for the French Air Force, and 110 C-160Ds for the Federal German Luftwaffe. Nine have also been delivered to the South African Air Force. The 4,072 cu ft (115.3 m^3) cabin can accommodate up to 93 troops or 81 paratroops; 62 casualty litters and their attendants; or a variety of jeeps, tractors, trucks or small armoured vehicles and their crews. All doors and the cabin floor are at truck-bed height, and individual loads of up to 17,640 lb (8,000 kg) can be air-dropped through the ramp-door at the rear of the cabin.

SHORT BELFAST

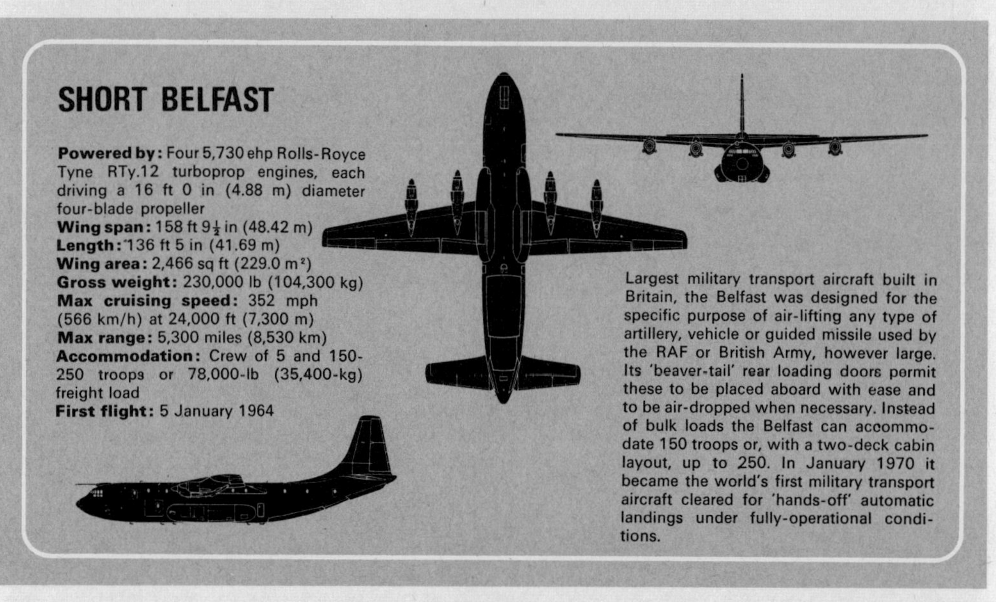

Powered by: Four 5,730 ehp Rolls-Royce Tyne RTy.12 turboprop engines, each driving a 16 ft 0 in (4.88 m) diameter four-blade propeller
Wing span: 158 ft 9½ in (48.42 m)
Length: 136 ft 5 in (41.69 m)
Wing area: 2,466 sq ft (229.0 m^2)
Gross weight: 230,000 lb (104,300 kg)
Max cruising speed: 352 mph (566 km/h) at 24,000 ft (7,300 m)
Max range: 5,300 miles (8,530 km)
Accommodation: Crew of 5 and 150-250 troops or 78,000-lb (35,400-kg) freight load
First flight: 5 January 1964

Largest military transport aircraft built in Britain, the Belfast was designed for the specific purpose of air-lifting any type of artillery, vehicle or guided missile used by the RAF or British Army, however large. Its 'beaver-tail' rear loading doors permit these to be placed aboard with ease and to be air-dropped when necessary. Instead of bulk loads the Belfast can accommodate 150 troops or, with a two-deck cabin layout, up to 250. In January 1970 it became the world's first military transport aircraft cleared for 'hands-off' automatic landings under fully-operational conditions.

LOCKHEED C-141A STARLIFTER

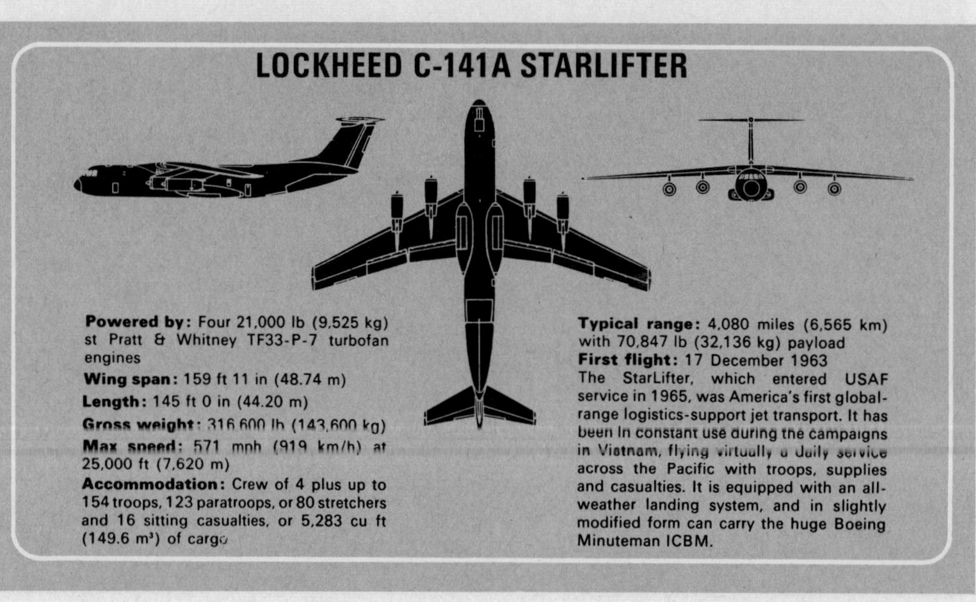

Powered by: Four 21,000 lb (9,525 kg) st Pratt & Whitney TF33-P-7 turbofan engines
Wing span: 159 ft 11 in (48.74 m)
Length: 145 ft 0 in (44.20 m)
Gross weight: 316,600 lb (143,600 kg)
Max speed: 571 mph (919 km/h) at 25,000 ft (7,620 m)
Accommodation: Crew of 4 plus up to 154 troops, 123 paratroops, or 80 stretchers and 16 sitting casualties, or 5,283 cu ft (149.6 m^3) of cargo
Typical range: 4,080 miles (6,565 km) with 70,847 lb (32,136 kg) payload
First flight: 17 December 1963

The StarLifter, which entered USAF service in 1965, was America's first global-range logistics-support jet transport. It has been in constant use during the campaigns in Vietnam, flying virtually a daily service across the Pacific with troops, supplies and casualties. It is equipped with an all-weather landing system, and in slightly modified form can carry the huge Boeing Minuteman ICBM.

Transall C-160D

Short Belfast

Lockheed C-141A StarLifter

NORTH AMERICAN XB-70 VALKYRIE

Powered by: Six 31,000 lb (14,060 kg) st General Electric YJ93-GE-3 afterburning turbojet engines
Wing span: 105 ft 0 in (32.00 m)
Length: 196 ft 0 in (59.74 m) incl nose probe
Wing area: 6,297.15 sq ft (585.02 m²)
Typical gross weight: 400,000 lb (181,440 kg)
Max speed: over 2,000 mph (3,220 km/h) at 70,000 ft (21,300 m) (Mach 3)
Accommodation: Crew of 2
First flight: 21 September 1964
The XB-70 was designed originally to succeed the B-52 Stratofortress as the USAF's long-range strategic bomber, but this programme was cancelled in 1963 and the two prototypes were used instead for research into the aerodynamics of flight at high supersonic speeds. The thin movable foreplane, fitted with flaps, assisted lift control and trim during supersonic flight, while the tips of the main delta wings could be drooped to aid stability and manoeuvrability.

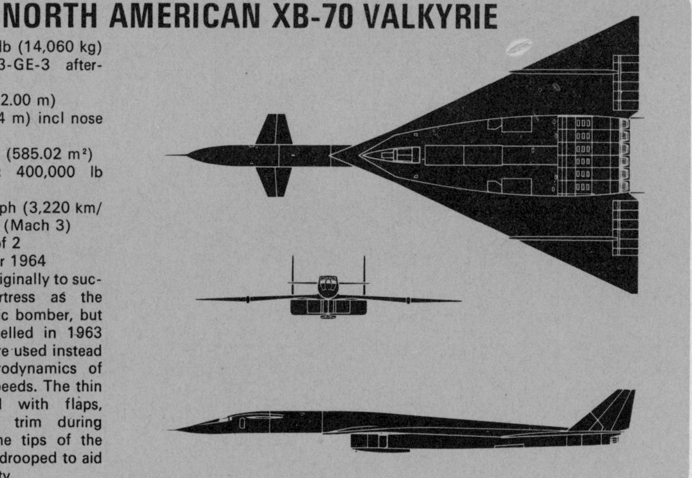

LOCKHEED SR-71

Powered by: Two 32,500 lb (14,740 kg) st Pratt & Whitney J58 (JT11D-20B) afterburning turbojet engines
Wing span: 55 ft 7 in (16.95 m)
Length: 107 ft 5 in (32.74 m)
Height: 18 ft 6 in (5.64 m)
Max speed (YF-12A world record): 2,070.102 mph (3,331.507 km/h) over a 15-25 km course at unlimited altitude
Accommodation: Crew of 2
First flight: 22 December 1964
The SR-71 stems from the Lockheed A-11 design, which first appeared in the form of three YF-12A fighter prototypes for evaluation by the US Air Force. These had small underfins beneath each half of the tail assembly, and the fuselage side fairings ended just forward of the front cockpit. Eight Hughes AIM-47A air-to-air missiles formed the armament of the fighter version. In the SR-71 the underfins are deleted and the fuselage fairings continue unbroken to the tip of the nose. The operational reconnaissance model is the SR-71A; two training versions, the SR-71B and SR-71C, have been built.

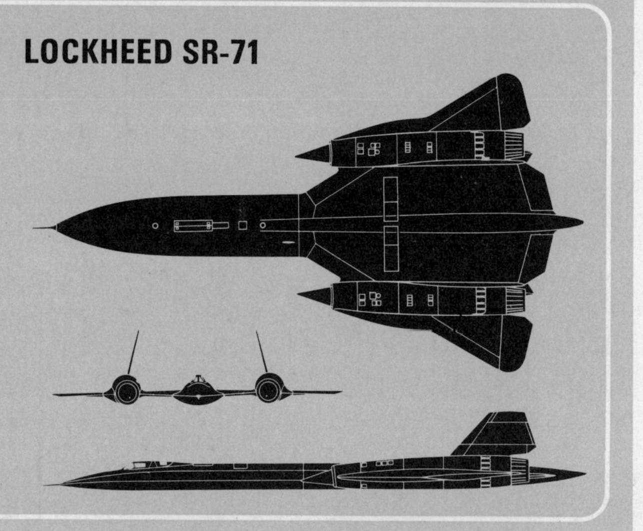

MIKOYAN E-266 (MiG-23)

Powered by: Two 24,250 lb (11,000 kg) st afterburning turbojet engines; provision for rocket-assisted take-off gear
Wing span: approx 40 ft 0 in (12.20 m)
Length: approx 69 ft 0 in (21.00 m)
Speed (1967 closed-circuit record): 1,814.81 mph (2,920.67 km/h) over a 621-mile (1,000-km) course
Accommodation: Crew of 1
A speed of 1,441.5 mph (2,320 km/h) over a 1,000-km closed-circuit course with a 4,409-lb (2,000-kg) payload in April 1965 gave the world its first intimation of the potential performance of this advanced Soviet aircraft, which has since been identified as the MiG-23 twin-engined fighter (code-named 'Foxbat' by the NATO authorities). In October 1967 a similar aircraft raised this record to the figure given above, shortly after establishing a 310-mile (500-km) closed-circuit speed record (without payload) of 1,852.61 mph (2,981.5 km/h). In the same month the E-266 also set a payload-to-height record by lifting a 2,000-kg load to an altitude of 98,349 ft (29,977 m). These records remained unbroken at the end of 1970.

North American XB-70 Valkyrie, with wingtips drooped

Lockheed SR-71A

MiG-23

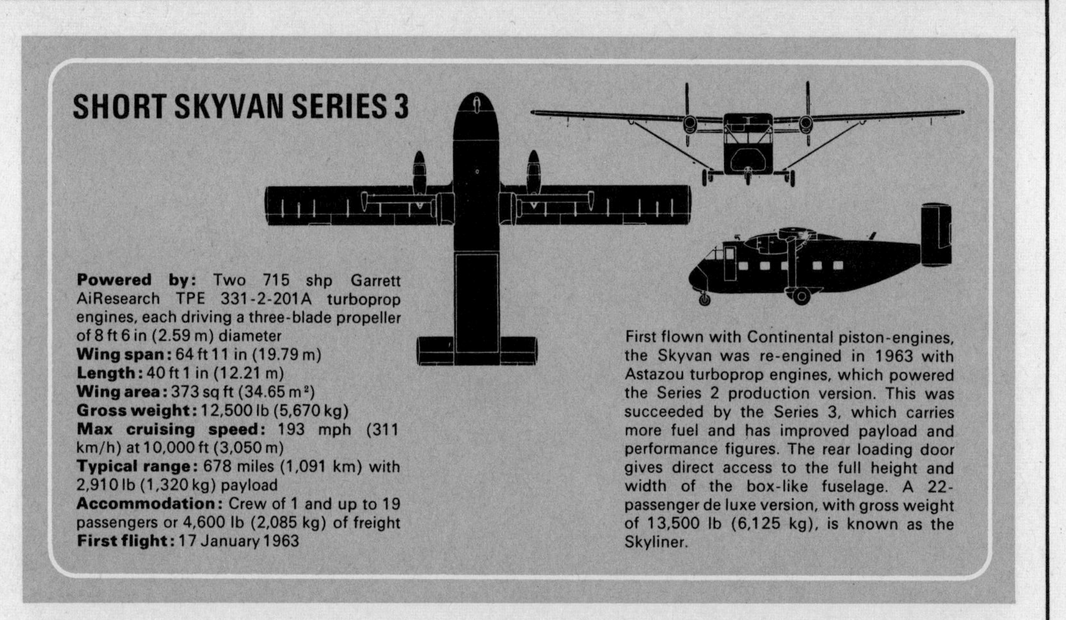

SHORT SKYVAN SERIES 3

Powered by: Two 715 shp Garrett AiResearch TPE 331-2-201A turboprop engines, each driving a three-blade propeller of 8 ft 6 in (2.59 m) diameter
Wing span: 64 ft 11 in (19.79 m)
Length: 40 ft 1 in (12.21 m)
Wing area: 373 sq ft (34.65 m²)
Gross weight: 12,500 lb (5,670 kg)
Max cruising speed: 193 mph (311 km/h) at 10,000 ft (3,050 m)
Typical range: 678 miles (1,091 km) with 2,910 lb (1,320 kg) payload
Accommodation: Crew of 1 and up to 19 passengers or 4,600 lb (2,085 kg) of freight
First flight: 17 January 1963

First flown with Continental piston-engines, the Skyvan was re-engined in 1963 with Astazou turboprop engines, which powered the Series 2 production version. This was succeeded by the Series 3, which carries more fuel and has improved payload and performance figures. The rear loading door gives direct access to the full height and width of the box-like fuselage. A 22-passenger de luxe version, with gross weight of 13,500 lb (6,125 kg), is known as the Skyliner.

DHC-6 TWIN OTTER

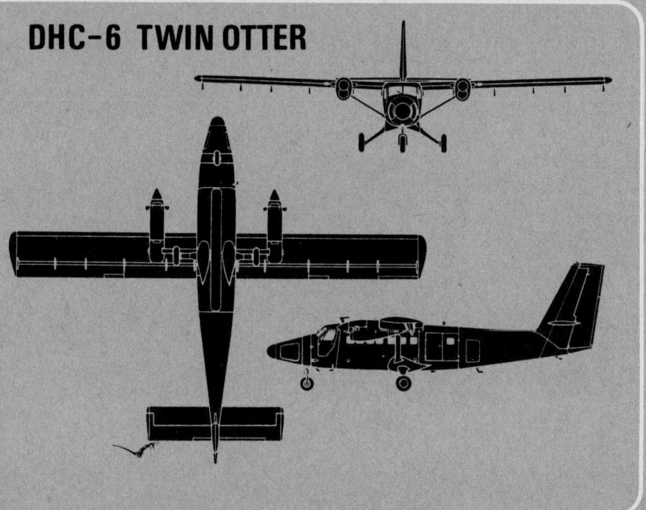

Powered by: Two 652 eshp Pratt & Whitney (UACL) PT6A-27 turboprop engines, each driving an 8 ft 6 in (2.59 m) diameter three-blade propeller
Wing span: 65 ft 0 in (19.81 m)
Length: 51 ft 9 in (15.77 m)
Wing area: 420 sq ft (39.02 m²)
Gross weight: 12,500 lb (5,670 kg)
Max cruising speed: 210 mph (338 km/h) at 10,000 ft (3,050 m)
Range: 745 miles (1,198 km) with 3,250 lb (1,474 kg) payload
Accommodation: Crew of 1 or 2 and up to 20 passengers or equivalent freight load
First flight: 20 May 1965

Since the second World War the de Havilland Aircraft of Canada Ltd has become known as a manufacturer specialising in the design and production of small 'bush' aircraft (like the Beaver and Otter) and of the larger Caribou and Buffalo STOL transports. In the intermediate size range is the Twin Otter, of which approximately 300 had been sold by the end of 1970 to operators all over the world. It is available with wheel, ski or float undercarriage, and with freighter, survey, ambulance or executive interior layout.

BRITTEN-NORMAN BN-2A ISLANDER

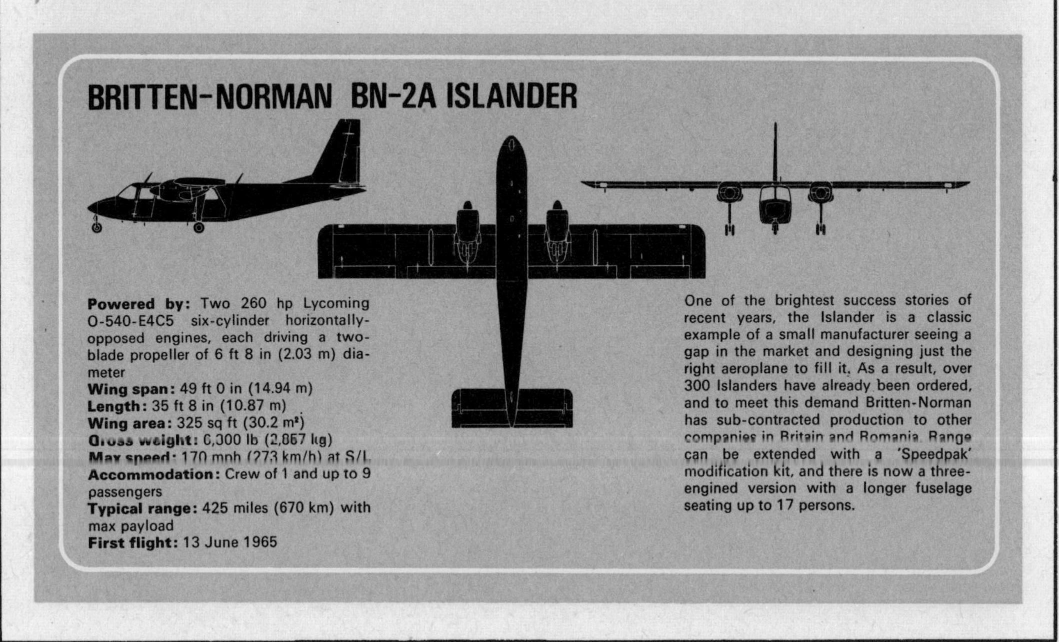

Powered by: Two 260 hp Lycoming O-540-E4C5 six-cylinder horizontally-opposed engines, each driving a two-blade propeller of 6 ft 8 in (2.03 m) diameter
Wing span: 49 ft 0 in (14.94 m)
Length: 35 ft 8 in (10.87 m)
Wing area: 325 sq ft (30.2 m²)
Gross weight: 6,300 lb (2,857 kg)
Max speed: 170 mph (273 km/h) at S/L
Accommodation: Crew of 1 and up to 9 passengers
Typical range: 425 miles (670 km) with max payload
First flight: 13 June 1965

One of the brightest success stories of recent years, the Islander is a classic example of a small manufacturer seeing a gap in the market and designing just the right aeroplane to fill it. As a result, over 300 Islanders have already been ordered, and to meet this demand Britten-Norman has sub-contracted production to other companies in Britain and Romania. Range can be extended with a 'Speedpak' modification kit, and there is now a three-engined version with a longer fuselage seating up to 17 persons.

Short Skyvan Series 3

de Havilland Canada Twin Otter Series 300

Britten-Norman Islander

KAMOV Ka-26

Powered by: Two 325 shp Vedeneev M-14V-26 fourteen-cylinder radial engines in externally-mounted pods
Rotor diameter: 42 ft 8 in (13.00 m) each
Fuselage length: 25 ft 5 in (7.75 m)
Rotor disc area: 1,428.7 sq ft (132.73 m²)
Gross weight: 7,165 lb (3,250 kg)
Max cruising speed: 93 mph (150 km/h)
Typical range: 250 miles (400 km) with 7 passengers
Accommodation: Crew of 1 or 2 and up to 7 passengers
First flight: 1965

One of the Soviet Union's most versatile helicopters, the Ka-26 has been in production since 1966 for a variety of duties. By using interchangeable rear-fuselage pods, it can be adapted quickly to serve as a passenger transport, ambulance, agricultural aircraft, cargo-carrier or survey helicopter. For aerial survey it can be fitted with a cabin-mounted camera which can photograph 2 sq miles (5 km²) of territory in an hour at a scale of 1:10,000. The geophysical survey version carries a large 'hoop' aerial around the fuselage, an electro-magnetic receiver 'bird' (towed beneath the helicopter on a cable), and pulse-generating equipment inside the cabin.

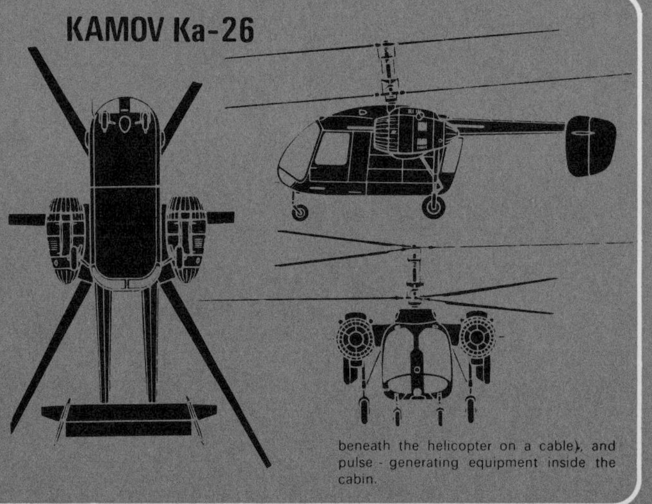

BELL AH-1 HUEYCOBRA

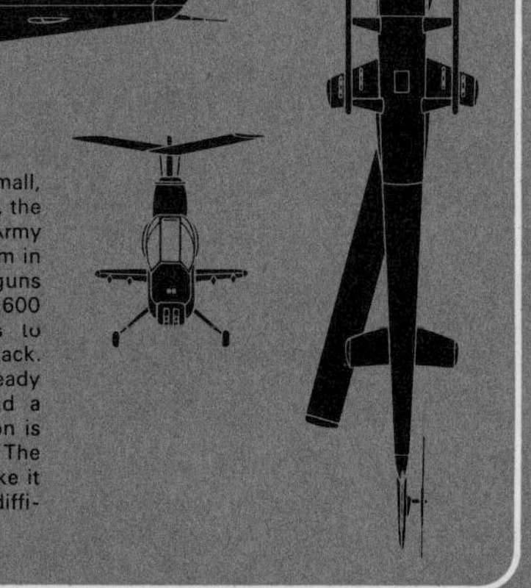

Powered by: One 1,400 shp Lycoming T53-L-13 turboshaft engine, derated to 1,100 shp
Main rotor diameter: 44 ft 0 in (13.41 m)
Fuselage length: 44 ft 5 in (13.54 m)
Main rotor disc area: 1,520.4 sq ft (141.2 m²)
Gross weight: 9,500 lb (4,309 kg)
Max speed: 219 mph (352 km/h)
Max range: 387 miles (622 km)
Armament: XM-28 'chin' turret, mounting either two 7.62-mm six-barrel Miniguns, two 40-mm grenade launchers, or one Minigun and one grenade launcher; racks under stub-wings for four rocket packs, two Minigun pods or two TOW missile pods
Accommodation: Crew of 2
First flight: 7 September 1965

Developed privately by Bell as a small, agile, well-armed 'gunship' helicopter, the HueyCobra was adopted by the US Army in 1966 and entered service in Vietnam in mid-1967 as the AH-1G. The Miniguns can carry out 'search' firing at 1,600 rounds per minute, increasing this to 4,000 rounds per minute in an attack. More than 1,000 HueyCobras have already been ordered for the US Army, and a twin-engined AH-1J SeaCobra version is being built for the US Marine Corps. The AH-1's small size and slim profile make it easy to conceal on the ground and difficult to hit in the air.

BEECH KING AIR

Powered by: Two 550 shp Pratt & Whitney (UACL) PT6A-20 turboprop engines, each driving a 7 ft 9 in (2.36 m) diameter three-blade propeller
Wing span: 50 ft 3 in (15.32 m)
Length: 36 ft 6 in (11.13 m)
Wing area: 293.9 sq ft (27.30 m²)
Gross weight: 9,650 lb (4,377 kg)
Max cruising speed: 256 mph (412 km/h) at 16,000 ft (4,875 m)
Typical range: 1,367 miles (2,200 km) at 16,000 ft (4,875 m)
Accommodation: Crew of 2 and up to 8 passengers
First flight: 20 January 1964

Typical of the range of twin-engined business aircraft currently available from US manufacturers, the King Air is a pressurised, turboprop-powered development of the earlier Queen Air, which first flew in 1958. More than 500 King Airs have been produced since 1964, including the improved Model A90 of 1966 and the B90 which was the current version in 1970. Beechcraft produces a whole family of twin-engined aircraft, ranging from the lightweight Baron and the slightly larger Duke to the Queen Air, King Air and the 15-passenger Model 99 'third-level' airliner.

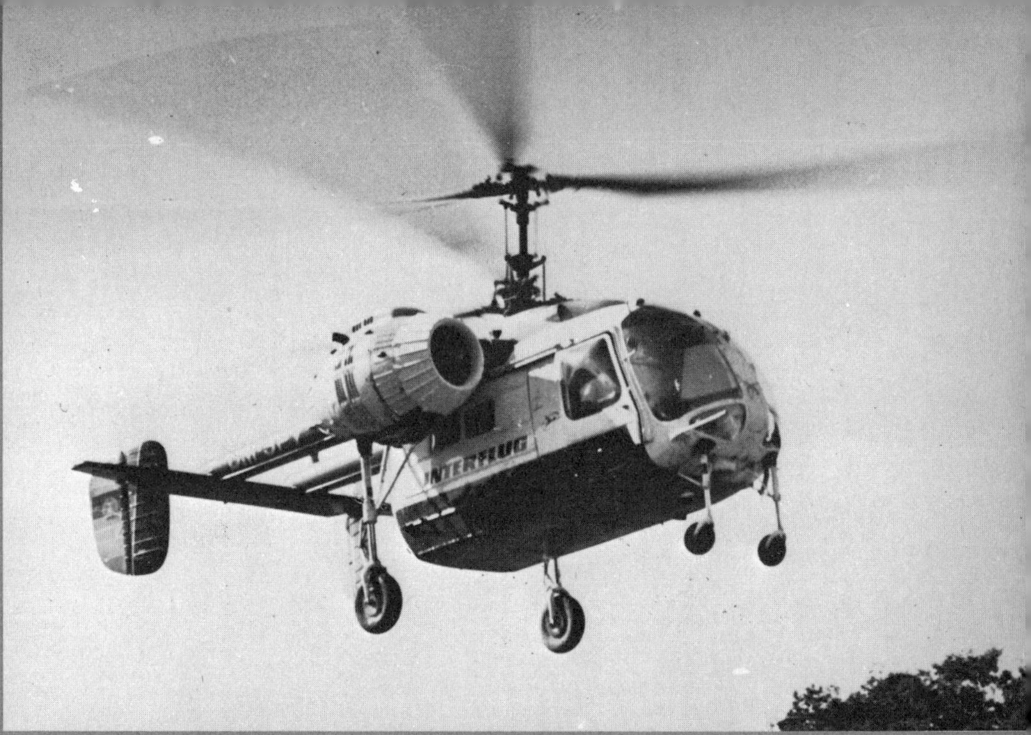

Ka-26, passenger version

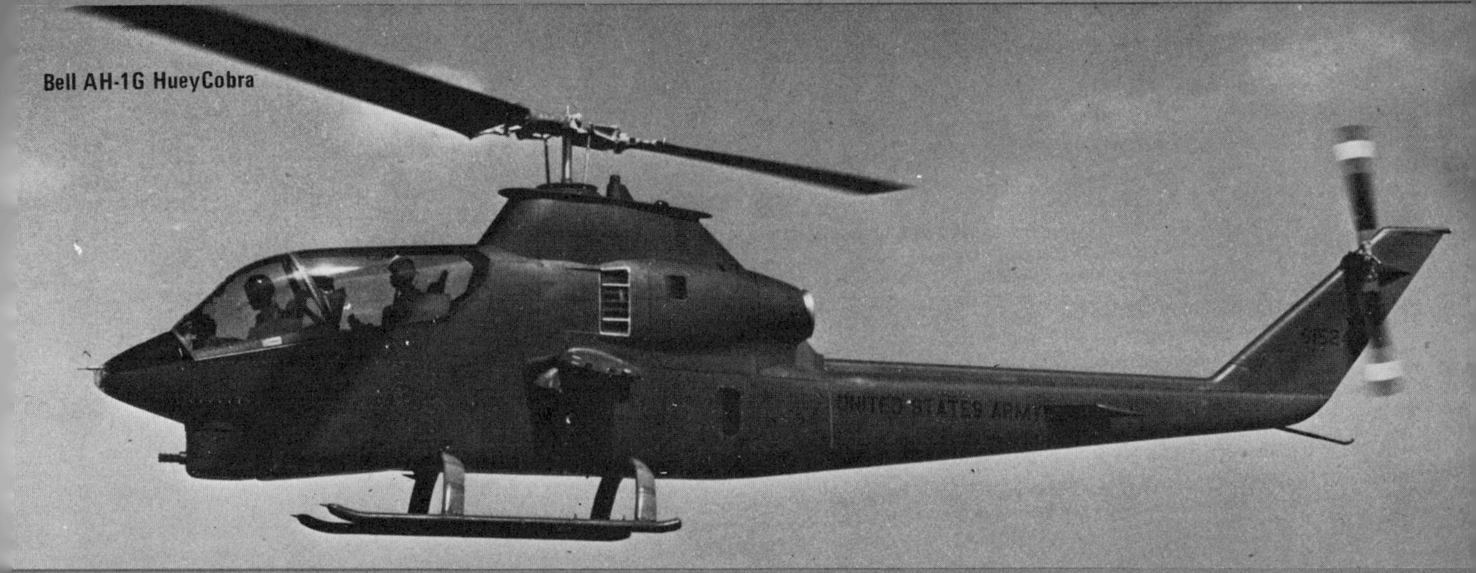

Bell AH-1G HueyCobra

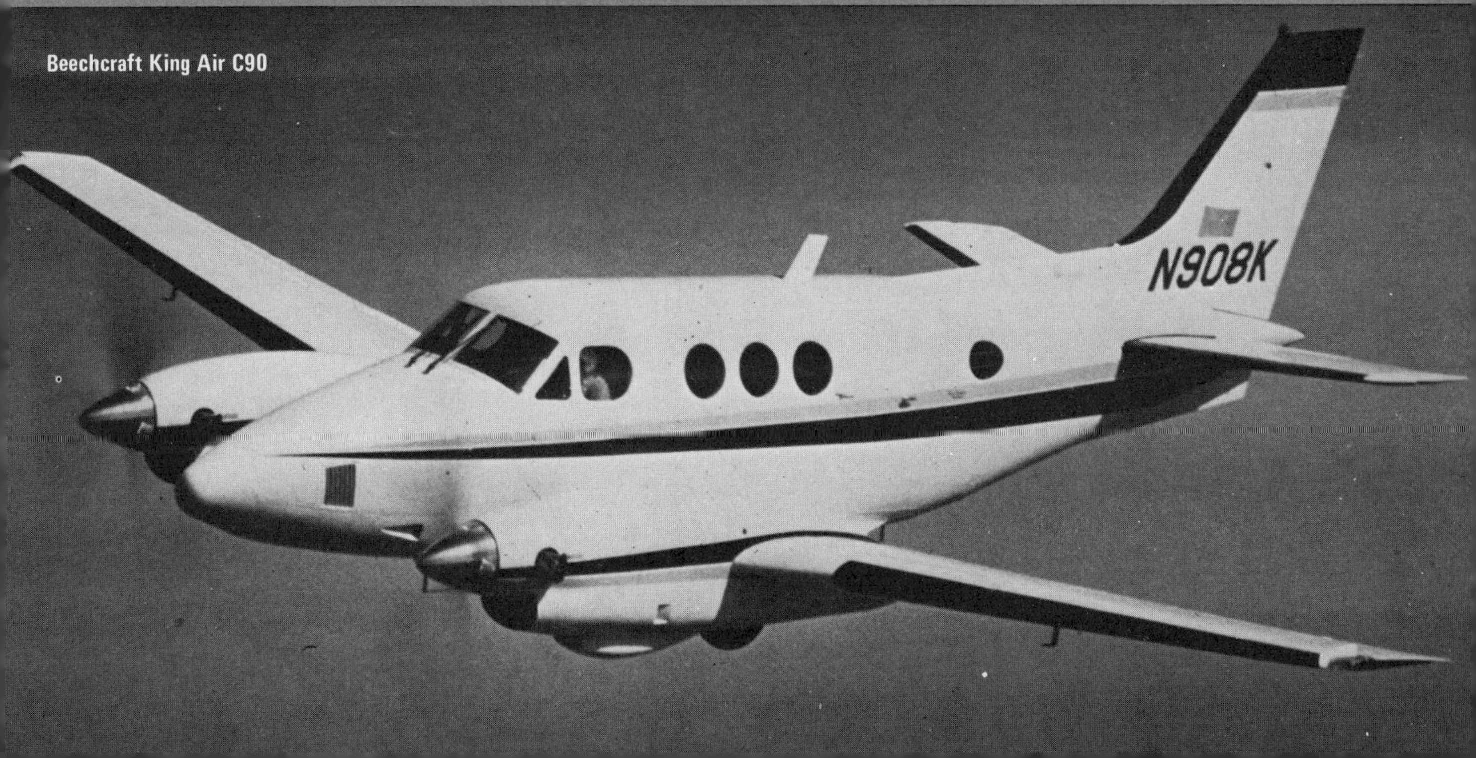

Beechcraft King Air C90

ANTONOV An-22 ANTEUS

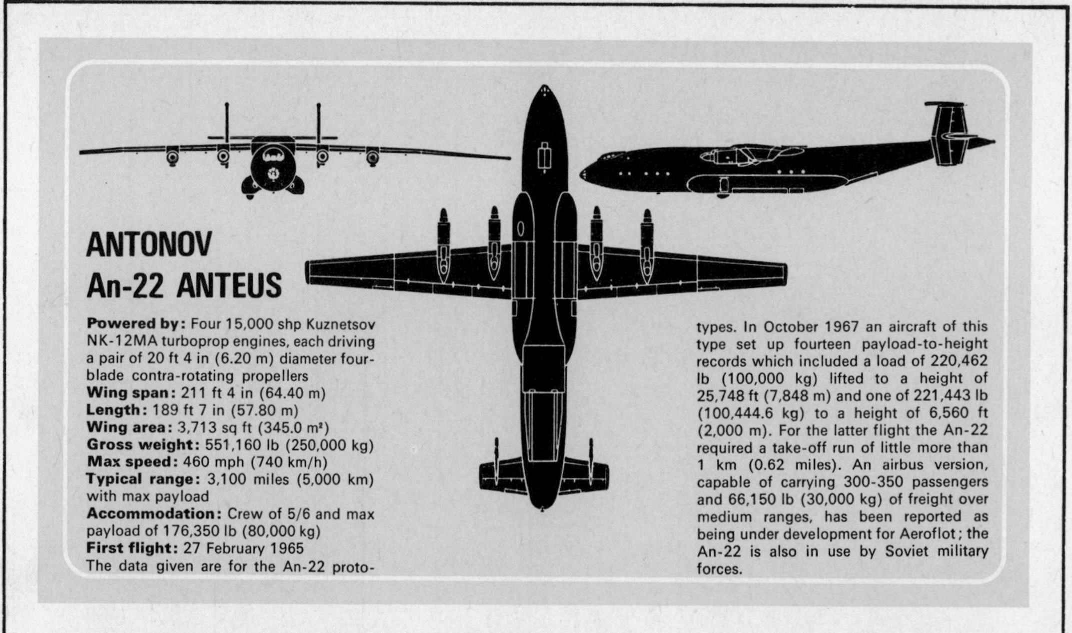

Powered by: Four 15,000 shp Kuznetsov NK-12MA turboprop engines, each driving a pair of 20 ft 4 in (6.20 m) diameter four-blade contra-rotating propellers
Wing span: 211 ft 4 in (64.40 m)
Length: 189 ft 7 in (57.80 m)
Wing area: 3,713 sq ft (345.0 m²)
Gross weight: 551,160 lb (250,000 kg)
Max speed: 460 mph (740 km/h)
Typical range: 3,100 miles (5,000 km) with max payload
Accommodation: Crew of 5/6 and max payload of 176,350 lb (80,000 kg)
First flight: 27 February 1965
The data given are for the An-22 prototypes. In October 1967 an aircraft of this type set up fourteen payload-to-height records which included a load of 220,462 lb (100,000 kg) lifted to a height of 25,748 ft (7,848 m) and one of 221,443 lb (100,444.6 kg) to a height of 6,560 ft (2,000 m). For the latter flight the An-22 required a take-off run of little more than 1 km (0.62 miles). An airbus version, capable of carrying 300-350 passengers and 66,150 lb (30,000 kg) of freight over medium ranges, has been reported as being under development for Aeroflot; the An-22 is also in use by Soviet military forces.

McDONNELL DOUGLAS DC-8 SUPER SIXTY

Powered by: Four 19,000 lb (8,618 kg) st Pratt & Whitney JT3D-7 turbofan engines
Wing span: 148 ft 5 in (45.23 m)
Length: 187 ft 5 in (57.12 m)
Wing area: 2,927 sq ft (271.9 m²)
Gross weight: 350,000 lb (158,760 kg)
Max cruising speed: 600 mph (965 km/h) at 30,000 ft (9,150 m)
Range: 4,500 miles (7,240 km) with max payload
Accommodation: Crew of 3/5 and up to 259 passengers
First flights: 30 May 1958 (first DC-8); 14 March 1966 (first Super 61)
Almost all modern airliners incorporate a 'built-in stretch' potential in their design, but in few cases is this so apparent as in the Super Sixty versions of the Douglas DC-8. There are three members of the series, the first being the Super 61, which combines the standard DC-8 wings with a 36 ft 8 in (11.18 m) longer fuselage. The fuselage of the Super 62 is only 6 ft 8 in (2.03 m) longer than standard, seating up to 189 passengers, but this version has a 6 ft 0 in (1.82 m) increase in wing span and greater fuel capacity. The silhouette shows the Super 63; data apply to the Super 63, which combines the wings of the 62 with the long fuselage of the 61.

BOEING 747

Powered by: Four 43,500 lb (19,730 kg) st Pratt & Whitney JT9D-3 turbofan engines
Wing span: 195 ft 8 in (59.64 m)
Length: 231 ft 4 in (70.51 m)
Gross weight: 710,000 lb (322,050 kg)
Max speed: 595 mph (958 km/h) at 30,000 ft (9,150 m)
Accommodation: Crew of 3 374-490 passengers or 200,000 lb (90,720 kg) of freight
Typical range: 5,790 miles (9,140 km) with 374 passengers
First flight: 9 February 1969
The data above apply to the basic Model 747, which entered airline service early in 1970. This version is known as the 747-100. Later variants include the 747-200, which is available in passenger, cargo or convertible versions, and the 747F all-freight version. More than 200 Boeing 747s had been ordered by early 1972.

Antonov An-22

McDonnell Douglas DC-8 Series 61F freighter

Boeing 747-100

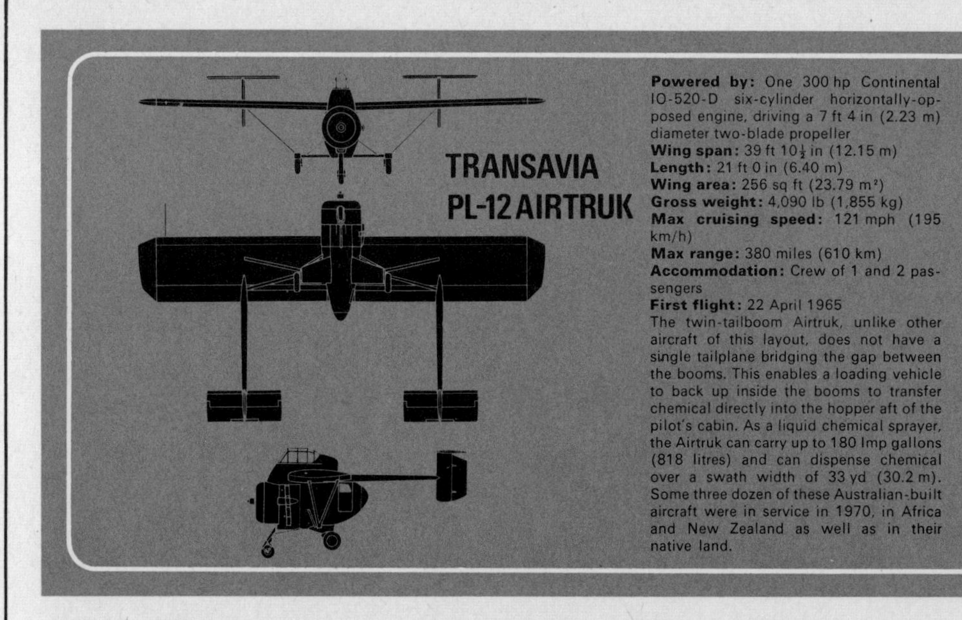

TRANSAVIA PL-12 AIRTRUK

Powered by: One 300 hp Continental IO-520-D six-cylinder horizontally-opposed engine, driving a 7 ft 4 in (2.23 m) diameter two-blade propeller
Wing span: 39 ft 10½ in (12.15 m)
Length: 21 ft 0 in (6.40 m)
Wing area: 256 sq ft (23.79 m²)
Gross weight: 4,090 lb (1,855 kg)
Max cruising speed: 121 mph (195 km/h)
Max range: 380 miles (610 km)
Accommodation: Crew of 1 and 2 passengers
First flight: 22 April 1965
The twin-tailboom Airtruk, unlike other aircraft of this layout, does not have a single tailplane bridging the gap between the booms. This enables a loading vehicle to back up inside the booms to transfer chemical directly into the hopper aft of the pilot's cabin. As a liquid chemical sprayer, the Airtruk can carry up to 180 Imp gallons (818 litres) and can dispense chemical over a swath width of 33 yd (30.2 m). Some three dozen of these Australian-built aircraft were in service in 1970, in Africa and New Zealand as well as in their native land.

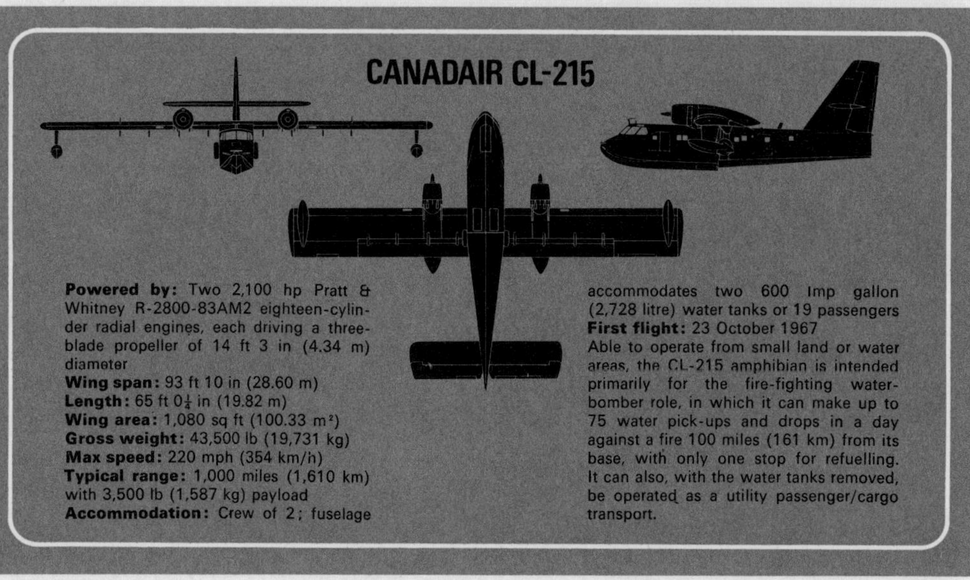

CANADAIR CL-215

Powered by: Two 2,100 hp Pratt & Whitney R-2800-83AM2 eighteen-cylinder radial engines, each driving a three-blade propeller of 14 ft 3 in (4.34 m) diameter
Wing span: 93 ft 10 in (28.60 m)
Length: 65 ft 0¼ in (19.82 m)
Wing area: 1,080 sq ft (100.33 m²)
Gross weight: 43,500 lb (19,731 kg)
Max speed: 220 mph (354 km/h)
Typical range: 1,000 miles (1,610 km) with 3,500 lb (1,587 kg) payload
Accommodation: Crew of 2; fuselage accommodates two 600 Imp gallon (2,728 litre) water tanks or 19 passengers
First flight: 23 October 1967
Able to operate from small land or water areas, the CL-215 amphibian is intended primarily for the fire-fighting water-bomber role, in which it can make up to 75 water pick-ups and drops in a day against a fire 100 miles (161 km) from its base, with only one stop for refuelling. It can also, with the water tanks removed, be operated as a utility passenger/cargo transport.

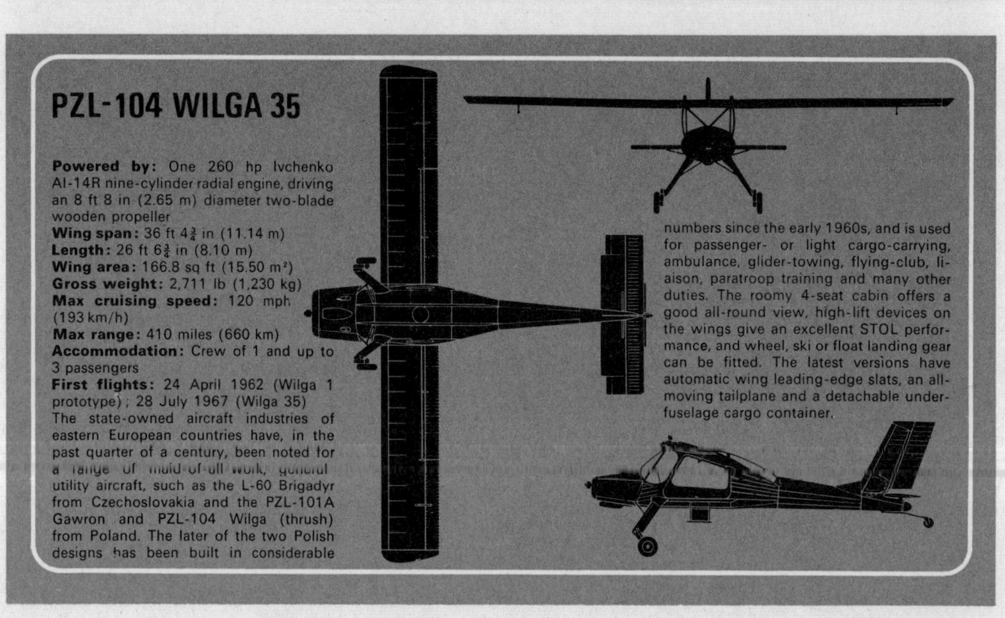

PZL-104 WILGA 35

Powered by: One 260 hp Ivchenko AI-14R nine-cylinder radial engine, driving an 8 ft 8 in (2.65 m) diameter two-blade wooden propeller
Wing span: 36 ft 4½ in (11.14 m)
Length: 26 ft 6¾ in (8.10 m)
Wing area: 166.8 sq ft (15.50 m²)
Gross weight: 2,711 lb (1,230 kg)
Max cruising speed: 120 mph (193 km/h)
Max range: 410 miles (660 km)
Accommodation: Crew of 1 and up to 3 passengers
First flights: 24 April 1962 (Wilga 1 prototype); 28 July 1967 (Wilga 35)
The state-owned aircraft industries of eastern European countries have, in the past quarter of a century, been noted for a range of maid-of-all-work, general utility aircraft, such as the L-60 Brigadyr from Czechoslovakia and the PZL-101A Gawron and PZL-104 Wilga (thrush) from Poland. The later of the two Polish designs has been built in considerable numbers since the early 1960s, and is used for passenger- or light cargo-carrying, ambulance, glider-towing, flying-club, liaison, paratroop training and many other duties. The roomy 4-seat cabin offers a good all-round view, high-lift devices on the wings give an excellent STOL performance, and wheel, ski or float landing gear can be fitted. The latest versions have automatic wing leading-edge slats, an all-moving tailplane and a detachable under-fuselage cargo container.

Transavia PL-12 Airtruk

Canadair CL-215

PZL-104 Wilga 3

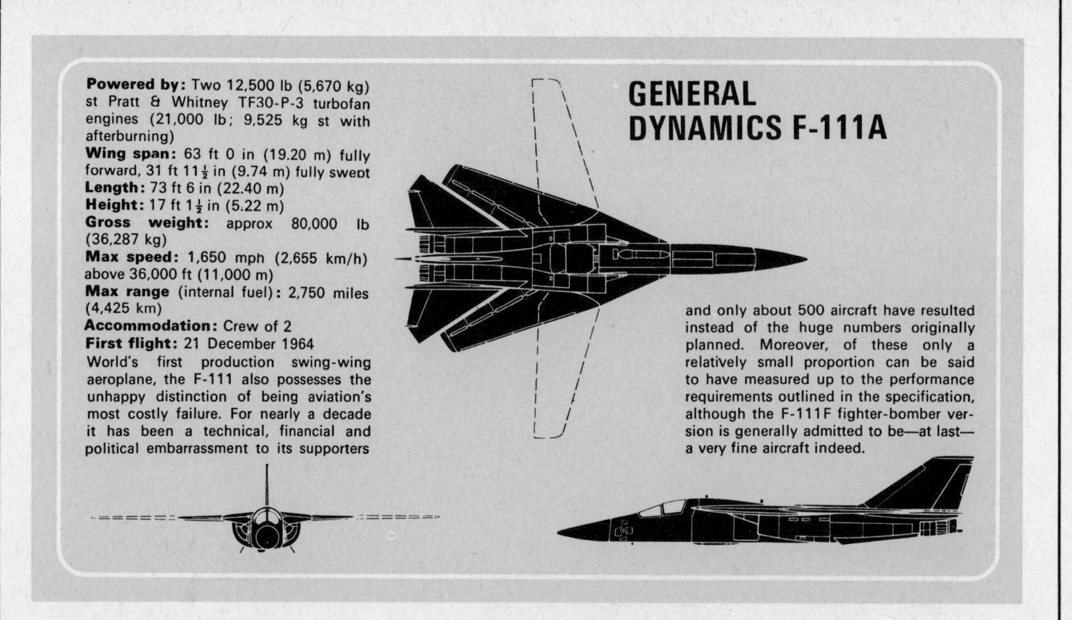

Powered by: Two 12,500 lb (5,670 kg) st Pratt & Whitney TF30-P-3 turbofan engines (21,000 lb; 9,525 kg st with afterburning)
Wing span: 63 ft 0 in (19.20 m) fully forward, 31 ft 11½ in (9.74 m) fully swept
Length: 73 ft 6 in (22.40 m)
Height: 17 ft 1½ in (5.22 m)
Gross weight: approx 80,000 lb (36,287 kg)
Max speed: 1,650 mph (2,655 km/h) above 36,000 ft (11,000 m)
Max range (internal fuel): 2,750 miles (4,425 km)
Accommodation: Crew of 2
First flight: 21 December 1964

World's first production swing-wing aeroplane, the F-111 also possesses the unhappy distinction of being aviation's most costly failure. For nearly a decade it has been a technical, financial and political embarrassment to its supporters and only about 500 aircraft have resulted instead of the huge numbers originally planned. Moreover, of these only a relatively small proportion can be said to have measured up to the performance requirements outlined in the specification, although the F-111F fighter-bomber version is generally admitted to be—at last—a very fine aircraft indeed.

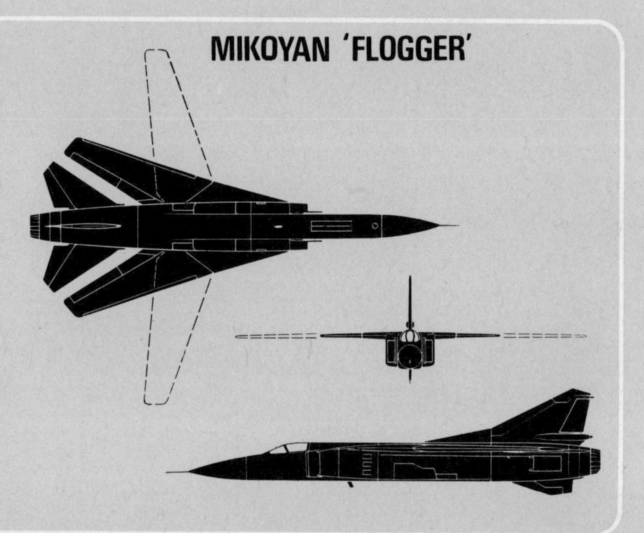

Powered by: One turbojet engine developing approx 29,760 lb (13,500 kg) st with afterburning
Wing span: approx 50 ft 0 in (15.25 m) fully forward, 29 ft 6 in (9.00 m) fully swept
Length: approx 57 ft 0 in (17.40 m)
Height: approx 15 ft 0 in (4.50 m)
Gross weight: approx 36,375 lb (16,500 kg)
Max speed: approx 1,650 mph (2,655 km/h) above 36,000 ft (11,000 m)
Accommodation: Crew of 1
First flight: 1967 (?)

Since the appearance of a single prototype at the Aviation Day Display near Moscow in 1967, little has been seen or heard of this variable-geometry fighter evolved by the Mikoyan design collective; but by early 1971 there were indications that it is in service in modest numbers with the Soviet Air Force. It is smaller than the F-111, having only a single crew member and a single engine, and is similar in size (and, presumably, in performance) to the original Mirage G swing-wing prototype built by Dassault in France.

Powered by: Two Turbo-Union (Rolls-Royce/MTU/Fiat) RB.199-34R after burning turbofan engines
Max speed: Above 1,320 mph (2,125 km/h) (Mach 2) at high altitude
Accommodation: Crew of 2
First flight: scheduled for 1974

Panavia is the European company formed in 1969 to design, develop and produce the MRCA (Multi-Role Combat Aircraft) for service with the air forces of Great Britain, Federal Germany and Italy. Total requirements for this aircraft are about 900, including 350-400 by Britain and up to 420 by Germany. By early 1971 work had begun on the construction of seven prototypes—three each in Britain and Germany and one in Italy. Five main roles are foreseen for the MRCA: close support, interdictor strike, air superiority, naval and reconnaissance, and each country will also require a trainer version. The only clue to the aircraft's size and weight given officially is the statement that it is 'no larger than the Mirage G and substantially lighter than the Phantom', but the provisional silhouette shows the general appearance of this two-seat swing-wing aircraft.

General Dynamics F-111A

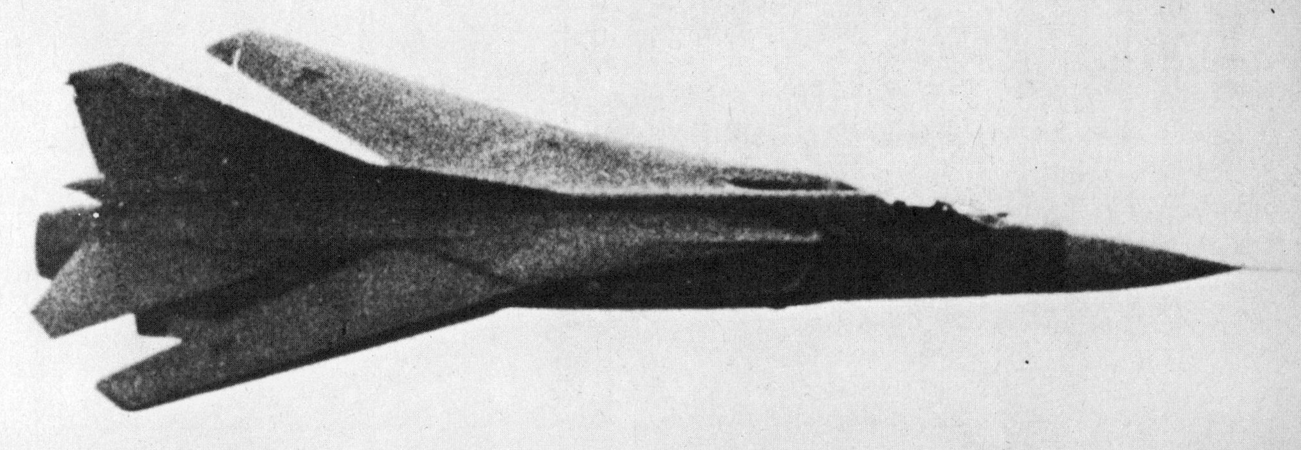

Mikoyan 'Flogger'

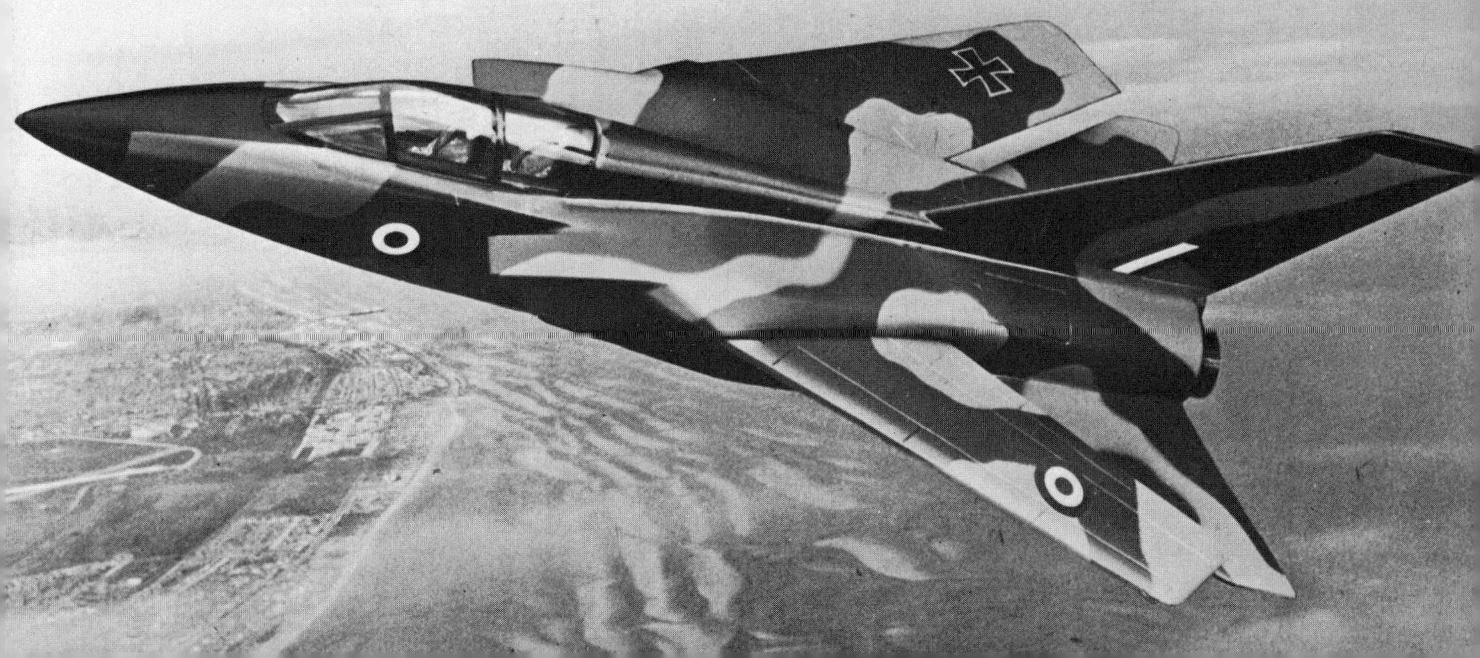

Panavia MRCA (artist's impression)

HAWKER SIDDELEY HARRIER GR Mk1

Powered by: One 19,000 lb (8,618 kg) st Rolls-Royce Bristol Pegasus Mk 101 vectored-thrust turbofan engine.
Wing span: 25 ft 3 in (7.70 m).
Length: 45 ft 8 in (13.92 m).
Gross weight: over 22,000 lb (9,979 kg)
Max. speed: over 720 mph (1,159 km/h).
Accommodation: Crew of 1.
Typical Armament: Two 30 mm Aden gun pods and one 1,000 lb (454 kg) bomb on under-fuselage pylons, plus two 1,000 lb bombs and two Matra launchers, each with 19 x 68-mm rockets, beneath wings.
Max. endurance: over 7 hr with in-flight refuelling.
First flight: 28 December 1967.

The GR Mk 1 is the single-seat close-support and reconnaissance version for the RAF, which has also ordered the 2-seat T Mk 2 for operational training. Export versions, which have the more powerful Pegasus 11 engine, are designated Mk 50 (single-seat) and Mk 51 (2-seat). US Marine Corps designation is AV-8A.

DORNIER Do 31 E3

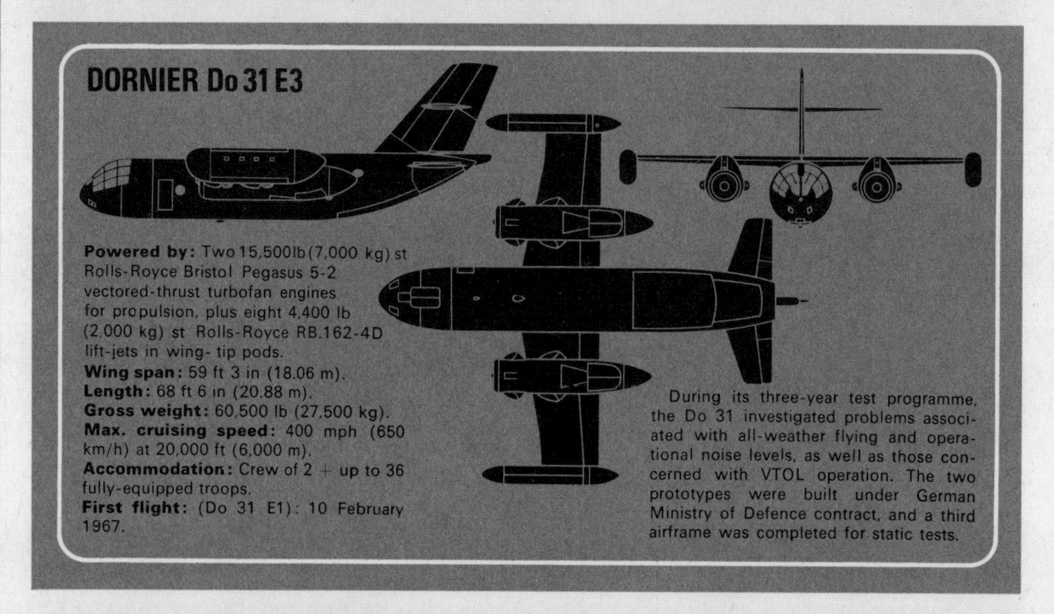

Powered by: Two 15,500lb (7,000 kg) st Rolls-Royce Bristol Pegasus 5-2 vectored-thrust turbofan engines for propulsion, plus eight 4,400 lb (2,000 kg) st Rolls-Royce RB.162-4D lift-jets in wing- tip pods.
Wing span: 59 ft 3 in (18.06 m).
Length: 68 ft 6 in (20.88 m).
Gross weight: 60,500 lb (27,500 kg).
Max. cruising speed: 400 mph (650 km/h) at 20,000 ft (6,000 m).
Accommodation: Crew of 2 + up to 36 fully-equipped troops.
First flight: (Do 31 E1): 10 February 1967.

During its three-year test programme, the Do 31 investigated problems associated with all-weather flying and operational noise levels, as well as those concerned with VTOL operation. The two prototypes were built under German Ministry of Defence contract, and a third airframe was completed for static tests.

YAKOVLEV 'FREEHAND'

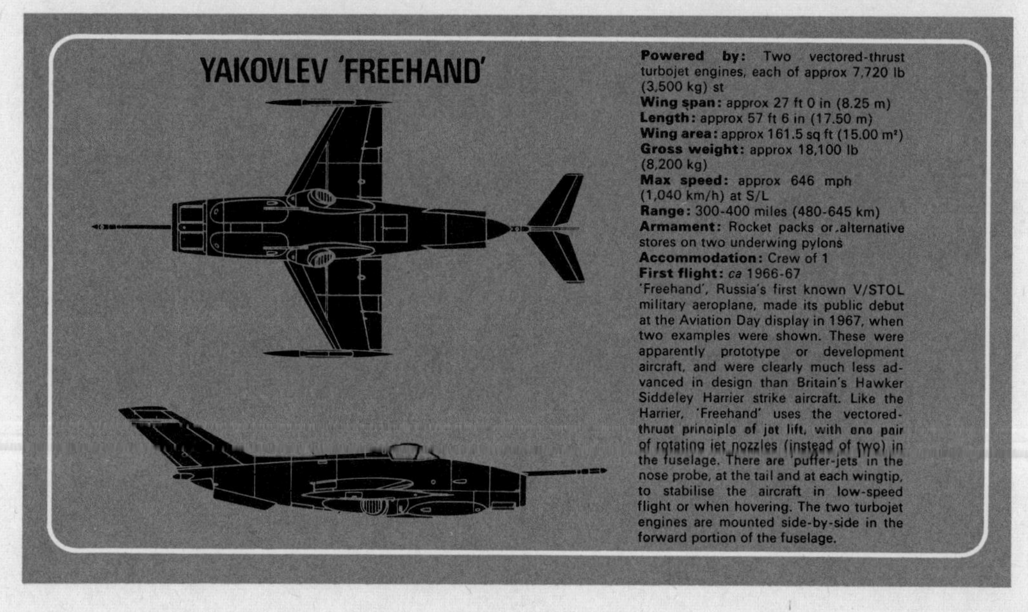

Powered by: Two vectored-thrust turbojet engines, each of approx 7,720 lb (3,500 kg) st
Wing span: approx 27 ft 0 in (8.25 m)
Length: approx 57 ft 6 in (17.50 m)
Wing area: approx 161.5 sq ft (15.00 m²)
Gross weight: approx 18,100 lb (8,200 kg)
Max speed: approx 646 mph (1,040 km/h) at S/L
Range: 300-400 miles (480-645 km)
Armament: Rocket packs or alternative stores on two underwing pylons
Accommodation: Crew of 1
First flight: *ca* 1966-67

'Freehand', Russia's first known V/STOL military aeroplane, made its public debut at the Aviation Day display in 1967, when two examples were shown. These were apparently prototype or development aircraft, and were clearly much less advanced in design than Britain's Hawker Siddeley Harrier strike aircraft. Like the Harrier, 'Freehand' uses the vectored-thrust principle of jet lift, with one pair of rotating jet nozzles (instead of two) in the fuselage. There are 'puffer-jets' in the nose probe, at the tail and at each wingtip, to stabilise the aircraft in low-speed flight or when hovering. The two turbojet engines are mounted side-by-side in the forward portion of the fuselage.

AV-8A Harrier in US Marine Corps insignia

Dornier Do 31 E3

Yakovlev 'Freehand' *(Tass)*

SAAB AJ 37 VIGGEN

Powered by: One 26,450 lb (12,000 kg) st Svenska Flygmotor RM8 afterburning turbofan engine (supersonic development of the Pratt & Whitney JT8D-22)
Wing span: 34 ft 9¼ in (10.60 m)
Length: 53 ft 5¾ in (16.30 m) incl nose probe
Height: 18 ft 4½ in (5.60 m)
Gross weight: approx 35,275 lb (16,000 kg)
Max speed: over 1,320 mph (2,125 km/h) at 36,000 ft (11,000 m) (Mach 2)
Typical combat radius: over 620 miles (1,000 km)
Armament: Wide assortment of guns, bombs, air-to-air or air-to-surface missiles on seven attachment points beneath wings and fuselage
Accommodation: Crew of 1 (2 in SK 37)
First flight: 8 February 1967
One of the most advanced combat aircraft currently in production anywhere in the world, the Viggen is a highly-automated integral part of Sweden's air defence system for the 1970s. It uses a canard foreplane, fitted with flaps, in conjunction with a large delta-shaped main wing, to obtain an excellent STOL performance, enabling it to use runways only 1,640 ft (500 m) long.

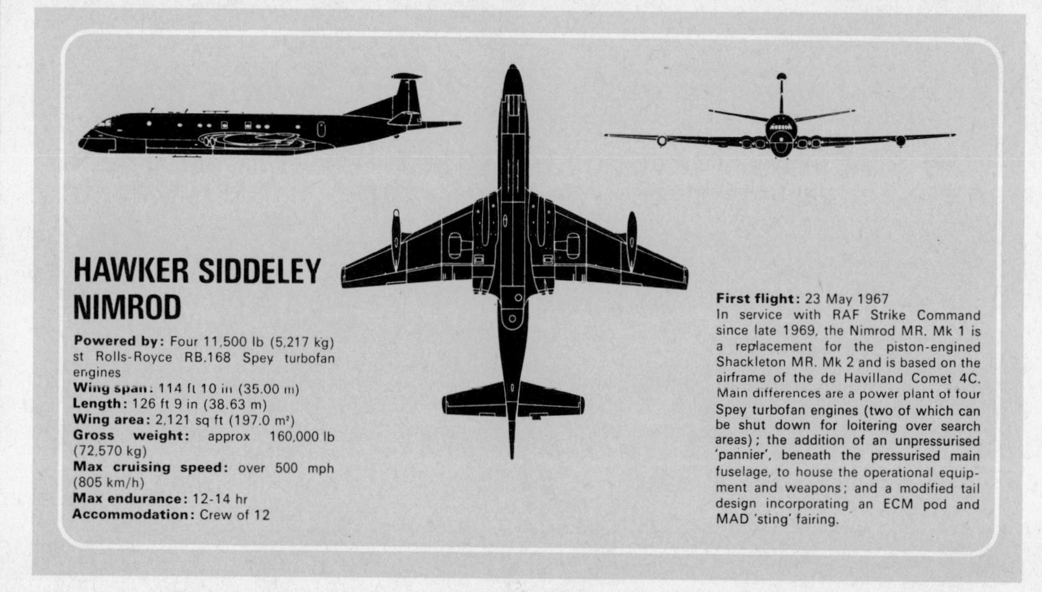

HAWKER SIDDELEY NIMROD

Powered by: Four 11,500 lb (5,217 kg) st Rolls-Royce RB.168 Spey turbofan engines
Wing span: 114 ft 10 in (35.00 m)
Length: 126 ft 9 in (38.63 m)
Wing area: 2,121 sq ft (197.0 m²)
Gross weight: approx 160,000 lb (72,570 kg)
Max cruising speed: over 500 mph (805 km/h)
Max endurance: 12-14 hr
Accommodation: Crew of 12
First flight: 23 May 1967
In service with RAF Strike Command since late 1969, the Nimrod MR. Mk 1 is a replacement for the piston-engined Shackleton MR. Mk 2 and is based on the airframe of the de Havilland Comet 4C. Main differences are a power plant of four Spey turbofan engines (two of which can be shut down for loitering over search areas); the addition of an unpressurised 'pannier', beneath the pressurised main fuselage, to house the operational equipment and weapons; and a modified tail design incorporating an ECM pod and MAD 'sting' fairing.

SEPECAT JAGUAR

Powered by: Two 6,950 lb (3,150 kg) st Rolls-Royce/Turboméca Adour afterburning turbofan engines
Wing span: 27 ft 10¼ in (8.49 m)
Length: 50 ft 11 in (15.52 m)

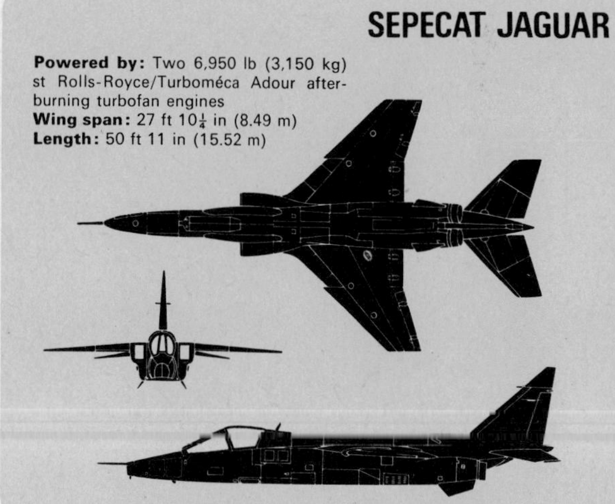

Wing area: 258.33 sq ft (24.00 m²)
Gross weight: 29,762 lb (13,500 kg)
Max speed: 1,120 mph (1,800 km/h) at 36,000 ft (11,000 m)
Typical combat radius: 775 miles (1,250 km)
Armament: Two 30-mm Aden cannon in fuselage and up to 10,000 lb (4,500 kg) of externally-mounted bombs, rockets or missiles in various combinations
Accommodation: Crew of 1 or 2
First flight: 29 March 1969 (first tactical prototype)
Evolved from an original French design, the Jaguar is being developed and produced by Breguet in France and BAC in Britain as a lightweight tactical support aircraft and two-seat advanced trainer for the British and French forces. A carrier-based version is also being produced for the French Navy. The Jaguar's maximum speed of Mach 1.7 is capable, with development, of being increased to more than Mach 2.

Saab AJ 37 Viggen

Hawker Siddeley Nimrod MR Mk 1

Sepecat Jaguar, British single-seat strike version

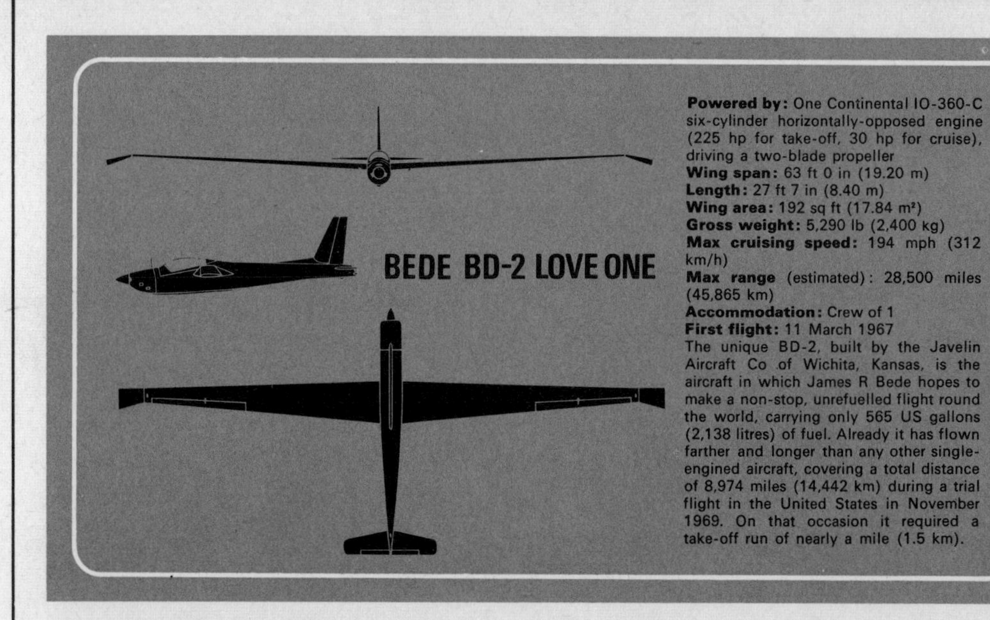

BEDE BD-2 LOVE ONE

Powered by: One Continental IO-360-C six-cylinder horizontally-opposed engine (225 hp for take-off, 30 hp for cruise), driving a two-blade propeller
Wing span: 63 ft 0 in (19.20 m)
Length: 27 ft 7 in (8.40 m)
Wing area: 192 sq ft (17.84 m²)
Gross weight: 5,290 lb (2,400 kg)
Max cruising speed: 194 mph (312 km/h)
Max range (estimated): 28,500 miles (45,865 km)
Accommodation: Crew of 1
First flight: 11 March 1967
The unique BD-2, built by the Javelin Aircraft Co of Wichita, Kansas, is the aircraft in which James R Bede hopes to make a non-stop, unrefuelled flight round the world, carrying only 565 US gallons (2,138 litres) of fuel. Already it has flown farther and longer than any other single-engined aircraft, covering a total distance of 8,974 miles (14,442 km) during a trial flight in the United States in November 1969. On that occasion it required a take-off run of nearly a mile (1.5 km).

EVANS VP-1

Powered by: One 40, 53 or 65 hp modified Volkswagen motor-car engine, driving a 4 ft 6 in (1.37 m) diameter two-blade propeller
Wing span: 24 ft 0 in (7.32 m)
Length: 18 ft 0 in (5.49 m)
Wing area: 100 sq ft (9.29 m²)
Gross weight: 750 lb (340 kg)
Rate of climb at S/L: 400 ft (122 m)/min
Accommodation: Crew of 1
Unashamedly sacrificing both appearance and performance to achieve simplicity of structure and maintenance, Mr Samuel Evans of La Jolla, California, designed his 'Volksplane' for the novice home-builder. Mr Evans, a Convair design engineer, took two years to evolve the design of the little aircraft, which is of all-wood construction and can take off in 450 ft (137 m) and land in 200 ft (61 m) under normal conditions. It is a strut-braced low-wing monoplane, with fixed landing gear and an all-moving tail unit.

MAHONEY SORCERESS 1

Powered by: One 125 hp Lycoming O-290-3 four-cylinder horizontally-opposed engine, driving a two-blade propeller
Wing span: 16 ft 0 in (4.88 m)
Length: 17 ft 0 in (5.18 m)
Wing area: 98 sq ft (9.10 m²)
Gross weight: 1,110 lb (503 kg)
Max speed: 202 mph (325 km/h)
Rate of climb at S/L: 1,495 ft (456 m)/min
Accommodation: Crew of 1
First flight: 1 August 1970
American home-builder Lee Mahoney, a member of the Professional Racing Pilots Association, has designed, built and flown one of the most unorthodox racing aircraft yet to appear in the 1970s, called the Sorceress. It is, in effect, a tandem-wing biplane with negative stagger, the lower-mounted front wing having an inverted gull form. Construction is all-metal, and fuel tanks are located in the fuselage and the rear wings.

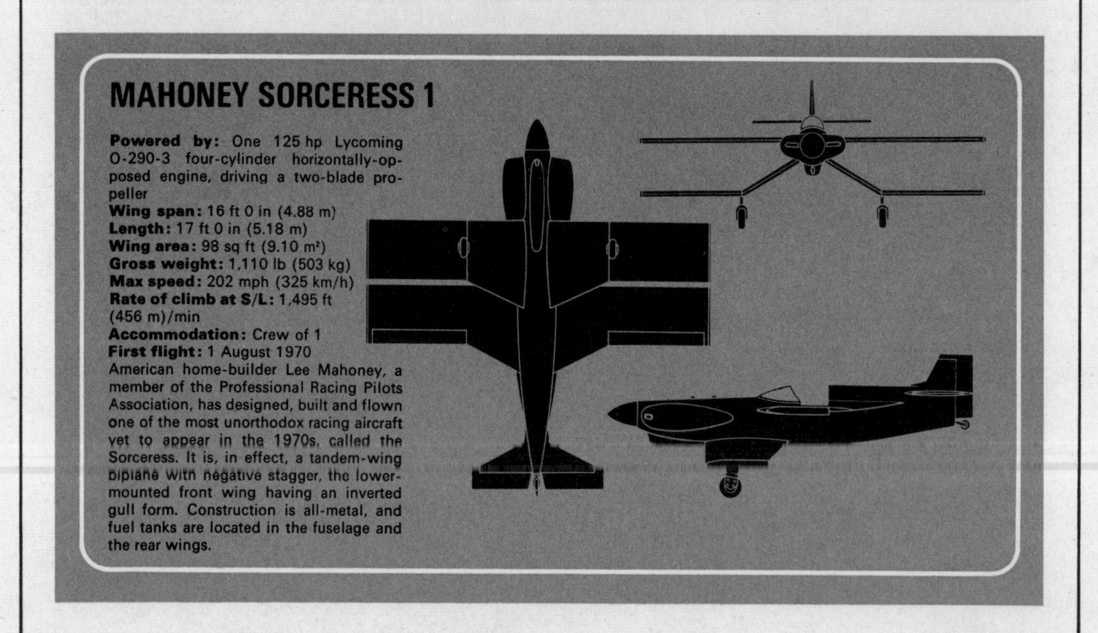

Bede BD-2 Love One, with wheeled take-off dolly still attached

Evans VP-1 *(Howard Levy)*

Mahoney Sorceress 1 *(Henry Artof)*

TUPOLEV Tu-144

Powered by: Four 38,580 lb (17,500 kg) st Kuznetsov NK-144 afterburning turbofan engines
Wing span: 90 ft $8\frac{1}{2}$ in (27.65 m)
Length: 190 ft $3\frac{1}{2}$ in (58.00 m)
Height: approx 43 ft 3 in (13.20 m)
Gross weight: 395,000 lb (179,150 kg)
Max cruising speed: 1,550 mph (2,500 km/h) at 65,000 ft (20,000 m)
Range: 4,040 miles (6,500 km) with 121 passengers
Accommodation: Crew of 3 and up to 130 passengers
First flight: 31 December 1968

Often nicknamed 'Concordski' by the western press, implying that it is a copy of the Anglo-French design, the Tu-144 was in fact the world's first supersonic transport aircraft to fly, preceding the first prototype Concorde by some two months. It flew at Mach 1 four months before the Concorde and at Mach 2 six months before its western rival; moreover, the entire test programme up to the autumn of 1971 had been carried out by a single prototype. A second and third aircraft joined the test programme subsequently, and deliveries of production Tu-144s are due to begin in 1974-75.

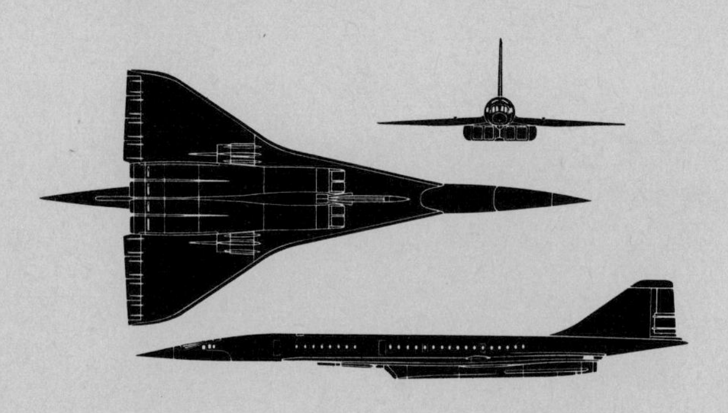

AÉROSPATIALE/BAC CONCORDE

Powered by: Four 38,050 lb (17,260 kg) st Rolls-Royce/SNECMA Olympus 593 Mk 602 afterburning turbojet engines
Wing span: 84 ft 0 in (25.60 m)
Length: 203 ft $11\frac{1}{2}$ in (62.17 m)
Wing area: 3,856 sq ft (358.25 m²)
Gross weight: 385,000 lb (174,640 kg)
Max cruising speed: 1,450 mph (2,333 km/h) at 54,500 ft (16,600 m)
Range: 4,020 miles (6,470 km) at Mach 2.05 cruise/climb with payload of 28,000 lb (12,700 kg)
Accommodation: Crew of 3 and 128-144 passengers
First flight: 2 March 1969

As the comparative data show, the Concorde and the Soviet Tu-144 supersonic transports are broadly comparable in terms of size, payload, engine power and performance. Main differences are the choice of turbofan engines to power the Soviet aircraft, which is designed for a slightly higher cruising Mach number with a slightly lower maximum passenger capacity. The Concorde first exceeded Mach 1 on 1 October 1969, and Mach 2 was passed during a test flight on 4 November 1970. Airline options on the Concorde totalled 74 aircraft by 1971, with deliveries due to begin in 1974. From the 41st aircraft onwards, Mk 612 engines of 39,940 lb (18,116 kg) st will be fitted.

DE HAVILLAND CANADA DHC-7

Powered by: Four 1,120 shp Pratt & Whitney (UACL) PT6A-50 turboprop engines, each driving an 11 ft 3 in (3.43 m) diameter four-blade propeller
Wing span: 93 ft 0 in (28.35 m)
Length: 80 ft 4 in (24.49 m)
Height: 26 ft 3 in (8.00 m)
Gross weight: 38,500 lb (17,463 kg)
Max cruising speed: 276 mph (444 km/h)
Range: 495 miles (795 km) with max passenger payload and typical reserves
Accommodation: Crew of 2 and 48 passengers

One trend likely to develop in commercial aviation is towards what is becoming known as the QTOL (Quiet Take-Off and Landing) transport aircraft. Among the first aircraft specifically designed to this philosophy is the DHC-7, a Canadian project which could operate from city STOLports with runways no longer than 2,000 ft (610 m). United Aircraft Corporation is collaborating with de Havilland Canada to produce an engine/propeller combination for the DHC-7 which would limit external noise to 95 PNdB at only 500 ft (152 m) from the aircraft during take-off and landing. In 1970 several airlines reserved delivery positions for the DHC-7 if the project goes ahead.

Tupolev Tu-144, first prototype *(Tass)*

Aérospatiale/BAC Concorde, second prototype

Artist's impression of the DHC-7

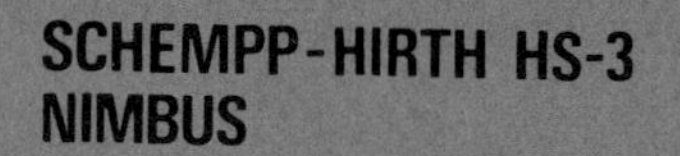

SCHEMPP-HIRTH HS-3 NIMBUS

The HS-3 Nimbus is a high-performance Open Class sailplane, and was designed by Dipl-Ing Klaus Holighaus, one of the co-designers of the Akaflieg Darmstadt D-36 Circe sailplane before he joined Schempp-Hirth KG in 1965. Construction is almost entirely of glass-fibre, with a foam-sandwich structure for the wings and tail unit. Piloted by George Moffat, a Nimbus was the outright winner of the World Gliding Championships held at Marfa, Texas, in the Summer of 1970.

Wing span: 72 ft 2 in (22.00 m)
Wing aspect ratio: 30.6
Length: 23 ft 11½ in (7.30 m)
Gross weight: 1,102 lb (500 kg)
Max speed: 137 mph (220 km/h) in rough or smooth air
Best glide ratio: 51 : 1 at 56 mph (90 km/h)
Accommodation: Crew of 1
First flight: January 1969

LOCKHEED YO-3A

Powered by: One 210 hp Continental horizontally-opposed piston-engine
Wing span: 57 ft 0 in (17.40 m)
Length: 30 ft (9.14 m)
Gross weight: 2,167 lb (983 kg)
Max speed: 149 mph (240 km/h)
Accommodation: Crew of 2
Armament: None

The YO-3A, based on the experimental Lockheed Q-Star, is a development aircraft for a new "quiet reconnaissance" type for the US Army. It is based on the wings and tail unit of the Schweizer SGS 2-32 sailplane, with a new fuselage, retractable landing gear and a heavily-muffled engine driving a three-blade propeller. With the engine cut, the YO-3A can glide over the reconnaissance area; the engine is restarted when clear of enemy territory to make the return journey.

NIHON UNIVERSITY NM-69 LINNET III

Power system: Pedal drive to two-blade pusher propeller, developing an estimated 0.4 hp for take-off and 0.3 hp for level flight
Wing span: 83 ft 0 in (25.30 m)
Length: 19 ft 2¾ in (5.86 m)
Gross weight: 230 lb (105 kg)
Cruising speed (estimated): 16 mph (26 km/h)
Accommodation: Crew of 1
Take-off run (estimated): 260 ft (80 m)
First flight: 26 March 1970

The Linnet series of man-powered aircraft has been designed and built by students of the Department of Mechanical Engineering at Nihon University, Japan, under the leadership of Dr Hidemasa Kimura. The earlier machines, whose designations indicate the year of their design, were the NM-63 Linnet I and NM-66 Linnet II. Construction is mainly of aluminium tubes, balsa wood and styrene paper.

Schempp-Hirth Nimbus II

Lockheed YO-3A

Nihon University NM-66 Linnet II

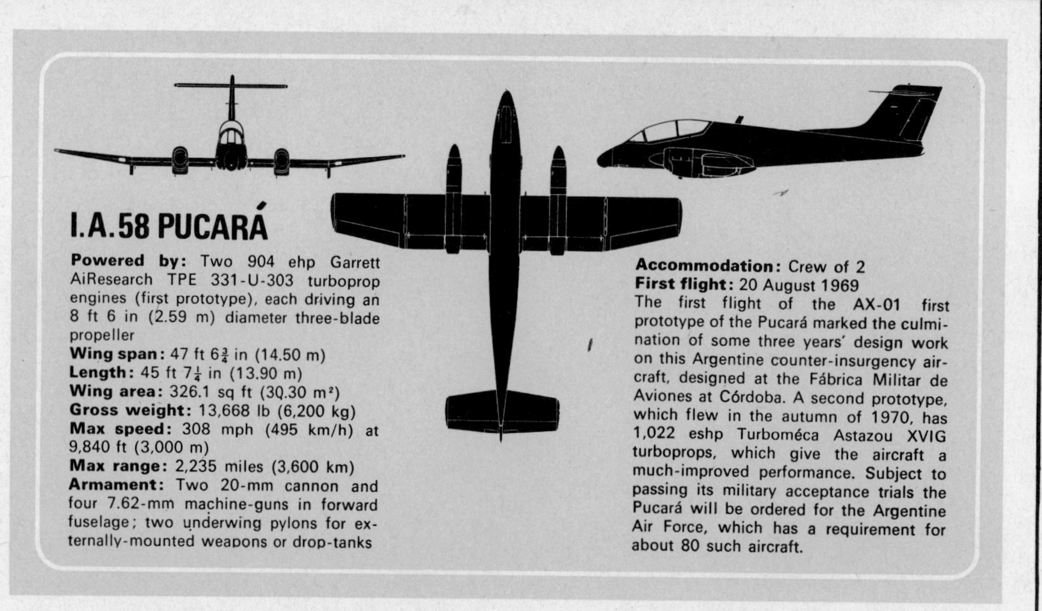

I.A.58 PUCARÁ

Powered by: Two 904 ehp Garrett AiResearch TPE 331-U-303 turboprop engines (first prototype), each driving an 8 ft 6 in (2.59 m) diameter three-blade propeller
Wing span: 47 ft $6\frac{3}{4}$ in (14.50 m)
Length: 45 ft $7\frac{1}{4}$ in (13.90 m)
Wing area: 326.1 sq ft (30.30 m²)
Gross weight: 13,668 lb (6,200 kg)
Max speed: 308 mph (495 km/h) at 9,840 ft (3,000 m)
Max range: 2,235 miles (3,600 km)
Armament: Two 20-mm cannon and four 7.62-mm machine-guns in forward fuselage; two underwing pylons for externally-mounted weapons or drop-tanks
Accommodation: Crew of 2
First flight: 20 August 1969

The first flight of the AX-01 first prototype of the Pucará marked the culmination of some three years' design work on this Argentine counter-insurgency aircraft, designed at the Fábrica Militar de Aviones at Córdoba. A second prototype, which flew in the autumn of 1970, has 1,022 eshp Turboméca Astazou XVIG turboprops, which give the aircraft a much-improved performance. Subject to passing its military acceptance trials the Pucará will be ordered for the Argentine Air Force, which has a requirement for about 80 such aircraft.

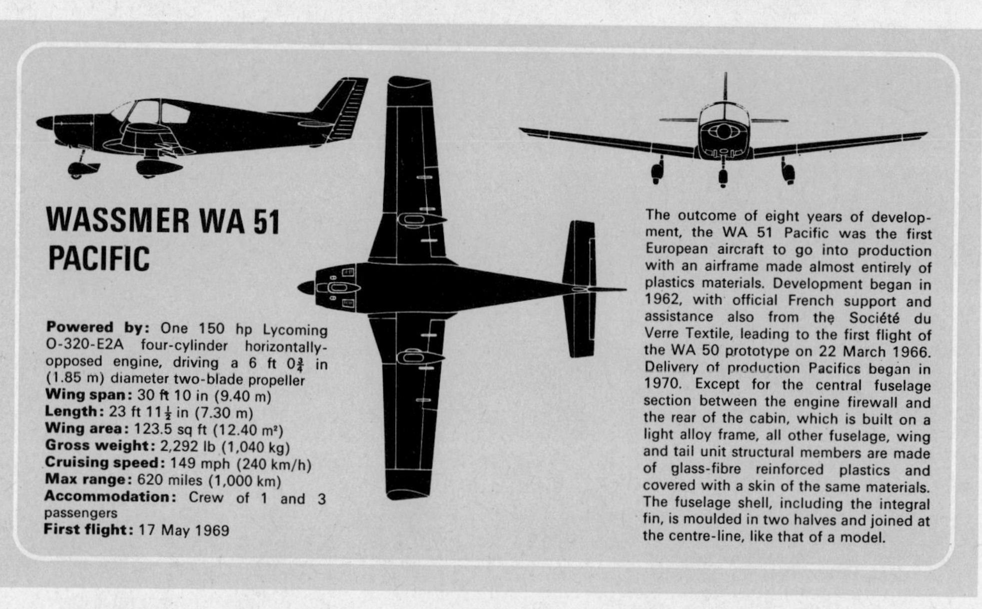

WASSMER WA 51 PACIFIC

Powered by: One 150 hp Lycoming O-320-E2A four-cylinder horizontally-opposed engine, driving a 6 ft $0\frac{3}{4}$ in (1.85 m) diameter two-blade propeller
Wing span: 30 ft 10 in (9.40 m)
Length: 23 ft $11\frac{1}{2}$ in (7.30 m)
Wing area: 123.5 sq ft (12.40 m²)
Gross weight: 2,292 lb (1,040 kg)
Cruising speed: 149 mph (240 km/h)
Max range: 620 miles (1,000 km)
Accommodation: Crew of 1 and 3 passengers
First flight: 17 May 1969

The outcome of eight years of development, the WA 51 Pacific was the first European aircraft to go into production with an airframe made almost entirely of plastics materials. Development began in 1962, with official French support and assistance also from the Société du Verre Textile, leading to the first flight of the WA 50 prototype on 22 March 1966. Delivery of production Pacifics began in 1970. Except for the central fuselage section between the engine firewall and the rear of the cabin, which is built on a light alloy frame, all other fuselage, wing and tail unit structural members are made of glass-fibre reinforced plastics and covered with a skin of the same materials. The fuselage shell, including the integral fin, is moulded in two halves and joined at the centre-line, like that of a model.

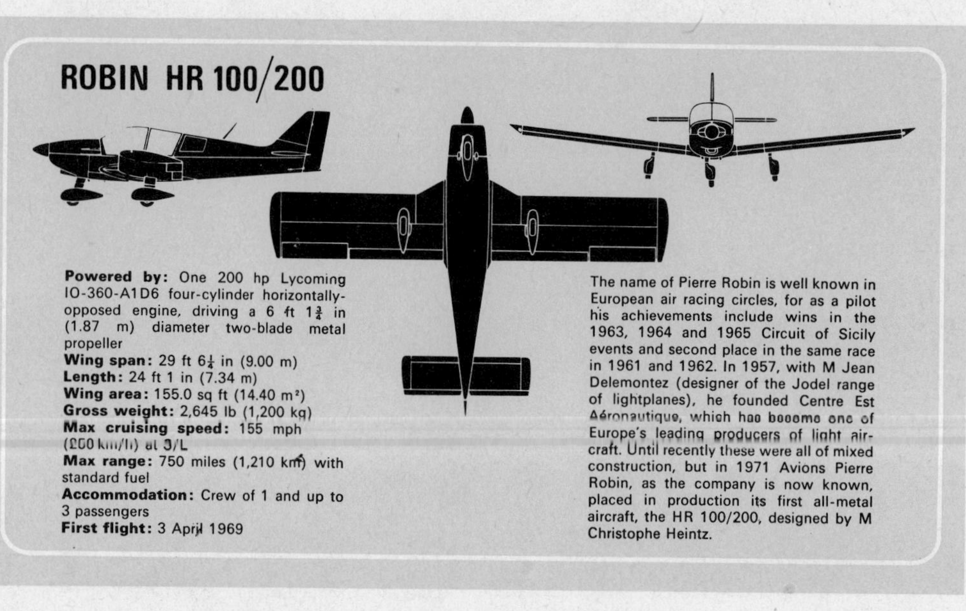

ROBIN HR 100/200

Powered by: One 200 hp Lycoming IO-360-A1D6 four-cylinder horizontally-opposed engine, driving a 6 ft $1\frac{3}{4}$ in (1.87 m) diameter two-blade metal propeller
Wing span: 29 ft $6\frac{1}{4}$ in (9.00 m)
Length: 24 ft 1 in (7.34 m)
Wing area: 155.0 sq ft (14.40 m²)
Gross weight: 2,645 lb (1,200 kg)
Max cruising speed: 155 mph (200 km/h) at S/L
Max range: 750 miles (1,210 km) with standard fuel
Accommodation: Crew of 1 and up to 3 passengers
First flight: 3 April 1969

The name of Pierre Robin is well known in European air racing circles, for as a pilot his achievements include wins in the 1963, 1964 and 1965 Circuit of Sicily events and second place in the same race in 1961 and 1962. In 1957, with M Jean Delemontez (designer of the Jodel range of lightplanes), he founded Centre Est Aéronautique, which has become one of Europe's leading producers of light aircraft. Until recently these were all of mixed construction, but in 1971 Avions Pierre Robin, as the company is now known, placed in production its first all-metal aircraft, the HR 100/200, designed by M Christophe Heintz.

I.A.58 Pucará, second prototype with Astazou engines

Wassmer WA 51 Pacific

Robin HR 100/200 Royale

McDONNELL DOUGLAS DC-10

Powered by: Three 40,000 lb (18,144 kg) st General Electric CF6-6D turbofan engines
Wing span: 155 ft 4 in (47.34 m)
Length: 181 ft $4\frac{3}{4}$ in (55.29 m)
Wing area: 3,861 sq ft (358.7 m^2)
Gross weight: 430,000 lb (195,045 kg)
Max cruising speed: 579 mph (932 km/h) at 31,000 ft (9,450 m)
Range: 2,430 miles (3,910 km) with max payload
Accommodation: Crew of 5 and up to 380 passengers
First flight: 29 August 1970

Second of the jumbo-sized American subsonic jet transports to enter service, the DC-10 was designed to meet an original requirement of American Airlines. After studying possible twin-engined configurations, a tri-jet layout was eventually adopted, and the DC-10 first entered service with American Airlines in August 1971. This version, to which the silhouette and data apply, is known as the Series 10. Other versions include the Series 20, which has increased wing span, longer range and JT9D engines; and the Series 30, which is similar but has CF6-50A engines. A Series 30F convertible cargo version is also available. By mid-1972, orders and options for all DC-10 versions totalled 240.

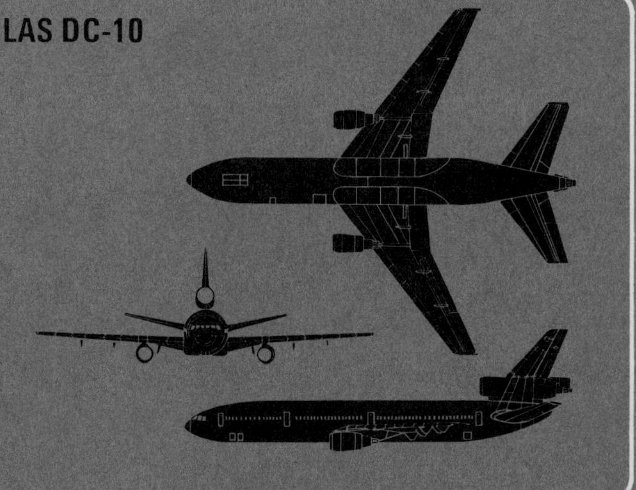

LOCKHEED L-1011-1 TRISTAR

Powered by: Three 40,600 lb (18,415 kg) st Rolls-Royce RB.211-22-02 three-shaft turbofan engines, one under each wing and one in rear fuselage
Wing span: 155 ft 4 in (47.34 m)
Length: 177 ft $8\frac{1}{2}$ in (54.16 m)
Wing area: 3,755 sq ft (348.85 m^2)
Gross weight: 409,000 lb (185.552 kg)
Max speed: 583 mph (939 km/h) at 30,000 ft (9,145 m)
Typical range: 3,287 miles (5,290 km) with max payload of 256 passengers and 5,000 lb (2,270 kg) of cargo
Accommodation: Crew of 13 (incl cabin attendants) and up to 345 passengers
First flight: 16 November 1970

Second of America's tri-jet high-capacity airbuses to fly, the Lockheed TriStar was conceived originally as a twin-turbofan transport. Orders and options for more than 140 of these huge aircraft had been placed by early 1972.

A 300 B AIRBUS

Powered by: Two 49,000 lb (22,226 kg) st General Electric CF6-50A turbofan engines
Wing span: 147 ft $1\frac{3}{4}$ in (44.84 m)
Length: 167 ft $2\frac{1}{4}$ in (50.96 m)
Wing area: 2,799 sq ft (260.0 m^2)
Gross weight: 291,000 lb (132,000 kg)
Max cruising speed: 582 mph (937 km/h) at 25,000 ft (7,620 m)
Range: 1,290 miles (2,070 km) with max payload of 62,000 lb (28,120 kg) and typical reserves
Accommodation: Crew of 2/3 and (typically) 261 passengers
First flight: scheduled for second half of 1972

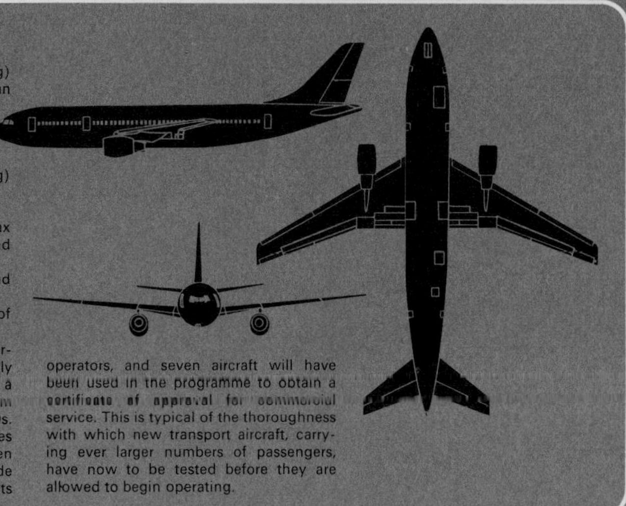

Known unofficially as the European Airbus, the A 300B is being developed jointly under French design leadership by a French/German/British/Dutch consortium for airline service in the mid-1970s. Although it entails no remarkable advances in design technology, it will have been under development for almost a decade before it begins to earn revenue for its operators, and seven aircraft will have been used in the programme to obtain a certificate of approval for commercial service. This is typical of the thoroughness with which new transport aircraft, carrying ever larger numbers of passengers, have now to be tested before they are allowed to begin operating.

McDonnell Douglas DC-10 Series 10

Lockheed L-1011-1 TriStar

Model of A 300B European Airbus

ALPHA JET

Powered by: Two 2,960 lb (1,345 kg) SNECMA/Turboméca Larzac 04 turbofan engines
Wing span: 30 ft 0½ in (9.16 m)
Length: 39 ft 6¼ in (12.05 m)
Wing area: 188.4 sq ft (17.50 m²)
Gross weight: 9,920 lb (4,500 kg)
Max speed: 560 mph (900 km/h) at 36,000 ft (11,000 m)
Typical endurance: 1 hr 30 min
Accommodation: Crew of 2
First flight: scheduled for early 1973

During the late 1960s Breguet in France and Dornier in Germany each evolved design proposals for a jet trainer to replace the long-serving Magister. Since both countries used the Magister for training, it was felt that a common design could be worked out on a collaborative basis, and an agreement to this effect was concluded in 1969. Outcome of this agreement is the Alpha Jet, whose basic design phase was completed in 1971. It will be suitable for both basic and advanced flying training, and for Germany will also be developed in a heavier version for close support duties, with externally-carried weapons.

GRUMMAN F-14A

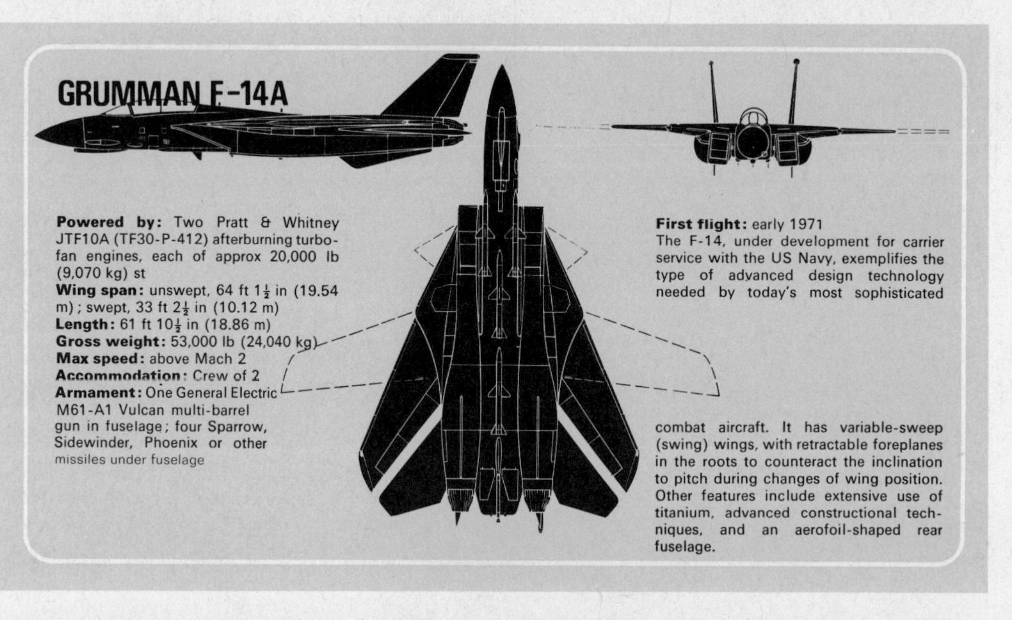

Powered by: Two Pratt & Whitney JTF10A (TF30-P-412) afterburning turbofan engines, each of approx 20,000 lb (9,070 kg) st
Wing span: unswept, 64 ft 1½ in (19.54 m); swept, 33 ft 2½ in (10.12 m)
Length: 61 ft 10½ in (18.86 m)
Gross weight: 53,000 lb (24,040 kg)
Max speed: above Mach 2
Accommodation: Crew of 2
Armament: One General Electric M61-A1 Vulcan multi-barrel gun in fuselage; four Sparrow, Sidewinder, Phoenix or other missiles under fuselage
First flight: early 1971

The F-14, under development for carrier service with the US Navy, exemplifies the type of advanced design technology needed by today's most sophisticated combat aircraft. It has variable-sweep (swing) wings, with retractable foreplanes in the roots to counteract the inclination to pitch during changes of wing position. Other features include extensive use of titanium, advanced constructional techniques, and an aerofoil-shaped rear fuselage.

McDONNELL DOUGLAS F-15 EAGLE

Powered by: Two approx 29,000 lb (13,155 kg) st Pratt & Whitney F100-PW-101 afterburning turbofan engines
Wing span: 42 ft 9¾ in (13.05 m)
Length: 63 ft 9¾ in (19.45 m)
Height: 18 ft 7¼ in (5.67 m)
Gross weight: approx 40,000 lb (18,144 kg)
Max speed: approx 1,650 mph (2,655 km/h) above 36,000 ft (11,000 m)
Armament: One internally-mounted rapid-firing gun; provision for various short/medium-range air-to-air weapons externally, plus provision for air-to-surface missiles
Accommodation: Crew of 1
First flight: scheduled for 1972

Dimensionally similar to the Soviet MiG-23 (page 158), to which it bears a broad superficial resemblance, the F-15 is under development as a short/medium-range all-weather fighter for USAF service from the mid-1970s. Its duties will include fighter sweep, escort and combat patrol, but it has been designed primarily for the air superiority role, with particular emphasis on manoeuvrability and acceleration. Twenty development aircraft (18 single-seat F-15As and 2 TF-15 2-seat trainers) are being built initially, and the ultimate requirement is for several hundred.

Mock-up of the Dassault-Breguet/Dornier Alpha Jet

Grumman F-14A Tomcat

Artist's impression of the McDonnell Douglas F-15A

APOLLO SPACECRAFT

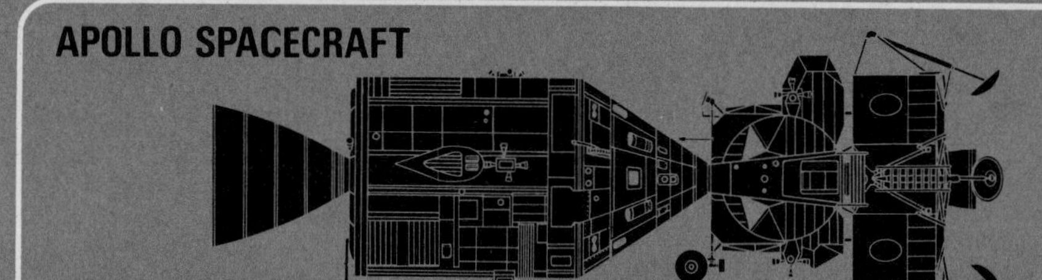

Engine thrust:
Saturn V launch vehicle (first stage) 7,500,000 lb (3,400,000 kg)
Service module 20,500 lb (9,300 kg)
Lunar module (descent stage) 9,700 lb (4,400 kg)
Lunar module (ascent stage) approx 3,500 lb (1,590 kg)
Length:
Saturn V launch vehicle (incl payload) 353 ft 5 in (107.7 m)
Command module 10 ft 7 in (3.23 m)
Service module 24 ft 9 in (7.54 m)
Lunar module 22 ft 11 in (7.00 m)
Diameter:
Saturn V launch vehicle 33 ft 0 in (10.06 m)
Command module 12 ft 9½ in (3.90 m)
Service module 12 ft 9½ in (3.90 m)
Lunar module (legs extended) 31 ft 0 in (9.45 m)
Gross weight:
Saturn V launch vehicle (incl payload) 6,100,000 lb (2,767,000 kg)
Command module 13,000 lb (5,900 kg)
Service module approx 53,000 lb (24,040 kg)
Lunar module 32,000 lb (14,515 kg)

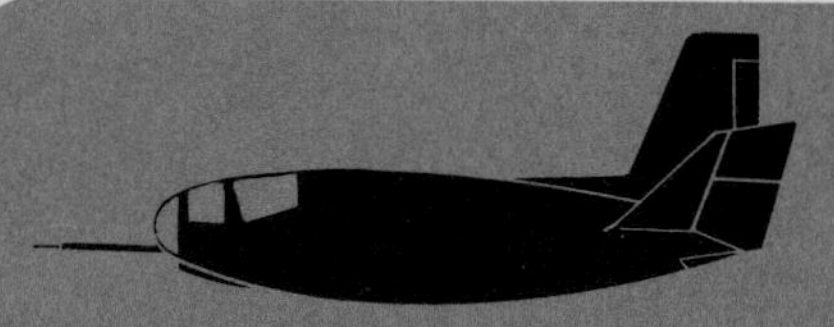

NORTHROP/NASA HL-10

Powered by: One 8,000 lb (3,630 kg) st Thiokol (Reaction Motors) liquid-propellant rocket engine
Max width: 15 ft 1 in (4.60 m) between fin tips
Length: 22 ft 2 in (6.76 m)
Planform area: 162 sq ft (15.05 m²)
Max launching weight: 9,400 lb (4,265 kg)
Max landing weight: 8,000 lb (3,630 kg)
Accommodation: Crew of 1
First flight: 22 December 1966 (unpowered)
The HL-10 is one of two broadly similar craft built by Northrop in recent years under NASA contracts to evaluate the concept of the wingless lifting-body re-entry vehicle. Both are roughly delta-shaped in planform and have a D-shaped cross-section when viewed from the front; but whereas the HL-10 has the curved side of the D on top, its stablemate, the M2-F3, has this side forming its undersurface. The craft are air-launched from a B-52 'mother-plane', and are being used as part of a programme to develop craft which can be piloted back from space through the Earth's atmosphere to land like a conventional aeroplane.

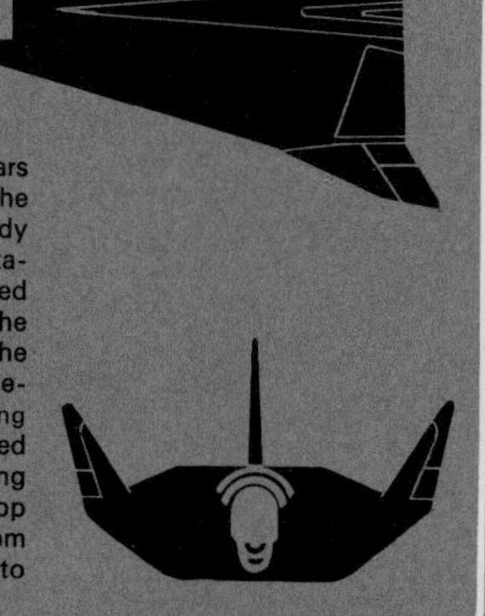

NASA SPACE SHUTTLE

The National Aeronautics and Space Administration's Space Shuttle will be a re-usable manned launch system which promises to reduce from $900 to $160 the cost of placing 1 lb (2.2 kg) of payload into a close Earth orbit. North American Rockwell is the prime contractor and integrator for the programme. The delta-winged flyback orbiter, designed to be re-used at least 100 times, is mounted on a huge expendable tank containing the liquid oxygen/liquid hydrogen main propellants: this tank it carries into orbit and subsequently discards. On the sides of the tank are two solid-propellant boosters, which operate in parallel with the main engines at lift-off and jettison at an altitude of about 25 miles (40 km). It is proposed to recover the boosters some 200 miles (320 km) down range after they have parachuted into the sea.
The data below are 1972 provisional figures and may change as the project develops:

ORBITER:
Main engines: Three 470,000 lb (213,190 kg) st Rocketdyne high-pressure rocket engines
Air-breathing engines: Two deployable turbofans, plus two fixed for horizontal flight tests and ferry purposes
Orbit manoeuvre engines: Two of 5,000 lb (2,268 kg) st each
Attitude control thrusters: Two sets of twelve 1,000 lb (453 kg) st engines in aft fuselage, and two sets of eight located forward, in the nose
Launch abort engines: Two 386,000 lb (175,100 kg) st solid-propellant units in external pods
Wing span: 79 ft (24.08 m)
Length: 110 ft (33.53 m)
Height: [illegible] ft (10.70 m) over vertical fin
Cargo bay: 60 x 15 ft (18.3 x 4.57 m)
Max payload: (delivered into due east low orbit): 65,000 lb (29,484 kg)
Accommodation: Crew of 2, plus 2 payload specialists on orbital flights
Max landing speed: 201 mph (324 km/h)
First horizontal flight: 1976, Edwards AFB, California
First vertical launch, unmanned: 1978, Kennedy Space Center, Florida
Full operational capability: 1980
EXPENDABLE TANK:
Length: 187 ft (57.00 m)
Diameter: 26 ft (7.92 m)
STRAP-ON BOOSTERS:
Thrust: 3,500,000 lb (1,587,600 kg) each for 110 sec
Length: 150 ft (45.72 m) each
Diameter: 13 ft (3.96 m) each

Launch of the Saturn V rocket carrying the Apollo 16 spacecraft, April 1972

Northrop/NASA HL-10

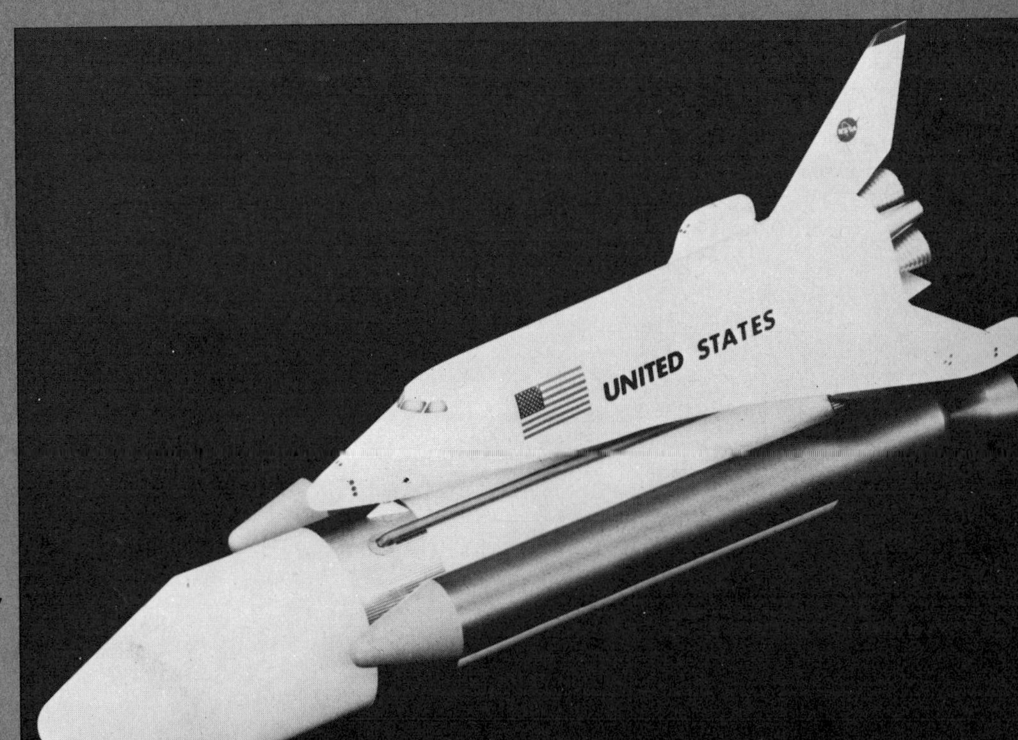

Model of the NASA Space Shuttle project, 1972

INDEX

The aircraft silhouettes in this book were prepared by **Dennis Punnett** and **John W. Wood**